Earth Ethics

A Case Method Approach

Ecology and Justice

An Orbis Series on Integral Ecology

The Orbis Series on Integral Ecology publishes books seeking to integrate an understanding of Earth's interconnected life systems with sustainable social, political, and economic systems that enhance the Earth community. Books in the series concentrate on ways to:

- reexamine human–Earth relations in light of contemporary cosmological and ecological science
- develop visions of common life marked by ecological integrity and social justice
- expand on the work of those exploring such fields as integral ecology, climate justice, Earth law, eco-feminism, and animal protection
- promote inclusive participatory strategies that enhance the struggle of Earth's poor and oppressed for ecological justice
- deepen appreciation for dialogue within and among religious traditions on issues of ecology and justice
- encourage spiritual discipline, social engagement, and the transformation of religion and society towards these ends.

Viewing the present moment as a time for fresh creativity and inspired by the encyclical *Laudato Si*, the series seeks authors who speak to eco-justice concerns and who bring into this dialogue perspectives from the Christian communities, from the world's religions, from secular and scientific circles, or from new paradigms of thought and action.

Earth Ethics

A Case Method Approach

**James B. Martin-Schramm
Daniel T. Spencer
Laura A. Stivers**

ORBIS BOOKS
Maryknoll, New York 10545

Founded in 1970, Orbis Books endeavors to publish works that enlighten the mind, nourish the spirit, and challenge the conscience. The publishing arm of the Maryknoll Fathers and Brothers, Orbis seeks to explore the global dimensions of the Christian faith and mission, to invite dialogue with diverse cultures and religious traditions, and to serve the cause of reconciliation and peace. The books published reflect the views of their authors and do not represent the official position of the Maryknoll Society. To learn more about Maryknoll and Orbis Books, please visit our website at www.maryknollsociety.org.

Library of Congress Cataloging-in-Publication Data

Martin-Schramm, James B.
   [Christian environmental ethics]
   Earth ethics : a case method approach / James B. Martin-Schramm, Daniel T. Spencer, Laura A. Stivers.
     pages cm
   Rev. ed. of: Christian environmental ethics : a case method approach. c2003.
   Includes bibliographical references and index.
   ISBN 978-1-62698-156-0 (pbk.)
   1. Human ecology—Religious aspects—Christianity—Case studies. 2. Environmental ethics—Case studies.   3. Christian ethics—Case studies. I. Title.
BT695.5.M37 2015
241'.691—dc23
                                                   2015019297

For
Robert L. Stivers
Mentor, Friend, and Father

and

For
Our Students
Past, Present, and Future

Contents

Acknowledgments

We have dedicated this revised volume to Bob Stivers, who was a co-author of the original edition and one of the pioneers of the case-based approach to Christian ethics. Bob has had an impact on each of our lives in various ways. He has also touched the lives of so many as a fine teacher, wise mentor, and good friend. Thanks, Bob!

We also dedicate this book to our students who have taught us so much over the years and who keep pushing us to master the art of teaching. We are grateful for the many ways our students have enriched our lives and look forward to the next generation.

Many people assisted our research and several also read drafts of the cases and commentaries we developed. Jim expresses his gratitude to the following friends and colleagues for their very helpful assistance: Erik Baack, Stratis Giannakouros, Steve Holland, Jon Jensen, Karen Martin-Schramm, Craig Mosher, Laura Peterson, and Maren Stumme-Diers. Jim is also very grateful for current and former students who provided terrific feedback on cases and commentaries: Callie Mabry, Emily Mueller, Jessa Anderson-Reitz, and Sam Wettach. A special word of thanks goes to Jim's student research assistant, Jamie Stallman. He did excellent research for some of the cases, read and commented on almost every chapter, and helped develop the first case, "Maybe One: Population Growth, Material Consumption, and Climate Change."

Laura thanks Lynn Sondag, Rebecca Todd Peters, Kevin O'Brien, Mark Stivers, Judy Slater, Robin Blakeman, Betty Pagett, Kiki La Porta, Bill Carney, and Susan Adams for their insight and support on the cases.

Dan thanks the members of his fall 2014 class, Earth Ethics: Moral Dimensions of Environmental Issues, for piloting several of the cases and providing feedback on the manuscript. Neva Hassanein, Crissie McMullan, Eric Nelson, Barbara Rossing, and Martha Spencer provided helpful feedback on several cases and commentaries. Dan especially thanks Deb Ford, executive director of the Playa Retreat Community in Summer Lake, Oregon, for granting him a two-week writing residency in July 2014, and his fellow members of the residency who inspired him with all of their creative work.

Finally, Jim also wants to thank Luther College for awarding him a full-year sabbatical leave to complete this project and the college's Paideia program for a grant that helped defray some of the related expenses. We are all fortunate to teach at institutions that value scholarship and its direct relationship to teaching.

James B. Martin-Schramm, Luther College
Daniel T. Spencer, University of Montana
Laura A. Stivers, Dominican University of California

Introduction

This book grew out of the classroom and has been revised based on feedback over the past decade from our students and also from colleagues in various fields. We have retained the case method approach because we have found it to be the best way to grapple with issues in applied ethics for several reasons. First, the cases educate readers about several social and environmental issues. They are all based on real dilemmas and current moral challenges. Second, the cases immerse readers into the complexities of an array of contemporary issues, especially their various dimensions, via the perspectives of multiple stakeholders. Third, the case commentaries provide ethical frameworks, concepts, and methods for understanding and analyzing the ethical dimensions of current issues raised by the cases. Readers have to step into the shoes of the main figures and quickly enter the messy complexity of ethics. Fourth, the cases and commentaries can also serve as a starting point for further research to gain greater knowledge and perspectives about the issues, and to update relevant background information.

Since ethics is inherently an interdisciplinary exercise, we have expanded the audience for this book to include not only those engaged in religious studies, but also those engaged in philosophical ethics and environmental studies. Our students have always come from a variety of disciplines in the humanities, natural sciences, and mathematics, as well as the social sciences. It is our hope that this book will continue to foster critical thinking and student-directed learning in a variety of fields. This casebook will probably work best, however, when it is paired with other books in specific disciplines that help students engage underlying ideas in greater depth.

We have also expanded our discussion of the ethic of ecological justice as the ethical framework because it provides a common moral vocabulary to engage in civil discourse about the issues in this book. The ethic addresses human-caused problems that threaten both human and natural communities. The ethic unites what are often viewed as separate fields of social ethics and environmental ethics because our moral obligations to other human beings cannot be separated from the welfare of other creatures in the community of life and the ecological systems that sustain us. We all share one planet, after all. Ecological well-being is the foundation for social well-being. Our ethical obligations overlap and are interconnected. Often the same logic of domination justifies exploitation of people and the planet. We signal this reality in the new title for this book, *Earth Ethics*.[1] In our view, the term *environmental ethics* is too small to denote the scope and magnitude of the challenges we face. Our friend, colleague, and mentor, Larry Rasmussen, coined the term *Earth ethics* when Orbis Books published *Earth Community, Earth Ethics* two decades ago. To make this distinction clear, Rasmussen writes,

> "Environment" means that which surrounds us. It is a world separate from ourselves, outside us. The true state of affairs, however, is far more interesting and intimate. The world around us is also within. We are an expression of it; it is an expression of us. We are made of it; we eat, drink, and breathe it. . . . None of this intimacy is carried by the word "environment." Nor does our responsibility ring as clear as it ought when we name our woe "the environmental crisis" and offer "environmental ethics" as the antidote. . . . Earth—all of it—is a community without an exit. Our problems—people-to-people and humankind-to-otherkind—are genuinely ours all together, for worse and for better.[2]

Wicked Ethical Problems in the Anthropocene Age

It is hard to find any part of Earth that is unaffected by the consequences of human activity since the rise of the Industrial Revolution, and those impacts are increasing at a significant rate. The International Geosphere-Biosphere Programme has illustrated these realities in two sets of graphs.[3] The first set below explores the increasing rates of change in human activity in a wide range of areas ranging from population growth and economic activity to water use, paper consumption, tourism, and the use of motor vehicles. All of these graphs have one thing in common—an exponential rate of growth since the middle of the twentieth century (Figure 1).

Figure 1. Increasing rates of change in human activity since the beginning of the Industrial Revolution

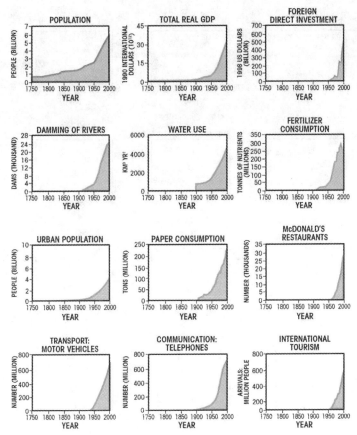

Source: W. L. Steffen et al., *Global Change and the Earth System* (Berlin: Springer, 2004), 132. Used with permission.

Not surprisingly, this rapid rate of growth in human activities has had an enormous impact on Earth's ecological systems. The second set of graphs begins by plotting increasing concentrations of greenhouse gases and then surveys impacts on oceans, terrestrial ecosystems, and global biodiversity. The exponential rate of impact mirrors the first set of graphs (Figure 2).

Figure 2. Global-scale changes in the Earth system as a result of the dramatic increase in human activity

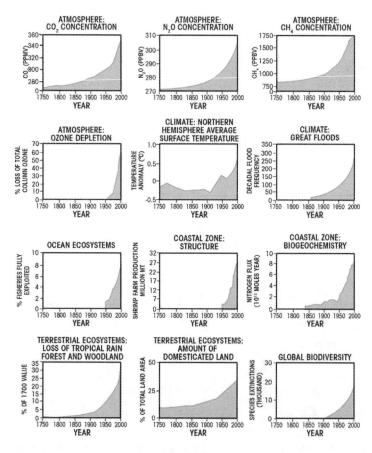

Source: W. L. Steffen et al., *Global Change and the Earth System* (Berlin: Springer, 2004), 133. Used with permission.

The pervasive impact of one species, *Homo sapiens*, is leading many scientists to conclude that we have entered a new era of planetary history—the Anthropocene. For example, a subset of geologists and other scientists affiliated with the International Commission on Stratigraphy is examining whether human impacts caused by colonization, agriculture, urbanization, and global warming have caused sufficient change to leave a discernible trace in layered rocks.[4] Geologists have marked similar epochal moments by inserting a golden disk into the relevant layer of rocks to physically point out where one scientific time period ends and another begins. John Kress, acting undersecretary of science for the Smithsonian, suggests the point of demarcation for the Anthropocene is "going to be a layer of plastic that covers the planet, if not a layer of (heat-trapping) carbon."[5]

If one of the distinguishing features of the twentieth century was technological change, it is now clear that the twenty-first century will be marked by unprecedented climate change. Two recent studies have sounded the alarm bells. In 2013–14 the UN Intergovernmental Panel on Climate Change (IPCC) issued its Fifth Assessment Report in four volumes.[6] The following are two of the headline statements for policy makers issued in conjunction with release of the synthesis report:[7]

- Human influence on the climate system is clear, and recent anthropogenic emissions of greenhouse gases are the highest in history. Recent climate changes have had widespread impacts on human and natural systems.
- Continued emission of greenhouse gases will cause further warming and long-lasting changes in all components of the climate system, increasing the likelihood of severe, pervasive, and irreversible impacts for people and ecosystems. Limiting climate change would require substantial and sustained reductions in greenhouse gas emissions, which, together with adaptation, can limit climate change risks.

The IPCC report emphasizes Earth's atmosphere has warmed about 1.5° Fahrenheit (F) (0.85° Celsius [C]) since 1880. If carbon dioxide and other greenhouse gases continue to be emitted at the current rate, temperatures will rise 3.6°F by 2050. By 2100, temperatures could be 6.7°F warmer. This rate of warming is unprecedented in human history and throughout most of the planet's history as well. The report emphasizes that failure to reduce greenhouse gas emissions will lead to food shortages due to disrupted and reduced agricultural production, refugee crises spurred by the flooding of major cities and low-lying areas, rapid extinction of many plant and animal species, and an increase in heat waves that will make it dangerous for people to be outside during the hottest times of the year. In order to limit warming to 3.6°F (2°C), the report states global greenhouse gas emissions must be reduced 40 to 70 percent below preindustrial levels by 2050, and by the end of the twenty-first century, the nations of the world would have to remove more carbon dioxide from the atmosphere than they are emitting. Given the current rapid increase in emissions, such a reduction seems almost impossible but also clearly vital.

The US Global Change Research Program issued its own major report about climate change in May 2014.[8] The twelve key findings in the third National Climate Assessment for the United States are very similar to those in the IPCC's Fifth Assessment Report:

Global climate is changing, and this is apparent across the United States in a wide range of observations. The global warming of the past fifty years is primarily due to human activities, predominantly the burning of fossil fuels.

1. Some extreme weather and climate events have increased in recent decades, and new and stronger evidence confirms that some of these increases are related to human activities.
2. Human-induced climate change is projected to continue, and it will accelerate significantly if global emissions of heat-trapping gases continue to increase.
3. Impacts related to climate change are already evident in many sectors and are expected to become increasingly disruptive across the nation throughout this century and beyond.
4. Climate change threatens human health and well-being in many ways, including through more extreme weather events and wildfires; decreased air quality; and diseases transmitted by insects, food, and water.
5. Infrastructure is being damaged by sea level rise, heavy downpours, and extreme heat; damages are projected to increase with continued climate change.
6. Water quality and water supply reliability are jeopardized by climate change in a variety of ways that affect ecosystems and livelihoods.
7. Climate disruptions to agriculture have been increasing and are projected to become more severe over this century.
8. Climate change poses particular threats to indigenous peoples' health, well-being, and ways of life.
9. Ecosystems and the benefits they provide to society are being affected by climate change. The capacity of ecosystems to buffer the impacts of extreme events like fires, floods, and severe storms is being overwhelmed.
10. Ocean waters are becoming warmer and more acidic, broadly affecting ocean circulation, chemistry, ecosystems, and marine life.
11. Planning for adaptation (to address and prepare for impacts) and mitigation (to reduce future climate change, for example, by cutting emissions) is becoming more widespread, but current implementation efforts are insufficient to avoid increasingly negative social, environmental, and economic consequences.

These two reports make it clear that climate change will exacerbate all current social and environmental problems, and also will likely create new problems we have not yet faced. Some have referred to problems caused by typical yet complex patterns of human reproduction, industrial production, and material consumption as "wicked problems" because they are not ordinarily the consequence of intentional malice, but rather the unintended result of our daily activities and unspoken assumptions.[9] For example, no one intends to contribute to global warming by having children. Nor do people intend to harm the planet by driving to work or heating their home or office. The reality, however, is that for most people, most of the time, engaging in these activities involves the combustion of fossil fuel and the emission of greenhouse gases.

There are a host of wicked social and environmental problems, and several are encountered via the cases in this book. These problems are wicked rather than tame because they are hard to define, and their solutions are hard to discern. For example, climate change is a problem in many different ways. It is hard to understand scientifically; its impacts are hard to calculate socially, economically, and politically; and assigning responsibility for mitigation and adaptation is proving difficult ethically. The reality is that there is no single, simple solution to the complicated problem of climate change.

Complexity is certainly one thing that makes some problems wicked. Another key factor is that solving them will require us to examine (and perhaps jettison) worldviews and assumptions that have given rise to them. Wicked problems lead us to challenge fundamental philosophical, religious, ethical, and social assumptions. Wicked problems are especially difficult because they challenge us to change our minds so that our behaviors change as well.

An Overview of *Earth Ethics*

This volume utilizes a case method approach to explore several wickedly complicated and interwoven problems in social and environmental ethics and provides resources for engaging in ethical reflection about them. The first three chapters provide foundations for moral deliberation about these issues.

Chapter 1 explores the context for Earth ethics by examining four interrelated causes of environmental degradation in population growth, consumption patterns, production technologies, and fundamental economic and political assumptions. The chapter also identifies various attitudes toward nature and explores a spectrum of perspectives about the relationship of nature and society.

Chapter 2 explores two sets of diverse perspectives for Earth ethics. Mind-sets and worldviews are important because how one frames a problem can determine whether an ethical issue is even perceived. The chapter begins by examining four key perspectives on the economy and the environment (free market, conservation, preservation, and critical ecology) developed in North America during the twentieth century. Next we review four similar perspectives (market liberal, institutionalist, bioenvironmentalist, and social green) associated with economic globalization. The chapter concludes by exploring ethical assumptions associated with both sets of perspectives and their contrasting visions of what constitutes *the good life*. While individuals and issues rarely fit neatly into just one of these categories, understanding the assumptions and values each holds can shed light on the range of perspectives and issues in each case.

Chapter 3 offers ethical resources for Earth ethics. It begins by exploring foundations for an ethic of ecological justice to unite the separate disciplines of environmental ethics and social ethics into one integrated scope of moral concern. The rest of the chapter outlines the benefits of a case study approach to ethics and offers a method to engage in moral deliberation about the cases in this volume. This three-stage method requires careful analysis of a case and its primary moral problem before engaging in an assessment of the alternatives and discernment of relevant moral norms and values to make an ethical judgment about the best course of action.

The bulk of this volume consists of nine cases that address different and difficult issues in social and environmental ethics. All of the cases are based on actual situations. Names and places have been changed when necessary to protect the privacy of those involved, but the ethical problems and moral dilemmas posed by the cases are real. Each case is accompanied by a commentary that provides important background information along with normative material that can aid in ethical assessment of the problems. None of the commentaries, however, take a definitive stance with regard to how the case should be resolved ethically. This is left up to the reader. The purpose of this volume is to equip readers with skills to do moral deliberation.

The first case, "Maybe One," is set at a university in Boston. After a letter in the university newspaper blames most of the world's ecological woes on increasing greenhouse gas emissions in China and population growth in other developing nations, the International Students Association invites five students from different parts of the world to participate in a panel discussion focused on personal and structural factors related to population growth, material consumption, and climate change. One of the invited panelists is a graduate student in demography from Maine who is engaged to be married. While he and his partner are committed to living a low-consumption, low-carbon lifestyle, they appear divided over how many children they may have once they are ready to start a family. Beyond the personal aspects, he is not sure what to say about structural factors that drive population growth, material consumption, and climate change. Conversations with friends and family lead him to think about gender equality, the impact of poverty on population growth, and the need for carbon pricing to reduce greenhouse gas emissions. The case requires readers to grapple with personal and delicate matters while also prompting ethical reflection about the some of the largest and most complicated issues of our day.

Personal consumption decisions set within the context of broader policy are also central to the second case, "Moral Eating." Here the daily choices we make about what foods to eat intersect with the reality of how food is produced in the modern industrial agriculture system. Through a class project, a student in Iowa learns about the conditions of animals raised in concentrated animal feeding operations and becomes a vegetarian in response. He enrolls at the University of Montana to study sustainable agriculture as an alternative to factory farms and joins a student effort to remove meat from the university dining hall. Exposed to other alternatives for raising animals, such as grass-fed cattle and the role animals can play in small-scale sustainable farming, he wrestles with whether or not it is ethical to eat meat. The commentary provides background on the industrial agriculture system with an emphasis on how animals are treated, and explores a range of ethical issues from animal rights and welfare to sustainability and justice concerns in agriculture. Readers wrestle with decisions about personal consumption as well as systemic and institutional issues connected to animal well-being and just and sustainable uses of resources.

The third case continues the focus on food. "Harvesting Controversy" focuses on the potential genetically modified crops pose for increasing food production in sub-Saharan Africa—the only region in the world where hunger is on the increase. The case is set in the United States and revolves around a Hunger Concerns group on a college campus that suddenly finds itself embroiled in a debate about genetically modified (GM) crops. Some members believe these technological innovations could play a significant role in reducing hunger. Others are concerned about dangers GM crops pose to human and ecological health. A crisis erupts when one member suggests the group join a Greenpeace campaign to ban genetically modified corn in Mexico. The commentary provides background information about biotechnology in agriculture and assesses ethical issues posed by the case. One of the unique features of this case is that it forces readers to grapple with respect for national sovereignty. Do citizens in developed nations have any moral right to tell other nations what to do about GM foods?

The fourth case, "Klamath Crisis," focuses on the protection of endangered species and water rights disputes in the western United States. For over a century, the Bureau of Reclamation's Klamath Project provided water for irrigation to farmers in the arid Klamath Basin of northern California and southern Oregon, creating a thriving agricultural economy. Overallocation of water combined with persistent drought in the 1980s, however, caused native fish populations in the Klamath River watershed to plummet, leading to the listing of several fish species under the Endangered Species Act (ESA) in the 1990s. By 2001 the lack of water to support fish populations led federal agencies to shut off the irrigation system, depriving farmers of water needed for their crops. Long-brewing tensions exploded into social protest and unrest. Farmers forcibly reopened the irrigation headgates to return water to the canals, launching a decade of protest and polarization that pitted environmentalists, Native Americans, farmers, and salmon fishermen against each other. Several years of difficult negotiations and collaboration between different stakeholders led US senators in Oregon and California to introduce the Klamath Basin Water Recovery and Economic Restoration Act of 2014. The proposed legislation has satisfied some, but not all, of the Basin's residents. A recent college graduate working with the US FoodCorps in Klamath Falls finds herself caught up in debates about the proposed legislation and is asked to choose sides. The case and commentary explore the difficult choices and trade-offs in the American West around the role of increasingly limited water in conservation, endangered species protection, and economic development.

The fifth case, "Blown Away," is the first of three that address specific energy-related issues. The case examines the impact of mountaintop removal coal mining on Appalachia and explores, in part, fossil fuel divestment campaigns on college campuses. In the case, a student in an environmental ethics class joins ten other students on a three-day field trip to West Virginia to view mountaintop removal firsthand and to participate in a walking, educational prayer vigil on Kayford Mountain—a site of massive destruction from mining. After the trip, some of the students create a campus environmental club to launch a campaign to get their university to divest its endowment from fossil fuels, and they organize a panel to educate fellow classmates on the issue. Panel remarks lead the student to question which aspects of energy policy and sustainability are most important and whether divestment from fossil fuels should be the primary focus. She wonders whether changes to local, state, national, and/or international energy policy should instead be central or whether encouraging students at her university to live more sustainably should be the starting point.

The next case, "Fractured Options," explores various methods a college in the Upper Midwest can use to reduce its greenhouse gas emissions to achieve carbon neutrality. The school has already reduced its emissions 40 percent via investments in energy efficiency and renewable energy. The question is whether the college should invest in a natural gas-fired combined heat and power plant (CHP) to reduce emissions further or pursue other options such as a biomass heating plant that may be as effective but more costly. CHP systems are in many respects the epitome of energy efficiency, but in this case the natural gas fuel stock is increasingly being derived from the controversial practice of hydraulic fracturing. The case examines various environmental and social issues related to fracking—

especially whether methane leakage rates from natural gas drilling and distribution systems actually produce more rather than less greenhouse gas emissions in the United States. It also makes clear that *every* solution has some negative environmental and social side effects, so readers must weigh multiple issues to decide the best course of action.

In "Hot Spot" the focus is on the storage and long-term disposal of high-level nuclear waste. While many know that the United States intends to bury high-level nuclear waste deep underground in Yucca Mountain, few are aware that a consortium of electric utilities that own and operate several nuclear reactors received a license from the Nuclear Regulatory Commission to store most of the nation's current stockpile of spent nuclear fuel on the Skull Valley Goshute Indian Reservation in Utah. The problem is that the project has been delayed for various reasons, and now the lease agreement with the tribe has run out. In the case, a college student in an environmental ethics class must write a paper on the topic of nuclear waste storage. She must decide whether it would be better to find a different site through a consent-based approach to the storage and disposal of spent nuclear fuel or whether it would be acceptable to store the waste on the tribe's reservation for up to forty years. She feels torn between her desire to defend the sovereignty of the tribe and her concern that they may be victims of environmental racism. The commentary addresses these concerns along with the broader question of how best to share the burden of high-level nuclear waste disposal.

The eighth case, "Smart Growth," grapples with sustainable development and social equity in the San Francisco Bay Area in California. At the center of the debate is a smart growth development plan that was approved in July 2013 to reduce greenhouse gas emissions. The plan requires each metropolitan area to have sustainable strategies that encourage future development to be in areas that are accessible via walking and biking, and close to public transit, jobs, schools, and other amenities. The goal is for various area plans to include an emphasis on affordable housing and public transportation as well as preservation of agriculture and open space. Communities that agree to be designated as Priority Development Areas (PDA) can receive transportation grants. Public debate gets heated between environmentalists and social justice advocates who support smart growth strategies with an emphasis on equity and some neighborhood residents who are opposed to new development, especially public transportation and higher-density affordable housing. In the case, a single mother living in a neighborhood being proposed as a PDA considers the potential social and environmental justice impacts of smart growth in relation to the individual well-being of her own family and neighborhood.

The last case, "Wearing Injustice," returns to personal and institutional consumption decisions by exploring workers' rights in the garment industry. A college student enrolls in a travel seminar to Central America where she meets workers in the textile factories that produce clothing for export to the United States. Deeply concerned about the low salaries and poor working conditions for the workers, and realizing that poor people worldwide produce all of her clothing in similar conditions, she joins an antisweatshop student movement on her college campus. They are pressuring the university administration to join the Worker Rights Consortium and the Designated Suppliers Program to assure that all the clothing that bears the university's name or logo is produced in *sweat-free* conditions where worker rights are protected and workers earn a livable wage. When the administration refuses, she faces the difficult choice about whether to participate in acts of civil disobedience to pressure the university, knowing the repercussions of her actions could threaten her ability to graduate or continue to receive her student loans.

The volume concludes with an appendix that contains various teaching resources for courses that explore issues in Earth ethics. These resources include the description of an ecological autobiography assignment as well as several spectrum exercises that help students physically locate themselves in key debates in social and environmental ethics. In addition, the appendix contains instructions for examining power dynamics in cases as well as guidelines for how students can write brief papers or make group presentations about the cases.

Notes

[1] James B. Martin-Schramm and Robert L. Stivers, *Christian Environmental Ethics: A Case Method Approach* (Maryknoll, NY: Orbis Books, 2003).

[2] Larry L. Rasmussen, *Earth Community, Earth Ethics* (Maryknoll, NY: Orbis Books, 1996), xii.

[3] W. L. Steffen et al., *Global Change and the Earth System* (Berlin: Springer, 2004), 132–33.

[4] Working Group on the "Anthropocene," Subcommission on Quaternary Stratigraphy, http://quaternary.stratigraphy.org.

[5] "Anthropocene: Welcome to the Age of Humans," *US News and World Report*, October 17, 2014, http://www.usnews.com.

[6] Intergovernmental Panel on Climate Change, Fifth Assessment Report (AR5), http://www.ipcc.ch/report/ar5.

[7] IPCC Secretariat, "Headline Statements from the Summary for Policymakers," *Climate Change 2014: Synthesis Report*, http://www.ipcc.ch.

[8] Jerry M. Melillo, Terese (T. C.) Richmond, and Gary W. Yohe, eds., 2014: *Climate Change Impacts in the United States: The Third National Climate Assessment*. US Global Change Research Program, http://nca2014.globalchange.gov/.

[9] Urban planner and designer Horst Rittel coined the term *wicked problem* in 1973 while discussing limitations of a linear systems approach to urban planning and design. See Horst W. Rittel and Melvin M. Webber, "Dilemmas in a General Theory of Planning," *Policy Sciences* 4 (1973): 155, 160–67. See also Willis Jenkins, *The Future of Ethics: Sustainability, Social Justice, and Religious Creativity* (Washington, DC: Georgetown University Press, 2013), 149–80.

Part I

CONTEXT, PERSPECTIVES, AND RESOURCES FOR EARTH ETHICS

1

Context for Earth Ethics

Until recently, humans and their evolutionary ancestors fit into ecosystems. Now the reverse is true. This reversal represents a revolution in the natural history of this planet. In a short period of time, the human species has emerged as the dominant species in almost all ecosystems. This domination has led to the degradation of the natural environment and now threatens the ecological systems that support the diversity of life on Earth.

Humans originally subsisted as hunters and gatherers near the top of food chains. They had the numbers, knowledge, and tools to cause only local damage, and then they would move on and allow degraded systems to recover. They were closely connected to nature and lived in rough harmony with it—rough because changing environmental conditions were not always conducive to easy living, and other species competed for scarce resources. In time, humans took to agriculture and developed new knowledge and more powerful tools. Populations increased and new forms of social organization, usually more hierarchical and unequal, emerged. New ideas about the uniqueness of humans and their special status replaced old ideas that had connected humans to nature and encouraged respect.

Further in time, humans discovered that scientific reason could be harnessed with tool making to vastly increase human power over nature. Changing ideas about economic and political relationships (notably capitalism and democracy), a shift to individualistic and materialistic attitudes, and an increased anthropocentric emphasis gave direction to this augmented power. In the space of about three hundred years the Industrial Revolution, as these changes came to be known, dramatically changed the face of Earth. In addition, the Enlightenment and industrialism caused a critical shift in human attitudes toward nature. While the Enlightenment, with its emphasis on equality and human dignity, was important for human liberation, it gave humans a central role and gave superior value to human reason. A mechanistic and utilitarian view of nature emerged: *nonhuman* living organisms were viewed as machines, constructed from separate parts, with no ability to reason or feel; all of nature was viewed merely as resource for human use and defined by what it was not.

The emergence of human consciousness in the evolutionary process is a momentous event. The possibility of increased freedom from starvation, poverty, disease, and death is to be prized. The arts have flourished. Humans have probed nature and discovered many of its inner workings. Individual rights have become increasingly respected. Capitalism has channeled self-interest into the production of goods and services. The list goes on. Some humans have benefited handsomely in pursuit of their material interests and control of nature, but others are bearing the brunt of that success.

Increased material well-being through capitalist economic growth has, among other things, reduced habitat for animals and plants, changed climate, polluted air and water, and created a burden of toxic wastes for future generations. It has also destroyed indigenous cultures and societies that had more sustainable ways of living, and caused increased poverty and disease for many across the globe. Another revolution, the environmental or ecological revolution, has begun and is now in conflict with capitalist perceptions of success and capitalism's focus on increased economic growth based on exploitation of Earth as well as marginalized humans. What remains to be seen is whether humans can renegotiate our fit into natural ecosystems before those systems force the issue. Climate change is clearly a game changer. This renegotiation toward sustainability will not be smooth or easy, especially for those people and societies who have the largest changes to make. Success is not assured. Little in the past prepares humans for the needed changes.

Causes of Environmental Degradation

Environmental degradation is a product of five interrelated causes: (1) too many people, (2) some of whom are consuming too much, (3) using powerful technologies that frequently damage nature's ecosystems, (4) supported by economic and political systems that permit and even encourage degradation, who are (5) informed by anthropocentric attitudes toward nature.

Population

The world's human population is now over seven billion and increasing at an annual rate of about 1.2 percent. Birth rates in most developed nations have declined to the point where they are in rough equilibrium with previously lowered death rates, so that almost all future population increase in these countries will come from immigration. This stabilization, often referred to as the *demographic transition*, was brought on largely by economic factors and was completed only after a large increase in population, the consumption of substantial resources, and the creation of considerable pollution.

Birth rates in most underdeveloped nations are declining but still exceed death rates, so that population continues to increase, in some countries in Africa at a rate over 3 percent. While prospects for lower birth rates in some countries like Niger and Somalia are not good, other countries like China and Bangladesh have made significant strides—though not without controversy. China's *one-child* policy produced a host of human rights violations in the past, and Bangladesh's success at reducing fertility was not always accompanied by other gains in social development.

The primary factor that is driving global population growth, however, is not the birth rate, but rather a phenomenon described as *demographic momentum*. On average, women around the world are giving birth to fewer children than they ever have before. Over the last 50 years, the fertility rate has dropped from over 6 children per woman to an average of 2.5 children today. Over this same period of time, however, the age structure in nations with high rates of population growth changed. For example, approximately 43 percent of sub-Saharan Africa is under the age of fifteen, and these young women and men are now entering the prime years of their reproductive lives. When this skewed age structure is combined with declining fertility rates, the result is more young couples having fewer children than their parents did, yet more people are having children. On the basis of this structural reality in global demographics, the United Nations projects that Earth's human population will almost certainly grow to nine billion people by 2050 before it begins to stabilize over the course of the following century.

Looking only at the numbers, the all too obvious pollution in the overcrowded cities of underdeveloped countries, and the pressures put on habitat by impoverished peoples, a popular attitude is to blame the world's ecological woes on global population growth. While there is an ounce of truth in this attitude, it misses the enormous degradation heaped on ecosystems by the activities of more affluent peoples. But the ounce of truth is that large and increasing numbers of people do place a burden on ecosystems. The great migration of poor people from rural areas with dense populations and little available land for subsistence farming takes a heavy toll socially and ecologically. Migrating to urban areas, poor people expand slums on land with alternative uses. Migrating to other less densely populated rural areas, desperate people move into pristine habitats and often set in motion a destructive cycle. Forests are cut down or burned. Soils are cropped until exhausted and then converted to grazing before they are taken over by more wealthy ranchers. The poor, driven by survival needs, squeezed by opportunistic ranchers, and encouraged by governments, move on to degrade still other habitats.

The social pressures on these poor people are immense. Poverty and lack of opportunities, especially for women, often limit women to child-bearing. Two-tiered social systems, with a few rich and many poor and held in place by custom, religion, and brute force, make little land available to the poor, increase their desperation, and force them to degrade their environments in the name of survival. Yes, expanding numbers of poor people do destroy ecosystems, but the cause is not so much population growth as it is oppressive economic and political systems.

The tendency to blame poor people is rendered even less viable by the knowledge of what is possible. Social development projects backed by appropriate environmental and population policies, adequate financing, land reform, and local control have been successful in lowering birth rates and reducing the degradation of ecosystems. Devising programs that address the needs of women and girl children is especially important. Increasing population does not necessarily have to mean increasing environmental degradation.

Consumption

Far and away the largest pressure on ecosystems comes from the consumption of people in wealthy countries. The quantities are staggering by any historical measure with the infrastructure needed to support this consumption adding additional burdens. Only 12 percent of the world's population lives in North America and Western Europe, yet they account for 60 percent of private consumption spending. The United States alone, only 5 percent of global population, uses about a quarter of the world's fossil fuel resources.[1] If everyone in the world consumed as much as Americans, we would currently need four Earths![2]

Many observers have commented on the extraordinary levels of current consumption in rich countries. Some celebrate it. Others are critical not only of the environmental degradation that results, but also of the human injustices that accompany it. One-third of the global population living in South Asia and sub-Saharan Africa account for only 3.2 percent of consumption, and 825 million people in the world are undernourished.[3] The historical changes that produced these levels of consumption are complex.

Rather than explore causes and the checkered history of increasing levels of material wealth, two general observations are in order. First, high levels of consumption are critical to the functioning of modern capitalism and the global economy in which virtually all nations participate today. High levels of demand are necessary to consume the large quantities of material objects that the system produces. If demand slackens, producers accumulate excess inventory and cut back purchases to reduce costs. Suppliers in turn cut back their production and lay off workers. This is devastating to workers because they are dependent on jobs to provide the income to purchase not only vast quantities of consumer goods, but also basic necessities. So, however virtuous frugality may be, in market societies it produces unemployment and economic hardship for some. High levels of consumption are tied to self-interest and become very difficult to alter.

One way to avoid degrading nature is to reduce the environmental impact of production and consumption. This will no doubt help, but less clear is whether it will be enough. The sheer volume itself may overwhelm ecosystems, even though pollution per unit of production is reduced. If this is the case, those in rich countries face a difficult dilemma. Reduce consumption and slow down the economy, or press on hoping that new technology reduces environmental degradation. Perhaps a combination of frugality, creative stewardship, and new technologies will work.

Second, although numerous studies reveal that increasing levels of consumption generally do not increase personal satisfaction, consumers act as if they do. Trying to convince them otherwise elicits incredulity and accusations of elitism. Dialogue ceases and the parties retreat behind their right to individual expression that modern culture has few resources to adjudicate. Calling this apparent satisfaction spirit-numbing and excessively materialistic, caricatures of consumption as addiction, and the use of satirical terms such as *affluenza* elicit further incredulity. While the average American or European consumes substantially more than the majority of people in developing countries, China and India now claim more than 20 percent of the global consumer class (362 million). In China alone, auto sales increased fourfold in the last ten years.[4] The Chinese also want the freedom of individual car ownership, but the resulting traffic jams, smog, and pollution decrease human well-being.

Technology

While some animals use tools to modify their environments, the human use of technology sets *Homo sapiens* apart from other species in significant ways. Humans apply scientific knowledge to develop and utilize technology in a systematic fashion to address practical problems and achieve desired ends. In addition to this functional description, modern technology is also a pervasive pattern that shapes, constrains, and mediates our experiences of the world. As a contemporary philosopher of technology observes,

> Human life is thoroughly mediated by technology. It is hard even to imagine a life that didn't involve at least some tools and devices. Today, it is even harder to imagine a life without complex technological systems of energy, transportation, waste management, and production. Our world is mostly a constructed environment, and our technologies and technological systems form the background, context, and medium for lives.[5]

The influence of technology is pervasive in our contemporary world. Yet humans create technology, and the tendency to give technology a life of its own must be countered with the insistence that technological systems are human systems.

Indeed the essence of technology is human reason that shapes artifacts and devices to produce services and experiences that in turn reshape our world. Humans devise tools based on scientific understandings, order them with techniques, and implement them to solve problems of production and remedy the historical miseries of hunger, disease, and confinement. That technology seems at times to take on a life of its own only testifies to the power of modern technological processes and the pervasive patterns of technology that order our lives, from personal devices, such as cell phones, computers, and televisions, to the structural fabric of the Internet, energy, and transportation systems. Technology shapes the social and natural environments in which we live and in turn influences the ways we perceive and interact with each other and the rest of the natural world. Technological momentum is so great today that it is arguably the number one force driving human society and environmental degradation.

Technology as a human process is remarkably ambiguous. Technologies offer (1) increased access to multiple levels of experience, yet the dominance of narrow technical reason; (2) greater wealth, yet greater inequality; (3) more freedom, yet increased and more concentrated control and manipulation; (4) more variety, yet the cutting off of traditional choices; 5) more frequent interaction, yet the neglect of community and the increased power of impersonal bureaucracies; (6) greater potential to improve the well-being of all people, yet control by elites pursuing narrow interests; (7) greater control of nature, yet the degradation of ecosystems; (8) the promise of mastery, yet the feeling that things are out of control; (9) apparently limitless power such as nuclear energy, yet the possibility of total destruction; (10) replacing encounters with actual people and nature with immersion into virtual reality.

A number of these ambiguities are central to understanding environmental degradation and community breakdown, especially the fifth, sixth, seventh, eighth, and tenth. The basic paradox of higher standards of living, greater choice, more leisure, and improved communications, yet greater alienation, the loss of community integrity, and the degradation of nature are particularly striking. The very technologies that have improved human life and created the most economic growth have also consumed huge amounts of energy and created the most pollution. These same technologies that promise greater and faster connection with each other paradoxically leave us feeling isolated and alienated from community and Earth.

While devices find their origin in a single person or a group of inventors, decisions about the specific use of these technological inventions are made by corporations. Their decisions are made primarily on calculations of short-term economic return to their organizations, which in turn are driven by the basic imperatives of technology: efficiency and control. Corporate leaders give relatively less attention to persons, communities, and ecosystems as they substitute capital for people, move investments freely, and use resources. Modern technology focuses our attention on the devices and goods it produces to increase our work and pleasure, while hiding the means that produce them—often crushing factory conditions in developing nations and rapacious exploitation of nature. Where once production and consumption of goods and services were both present to the people and communities that produced them, in the global economy consumption is severed from production. Focus is placed on the endless array of commodities produced by dazzling new technologies, while social and ecological costs are hidden from the consumer.

The impacts of modern technologies on ecosystems have been enormous. Take, for example, Earth's forests. The technologies that have made the harvest of ancient forest tracts possible in a short period of time are easy to pinpoint: the chainsaw, road building equipment, draglines, and the truck revolutionized timber harvests. Underlying these technologies were the skills of the large equipment operator, the expert tree faller, the accountant, the administrator, and the ideology of scientific management. Species and ecosystems have no defense against this kind of power. Evolutionary processes could not prepare other species and ecosystems for the onslaught of human reason augmented by the capacity to invent tools. Of special importance to the degradation of forest communities and ecosystems is the road building made possible by bulldozers, road graders, and other heavy equipment. Where roads go, immigrants go, forests go down, and forest dwellers go out.

To be sure this discussion of technology is an oversimplification. Nevertheless, the great productive technologies and the organizations that manage them are a significant part of the problem for the natural environment. Whether the public can balance the power that has accrued to these large corporations, and redirect the technological process to other ends, remains an open question and a matter of intense political conflict. The current battles over globalization are examples of this conflict. Even more challenging may be recognizing the pervasive ways technology now patterns and commodifies our lives, reconfiguring social patterns and how we even perceive the natural world. Why bother with the discomforts of experiencing nature directly when devices can deliver it to you instantly in brilliant color, high-definition resolution, and in three dimensions? How can we care for a natural world that increasingly we are distanced from and understand and experience less and less?

Economics and Politics

The social systems that have been most successful in organizing these powerful technologies for the production of goods and services are capitalism and democracy. In a series of gradual developments beginning in the sixteenth century in Western Europe, capitalism and democracy replaced a hierarchical, feudal system based on land. Today this outcome is called modernity and has become a global phenomenon.

Capitalism is an economic system that harnesses human competitive instincts and self-interest for the social good of greater production. Decentralized free markets, private property, profit, the limited liability of corporations, patents, and the enforcement of contracts are among the mechanisms by which self-interest has been channeled into the acquisition of wealth. By any measure, this system has been successful in producing massive quantities of material goods and in shifting the definition of human well-being in a materialistic direction.

Democracy is a political system that places sovereignty in the hands of the many and their elected representatives. As developed in Western countries, it has functioned, among other things, to support capitalism; to ameliorate accumulations of power; and to give voice to a wide range of people who had not previously participated in decisions that affected their lives. It has accomplished these tasks tolerably well, certainly better than alternative political systems.

Many celebrate capitalism and democracy to the point of missing serious shortcomings. One shortcoming is the current incapacity of these systems to limit self-interest. If the pursuit of self-interest is one key to the success of capitalism, too much self-interest undermines this success. Take, for example, the pursuit of profit. Profits are essential to the financial health of economic enterprises. Profits play a vital role as a signaling device in the efficient allocation of resources. Profits are essential to the continuing ability of a firm to pay workers and thus to distribute income and to create the demand that produces the profits in the first place. Managers must therefore have profit as their primary motivation.

Other things being equal, profits increase as sales increase or costs are reduced. Among the costs of production are the acquisition of resources, the payment of wages, and the disposal of wastes. Managers in the pursuit of profit to satisfy their own self-interest and that of stockholders therefore have an incentive to acquire resources cheaply, to reduce wages, and to pass the cost of waste removal on to the public in the form of pollution. These activities, if pursued vigorously, degrade communities and ecosystems. The competition of firms in an industry adds to these pressures. If the managers of one firm pay the full cost of resource extraction, decent wages, and all pollution costs while competitors do not, obviously they will be at a disadvantage and lose market share or be forced to reduce profits. Industry-wide agreements are one way to avoid this. Governmental regulation is another. The organization of workers in unions and the counterbalancing of corporate power by nongovernmental groups are still others. Industry-wide agreements are hard to come by and may be illegal, however. Governmental regulation is anathema to managers and against the ethos of free markets. Unions and nongovernmental groups are difficult to organize and frequently lack financial resources. Profit is not an evil, but its aggressive pursuit may lead to destructive resource extraction, low wages, and the pollution of ecosystems.

A second shortcoming is the narrow focus of these systems on human material well-being to the neglect of spiritual well-being and the flourishing of biotic communities. These systems are so powerful in the present day, and the material objects that are their fruits so alluring, that materialism has become a dominant global influence.

A third shortcoming that has contributed especially to environmental degradation is the great emphasis on economic growth. Markets work, of course, whether or not there is an increase in production. Capitalism in its modern form seems most stable in economic terms, however, when there is moderate growth. Inflation is usually low and employment levels high with moderate growth in the gross domestic product (GDP). The added wealth or extra product created by growth increases the resources for solving social problems.

In the United States, economic growth has become the most important social goal, and the federal government has assumed responsibility for achieving it. Elected officials consider it their number one priority. Reelection frequently depends on it. As the saying goes, "the business of America is business." An ideology of *economism*—organizing societies and economies around endless economic growth—has also become the goal of global capitalism. Globally, this ideology is forced on indebted developing countries, that, to remain in the global market and not default on their loans, must undergo a *structural adjustment* of their economies as stipulated by the International Monetary Fund (IMF). Structural adjustment programs promote increased private, often corporate, investment and decreased government regulation and provision of social safety nets, through privatization, export-led development, cuts in subsidies and wages, and currency devaluation. Subsistence agriculture and other forms of noncapitalist activity are discouraged because they do not increase economic growth or bring foreign currency to pay off interest on loans.

The added production and consumption produced by economic growth puts increased pressure on resource extraction. It also creates waste in abundance. The sheer volume of it all may itself overwhelm the capacity of the Earth to yield resources and absorb waste, not to mention the impacts on specific ecosystems.

In addition, the pursuit of economic growth, in general, without evaluation of the various elements that go into it, leads to a bias in favor of ever-greater production and consumption no matter how it is produced. Some forms of production and consumption increase human and ecosystem well-being, for example, the planting of trees in urban environments. Others are destructive, for example, the production of toxic wastes and the consumption of products made with them and the burning of fossil fuels with the release of carbon dioxide. The present pursuit of economic growth ignores these distinctions, converting all forms of growth to the quantitative measure of money. Markets make no distinctions either. The only way to be more discriminating and to prevent degradation of the environment is to alter ways of counting what goes into the GDP, to regulate markets, or to restrict producers. Producers resist such actions and have powerful ideological and political weapons to influence outcomes.

A fourth shortcoming in the evolution of market capitalism is the aggregation of economic and political power in the large transnational corporations (TNCs) that dominate the global economy. While such aggregation is not necessary to capitalism, it has been central to global capitalism. In some industries this aggregation results in monopolistic practices and reduced efficiency. The problem for the environment comes when this power is coupled with the pursuit of self-interest and the mobility of capital. Fifty-one of the largest economies in the world are corporations, and the top five hundred TNCs account for nearly 70 percent of worldwide trade.[6] Environmental regulation is thwarted and democracies are weakened when TNCs have such power.

The self-interest of corporate managers is the reduction in the costs of production, conversion of nature's resources into material products, the rapid passing of these products through markets, the encouragement of consumers to buy the products, and the removal of impediments to freedom of action. An international organization, made up of member nations, the World Trade Organization (WTO), was established in 1995 to promote free trade and a vision of a single, integrated, capitalist, global economy. The organization, influenced heavily by TNCs and wealthier countries, acts as judge and jury by enforcing trade sanctions on countries that violate the international trade rules legislated by the WTO. Its negotiations are conducted behind closed doors. As a result, environmentalists, labor leaders, and other critics have argued the organization is undemocratic and simply a hand tool of corporate behemoths to the detriment of the environment and people across the globe.

That the managers of TNCs are self-interested is no surprise. Nor does it necessarily make them bad citizens. Many TNCs pay key personnel well, voluntarily undertake pollution abatement measures, and give to established charities. The problem is the social primacy of their basic interests, the incentives to pay low wages and pollute, and the overall power they have accumulated. The situation is one of unbalanced power.

The forces that might counterbalance this power are either captive or weak. In the United States, the federal government played this role from roughly 1930 to 1980. Subsequent government bashing, the influence of campaign contributions, threats to move production facilities elsewhere, and the ideology of free-market capitalism largely removed the federal government, not to mention local governments, as an effective counter force. Labor unions and nongovernmental organizations have relatively little power, however much they are portrayed as powerful enemies. They remain as potential countervailing powers, however, and were they to pool their strengths could serve such a role. Resistance by these groups at key international economic meetings is some indication that such pooling is taking place.

While democracy retains a capacity to restrain TNCs, in most developed countries elected officials are in their service, maintained, among other things, by campaign contributions and the pervasive ideology of economism. Certain structural features of democracies also help to maintain this arrangement. The separation of powers at the heart of the US Constitution was designed to prevent tyranny, but it also serves to protect entrenched interests. The fragmentation of private property arrangements makes concerted action in ecosystems such as watersheds almost impossible. Private property rights give considerable leeway for individuals to misuse the land. Water rights legislation inhibits conservation of water resources. Antiquated mining laws and grazing rights on public lands encourage misuse of the commons. Polluters must be proven guilty in legal actions instead of having to demonstrate their operations are clean before production starts or continues. Producers are seldom required to test new products for polluting side effects.

Environmental degradation is not solely a consequence of democracy. Communist-led China and nations under dictatorships also have serious environmental destruction. Economic globalization has been designed, with the assistance of the WTO, the IMF, and large financial institutions, to benefit TNCs as the main agents of economic growth. While national sovereignty is compromised by this disproportionate power of TNCs (globalization has been referred to as a *Golden Straightjacket*),[7] national leaders and other elites do not want to be excluded from the global market either. Thus, they support policies that cause or allow environmental destruction and human exploitation.

Attitudes toward Nature

Some observers would end the discussion of causes at this point, maintaining that ideas and values count very little in outcomes. What makes the present stress on production and consumption so strong, however, is the integration of ideas, values, and material structures. Ideas matter. Modern capitalism, for example, is not only a way to organize production. It is also a system of ideas, and the two together have proven to be extremely powerful. The system of ideas includes a constellation of attitudes toward nature. For humans to be in a caring relation to nature, these attitudes must change. For some, this means radical change and the adoption of polar opposite attitudes. For others, a synthesis of old and new attitudes is needed to care for both humans and nature.

Among the many stars in this constellation of attitudes, five warrant discussion. They are the attitudes of anthropocentrism, hierarchy, dualism, domination, and atomism. Their polar counterparts are biocentrism, egalitarianism, connection, cooperation, and holism.

Anthropocentric Attitudes

Anthropocentrism means human centered, and is more or less a summation of the entire constellation, since all five dominant attitudes toward nature primarily serve human beings. That human beings, like all other species, are species centric is no surprise. Individuals of all species concentrate on survival and reproduction and so unconsciously promote the well-being of their own kind. They are normally interested in individuals of another species only as a resource; otherwise they are indifferent. In other words, one species has only a use or utilitarian value for another, and with anthropocentrism other species are counted only as they serve human interests. That they also have intrinsic value, that is, value in and of themselves, is one of the changes in attitudes under current consideration.

Jewish and Christian traditions have contributed to anthropocentrism. The doctrine of creation in both traditions places humans at the apex of the creative process. The Book of Genesis gives dominion to human beings. With the exception of the covenant after the flood in Genesis 9 where God enters into relationship with Noah and his descendants and also independently with nature, the great covenants of the Bible are between God and humans. Judaism was forged in the crucible of conflict with Canaanite nature religions. That the Hebrews made human history, not nature, the stage of God's activity is understandable in this context. Nature becomes the backdrop for the God–human drama. Human sin in both traditions is the central problem. In the aftermath of the Reformation, individual salvation emerged as a central feature of Protestantism. Ecotheologians today are offering alternative interpretations of concepts like dominion and salvation that emphasize human interdependence with nature and human responsibility to be in right relationship with Earth and all of its inhabitants.

Strong anthropocentric attitudes did minimal harm to ecosystems when humans wielded little power. They are problematic in the present context when humans have the power to exploit all ecosystems. In this new situation, utilitarian attitudes lead to the devaluing of nature and consequently to exploitation. Ultimately, they undermine human survival itself, since humans are dependent on healthy ecosystems. Strong anthropocentric attitudes are also spiritually numbing because they tend to reduce human interaction with and appreciation of nature.

Biocentrism and ecocentrism are alternative ways of viewing the natural world. Biocentrism extends inherent value to all life in nature. An individualistic form of biocentrism coincides with an animal rights perspective, with some advocates giving equal value to all life and others giving equal value to beings with sentience. A more holistic form of biocentrism, usually labeled ecological holism or ecocentrism, focuses on protecting natural entities such as species, ecosystems, and landscapes. In environmentalist Aldo Leopold's words, "Actions are right insofar as they have a tendency to preserve the integrity, stability, and beauty of biotic communities."[8]

Hierarchical Attitudes

A hierarchical pattern of social organization and thought with a few males at the apex of the power pyramid characterizes many societies since the beginning of the Agricultural Revolution about twelve thousand years ago. Food surpluses from the rise of agriculture made possible the move away from more egalitarian hunter and gatherer societies to socially stratified and patriarchal societies. Religious traditions evolved to reflect and sanctify these changes. It is certainly characteristic of mainline Western religious traditions, where God as father or monarch rules in righteous supremacy over a *great chain of being* with males above females, humans above all other species, sentient species above plants, and plants above single-celled organisms. Dirt and rocks have little worth.

One reason for hierarchy is clear. It serves those who are socially powerful as a system of order. Through inheritance, competitive struggle, and sometimes even the *consent* of the dominated, individuals and groups attain positions of power, surround themselves with the trappings of authority, claim superiority for themselves, and maintain their positions with physical and ideological forms of coercion. Elite groups can usually maintain themselves as long as they do not become too oppressive, which is a constant tendency, of course. Humans need order, and a benevolent hierarchy often seems to satisfy this need.

In addition, hierarchical forms take many shapes, not all of which are oppressive. Intelligent and compassionate people should play leadership roles as a matter of responsibility. In complex societies, the exercise of political power requires decision making and a division of labor.

Today hierarchical attitudes toward nature are clothed in the garb of scientific management. This perspective urges the use of resources to promote human well-being but in a way that conserves these resources for the future. This is an attractive perspective. Humans do need to use resources but must refrain from destroying basic life support systems. Science and technology are critical to this endeavor. Use implies some sort of management, and good management is better than bad.

In the present context, however, scientific management is also an ideology that disguises and justifies hierarchical domination. At its worst, this ideology sees nature in a utilitarian way as a resource rightly exploited by a superior human species. Managers easily lose restraint and responsibility as superiority justifies the exploitation of nature and assuages guilt. The sense of superiority is also used to justify the culture/nature hierarchy. This sense is variously stated. In the biblical tradition, humans alone are created in the image of God and thus seen as superior. In the Western philosophical tradition, humans alone possess the capacity to reason, and this attribute gives them superiority. There are, however, other ways to interpret what it means to be created in the image of God, and a case must be made for equating an ability to reason with higher worth.

A biocentric perspective rejects superiority outright and substitutes notions of equality. The capacity to experience pleasure and pain or sentience is often substituted for reason as the decisive moral capacity. All sentient creatures have intrinsic worth. Alternatively, animals are invested with rights appropriate to their capacities, rights that humans are to respect. Essentially what is needed is an attitude of respect and care for humans and nature, an attitude that affirms ecologically sensitive scientific knowledge and management techniques as well as the preservation of species and ecosystems.

Dualistic Attitudes

Dualism is the tendency to divide reality into polar opposites: one pole superior and the other inferior (hierarchy). The great dualisms of the Western tradition are familiar: God and world, heaven and Earth, spirit–soul–mind and nature–body–matter, men and women, good and evil, winners and losers, and culture and nature.[9]

Perceiving the world through the lens of paired qualities or tensions can be appropriate. Dualism has been the bedrock of some very creative efforts in philosophy, for example, those attributed to Plato. Dualisms simplify what is often a very complex reality. In times of personal and social crisis, the image of a perfect realm apart can secure meaning and purpose. Over against the fear of death and the vicissitudes of life, the same image offers hope. Finally, this way of thinking sheds light on important distinctions and differences. Dualism need not be about binary opposition. In Eastern philosophy and culture, each side of a dualism, while different, has equal power and importance. For example, the yin/yang symbol denotes balance, where two opposites coexist in harmony and depend on one another. The dualistic frame of mind is deeply troubling, however, when polar opposites are disconnected, value judgments place one pole above the other, and social customs and attitudes toward nature are formed on these judgments. The oppression of people and the degradation of nature are almost inevitable under these circumstances.

The culture/nature and spirit/matter dualisms that inform both Western thought, in general, and Christianity in particular are the dualisms most relevant to environmental concerns. In these dualisms, spirit is superior to matter as culture is to nature and is identified with males. Women and nature are further identified with matter. What emerges from the hierarchical dualism is not only the devaluing of women and nature and their consequent oppression, but an escapist mentality. The self needs liberation from the material world for life in an ideal spiritual realm in heaven, an attitude that is hardly conducive to good stewardship on Earth.

Dualism also brings disconnection. Humans have embraced this with a vengeance, sealing themselves off in air-conditioned chambers. The shopping mall becomes the place for hiking. The elaborate coffin becomes the way to avoid bodily disintegration. Nature is viewed as real estate, and the spirit goes out of the land. According to Carolyn Merchant,

> [The] nature/culture dualism is a key factor in Western civilization's advance at the expense of nature. As the unifying bonds of the older hierarchical cosmos were severed, European culture increasingly set itself above and apart from all that was symbolized by nature. Similarly, in America the nature/culture dichotomy was basic to the tension between civilization and the frontier in westward expansion and helped to justify the continuing exploitation of nature's resources. Much of American literature is founded on the underlying assumption of the superiority of culture to nature. If nature and women, Indians and blacks are to be liberated from the strictures of this ideology, a radical critique of the very categories "nature" and "culture," as organizing concepts in all disciplines, must be undertaken.[10]

An end to the oppression of women and other groups thought to be different and inferior, to the degradation of nature, and to the disconnection of humans from nature is long overdue. Reconnection to nature need not mean a return to primitive living, although some may well seek to simplify their lives by living close to nature. It means being open to spirit in nature, an intention to care for nature, practices that end degradation of species and ecosystems, and a revaluing of matter.

Dominating Attitudes

All organisms modify the environments in which they live. While humans have manipulated nature ever since the first tool user, at issue is *how* they modify nature. The gains for human well-being have been substantial, especially in the last few centuries. Disease control, better nutrition, and greater mobility are obvious examples. The gains legitimated the manipulation as long as the so-called side effects were ignored. Today the side effects can no longer be ignored. They have become main effects. Manipulation and control are giving way to domination and even exploitation.

Anthropocentrism, hierarchy, and dualism merge to contribute to domination, which also has a life of its own as an attitude. From anthropocentrism comes a disregard for nature and other forms of life. They are a backdrop, something to be used. From hierarchy come gradations of superior and inferior, and from dualism the separation of humans from the rest of nature. The domination and exploitation of nature follow easily from each of these attitudes and from their combined effects. The desire to dominate is also rooted in anxieties about death and scarce resources.

Judaism and Christianity have added to this dominating tendency by offering a particular interpretation to Genesis 1:26-28 and other texts that speak of dominion. Different interpretations notwithstanding, dominion has been widely interpreted as domination. Since the Industrial Revolution, this interpretation has been quite common. Even the notion of stewardship has been interpreted as domination. In the United States, attitudes emerged that viewed nature as uncivilized, alien, and an enemy to be conquered. The wild, uncivilized West was unfavorably compared to the more urban and civilized East. The frontier needed to be pushed back, Native Americans *civilized*, and the forest turned into a garden.

Such attitudes have had devastating consequences for Native Americans and, coupled with the increasing power of human technologies, have led to equally devastating consequences for nature. Today climate is altered at a global scale, animal habitat lost, species extinguished, ozone depleted, and streams polluted. Ultimately, this attitude encourages a false sense of security that technology and scientific management will fix all problems.

Darwinian-based ideas of survival of the fittest and competition are yielding to new biological observations of cooperation in nature. The idea of humans as alien exploiters is yielding to one of participation and cooperation in ecosystems. Much more nature-friendly attitudes in religion have also emerged to counter domination. Some Christians, Jews, and Muslims have gone back to stewardship understood not as domination but as caring for and cooperating with nature.

Atomistic and Individualistic Attitudes

Holistic and communal ways of thinking have traditionally character-ized human societies. The modern emphasis on the individual and the division of knowledge into parts is relatively recent. In the West, it is a product, among other things, of the Scientific Revolution, the emergence of a large commercial class, and the religious preoccupation with individual salvation that grew out of the Reformation.

Great advances in knowledge were made when scientists became spe-cialists in ever-smaller areas of observation. To control nature perceived as a machine, scientists learned to investigate its parts and, in so doing, to divide and subdivide the totality of nature into specialized areas of study. They probed deeply and systematically. They simplified as much as possible into mathematical laws and principles. They tested and verified by experimenting.

Soon this atomistic, quantifiable, and empirical way of thinking came to dominate most fields of study in the academy, and the academy orga-nized itself on the basis of distinct fields. Holistic and integrated modes of thinking receded. In the field of economics, arguably the field with the most social influence today, the focus shifted to individual consumers in competition and invested with legal and property rights. Huge gains in production and real progress in limiting the arbitrary powers of the state followed. A new middle class swelled in numbers and challenged the or-ganic and communal ways of feudalism. The new emphasis on individual salvation turned consciousness inward to the self and outward to heaven and away from Earth. New secular modes of thought pushed the church from center to periphery.

The problem for society and the environment stems from their holistic natures. Both require integration if they are to function well. Broken up like Humpty Dumpty they are difficult to piece together again, especially when individuals view themselves in competition on isolated paths through a hostile environment. To solve major environmental problems, specialists need to integrate their specialties. To pursue the common good, individuals expressing a plurality of views must come to agreement. To reintegrate fragmented ecosystems, such as watersheds, planners must pull thousands of property owners together. For these tasks, more holistic, integrated, and communal attitudes are required.

In the current situation, there is no moving on, no place for the indi-vidual to escape since humans have occupied and exhausted most natural environments. The frontiers that only a century ago beckoned individuals are all gone. Individualism is a limiting way of life when the individual is divorced from social life.

In moving to more holistic, integrated, and communal attitudes, the methods of science will remain critical, however. A smothering sort of communalism is no replacement for individualism. Societies need to protect the hard-won rights of individuals. The vision is rather one of synthesis and reintegration, of individuals deeply imbued with social consciousness and toleration, and of ecosystems with humans as integrated parts.

Conclusion

While these five attitudes toward nature are not the only attitudes contributing to environmental degradation, they are the most important and demonstrate that part of the problem is the way humans think about nature. These attitudes were foundational for immense economic growth and development that brought prosperity to some, but they were also used as justification for human oppression and environmental destruction. Many current environmental difficulties are a result of what humans have done well. This realization presents a fundamental dilemma. How are humans to preserve what contributes to their well-being while preserving the natural environment and increasing social justice?

In terms of attitudes toward nature, individuals and groups need to move beyond the either/or of polar opposites. Another way of viewing these attitudes is to see them on a continuum, to which we turn in the next chapter.

Notes

[1]Worldwatch Institute, "The State of Consumption Today" (June 2014), http://www.worldwatch.org.

[2]Global Footprint Network, "Global Footprint Basics: Introduction," http://www.footprintnetwork.org.

[3]Ibid.

[4]"Car Makers Renew Efforts to Woo First-Time Buyers in China," *Wall Street Journal*, April 18, 2014, http://online.wsj.com.

[5]Arum Kumar Tripathi, "Culture of Embodiment and Technology Reflection," http://www.childresearch.net.

[6]World Trade Organization, "Trade Liberalisation Statistics," http://www.gatt.org.

[7]Thomas Friedman, *The Lexus and the Olive Tree* (New York: Anchor Books, 2000), 86–87.

[8]Aldo Leopold, *Sand County Almanac* (New York: Ballantine Books, 1986), 262.

[9]Michael Northcott traces the origins of these dualisms and their heightened power since the Enlightenment in *A Political Theology of Climate Change* (Grand Rapids: Wm. B. Eerdmans, 2013). For a scathing critique of hierarchy and dualism, see Beverly W. Harrison, *Making the Connections: Essays in Feminist Social Ethics*, ed. Carol S. Robb (Boston: Beacon Press, 1985), 25–30.

[10]Carolyn Merchant. *The Death of Nature: Women, Ecology, and the Scientific Revolution* (San Francisco: Harper & Row, 1980), 143ff.

2

Perspectives on Earth Ethics

We ended the first chapter by discussing differing attitudes about nature, and how they shape different approaches to understanding and resolving environmental problems. Individuals and groups need to move beyond either/or polar opposites. A better way of viewing these attitudes is to see them as ends on a continuum of perspectives.

We begin this chapter by looking at four key perspectives about nature that have emerged in the North American context in the past century and continue to influence debates about the environment. Next we review four global perspectives associated with economic globalization. Finally, the chapter concludes by exploring ethical assumptions associated with both sets of perspectives and their contrasting visions of what constitutes *the good life*.

Four North American Perspectives

When viewing attitudes toward nature, the continuum perspective mapped in Table 1, below, reveals that environmental debates are informed by quite different perspectives. Ships pass in the night when those in conflict are not aware of the basic assumptions that shape their perspectives and those of others. During the twentieth century, four main perspectives emerged in North American environmental disputes that continue to affect environmental debates. While distinct, these perspectives overlap, and individuals sometimes find themselves integrating aspects of each. While these perspectives emerged first in the North American context, they have been influential in debates about environmental issues globally as well. In this chapter we examine these four perspectives before looking at how the current context of globalization has led to additional perspectives.

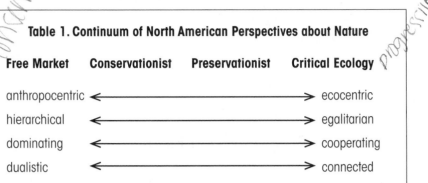

Table 1. Continuum of North American Perspectives about Nature

Free Market	Conservationist	Preservationist	Critical Ecology
anthropocentric	←	→	ecocentric
hierarchical	←	→	egalitarian
dominating	←	→	cooperating
dualistic	←	→	connected
atomistic	←	→	holistic

The attitudes toward nature and society discussed in the preceding chapter are central to these perspectives. The perspectives also include competing economic and political philosophies, positive and negative evaluations of the modern technological process, and different attitudes toward materialism and spirituality.

These four perspectives are *free market, conservation, preservation,* and *critical ecology.*[1] The first three perspectives are relatively coherent and developed as modern perspectives over the last century and a half. The fourth is more recent, very much in process, and finds advocates in a multiplicity of movements.

The first task is to locate these groups on the continuum of attitudes toward nature. Free market advocates generally line up on one side of the continuum, critical ecology advocates on the other, with preservationists and conservationists in the middle. To set this continuum in the context of US politics and economics, those on the free market side of the continuum tend to be more conservative; those on the critical ecology side are more progressive.

Free Market

Advocates of a *free market* perspective arrived with early European settlers, and their attitudes toward nature and society set the terms of the debate. Free market advocates are sometimes called developmentalists because the essence of their perspective is the development of nature's resources for human well-being. In the North American experience, especially in the nineteenth century, this perspective is sometimes referred to as exploitationist to highlight its characteristic attitude toward resource extraction: exploitation with little regard for environmental consequences.

In more moderate forms, free market advocates seek the improvement of human well-being through the creation of goods and capital within

mark ... ms
of th ... sly
succ ... by
transforming the shape of society and the face of nature.

As for the environmental destruction that has accompanied economic growth and resource extraction, advocates of the free market perspective either claim it is overstated, describing it as an externality or side effect, or are optimistic about technological remedies. Theirs is a faith in human ingenuity, the efficacy of technology, the efficiency of markets, and predictability of entrepreneurs responding to competitive pressures. In their view, prices, on the basis of supply and demand, signal what is in scarce supply. Entrepreneurs and corporations will respond to these signals out of self-interest, devise and put into service new and improved technologies as needed to replace dwindling resources, and thus remove or alleviate supply problems.

An example of new technologies substituting for natural resources is the production of agricultural fertilizers, the basis of much of the increase in modern agricultural output. Nitrogen is a limiting nutrient in plant growth, and it is difficult to fix in usable form at large scales. Throughout the nineteenth century, production of fertilizer depended on the mining of guano (bird manure), typically found on remote islands where birds congregate in large numbers. Limitations on the availability of guano in turn limited fertilizer and agricultural production. In 1918, the chemist Fritz Haber invented the Haber-Bosch process to convert atmospheric nitrogen to ammonia, thus making the nitrogen available for fertilizers. This new technology rapidly increased the production of fertilizers, making possible dramatic increases in crop production throughout the twentieth century while greatly reducing the environmentally destructive mining of guano. Free market advocates argue that in just such ways, by combining new technologies with market economies, societies are kept on an upward trajectory of economic growth and increased well-being.

Those problems for which there are no market solutions, for example, the enforcement of contracts, will require government intervention, but such intervention should be kept to a minimum and employ market mechanisms wherever possible. The resource extractor should have the maximum room to maneuver.

In this perspective the uneven distribution of costs and benefits that result from the free play of market forces is either temporary or the price society pays for *the rising tide that raises all boats*. It is temporary, especially in poorer countries, as a step on the ladder to affluence. A short period of inequality and environmental degradation is a prelude to the affluence that will follow when the full potential of economic expansion is realized. In the long run, the free play of market forces is the best way to improve human well-being because it harnesses individual self-interest for the social good. It is also the best way to protect the environment because affluent societies are more likely to care about healthy environments, and economic growth provides them with the resources needed to protect and clean up the environment.

Free market advocates are unabashedly (anthropocentric.) Jobs and human material well-being are the first priority. Humans are superior to other species and have the right to dominate nature for their own well-being. Nature is distinct from culture with little or no intrinsic value, only utilitarian value for human beings. This value is measurable in terms of dollars and compared to other uses of resources similarly valued. Land and resources are factors of production and are considered as costs in the same way as labor and capital. Property rights are essential to protect the individual against encroachment from other individuals and government and to allow markets to function properly.

Increasingly this perspective is under critical scrutiny. Critics are skeptical about the claims made for the market system and modern technology. Side effects are seen as main effects, externalities are seen as intrinsic to the system. Critics reject the reduction of nature to a factor of production and its quantification solely in dollar terms.[2] Others find unsatisfying the hierarchical, dominating, dualistic, atomistic, and anthropocentric attitudes at the heart of the free market perspective.

Conservation

Conservationists get their name from the movement in the late nineteenth and early twentieth centuries led in the United States by Gifford Pinchot to conserve resources for human use. Many conservationists share with free market advocates anthropocentric ideas and values. Nature is there for human use; only this must be wise use governed by the best science-based management practices. Conservationists emphasize scientific management and control based on the science of ecology, confident that the judicious use of technology will allow increases in the use of resources without degrading the capacity of ecosystems to continue producing.

Like the free market perspective, conservationists seek to control nature, but unlike the advocates of the free market, they often draw on government agencies, regulations, and resources to control it rationally for sustained use over time. Rational control presents problems, of course. Scientific understanding may be poor or in dispute yet used as if it were objective. Ideology and political give and take can cloud rationality. The lure of higher income can bias objectivity.

Conservationists have less faith than free market advocates in market mechanisms and promote governmental interference in markets to ensure environmental quality. Indeed, conservationists came to prominence in opposition to *cut and run* forest practices and the abuses of corporate power in the late nineteenth century. Governmental intervention was necessary then, according to the conservationists, to avoid the degrading side effects of unregulated resource extraction and markets. The formation of the US Forest Service and the subsequent assignment of vast tracts of forests in the United States to it for management was due to their efforts. Their emphasis on governmental intervention and management also contributed to the acceptance of government as a countervailing power to big business that culminated in the New Deal.

Conservationists are largely utilitarians. They are more holistic than market liberals, focusing less on individual property rights than on the greatest good for the human community as a whole. They believe that nature is to be used in accordance with utilitarian principles to maximize human well-being. As articulated by Gifford Pinchot, for example, the Forest Service is to produce "the greatest good for the greatest number [of humans] over the longest period of time."[3] Like market liberals, jobs and economic growth are important to conservationists but not at the expense of healthy ecosystems. Resource use must be governed by the principle of sustainability, which is best calculated by scientifically trained managers.

In their stress on the good of the human community and in their regard for the future of healthy ecosystems, conservationists are less anthropocentric, dualistic, and atomistic than free market advocates and take a longer-term outlook. Healthy ecosystems and human communities should be managed for the long-term sustenance of humans, and to some minimum degree humans have to cooperate with nature in the development of resources. So while largely anthropocentric, conservationists exhibit some regard for the biosphere and do not separate themselves as thoroughly as free market advocates from it.

Nevertheless, hierarchy, dualism, and domination lurk in notions such as scientific management. The scientific mind is seen as superior to the matter of nature's processes and is assigned the task of controlling it. Technology is the means of control. Nature is a resource with utilitarian, not necessarily intrinsic, value. The free market perspective is sometimes disguised in conservationist garb, and claims for scientific management and sustainability are made to cover degrading environmental practices.

Preservation

With *preservationists* comes marked difference, although at the margin with conservationists there is similarity. The essence of the preservationist perspective is the protection of ecosystems, species, and individuals of a species from degrading human practices. Preservationists thus share with many conservationists a passion for protecting the environment and sometimes even use the anthropocentric and utilitarian appeals of the conservationists to achieve their ends. Most preservationists also accept the need to give over part of nature to human resource extraction, that part being guided by best resource management practices.

Indeed, the preservationist perspective in the United States emerged out of the conservationist movement, and early on in the twentieth century, preservationists were allies of conservationists in opposition to exploitation. The event that gave birth to the preservationist movement is generally recognized to be the fight over Hetch Hetchy Dam in Yosemite National Park, a fight that ended in 1913 with a decision by Congress in favor of the dam. This battle pitted Gifford Pinchot against John Muir, who pressed for the preservation of Hetch Hetchy Valley in its pristine state. While supportive of the conservationists' introduction of scientific management in the extraction of natural resources, Muir argued with religious fervor for set-asides, such as national parks. These areas should be preserved undisturbed and never appropriated for human exploitation. They are valuable in and of themselves and deserve protection. Material abundance and utilitarian arguments do not trump the intrinsic value of these places.[4]

Preservationists are responsible for the creation of the extensive National Wilderness Preservation System under the Wilderness Act of 1964 that, to date, has set aside nearly 110 million acres of land in the United States for permanent wilderness protection.[5] John Muir was also one of the founders of the Sierra Club, which is today among the nation's most important environmental groups. Initially a wilderness venture society, today the Sierra Club is a bastion of the preservationist perspective and a group with considerable political power.

To those on the conservationist side of the continuum, preservationists push too hard for set-asides, for taking land and resources out of the economic cycle where they serve the production of wealth. To those with critical ecology perspectives, preservationists are too timid and too supportive of the economic and political status quo, however near they may be in terms of basic perspective.

With the preservationists there is a decided shift to the critical ecology side of the continuum in terms of attitudes toward nature. Preservationists are biocentric and ecocentric, at least in terms of species and ecosystems. In preserves, intact and untouched ecosystems should be the norm. All species should be protected from extinction; and while humans may enjoy the preserves and admire other species, that is, consider them for their value to human interests, ecosystems, species, and individuals of a species also have intrinsic value—value for their own sake apart from human interest. Ecosystems are especially important to protect and preserve because they are the foundation of everything else. They should be left intact to continue their biotic processes.

Some preservationists would carry this even further as a principle for relationships to all ecosystems. Ecocentrism means that the needs of evolving ecosystems and species come before all but the most basic of human needs. Other preservationists would hold human needs in some sort of balance with the preservation of ecosystems and species.

As this indicates, preservationists are far less hierarchical. Viewed ecologically, humans are one species among many. All forms of life have intrinsic value as well as value for the greater ecological whole. The emergence of human intelligence is an amazing and perhaps unique product of evolutionary history, but ethically, its main importance is to convey a sense of responsibility rather than a hierarchical sense of moral superiority over other species.

With the preservationists dualism and domination recede. Humans are part of nature and completely dependent on ecosystems. Domination yields to cooperation, dualism to connectedness and integration, not only for reasons of survival, but also for spiritual well-being.

Among preservationists, the spiritual motif is quite strong. Muir was a pantheist who was deeply influenced by his Christian upbringing. Many preservationists claim to encounter God in nature and see their relationship to, and participation in, nature in spiritual terms. This is a far cry from the scientific and managerial approach of conservationists and the economic approach of the free market advocates.

In their stress on ecosystems, species, and humans in community, preservationists are more holistic and communitarian, less individualistic and atomistic. Preservationists are strong supporters of so-called landscape, watershed, and ecosystem management approaches that have been prominent in recent environmental discussions. By management, of course, they mean something quite different from the economic management of free market advocates and the scientific management of the conservationists. While not rejecting these forms of management, they want to expand them by looking at all elements in an ecosystem and the complex interactions that take place there. Management in this view may also mean *not* managing, that is, letting be—or rather managing *human* behaviors to give wild nature the space and freedom it needs to evolve on its own terms. In keeping also with this emphasis on whole systems and species, preservationists play down the importance of individuals, thereby creating space for conflict with those who focus on animal rights or human property rights.

Preservationists are critical of the current preoccupation with economic growth, especially forms that cause environmental degradation. Affluence is not a priority. They place little trust in markets, convinced that the market system left to itself is incapable of accounting for noneconomic, nonquantifiable goods. Preservationists frequently turn to government to regulate markets and to protect ecosystems, although with less confidence than the conservationists.

Finally, preservationists do not hold modern technology in the same high esteem as free market advocates and conservationists. While not Luddites, they view the introduction of new technology and new management schemes with suspicion because of the historical role technology has played in environmental degradation.

Critical Ecology

The fourth perspective on this continuum is more difficult to pin down. *Critical ecology* is actually a group or cluster of perspectives that share in common a strong criticism of dominant social arrangements and values. In environmental conflicts this cluster has been influential in shaping ideas and values but marginal in terms of social policy, highly publicized interventions by various direct action groups notwithstanding. Carolyn Merchant's delineation of the various groups in this cluster is useful.[6]

1. *Deep ecologists* call for a new ecological paradigm to replace the dominant mechanistic paradigm. Opposed to reformist efforts of conservationists and preservationists they call *shallow ecology*, deep ecologists reverse the attitudes toward nature of the free market advocates and emphasize the equal intrinsic value of all forms of life. The crisis is so deep that only a radical transformation in thinking and being will be sufficient.
2. *Spiritual ecologists* focus on a transformation of consciousness, especially religious consciousness. Some raise up older forms of nature spirituality, such as *goddess* and Native American forms of worship, others Eastern religions, and still others neglected currents in Christianity.
3. *Social ecologists* stress the shortcomings of the market system and the political and economic thought of the free market perspective. Critical of all forms of social hierarchy, they also work hard to keep justice and ecology together. They envision a world where basic human needs are met through an economic restructuring that is environmentally sustainable and grounded in networks of decentralized, localized communities.
4. *Ecofeminists* are concerned about environmental degradation that affects bodily integrity and about women's roles in social institutions. Ecofeminists also insist that assaults on nature and women are linked historically and are the result of androcentric (male-centered) rather than simply anthropocentric thinking. Women and nature are both victims of the same domination that stems from patriarchal ideas and institutions. Women's ways of knowing, which are closely aligned with the attitudes on the critical ecology side of

the continuum, offer alternatives that will liberate both oppressed women and degraded ecosystems.

5. *Green political movements* advocate direct action or grassroots confrontation in contrast to mainline environmentalists who pursue a reformist agenda through the legislative process. Groups like Earth First! and Greenpeace find the reformist agenda too timid and have used confrontational forms of involvement instead. While not so much a perspective, those in green political movements accept and are motivated by the attitudes toward nature on the critical ecology side of the continuum.

6. *Environmental justice* advocates agree with a radical critique of corporate and governmental practices but integrate social justice and environmental concerns to advocate for the well-being of socially and economically marginalized communities that typically bear the brunt of ecological degradation and the toxic byproducts of industrial society. The environmental justice movement is critical of mainstream environmental groups that focus on the well-being of nature, while ignoring the concentration of environmental and social injustices among the poor and communities of color. Rather than focusing on preserving pristine nature as separate from humans, environmental justice defines the environment as where humans "live, work, play, worship and go to school, as well as the physical and natural world."[7] With its focus on healthy environments and the well-being of marginalized communities, advocates of environmental justice tend to be more anthropocentric than other groups in the critical ecology cluster.

Diverse as they are, the movements and perspectives in this critical ecology grouping share a criticism of current directions and attitudes. Standing as they do at the opposite end of the continuum from free market advocates, these critical perspectives exhibit little faith in the market system. Whereas free market advocates and conservationists rely on economic and scientific arguments and appeal to balancing conflicting claims, those who utilize these critical perspectives tend to argue from different ethical foundations, stressing holistic and community well-being as opposed to personal property rights. Among spiritual ecologists and those of a religious bent, appeals to theology and a human spiritual connection to nature are frequent. Balancing opposing perspectives and claims is not a high priority. There are tensions, however, among those who share aspects of the critical ecology perspective. For example, the stress on nature is stronger among deep ecologists and spiritual ecologists, while social justice is of equal or greater concern among social ecologists, ecofeminists, and those in the environmental justice movement.

As for attitudes toward nature, most are decidedly biocentric or eco-centric because they see humans not as separate from but deeply embedded in and dependent on ecosystems. They assume the intrinsic value of individuals of a species, species themselves, and ecosystems. They prefer to keep the use of nature to a minimum. Some environmental justice advocates focus more on healthy environments for human well-being than protection of nature.

Instead of domination, those in the critical ecology position advocate cooperation with nature. They raise up such alternatives as appropriate technology, soft energy paths, integrated pest management, and renewable energy sources. These emphases are not antitechnological, as free market advocates sometimes claim, but pro–alternative technology. This theme of cooperation is accompanied by notions of integration and connectedness. The classic dualisms of Western thought are rejected out of hand.

Their emphasis on community, species, ecosystems, and environmental justice stands in contrast to the atomism and individualism at the other end of the continuum. From the science of ecology, those in the cluster borrow holistic categories. They see the individual person as part of both human communities and the larger biosphere and argue for both justice and sustainability. They talk little about economic growth as a policy goal. Sufficiency and frugality become guides for personal consumption.

Opponents often lump those in this cluster with preservationists and accuse both of elitism. While it is true that many environmentalists come from more affluent sectors of society, and some have been insensitive to workers, this criticism is often ideologically driven and misses the elitism of those who make the criticism. It also overlooks the fact that humans do in fact depend on healthy ecosystems whether or not environmentalists are elitist. Last of all, it is typically poor women of color and socially marginalized Native Americans who are leading the environmental justice movement, often in alliance with others in the critical ecology camp.

Four Global Perspectives

With the fall of the Berlin Wall in 1989, the subsequent rapid dissolution of the Soviet bloc of socialist nations, and the shift of communist China toward market economic policies in the 1990s, the world moved rapidly toward an integrated global capitalist economy. Within this new context of economic globalization we see several different environmental positions. Like the free market perspective in North America, some see the global economy and the economic growth it generates as key to resolving environmental and social development issues; others see it as the root cause of these problems and look to reform or transform the global economy to better achieve long-term environmental sustainability with social justice. These positions show some continuity with the earlier environmental stances described above that emerged in the context of environmental debates in the United States during the twentieth century, but they also have several distinctive elements that inform analysis of a range of contemporary environmental issues that increasingly have a global dimension. Clear ethical analysis requires understanding the global context and the dynamics of the global economy to address the interplay of current environmental and social justice issues.

Several scholars have grouped these emerging environmental perspectives into four broad categories: *market liberal, institutionalist, bioenvironmentalist,* and *social green.* Market liberals and institutionalists both see economic growth through free market economies as key to resolving environmental and social justice issues; hence, they are broadly in favor of a global capitalist economy. They differ, however, on the shape the global economy should take, and particularly on the role of government intervention and regulation of economic relations. Bioenvironmentalists and social greens unite in their opposition to the global economy specifically and many aspects of free market capitalism more broadly. They see capitalist economics, dependent on ever-increasing growth and consumption, as unsustainable in a world of ecological limits and exploitative of the poor and marginalized, particularly in the nations of the Global South.[9]

In outlining the four positions, we focus on how each frames environmental issues and how they should be resolved. We identify key assumptions that inform each position and shape how each perspective responds to environmental issues. As we saw with the four North American perspectives, how we frame issues largely shapes how we believe we should respond. Discerning the values and assumptions in each position can help us to shape our own ethical analysis and response.

Market Liberal

Market liberals believe that poverty and lack of economic growth are the primary causes of most environmental problems globally. Due to pressing survival needs, poor people often degrade the environment, which leads to a vicious cycle of greater poverty and environmental degradation. Economic growth and high per capita incomes are critical to alleviate poverty and improve human welfare; growth also provides the economic resources needed to address environmental issues. Market liberals argue for market economies free from government regulation as key to economic growth and an efficient use of natural resources. Hence, market liberals favor economic globalization and see it as the best way to spread the benefits of economic growth and new technologies to underdeveloped regions of the world.

Market liberals do not deny the reality of environmental problems, but rather see them resulting from a lack of economic growth, the effects of poverty, market failures, and bad government policies. They believe environmental problems are best addressed within the free market system by reforming economic policies and stimulating economic growth that raises income levels of the poor. Market liberals reject apocalyptic environmental scenarios, and they put great faith in market economics, entrepreneurship, and better technologies to provide solutions to current and future environmental issues. They argue that government regulations that restrict the dynamics of the market only exacerbate our abilities to deal successfully with environmental problems. Where government is involved, it should use market-based tools based primarily on positive incentives to encourage more environmentally sustainable activities without muzzling the genius of the market to provide new ideas and technologies to improve human welfare. Like free market advocates, market liberals are unabashedly anthropocentric and see capitalist globalization based on free trade as the best way to meet human needs and use natural resources efficiently.

Institutionalist

Institutionalists share with market liberals faith in neoclassical economics and market economies, but they argue that governments and international development and finance institutions play a critical role in distributing the benefits of economic growth more equitably and sustainably. They focus on political science and international relations as necessary complements to economics for how the global economy should be shaped and governed.[10]

For institutionalists, globalization is necessary to provide the economic growth and resources needed for sustainable development, but it must be guided by international cooperation. Therefore institutionalists are strong proponents of joint international efforts, such as the United Nations Framework Convention on Climate Change, to address climate change, and international institutions, such as the UN Environmental Programme and World Bank, to direct development programs. Institutionalists also see unfettered globalization as exacerbating global environmental problems, such as the unsustainable use of resources, or contamination of global commons, such as oceans and the atmosphere. Many support a precautionary approach, urging states to take collective action at the international level to prevent further environmental degradation. While institutionalists pay closer attention to environmental sustainability and well-being than do market liberals, both are anthropocentric, with institutionalists prioritizing human well-being with social equity and seeing healthy environments as a key means to achieve both.

Bioenvironmentalist

Bioenvironmentalists frame environmental and social issues through an ecological rather than an economic lens. They root their analysis first and foremost in the natural laws of biology and ecology, stressing the biological limits of the Earth to support all forms of life, not only humanity. They emphasize that humans and our societies are *not* exempt from ecological laws and limits; therefore the ways we structure our economic and social relations must fit within and conform to Earth's limits. Bioenvironmentalists argue that the global capitalist economy does just the opposite: by fostering perpetual economic growth and ever-increasing levels of human consumption, it already exceeds the carrying capacity of both the planet and most ecosystems within it, and is moving the planet rapidly toward ecological collapse. Thus, bioenvironmentalists see the global economy and the high rates of consumption it fosters as a key—if not *the* key—cause of a wide array of environmental problems.

In contrast to the first two positions, bioenvironmentalists typically are either biocentric or ecocentric—recognizing the moral value of whole ecosystems and the need for humans to adapt *within* the greater ecological whole. They are critical of anthropocentrism as the principal cause of modernity's unsustainable ways of living. Where market liberals see economic growth as the primary element that provides resources to address environmental problems, bioenvironmentalists see growth as driving the unsustainable consumption of natural resources and increasing waste and pollution. Therefore, trying to meet the economic needs of poor nations by integrating them further into the global economy only increases the unsustainable demands made on Earth's ecosystems and accelerates the ecological crisis.

Bioenvironmentalists argue that only when we curb the twin problems of economic and population growth will we be able to resolve pressing environmental issues. We need to rethink concepts such as *progress* and *standard of living* to move them away from increasing levels of consumption and toward ecologically sustainable patterns of living. Linking population growth and consumption with ecological degradation, bioenvironmentalists argue for measures to lower population growth rates in poor countries and to limit immigration to wealthy nations with higher consumption rates.

Social Greens

Social greens emphasize the links between environmental and social problems. Similar to many of the proponents of critical ecology discussed earlier, they draw on radical social and economic theories to flesh out root causes that generate both ecological degradation and human exploitation. Like bioenvironmentalists, social greens critique globalization for spreading large-scale industrialism that is inherently exploitative of both the poor and the environment in poor countries. Yet whereas bioenvironmentalists focus primarily on ecological limits and sustainability, social greens focus on economic justice concerns and the welfare of the poor. Hence, they are perhaps closest to the perspectives of social ecology and environmental justice in the North American context. Many social greens draw on Marxist thinking that claims capitalism is the primary cause of social and environmental injustice in a globalized world. What unites social greens is their conviction that the socioeconomic structures of globalization generate broad environmental injustices, linking rising social inequality and exploitation with increasing levels of ecological degradation.

Whereas market liberals see transnational corporations as the central actors to spread both wealth and technology to poor nations, social greens see the concentration of economic and political power in corporations as one of the main drivers of environmental injustice.[11] Many see globalization as *neocolonialism*—a set of global economic and political structures that continues the unjust colonial paradigm that benefits the Global North at the expense of the Global South.[12] In response, social greens argue for a *reverse economic globalization* or a *grassroots globalization from below* to reverse perceived environmental injustices stemming from capitalist globalization.

Social greens favor localization—restoring local community autonomy and relations to the natural environment, and empowering the socially marginalized to generate genuinely democratic societies freed from the hegemony of corporations in a corporate global economy. Both social greens and some bioenvironmentalists argue for bioregionalism, that is, developing our communities, societies, and economies *within* the ecological rhythms and limits of the bioregions that contain them. They also favor small-scale community development, where *progress* is equated with increasing qualitative goods such as a stronger sense of community rather than simply consuming more goods and services. Social greens often link cultural diversity with biological diversity: only by protecting the range of cultural diversities that are locally adapted to place can the biological diversity of those places be protected and maintained.

Table 2 outlines the view of these four global environmental perspectives in relation to four key areas.

Table 2. Four Global Environmental Perspectives

	Market Liberal	Institutionalist	Bio-environmentalist	Social Green
Focus	Economies	Institutions	Ecosystems	Justice
Causes of Problems	Poverty; weak economic growth	Weak institutions and governance; Social inequity	Anthropocentrism; Population and consumption	Exploitation and ecological injustice
Impact of Globaliza-tion	Source of progress through economic growth and technology	Enhances opportunities for global cooperation	Drives unsustainable growth, trade, debt, and investment; Growing ecological degradation	Accelerates exploitation, inequalities, and environmental injustice
Solutions	Promote economic growth to alleviate poverty; Better technology and economic efficiency	Link economic growth to social equity through institutions	New global economy with limits to growth; Limit population growth and consumption	Reverse economic globalization; Promote localization and environmental justice

Adapted from Clapp and Dauvergne, *Paths to a Green World,* 16–17.

How do these four global positions compare to the four North American perspectives described earlier in the chapter? The free market and market liberal perspectives are virtually identical: both view the natural world as a source of resources for human use and development, and argue that a market economy largely free of government regulation is the best way to promote human well-being and an efficient use of natural resources. The institutionalist perspective parallels conservation in its concern for the wise use of natural resources to promote human well-being but puts much more attention on issues of holistic human development and social equity and the importance of government and international institutions to bring these about. Bioenvironmentalists share the preservationist concern for protecting wild nature and ecosystems. Where North American preservationists work largely through the legislative and court systems to protect nature and species, bioenvironmentalists focus more on global issues of population growth and consumption, as well as globalization driving unsustainable economic growth, as the principal causes of declining biodiversity and habitat loss. Social greens share with social ecology and the North American environmental justice movement a strong linkage between social justice and environmental sustainability for marginalized communities. Like Native Americans working for environmental justice, social greens promote local and indigenous knowledge systems while working to restore local community autonomy and bioregional forms of governance.

Moral Norms and Visions for Living the Good Life

Having surveyed different approaches to environmental issues within our North American and global contexts, we turn now to examine some of the moral assumptions and values each is built on. Understanding the moral underpinnings of each position can help guide our ethical analysis of the specific issues we confront in the case studies.

In her ethical analysis of the four global approaches, Christian ethicist Rebecca Todd Peters notes that implicit in each perspective is a moral vision of the good life. That is, each position argues for how we should respond to current issues and problems based on a set of beliefs and values about the meaning of human life. The question of what constitutes a *good life* for humans and how to achieve it is an ancient one in the Western ethical tradition, dating back to both the Greek philosopher Aristotle in the fourth century BCE, who made it the central question of his *Nicomachean Ethics*,[13] as well as the Hebrew prophets, who critiqued Israel's leaders for straying from the covenant given by God to Moses on Mt. Sinai.

Three questions get at important dimensions of any moral view of the good life: What is each perspective's understanding of the context needed to exercise moral agency? How does each perspective view humanity's purpose—our end, or *telos*? And what constitutes human flourishing?[14] Let's take a look at each question for what it reveals about doing ethical analysis and then see what insights they can shed on the four positions.

Exercising moral agency—the ability for humans to reflect thoughtfully on issues and then to act on them—is perhaps the central premise of doing ethics. In contrast to most other members of the animal world who act largely in response to instinct, humans must understand and interpret our worlds in order to know how to respond to them—how to live. Hence, the ability to make sense of and choose how to respond to both our physical and social environments is a key dimension of what it means to be human, and how we exercise this shapes our moral agency. Often the social context shapes how and to what extent individuals are able to exercise moral agency.

Once we have a sense of how individuals exercise moral agency within each position, we can look at the second broader question that is implicit in any view of the good life: What is humanity's purpose or *telos*? For Aristotle, humanity's purpose was living a life of *eudemonia*, happiness or human flourishing. A person achieved this through developing his or her character, practicing and embodying virtues or positive character traits such as integrity, courage, honesty, and temperance. Divine purpose or *telos* for the ancient Hebrews meant living in accordance with God's covenant as set forth in the commandments in the Torah or the Law. The

Hebrew people achieved this through following God's call to justice, integrity, and community in diverse times and settings, living according to God's vision of *shalom* as set forth in the scriptures. How do each of these four positions address the questions of what make humans happy or what gives meaning to our lives?

What we understand the purpose or *telos* of life to be informs the third question of what constitutes human flourishing. Every tradition's vision of the good life moves beyond merely meeting the basic conditions of survival—although these form a necessary foundation—to what allows humans to thrive and flourish. Though there are often environmental and social constraints on achieving the conditions for flourishing, how we understand what constitutes human flourishing can tell us a great deal about how we respond to particular environmental problems. Do the resolutions we propose further the conditions for human flourishing (and the flourishing of *otherkind*), and, if so, how and for whom?

There is one additional element of these positions that can help us deepen our ethical analysis in the case studies that follow. Each position is largely generated by and reflects the interests of a particular *standpoint* or *social location* in society. How we understand the world and the issues within it often is shaped by our experiences within it—and this is shaped by social factors such as our income level, gender, race, sexual orientation, level of education, and geographic location. Hence, a young female factory worker producing clothing in a sweatshop in Bangladesh may have a very different view of the benefits and costs of the global economy than a young woman of the same age who buys that piece of clothing in a US boutique. Our different social locations often provide us with very different levels of power and access in the world, and these differences are reflected in the case studies in the different levels of power and access the various actors are able to exercise in each case. Understanding the social locations of the four models can also help us understand who has influence in formulating and propagating each model and why.

Turning now to examining the vision of the good life implicit in each of our models, the first position, free market advocates and market liberals, represents the dominant position in the world today. Since the late 1970s, free market advocates and market liberals have generally advocated the economic model of *neoliberalism* that seeks to develop a single integrated global capitalist economy, free of government regulation and rooted in trade liberalization to foster economic growth. Globally market liberals favor free trade, and most view transnational and multinational corporations as the *engine* of the global economy. International finance organizations, such as the World Trade Organization and the International Monetary Fund, shape the global economy to facilitate cross-border investments by transnational corporations in the belief that the resultant economic growth will benefit everyone.[15]

The vision of the good life that undergirds the free market and market liberal positions is rooted in the belief that each person who is willing to work hard and accept responsibility for his or her position will be rewarded with a life of success and happiness. Hence, individual responsibility and hard work are central values. The free market positions advocate Adam Smith's *invisible hand* where the common good is achieved best by each individual pursuing his or her own self-interest. Hence, *individualism* forms the context for moral agency. Respect for individual moral agency free from government constraint is the foundational moral premise of the free market and market liberal positions.

What, then, is humanity's purpose or *telos* within these free market models? The value of *prosperity* most encapsulates their vision in neoliberalism: "Prosperity represents the rewards of working hard and leading the good life."[16] Central to maximizing prosperity is respect for, and protection of, private property rights, which also allows individuals to pass on wealth to family members, thus assuring that each generation has a higher standard of living than the one that precedes it—but also exacerbating already existing income inequalities. As Enlightenment figures, such as John Locke and Thomas Jefferson, argued, a key role for government, then, is protecting private property so that individuals may enjoy the fruits of their labors in security.

What enables human flourishing in the free market context? *Individual freedom.* Here freedom is understood primarily as *liberty*—the freedom to act as one chooses, free from constraint and control, particularly by the government. Respect for human dignity is expressed through respect for individual human autonomy and freedom. Government does have an important role in this, but as the economist Milton Friedman argued, the primary role of government is to establish and maintain the conditions for a free market where individuals can choose what to purchase and how to act free from government coercion and control.

With this vision of the good life rooted in individualism, prosperity, and freedom, we can understand the free market and market liberal responses to environmental issues with their preference for market mechanisms and government actions limited largely to providing market-based incentives to accomplish environmental goals. Government limitations on either individuals or the market are seen as unjustified intrusions on human freedom and as ineffective in achieving environmental goals.

Institutionalist and conservationist positions share with the free market positions confidence in capitalism to provide the economic resources necessary for the good life, but their emphasis on conserving and using resources for the common good tempers a focus solely on individual property rights and freedom from government constraints. Internationally, the social location of the institutionalist position is reflected in its name: this approach comes largely from persons located in international agencies, institutions, and nongovernmental organizations concerned with economic and social development of poor nations. While conservationists focus primarily on the sustainable use of resources in economic development, institutionalists go further to emphasize the *holistic social development* of poor people in poor nations, as reflected in the work of the UN Development Programme (UNDP) in its annual *Human Development Report* or the World Bank with its motto—"Our dream is a world without poverty."

Concern for the common good and the holistic development of the poor is reflected in the three central values underlying the institutionalist vision of the good life. As in the market liberal perspective, *responsibility* is a central value, but rather than focusing on responsibility for one's individual choices and actions, institutionalists focus on the moral responsibility for the well-being of our neighbor. Hence, institutionalists argue "that people possess a certain amount of responsibility toward their fellow human beings and increasingly toward the environment."[17] This ethic of responsibility for the well-being of others also reflects the institutionalist view of humanity's *telos* as *progress*. As in the World Bank's conviction that a world without poverty is possible, they argue for a life for everyone that is free from want, suffering, and untimely death, where development attends to the holistic needs of persons: not only physical needs, but mental, emotional, and spiritual as well.[18] Hence, the institutionalist vision of humanity's purpose goes well beyond the market liberal vision of individual prosperity to include a social, communal dimension. The UNDP argues: "The real wealth of a nation is its people. And the purpose of development is to create an enabling environment for people to enjoy long, healthy and creative lives. This simple but powerful truth is too often forgotten in the pursuit of material and financial wealth."[19]

An additional focus of the institutionalist position that separates it from the free market perspectives, as well as conservationism, is its attention to increasing social and economic inequality between and within nations. Therefore, rather than focusing on individual freedom as what constitutes human flourishing, institutionalists give more weight to the value of *equity*—the fair and just distribution of both the benefits and burdens of the global economy. Here the role of governments and good governance is critical to steer the global economy into a fairer distribution of both its costs and benefits. Institutionalists join market liberals in arguing for free market economies as the best way to address social and environmental problems, but they contend that governments are a necessary partner with markets to achieve needed holistic development goals where the values of responsibility for our neighbor, and progress and equity for all can be achieved.

The two positions that generally oppose the global economy—bioenvironmentalists and social greens—share many concerns and values, but their focus and emphases differ. Because bioenvironmentalists prioritize the ecological well-being of the planet, they criticize the free market, conservationist, and institutionalist positions for their reliance on what theologian John Cobb calls the ideology of economism: "that attention to the expansion of the economy should be the primary political, economic, and social consideration."[20] Cobb argues that economism as a governing ideology is both "morally bankrupt" in that it privileges accumulation of wealth (especially for the already wealthy) over the well-being of people and ecosystems, and "functionally bankrupt" because it increases the affluence of the already affluent while increasing the gap in social and economic inequality between rich and poor.

Though bioenvironmentalists are found across the planet, this position's social location is primarily in the Global North among citizens and organizations who are deeply concerned by the growing global ecological crisis that threatens not just human life, but the viability of many forms of life. Hence bioenvironmentalists share many of the concerns and perspectives of the cluster of positions in critical ecology. Bioenvironmentalists use an explicitly ecocentric framework to envision the good life for the planet. Like deep ecologists and ecofeminists, they see moral agency as rooted in *mutuality*, where people are seen as fundamentally relational, not only within human societies, but also embedded in larger ecosystems. Like the institutionalists, bioenvironmentalists emphasize the common good, but they expand the common good to include all of Earth and its creatures.

Much like critical ecology that links social justice to ecology, bioenvironmentalists see humanity's purpose as establishing *right-relatedness* or *ecojustice* with all creatures of the Earth. Ethicist Larry Rasmussen describes ecojustice as meaning "essentially that we share one another's fate and are obligated by creation itself to promote one another's well-being."[21] From the values of mutuality and ecojustice comes the bioenvironmentalist claim that *sustainability* is what constitutes the context for flourishing—flourishing for *both* humans and the broader creation since they are inextricably intertwined.

Sharing much in common with the bioenvironmentalist position, social greens typically are located in grassroots communities in the Global South or in communities that express active solidarity with the anticolonial struggles of the Global South. Given their shared historical context of struggle against European colonialism and racism, like their North American counterparts in the environmental justice movement, social greens link problems of social justice and ecological degradation. Hence, as noted above, social greens typically see the global economy as a form of neocolonialism rooted in ongoing exploitation of poor nations and their environments in the Global South. In addition to exposing and critiquing the economic exploitation of the global economy, social greens argue that globalization includes cultural colonization where the export of Western values, lifestyles, and consumerism undermines local and indigenous cultures and communities.

The social green vision of the good life therefore involves resisting the multidimensional penetration of globalization and reinvigorating local and indigenous ways of life. In contrast to the Western focus on individual autonomy and freedom as the context for moral agency, social greens argue for *community*, maintaining that "one's position as a member of a community is the most significant factor in evaluating personal choices and decisions."[22] Like the environmental justice position in North America, social greens emphasize healthy human communities and environments as the critical grounding for moral agency, and therefore often have a more anthropocentric tone than some of their allies in the critical ecology camp. Thus humanity's purpose is being embedded in healthy environments and maintaining vibrant local *cultures*. Respecting a diversity of cultures that is tied deeply to the places and lands that gave birth to it is linked to maintaining the ecological integrity of these places. To achieve this, *communal autonomy* is understood as what constitutes human flourishing, and integrates the flourishing of human communities with the Earth's flourishing in local ecosystems and bioregions. This vision explicitly opposes a globalized economy that prioritizes the agency and well-being of corporations and profit, often at the expense of local cultures, communities, and ecosystems. There will necessarily be diversity in how vision manifests itself, reflecting the variety of many local and indigenous cultures.

Table 3 outlines the primary moral norms and visions of the four global environmental perspectives in relation to three questions about what constitutes the good life.

Table 3

Moral Norms and Visions of Four Global Environmental Perspectives				
	Market Liberal	**Institutionalist**	**Bioenvironmentalist**	**Social Green**
1. What is the context for moral agency?	Individual responsibility	Responsibility for others' well-being	Mutuality and relationality	Community
2. What is humanity's *telos*?	Increase prosperity	Social progress	Ecojustice	Flourishing local culture and environment
3. What moral norms constitute human flourishing?	Individual freedom as liberty	Social and economic equity	Sustainability	Communal autonomy

Adapted from Peters, *In Search of the Good Life.*

Guidelines for Earth Ethics

The question remains: What should be done by individuals in communities and ecosystems? *Should* signals ethics, and useful to doing ethics are norms to guide ethical acts directly or to inform the setting of goals.

To start gathering appropriate norms, a task that is the focus of the next chapter, the foregoing analysis of causes and perspectives is helpful. The analysis has frequently used normative language, and several norms are readily apparent. Each of the North American and global perspectives is itself a normative perspective insofar as each commends a version of *the good life*. Students of environmental ethics need to locate themselves on the continuum of perspectives or select features from each of the perspectives to arrive at their own distinct position. Included also in these perspectives are attitudes toward nature and human community. These attitudes are normative attitudes, and students should appropriate them to form their own guidelines for thought and action. A series of spectrum exercises included in the appendix to this volume helps students physically locate themselves in a range of views related to key debates in environmental ethics.

We the authors of this volume stand toward the critical ecology side of the continuum, although we draw insights from all perspectives. We think that resource use should be reduced and extraction governed by strict conservationist principles. We think endangered and vital ecosystems should be preserved intact. We think that those attitudes toward nature and human community on the critical ecology side of the continuum should more and more guide social policy, but not to the exclusion of human need. Humans count. Sufficiency, not luxury, should guide our use of nature, however. Human justice should be a major consideration in environmental decisions. We do not trust in the so-called technological fix, but we do believe that science and technology are vital to sufficient production, as are the insights of economists.

We think increased spirituality is badly needed to correct today's materialism. In environmental ethics, this means finding a deep spiritual sense in nature. We believe a sense of the sacred is present in natural processes and can be found there by cultivating sensitivity and care. Finally, we think ethical norms developed by humans for application in society may be extended to the natural world after allowances are made for significant differences. It is to the task of developing specific ethical norms and a method for working through environmental issues via case studies that we turn in the next chapter.

Notes

[1]Adapted from Douglas E. Booth, *Valuing Nature: The Decline and Preservation of Old-Growth Forests* (Lanham, MD: Rowman & Littlefield, 1994); and Carolyn Merchant, *Radical Ecology* (New York: Routledge, Chapman & Hall, 1992).

[2]The growing field of natural capitalism, for example, argues that while market economies are important, nature must be understood along with labor, finance, and manufactured goods as *capital* to be preserved for the services each provides, rather than inexhaustible resources to be exploited at will. See Paul Hawken, Amory Lovins, and L. Hunter Lovins, *Natural Capitalism: Creating the Next Industrial Revolution* (Boston: Little, Brown, 1999); and Paul Hawken, *The Ecology of Commerce: A Declaration of Sustainability,* rev. ed. (New York: HarperBusiness, 2010).

[3]American Forests, "Lasting Legacies: Gifford Pinchot," http://www.americanforests.org.

[4]Because free market proponents are anthropocentric and generally do not recognize intrinsic value in nature, they see human-made capital and natural resources as substitutable; when natural resources dwindle, the market will incentivize creating technological substitutes. In contrast, biocentric and ecocentric perspectives recognize intrinsic value in nature and therefore reject substitutability. Instead they emphasize the need to preserve nature and the intrinsic value found in it. These differing views of utilitarian versus intrinsic value in nature underlie many of the conflicts between preservationists and free market and conservationist positions.

[5]For information on the Wilderness Act and the National Wilderness Preservation System, see Wilderness.net at http://www.wilderness.net/nwps/fastfacts.

[6]Merchant, *Radical Ecology*, chaps. 4–8.

[7]Introduction to *Toxic Wastes and Race at Twenty: 1987–2007* (Cleveland: United Church of Christ, 2007), 1, http://www.ucc.org.

[8]See in particular Jennifer Clapp and Peter Dauvergne, *Paths to a Green World: The Political Economy of the Global Environment,* 2nd ed. (Cambridge, MA: MIT Press, 2011). We follow the four-model typology outlined by Clapp and Dauvergne in what follows. For a similar typology that also includes ethical analysis of the four positions, see Rebecca Todd Peters, *In Search of the Good Life: The Ethics of Globalization* (New York: Continuum, 2004). We follow Peters for ethical analysis of the four models and providing a set of questions and categories that help to discern the ethical and moral assumptions embedded in each of the four positions described here. For a concise summary of Peters' typology, see Rebecca Todd Peters, "The Future of Globalization: Seeking Pathways of Transformation," *Journal of the Society of Christian Ethics* 24, no. 1 (2004): 105–33.

[9]The nations of Africa, Latin America, and the Caribbean, and much of Asia are often referred to collectively as the Global South. The Global South includes 157 of 184 recognized nation-states, and often the poorest and least economically and socially developed. The Global North refers to the economically developed countries of Europe, North America, and Japan, and often includes Australia and New Zealand, even though they are in the southern hemisphere. See Center for the Global South, http://www1.american.edu/academic.depts/acainst/cgs/.

[10]As political scientists Jennifer Clapp and Peter Dauvergne note, "Institutionalists . . . worry far more than market liberals about environmental scarcity, population growth, and the growing inequalities between and within states. But they do not see these problems as beyond hope. To address them, they stress the need for strong institutions and norms to protect the common good." Clapp and Dauvergne, *Paths to a Green World*, 7.

[11]See, for example, David Korten, *When Corporations Rule the World,* 2nd ed. (San Francisco: Berrett-Koehler, 2001); and David Korten, *The Great Turning: From Empire to Earth Community* (San Francisco: Berrett-Kohler, 2006).

[12]For globalization as neocolonialism, see Peters, *In Search of the Good Life,* especially Chapter 6, "Globalization as Neocolonialism." The list of social green concerns is long. See Clapp and Dauvergne, *Paths to a Green World*, 13.

[13]See Aristotle, *Nicomachean Ethics,* 2nd ed., Terence Irwin, trans. (Indianapolis: Hackett, 1999).

[14]Peters, *In Search of the Good Life,* 22.

[15]Ibid., 41–42.

[16]Ibid., 62.

[17]Ibid., 90.

[18]Ibid., 92.

[19]UN Development Programme, *Human Development Report 1999* (New York: Oxford University Press for the UN Development Programme, 1999), 1, cited in Peters, *In Search of the Good Life*, 92.

[20]Peters, *In Search of the Good Life*, 109.

[21]Larry Rasmussen, *Earth Community, Earth Ethics* (Maryknoll, NY: Orbis, 1996), 260.

[22]Peters, *In Search of the Good Life*, 160.

3

Resources for Earth Ethics

Human beings have developed a variety of cultural traditions since the advent of agriculture some thousand years ago. Most of these traditions developed in social and natural settings quite different from today. Human numbers were much lower, most people lived in rural areas, and social organizations were much simpler. Social stability, buttressed by religious traditions, mattered a great deal because disease, drought, and physical disruption were always threats. Subsistence ways of living were typical. Technologies were relatively unsophisticated and weak. The primary environmental problem was how nature was affecting humanity, not the reverse, as is the case today. All this has changed over the past two hundred years or so.

Given this historical context, it is somewhat surprising that nature has played a secondary role in most Western religious traditions, and it is disappointing that these traditions tend to pay scant attention to today's environmental problems. Humans are the chief concern of these traditions, with nature serving mostly as a backdrop for the human drama. While nature has been assumed as the basis of all life through the centuries, it has not been at the center of most deliberations. The anthropocentric nature of Western thought, which many claim is rooted in Jewish and Christian traditions, has been a source of considerable criticism, some finding in it the primary cause of the environmental crisis.[1]

Today people of faith and others concerned about the fate of Earth are reinterpreting their own religious and philosophical traditions in light of environmentalism while weaving together an environmental ethic from neglected traditions that have appreciated nature. Key to this enterprise has been extending to nature ethical norms like justice, equality, and dignity originally used solely to inform human moral problems. This book utilizes an ethic of ecological justice that has deep roots in Western religious and philosophical traditions. The ethic offers a common moral vocabulary for civil discourse about complicated moral problems affecting human beings and the rest of life on Earth.[2]

The term *ethics* has a Greek root.[3] As a noun, *tō ethos* originally referred

45

to a stall for domesticated animals where animals received nourishment and protection. The stall or *stable* offered *stability* and security. The verb form, *eiōtha*, means *to be accustomed to*. The Latin parallel is *mos*, which serves as the root of the English words *mores*, *morality*, and *morale*. This is one of the oldest meanings of morality—behavior according to custom. Mores are customs. Routine, customary behavior does for human society what the stall does for domesticated animals: it provides stability and security. Most of the time customary moral behavior goes unquestioned because it serves its purpose, which is to protect life so that it may flourish. There are times, however, when it appears customary moral codes are failing to serve their purpose or are inconsistent with the ideals upon which they are based.

It was the Greeks who began to distinguish between morality as behavior according to custom and ethics as behavior according to reason. One engages in ethical reflection when one steps back from customary moral behavior to ask whether, in fact, that behavior is justified. In the end, this ethical reflection might reaffirm the moral views inherited from the past, but it might also recommend a departure from customary views to embrace a better form of morality that is more consistent with foundational ideals and more fitting for the times. Thus, ethics involves critical reflection on moral obligations, while morality refers to the standards communities use to guide human choices and actions. The cases and commentaries in this book lead readers to engage in ethical reflection about several issues that rest at the nexus of social justice and environmental concerns. This ethical reflection might lead to changed perceptions of what constitutes moral behavior to promote planetary well-being.

The Ethic of Ecological Justice

The ethic of ecological justice addresses human-caused problems that threaten both human and natural communities. The ethic tries to unite in one orbit of moral concern the separate fields of social ethics and environmental ethics. The ethic of ecological justice attempts to discern and adjudicate various responsibilities owed to the poor, to future generations, to sentient life, to organic life, to endangered species, and finally to ecosystems themselves. The word *ecological* highlights the value of other species and their habitats; the word *justice* points to the distinctly human realm and human relationships to the natural order.

Justice

The norm of justice used in the title of this ethical perspective is an inclusive concept. Its full meaning is given greater specificity by the four norms of sustainability, sufficiency, participation, and solidarity summarized below. Justice, however, is a major moral norm in its own right with a distinct history in Western philosophy and Christian ethics. While conceptions of justice differed in the Greco-Roman world, the Latin phrase *suum cuique* (to each his or her own) served as the primary foundation for reflections on justice. In Plato's dialogue, *The Republic*, Socrates argues "justice is when everyone minds his own business, and refrains from meddling in others' affairs."[4] Socrates goes on to argue that each person should receive "his own" (e.g., rights) and not be deprived of "his own" (e.g., property).[5] Aristotle explores this conception of distributive justice further in his *Nicomachean Ethics*.[6] Justice, for Aristotle, is one of four cardinal virtues that needs to be cultivated in *the good life*. The other cardinal virtues are prudence, fortitude, and moderation.

Christian traditions of justice have also deeply influenced Western views. Here justice is rooted in the very being of God. It is an essential part of God's triune community of love, and calls human beings to make fairness the touchstone of social relations as well as relations with other species and ecosystems. While related, justice and love are not synonyms. Justice involves a calculation of interests. Justice has a more impersonal quality than love because social groups are more its subject than individuals. Nevertheless, justice divorced from love easily deteriorates into a mere calculation of interests and finally into a cynical balancing of interest against interest. Without love inspiring justice, societies lack the push and pull of care and compassion to move them to higher levels of fairness. Love forces recognition of the needs of others. Love judges abuses of justice. Love lends passion to justice. Justice, in short, is love worked out in arenas where the needs of each individual are impossible to know.

For Aristotle, justice means "treating equals equally and unequals unequally."[7] This simple statement of the norm of justice hides the complexities of determining exactly who is equal and who is not as well as the grounds for justifying inequality. For example, women and slaves were not regarded as equals in Greco–Roman society. Modern interpretations of justice thus have emphasized freedom and equality as measures of justice. This has also led to the concept of equity, which is justice in actual situations where a degree of departure from freedom and equality are permitted in the name of achieving other social goods. So, for example, most societies give individuals with mental and physical impairments extra resources and justify it in the name of greater fairness. This is a departure from equal treatment but not from equitable treatment. The problem, of course, is that self-interested individuals and groups will often ask for departures from freedom and equality and use spurious justifications. This is one reason justice needs love as its foundation. Claims for justice require careful scrutiny.

Another problem with justice as it has been conceived in classical Western religious and philosophical traditions is that it has been utterly anthropocentric. One approach to ethics has focused on maximizing human welfare. A second approach has focused on respect for human dignity as the most important principle at the heart of justice. A third has focused on the cultivation of moral virtues and the formation of human moral character. All three approaches fail, however, to account for planetary well-being, which is the basis for all forms of life and any experience of human good. The ethic of ecological justice used in this book seeks to remedy this problem by drawing on a moral vision that extends to all members of the community of life and to the ecological systems that sustain that life.

In summary, justice requires a special concern for the poor, a rough calculation of freedom and equality, and a passion for establishing equitable relationships. The ethical aims of justice in the absence of other considerations should be to relieve the worst conditions of poverty, powerlessness, exploitation, and environmental degradation and provide for an equitable distribution of burdens and costs. The moral norms of sustainability, sufficiency, participation, and solidarity help to flesh out more fully what an ethic of ecological justice entails.

Biblical and Theological Foundations for Justice

The biblical basis for justice with its special sensitivity for the poor starts with God's liberation of the poor and oppressed slaves in Egypt and the establishment of a covenant, one of whose cardinal features is righteousness (Exodus 22:21–24). The biblical basis continues in the prophetic reinterpretation of the covenant. Micah summarized the law: "to do justice, and to love kindness, and to walk humbly with your God" (Micah 6:8). Amos was adamant that God's wrath befell Israel for its unrighteousness. Important for Amos among the transgressions of Israel were injustice and the failure to care for the poor (Amos 2:6, 8:4–8, 5:11). Isaiah and Jeremiah were no different (Isaiah 10:1–2; Jeremiah 22:13–17).

In the Christian scriptures the emphasis on justice is muted in comparison to the prophets, but the concern for the poor may be even stronger. Jesus himself was a poor man from a poor part of Israel. His mission was among the poor and directed to them (Luke 4:16–20). He blessed the poor and spoke God's judgment on the rich (Luke 6:20–26; Matthew 5:1–14).

The early church carried this tradition beyond the time of Jesus. Paul's concern is frequently for the weak members of the community. This is his concern as he addresses a question that now seems quaint: eating meat sacrificed to idols (1 Corinthians 8). He affirms the new freedom in faith that is one important foundation for political freedom. Freedom is not, however, a license to ignore or prosecute the weak in the pursuit of one's own consumption.

Paul is even more emphatic on equality, which together with freedom is the backbone of the modern concept of justice. His statement on the ideals of freedom and equality are among the strongest in the entire biblical witness

(Galatians 3:28). His commitment to freedom and equality is in no way diminished by his more conservative interpretations in actual situations where he may have felt the need to moderate his ideals for the sake of community harmony. Thus, while Paul seems to advise an inferior role for women (1 Corinthians 14:34–36) and urges a slave to return to his master (Philemon), his ringing affirmation of equality in Galatians has through the ages sustained Christians concerned about justice.

In the Christian community in Jerusalem (Acts 1–5), equality was apparently put into practice and also involved sharing. In this practice these early Christians set themselves apart from the prevailing Roman culture.

Sustainability

Sustainability may be defined as the long-range supply of sufficient resources to meet basic human needs and the evolutionary continuation of natural communities. It expresses a concern for future generations and the planet as a whole, and emphasizes that an acceptable quality of life for present generations must not jeopardize the prospects for future generations.

Sustainability is basically good stewardship and is a pressing concern today because of the human degradation of nature. It embodies an ongoing view of nature and society, a view in which ancestors and posterity are seen as sharing in present decisions. The present generation takes in trust a legacy from the past with the responsibility of passing it on in better or at least no worse condition. A concern for future generations is one aspect of love and justice. Sustainability precludes a shortsighted stress on economic growth that fundamentally harms ecological systems and any form of environmentalism that ignores human needs and costs.

The focus on future generations associated with sustainability has been controversial for at least two reasons. The first is because justice in the West has usually been associated with reciprocity. That is, if I want my rights to be respected, then I need to respect the rights of others. From this perspective, the problem with future generations is they can never do anything for present generations. Thus, champions of the free market and market liberalism have tended to discount or dismiss obligations to future generations. At best, advocates of conservation have focused on long-term management of natural resources to provide sustainable supplies for each generation of human communities. This leads to the second area of controversy. Deep ecologists, bioenvironmentalists, and many religious traditions have argued that all life has value, not merely human life. Thus, the norm of sustainability extends the scope of moral concern to the whole community of life. This extension of moral consideration can cause innumerable conflicts and problems as human needs and wants come into conflict with the interests of all other forms of life.

Biblical and Theological Foundations for Sustainability

There are several significant biblical and theological foundations for the norm of sustainability. The doctrine of creation affirms that God as Creator sustains God's creation. The creation is also good independently of human beings (Genesis 1). It is not simply there for human use, but possesses an autonomous status in the eyes of God. The goodness of matter is later picked up in Christian understandings of the incarnation and the sacraments.

Psalm 104 is a splendid hymn of praise that celebrates God's efforts at sustainability. "When you send forth your spirit . . . you renew the face of the ground" (Psalm 104:30). Similarly, Psalm 145 rejoices in the knowledge that God gives "them their food in due season" and "satisfies the desire of every living thing" (Psalm 145:15–16). The doctrine of creation also emphasizes the special vocation of humanity to assist God in the task of sustainability. In Genesis the first creation account describes the responsibility of stewardship in terms of "dominion" (Genesis 1:28) or responsible rule, and the second creation account refers to this task as "to till and keep it" (Genesis 2:15). In both cases, the stress is on humanity's stewardship of *God's* creation. The parable of the Good Steward in Luke also exemplifies this perspective. The steward is not the owner of the house but manages or sustains the household so that all may be fed and have enough (Luke 12:42). The Gospels offer several other vivid metaphors of stewardship. The shepherd cares for the lost sheep. The Earth is a vineyard, and humanity serves as its tenant.

The covenant theme is another important biblical and theological foundation for the norm of sustainability. The Noahic covenant (Genesis 9) celebrates God's "everlasting covenant between God and every living creation of all flesh that is on the Earth." The biblical writer repeats this formula several times in subsequent verses, as if to drive the point home. The text demonstrates God's concern for biodiversity and the preservation of all species (Genesis 9:16).

It is the Sinai covenant, however, that may best reveal the links between the concepts of covenant and sustainability. Whereas the prior covenants with Noah and Abraham were unilateral and unconditional declarations by God, the Sinai covenant featured the reciprocal and conditional participation of humanity in the covenant. "If you obey the commandments of the Lord your God . . . then you shall live" (Deuteronomy 30:16). Each of the Ten Commandments and all of the interpretations of these commandments in the subsequent Book of the Covenant were intended to sustain the life of the people of God in harmony with the well-being of Earth (Exodus 20–24).

At the heart of the Sinai covenant rested the twin concerns for righteousness (justice) and stewardship of Earth. Likewise the new covenant in Christ is very much linked to these twin concerns as well as to the reciprocal relation of human beings. In Romans 8:18 the whole creation suffers and in 8:22 "groans in travail." But suffering, according to Paul, does not lead to despair." The creation awaits in eager longing for the revealing of the children of God" (Romans 8:19), and "in this hope we are saved" (Romans 8:24).

Suffering, as in the suffering of Jesus Christ on the cross, points beyond to the hope that is already partially present. Part of this hope is a return to the good stewardship of Genesis 1 and 2 before the fall in Genesis 3.

Sufficiency

The norm of sufficiency emphasizes that all forms of life are entitled to share in the goods of Earth. To share in planetary goods, however, does not mean unlimited consumption, hoarding, or an inequitable distribution of Earth's goods. Rather it is defined in terms of basic needs, sharing, and equity. It repudiates wasteful and harmful consumption and encourages humility, frugality, and generosity. Only an ethic that stresses sufficiency, frugality, and generosity will ensure a sustainable future.

The norm of sufficiency challenges fundamental assumptions held by advocates of the free market who champion the benefits of economic growth. Market liberals and institutionalists have been preoccupied with improving human welfare through increased consumption. While this concern has benefited many and is still important for the poor, with increasing environmental awareness, preoccupation with endless economic growth is no longer appropriate. While other species are not equipped to practice frugality or simplicity, indeed to be ethical at all in a human sense, the norm of sufficiency does apply to humans in how they relate to other species. To care is to practice restraint. Various forms of critical ecology emphasize that humans should be frugal and share resources with plants and animals because all creatures deserve ethical consideration. A focus on sufficiency is part of what it means to practice justice.

It is important to note that sufficiency and sustainability are linked, for what the ethic of ecological justice seeks to sustain is the material and spiritual wherewithal to satisfy the basic needs of all forms of life. They are also linked through the increasing realization that present levels of human consumption, especially in affluent countries, are more than sufficient and in many respects are unsustainable. Finding agreement on such claims is easier said than done, however. For example, companies engaged in free market competition try to convert human wants into perceived needs through appealing advertising. In addition, conflicts will inherently arise when the basic needs of human communities come into conflict with the basic needs of endangered species.

Biblical and Theological Foundations for Sufficiency

This norm appears in the Bible in several places. As the people of God wander in the wilderness after the Exodus, God sends "enough" manna each day to sustain the community. Moses instructs the people to "gather as much of it as each of you need" (Exodus 16). The norm of sufficiency is also integral to the set of laws known as the jubilee legislation. These laws fostered stewardship of the land, care for animals and the poor, and a regular redistribution of wealth. In particular, the jubilee laws stressed the needs of the poor and wild animals to eat from fields left fallow every seven years (Exodus 23:11). All creatures were entitled to a sufficient amount of food to live.

In Christian scriptures, sufficiency is linked to abundance. Jesus says, "I came that you may have life, and have it abundantly" (John 10:10). Jesus rejected the notion, however, that the good life is to be found in the abundance of possessions (Luke 12:15). Instead, the good life is to be found in following Christ. Such a life results not in the hoarding of material wealth, but rather in sharing it so that others may have enough. Acts 1–5 reveals that this became the model for what amounted to the first Christian community in Jerusalem. They distributed their possessions "as they had need" (Acts 2:45). Paul also emphasized the relation of abundance to sufficiency: "God is able to provide you with every blessing in abundance, so that you may always have enough" (2 Corinthians 9:8).

The norm of sufficiency is also supported by biblical and theological understandings of wealth, consumption, and sharing. Two general and not altogether compatible attitudes dominate biblical writings on wealth and consumption. On the one hand, there is a qualified appreciation of wealth; on the other hand, there is a call to freedom from possessions that sometimes borders on deep suspicion. The Hebrew Bible generally takes the side of appreciating wealth, praising the rich who are just and placing a high estimate on riches gained through honest work.

Both sides are found in the teachings of Jesus. The announcement of the coming community of God carries with it a call for unparalleled righteousness, freedom from possessions, and complete trust in God. The service of God and the service of riches are incompatible (Matthew 6:24; Mark 8:36, 9:43–48, 10:17–25; Luke 12:15, 8:14, 11:18–23, 19:1–10). Jesus himself had no possessions and prodded his disciples into the renunciation of possessions and what later has been called holy poverty, that is, poverty that is freely chosen as a way of life (Matthew 8:20; Mark 1:16, 6:8ff.; Luke 9:3, 10:4).

On the other side, Jesus took for granted the owning of property and was apparently supported by women of means (Luke 8:2). He urged that possessions be used to help those in need (Luke 6:30, 8:2ff., 10:38ff.). He was fond of celebrations, talking often about feasts in the community of God.

The biblical witness on consumption follows much the same pattern. The basic issue has been between self-denial and contentment with a moderate level of consumption. The side of self-denial evolved into the monastic movement of later ages. The way of moderation is expressed well in 1 Timothy 6:6–8: "There is great gain in godliness with contentment; for we brought nothing into the world, and cannot take anything out of the world; but if you have food and clothing, with these we shall be content."

Sharing is an implication of neighbor love, hoarding a sign of selfishness and sin. Jesus repeatedly calls his disciples to give of themselves, even to the point of giving all they have to the poor. He shares bread and wine with them at the Last Supper. Paul in several letters urges Christians elsewhere to share with those in the Jerusalem community.

Participation

The norm of participation likewise stems from the affirmation of all forms of life and the call to justice. This affirmation and this call lead to the respect and inclusion of all forms of life in human decisions that affect their well-being. Voices should be heard, and, if not able to speak, which is the case for other species, then humans will have to represent their interests when those interests are at stake. Participation is concerned with empowerment and seeks to remove the obstacles to participating in decisions that affect lives.

Without some semblance of justice, there can be little participation in community. Extremes of wealth and poverty and disproportions of power create an envious and angry underclass without a stake in the community. Members of the environmental justice movement have emphasized that a rough equality of power and the experience of political freedom are prerequisites for genuine communities.

It is difficult to achieve participatory communities, the more so in industrialized societies even with their full range of communications. A multitude of decisions each requiring expert technical judgments and having wide-ranging consequences must be made in a timely way. Popular participation in decisions, especially when there is conflict, can paralyze essential processes. Expedience often results in the exclusion of certain voices and interests. Impersonal, functional ways of relating become easy and further reduce participation.

The norm of participation calls for a reversal of this trend. At minimum, it means having a voice in critical decisions that affect one's life. For environmental problems, it means having a say, for example, in the selection of energy and resource systems, the technologies these systems incorporate, and the distribution of benefits and burdens these systems create. All this implies free and open elections, democratic forms of government, responsible economic institutions, and a substantial dose of good will.

Finally there is the difficult problem of how to bring other species and ecosystems into human decision making. In one sense they are already included since there is no way to exclude them. Humans are inextricably part of nature, and many human decisions have environmental consequences that automatically include other species and ecosystems. The problem is the large number of negative consequences that threaten entire species and systems and ultimately the human species, for humans are dependent on other species and functioning ecosystems. The task is to reduce and eliminate where possible these negative consequences. One reason is obviously pragmatic. Humans are fouling our own nests. Beyond this anthropocentric reason, however, proponents of deep ecology emphasize the need to see plants, animals, and their communities as having interests that humans should respect. They have a dignity of their own kind. Many experience pleasure and pain. The norm of participation should be extended to include their interests, in effect to give other species a voice. Humans have an obligation to speak out for other forms of life that cannot defend themselves.

Biblical and Theological Foundations for Participation

The norm of participation is also grounded in the two creation accounts in Genesis. These accounts emphasize the value of everything in God's creation and the duty of humans to recognize the interests of all by acting as good stewards. Through their emphasis on humanity's creation in the image of God, the writers of Genesis underline the value of human life and the equality of women and men.

The prophets brought sharp condemnation upon kings and people of Israel for violating the covenant by neglecting the interests of the poor and vulnerable. They repudiated actions that disempowered people through the loss of land, corruption, theft, slavery, and militarism. The prophets spoke for those who had no voice and could no longer participate in the decisions that affected their lives (Amos 2:6–7; Isaiah 3:2–15; Hosea 10:12–14).

With Jesus comes a new emphasis, the kingdom or community of God (Mark 1:14–15). While the community of God is not to be equated to any community of human beings, it nevertheless is related. It serves as a general model for human communities and is to some degree realizable, although never totally.

The community of God has its source in a different kind of power, God's power of love and justice. This power alone is capable of producing genuine and satisfying human communities and right relations to nature's communities. The community of God cannot be engineered. Technology, material consumption, and economic growth may enhance human power but offer little help in developing participatory communities. Reliance on these powers alone can in fact make matters worse by creating divisions.

Jesus also stressed the beginning of the community of God in small things such as seeds that grow. He gathered a community largely of the poor and needy. He gave and found support in a small inner group of disciples. In this day of complex technologies, large corporations that dominate globalization, and mammoth bureaucracies, Jesus's stress seems out of place to many. In their pell-mell rush to increase the size and complexity of social organizations and technological processes, humans are missing something, however. For effective community and participation, size counts and must be limited in order for individuals to have significant and satisfying contacts. The concern for the poor evident in the Gospels is another support for the norm of participation.

Solidarity

The norm of solidarity reinforces the importance of considering the interests and welfare of all. Solidarity emphasizes the kinship and interdependence of all forms of life and encourages support and assistance for the most vulnerable, especially those who suffer. The norm highlights the communal nature of life in contrast to individualism and encourages individuals and groups to join in common cause with those who are victims of discrimination, abuse, and oppression. Underscoring the reciprocal relationship of individual welfare and the common good, solidarity calls for the powerful to share the plight of the powerless, for the rich to listen to the poor, and for humanity to recognize its fundamental interdependence with the rest of nature. The virtues of humility, compassion, courage, and generosity are all marks of the norm of solidarity.

Ecofeminists and members of the environmental justice movement have been the strongest champions of solidarity. Ecofeminists have emphasized that it is the same logic of domination that has justified the exploitation of women, other creatures, and the manifold resources of the planet. Advocates for environmental justice have similarly noted that marginalized people tend to be forcibly moved onto marginalized land where both are exploited by the rich and the powerful. While solidarity was one of the rallying cries of the French Revolution, social greens and others emphasize that the norm extends beyond the human community to all forms of life. Solidarity with those who suffer then leads to careful analysis of the systems and structures that cause this suffering and institutionalized violence.

Biblical and Theological Foundations for Solidarity

Both creation accounts in Genesis emphasize the profound relationality of all of God's creation. These two accounts point to the fundamental social and ecological context of existence. Humanity was created for community. This is the foundation of solidarity. While all forms of creation are unique, they are all related to each other as part of God's creation.

Understood in this context and in relation to the concept of stewardship in the Gospels, the *imago dei* tradition that has its origins in Genesis also serves as a foundation for solidarity. Creation in the image of God places humans not in a position over or apart from creation, but rather in the same loving relationship of God with creation. Just as God breathes life into the world (Genesis 7:15), humanity is given the special responsibility as God's stewards to nurture and sustain life.

In their descriptions of Jesus's life and ministry, the Gospels provide the clearest examples of compassionate solidarity. Jesus shows solidarity with the poor and oppressed; he puts their interests at the center of his preaching and ministry, eats with sinners, drinks from the cup of a gentile woman, meets with outcasts, heals lepers, and consistently speaks truth to power. Recognizing that Jesus was the model of solidarity, Paul used the metaphor of the body of Christ to emphasize the continuation of this solidarity within the Christian community. Writing to the Christians in Corinth, Paul stresses that by virtue of their baptisms they are all one "in Christ." Thus, if one member suffers, all suffer together; if one member is honored, all rejoice together (1 Corinthians 12:26). It would be hard to find a better metaphor to describe the character of compassionate solidarity.

The norm of solidarity also finds its home in a theology of the cross. The cross is the central symbol in Christianity. It points to a God who works in the world not in terms of power *over* but power *in, with, and under.* This is revolutionary. It upsets normal ways of conceiving power. God suffers with all living things that groan in travail (Romans 8). In the words of Jesus, "The last shall be first, and the first shall be last" (Matthew 19:30; Mark 10:31; Luke 13:30). The one who "was in the form of God . . . emptied himself, taking the form of a servant" (Philippians 2:6–7). The implication is clear. Christians are called to suffer with each other and the rest of the creation, to change their ways, and to enter a new life of solidarity and action to preserve and protect the entire creation.

While other norms will find their way into the commentaries on the cases in this volume, the ethic of ecological justice as outlined here is the normative perspective that informs and guides what follows. It has deep roots in Western religious and philosophical traditions, finds its context in current social and environmental situations, and looks to the future with a sense of inclusive justice, expectation, and hope.

The Case Study Approach

The previous section outlined an ethic of ecological justice; this section focuses on putting this ethic into action. In particular, this section explains the utility of the case study approach to issues in social and environmental ethics, and proposes a method to engage in ethical deliberation about the cases in this volume.

Case studies ground ethical reflection in reality. At the heart of Western approaches to ethics are broad injunctions expressed in simple phrases like *love your neighbor* or *do unto others as you would have them do unto you*. The problem is not identifying these norms so much as it is applying them to different situations. While many situations are similar, different details and relationships make for exceptional circumstances, conflicting norms, and moral ambiguity. Case studies are an effective tool for moral deliberation because they provide an opportunity to bring ethical resources from diverse traditions to bear on specific situations with all their differences.

Pedagogically, there are several advantages to the case study approach. Moral deliberation about specific cases tends to produce a greater degree of engaged learning and moves beyond merely theoretical reflection about broad topics or issues. All of the cases in this volume are based on real situations where individuals or groups have been faced with difficult ethical choices. Readers engaged in ethical reflection about these cases have to decide how the problems should best be resolved. Theoretical discussions become concrete when a decision has to be made. There are no places to hide. The case study approach requires a significant degree of accountability for one's ethical convictions.

Case studies promote engaged learning in other ways as well. The setting and circumstances of a case often require readers to enter foreign territory as they step into the shoes of various characters. These unfamiliar situations stimulate moral reflection in ways that familiar settings and problems do not. In addition, the use of cases in classroom settings encourages students to *apply* what they have learned in a course. In a case study approach, learning is not measured by how much information a student has been able to store up, but rather by how well a student can use that information to do ethics. This is a more complex and therefore more challenging task. Also, the discussion of cases can promote engaged learning as participants actively share their views with each other. Facilitated properly, discussion about cases can produce a community of moral discourse where all are engaged in ethical reflection.

Another advantage of the case study approach is that cases provide a setting to observe relationships between individuals and communities. Communities shape moral character, establish boundaries, produce loyalties, and create frameworks of accountability. Families normally serve as the most important community in moral formation, but peer groups, fellow students, co-workers, civic groups, religious organizations, and branches of the armed services are also examples of communities that shape the values and influence the choices of individuals. Case studies provide a means to examine ways communities influence individuals faced with important moral decisions. Often these communities produce mixed loyalties in individuals, thus complicating already difficult situations. For example, the lead character in "Smart Growth" (Chapter 11) is a champion of affordable housing, but she worries this may increase crime in her community and thus put her children at risk. Similarly, the lead character in "Moral Eating" (Chapter 5) feels loyalty to animals and the animal rights community but is also committed to local food and farming. Duties to communities can constrain the range of an individual's choices.

Cases also provide a way to see how individuals can shape and reform the values of the communities to which they are accountable. In fact, the values and ethical standards of communities and institutions only change when they are required to do so by forces from without or individuals from within. For example, in "Blown Away" (Chapter 8) students pressure their university to divest endowment holdings in fossil fuel stocks. In "Smart Growth" (Chapter 11), a vision for sustainable urban development promulgated in the state capital is upsetting some residents of an affluent community in the San Francisco Bay Area. These case studies reveal that ethical decisions are required of *both* individuals and communities.

This focus on ethical decision making leads to another advantage of case studies. Insofar as moral deliberation about cases requires an individual or group to think through and render ethical judgments, the case study method contributes to moral development. Obviously, character is shaped most significantly when the fires of experience test it, but not all lessons need to be learned the hard way. Case studies allow passions to be informed by reason and values to be clarified through judgments. Such ethical reflection can better prepare a person or a group for hard decisions that will eventually crop up in their lives.

The case study method is flexible and can be used in a variety of ways. The cases and commentaries in this volume were written with this in mind. In some situations, the reading of a case alone will be sufficient to stimulate moral deliberation about the issues posed. This would be true in settings like adult forums or in academic classrooms where the discussion about a case may simply inaugurate a new unit in a course. In other situations, readers of a case can extend the depth of their moral reflection by reading the accompanying commentary. The commentaries provide background information and identify normative elements to help those who are making ethical judgments about the case. For many of the cases, additional research into the issues can add depth and timeliness to ethical reflection. In academic settings, students might demonstrate this depth of ethical reflection in class presentations or brief papers in which they wrestle with the issues and propose a resolution to the case, or in term papers that reach conclusions by drawing on the fruits of additional research. Since ethical decisions are made not only by individuals, groups of students could also be assigned to a case and asked to reach consensus about how it should best be resolved.

A Three-Stage Method for Ethical Deliberation

In these and other ways, there are several advantages to using case studies to stimulate ethical reflection. Moral deliberation is most effective, however, when it is guided or structured in a particular way. This chapter offers a method that consists of three stages: analysis, assessment, and action (Figure 1). Factors related to each of these stages are illustrated by referencing cases in this volume. In addition, the appendix to this volume includes specific guidelines for ways this three-stage method can be used in classroom settings to structure moral deliberation about cases in written assignments and group presentations.

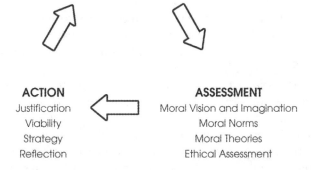

ANALYSIS
Personal Factors
Power Dynamics
Factual Information
Complicating Factors
Relationships
Ethical Issue(s)
Alternatives & Consequences

ACTION
Justification
Viability
Strategy
Reflection

ASSESSMENT
Moral Vision and Imagination
Moral Norms
Moral Theories
Ethical Assessment

Figure 1. Case studies and moral deliberation: a three-stage method

Stage I: Analysis

Good ethics depends on good information. Since ethical situations are always contextual, it is not possible to know what one ought to do until more is known about the circumstances that have produced an ethical problem. Norms like love, justice, and stewardship certainly exist to guide moral behavior, but varying circumstances often require that these norms be employed differently. There are several factors to consider when analyzing a case that is rooted in a specific set of circumstances.

Personal Factors. A starting point is with the person doing the analysis. All knowledge is filtered through the lens of personal experience and perception. These experiences, or lack thereof, do not necessarily *determine* the stance a person will take with regard to an ethical issue, but they will *influence*, to some degree, a person's analysis of the situation and assessment of the moral problem. Thus, it is helpful at the outset to reflect on ways one's personal experience may affect moral deliberation about the case. In "Maybe One" (Chapter 4), Greg finds himself thinking a lot about his personal experience with consumerism and what it was like to grow up with three siblings after he is asked by a student group to join a panel discussion about personal and structural causes of population growth, material consumption, and climate change. In "Moral Eating" (Chapter 5), Peter grapples with his vegetarianism as he learns more about small-scale, local agriculture and how well-managed cattle can mimic the ecosystem benefits of bison or elk. Again, these different experiences in life would not necessarily determine one's view about a case, but it is reasonable that these experiences could influence the way a person analyzes and assesses the case.

It can also matter if a person has something at stake with regard to the issues raised in a case. For example, in "Klamath Crisis" (Chapter 7), all of the stakeholders have a vested interest in how the Klamath Basin is managed. The same goes for "Smart Growth" (Chapter 11), where the designation of a part of Marin County as a Priority Development Area (PDA) could have significant impacts on those who live and work in this part of California. Vested interests can influence the way a person analyzes and assesses a case.

Consideration of personal factors is a good first step in the analysis of a case because it is helpful to become aware of any biases that may exist at the outset. These initial biases may be justified or rejected later during the assessment and action stages, but in an effort to be objective and fair, it is important to identify these factors as best one can in order to determine whether they play a significant role in moral deliberation. Friends and communities, as well as openness to differing perspectives, can help individuals overcome blindness to these biases.

Power Dynamics. Another important factor to consider when analyzing a case is the distribution of power between key players or stakeholders. Ethics is largely a pointless enterprise if those engaged in moral deliberation do not have the power they need to put their values into action. In ethics, this ability to implement ethical decisions is referred to as *moral agency.* It is helpful to identify the main characters or forces of power in a case and then develop a diagram that sketches the power dynamics between them. Do some individuals or groups harbor more power than others? Are they in a position of control over others? Do factors like poverty, ignorance, or race function in ways to disempower key players or stakeholders in the case? Questions like these help to diagram the power dynamics in a case.

Groups engaged in moral reflection about a case may want to develop three-dimensional diagrams by creating *human sculptures* to probe the significance that the distribution of power has in a case (see "Power Dynamic Exercise" in the appendix to this volume). In classroom settings, these sculptures tap into the creativity of students and allow them to step into a case physically in order to identify with certain characters or institutions in the case. It is one thing to look at a diagram that uses names or boxes to identify forces of power and arrows to indicate the power dynamics at play. It is another thing to see a person in a prone position with the foot of another on his or her chest, or to probe the complexity of power dynamics through the positioning of various individuals or representatives of institutions in a limited space. When shared with others, these diagrams and sculptures help identify forces that empower or disempower key players or stakeholders. They can also expose whose voices are heard or not heard within the case. Sometimes they help identify key stakeholders or forces that are invisible in the case as it is presented.

"Hot Spot" (Chapter 10) is a case that has complicated power dynamics. The case revolves around a small Native American tribe and a controversial proposal by a consortium of electric utilities to store spent nuclear fuel above ground on a portion of their reservation in Utah for up to forty years. The case has a long history. Key players include the tribe, the utility consortium, the Nuclear Regulatory Commission, various federal agencies, other citizens in Utah, Congress, and millions of American citizens who benefit from nuclear power but refuse to allow nuclear waste to be disposed of in their backyards. This is a complex case where time spent diagramming or sculpting the power dynamics would be helpful.

Factual Information. Power dynamics often play a major role in disputes about facts in a case. In order to do good analysis, it is imperative that factual information be understood as completely as possible. A good first step is to examine any historical roots to the problem. For example, there is no way to grapple with the issues in "Wearing Injustice?" (Chapter 12) without learning more about the dynamics of economic globalization and related impacts on working conditions in developing nations. The same can be said for "Moral Eating" (Chapter 5) and the history of food systems and food production in the United States.

A second step in the analysis of factual information is to determine which facts are in dispute. Facts are contested in virtually all of the cases in this volume. For example, in "Harvesting Controversy" (Chapter 6), opponents of genetically modified crops insist derived foods pose unacceptable threats to human and ecological health while proponents argue the evidence refutes these claims. In "Fractured Options" (Chapter 9), it is not clear how much methane is leaking into the atmosphere from the production and distribution of natural gas; thus, it is not clear that less carbon-intensive natural gas is truly reducing US greenhouse gas emissions by displacing emissions from coal-fired power plants.

In a few cases, however, the facts themselves are not in dispute, and yet people still differ radically. Here analysis needs to give attention to the way different worldviews and theoretical assumptions affect the way that characters in the case grapple with key facts. Every person uses various theories to organize factual information and knowledge. In turn, these theories and facts are perceived through broad worldviews and perspectives. Normally, people do not spend much time consciously reflecting about the theoretical framework that gives structure and meaning to their lives. Worldviews work best when they function invisibly in the background to provide coherence and structure to life. The problem comes when unexamined assumptions blind a person to other perspectives. Problems also arise when certain assumptions wind up being wrong or unproductive. Therefore, it is helpful to analyze the worldviews and broad theoretical frameworks used by key players in cases. It is also important to reflect on the way theories and worldviews shape the *reader's* analysis of facts in a case.

Chapter 2 identifies general attitudes toward nature that have played an important role in shaping the worldview of many people. The chapter also outlines several theoretical perspectives that influence the interpretation of factual information in cases dealing with environmental ethics. Several of these perspectives are at play in "Moral Eating" (Chapter 5), especially with regard to differing theoretical understandings of the value of other forms of life. It is no wonder that major disagreements exist because key figures in the case have very different assumptions about the relationship of humanity and nature. Good analysis of any case means giving attention to the way that different perspectives shape interpretation of the facts.

Complicating Factors. Power dynamics, theories, and worldviews are not the only things that make analysis difficult. Sometimes important information is unavailable, unfamiliar, technical, or very complex. For example, the commentary for "Fractured Options" (Chapter 9) notes the amount of methane leaking into the atmosphere is still a matter of scientific debate. The case also explores a topic (combined heat and power) that is likely unfamiliar to most readers. Similarly, "Harvesting Controversy" (Chapter 6) forces readers to grapple with the complicated science behind genetically modified crops. For those who lack a significant background in chemistry or genetics, it will require additional effort to understand important aspects of these cases. The same can be said for the legal, political, and social issues in "Klamath Crisis" (Chapter 7). In ethics, however, challenges associated with interdisciplinary work are unavoidable. It is precisely because ethical problems exist in the complexities of real life that good analysis will require grappling with unfamiliar, incomplete, or complicated information.

Relationships. Other factors that can complicate a case are relational or character dimensions that may influence the choices facing key players or stakeholders. In "Maybe One" (Chapter 4), Greg has to juggle his ethical commitments with his loyalty and affection for his future spouse, Sarah. A similar situation exists in "Harvesting Controversy" (Chapter 6) when Karen Lindstrom has to decide whether to risk losing a friendship by voting to join a Greenpeace campaign that seeks to ban genetically modified crops in Mexico. The very character of the Klamath Basin community is at stake in how water issues there are addressed, with long-term relationships already frayed from years of disputes. While some may see these relational issues as a complicating factor in the case, others may perceive the threat to a friendship or community as the primary moral problem that needs to be addressed.

Ethical Issue(s). The fact that people differ in terms of what they perceive to be a moral problem leads to the next step in the analysis of a case: Identification of the primary ethical issue that needs to be resolved. This step is crucial, of course, because it determines the set of alternatives that will be analyzed and assessed in the next phases of moral deliberation. In some cases, there may be more than one ethical issue that needs to be resolved. As noted above, those who analyze "Harvesting Controversy" (Chapter 6) from the perspective of Karen Lindstrom may not be able to divorce their ethical assessment of genetically modified crops from the impact this view could have on Karen's friendship with Josephine Omondi, a Kenyan student and ardent advocate for genetically modified agriculture in poor, developing nations.

More often, however, legitimate distinctions can be made between what constitutes the primary ethical problem in the case and other secondary problems that may justifiably receive less attention. For example, in "Wearing Injustice?" (Chapter 12) the primary issue revolves around whether the university will pledge not to source their apparel from companies that abuse workers, and the secondary issue revolves around the means of nonviolent resistance students are planning to engage in if the university fails to take the pledge. In all cases, the definition of the primary moral problem is key.

Alternatives and Consequences. Once the primary ethical issue has been identified, the last step in the analysis stage is to identify the options that exist to address this problem. Equally important is an analysis of the likely consequences associated with each option. Who will reap the benefits and bear the costs of each alternative? Alternatives that benefit a few at the expense of many, or benefit many at the expense of a few, deserve close scrutiny. Are there long-term consequences that must be weighed against potential short-term benefits? Sometimes resolving an ethical issue sets a precedent for future cases, so care must be taken to examine potential long-term consequences. Careful identification of alternatives and consideration of consequences is necessary in order to engage in ethical assessment of these options: the second stage of moral deliberation.

Sometimes the options appear to be few. For example, in "Klamath Crisis" (Chapter 7) Jennifer has to decide whether she will join a group either supporting or opposing the Klamath Basin Water Recovery and Economic Restoration Act. Nancy faces a similar choice in "Smart Growth" (Chapter 11)—whether to support or oppose the designation of a part of her community as a PDA in California.

Other cases present several alternatives. There are many personal and structural factors related to population growth, material consumption, and climate change that can be explored in "Maybe One" (Chapter 4). Similarly, there are lots of ways a college group can address mountaintop coal removal mining and related social and environmental issues in "Blown Away" (Chapter 8). In "Fractured Options" (Chapter 9), there are several ways the Energy and Climate Task Group at Vanguard College can go about reducing the college's greenhouse gas emissions, but no one option is sufficient to meet their goals and the consequences associated with one of the options are disputed. Nevertheless, good ethics requires as thorough consideration of alternatives and likely consequences as possible.

Stage II: Assessment

After the preparatory work is completed, a case is ready for ethical assessment. In this second stage of moral deliberation, each alternative and its related consequences are assessed in light of relevant moral norms, values, and principles. There are several factors to consider.

Moral Vision and Imagination. Just as theories shape the interpretation of facts, key stories, concepts, and ideas provide an ethical vision of the way life should be on Earth. For example, too often the biblical injunction to "have dominion . . . over every living thing that moves upon the Earth" (Genesis 1:28) has been used to justify the domination of both people and the planet. Moral visions matter. What if Jesus is the model of what it means to exercise dominion? That is, Jesus as Lord (*dominus*) reveals that dominion involves service to others rather than domination of them. Another source of moral vision might be found in the Greek concept, *oikos*, which means "house" or "household." *Oikos* is the root of "ecology," "economics," and "ecumenics." The *oikoumenē* refers to the entire habited planet. The reality is that all forms of life belong to the same household. Our economic, ecological, and spiritual lives are all intertwined. Equipped with such a concept, human beings might better be able to establish a truly ecological civilization due to the ecocentric (*oikocentric*) scope of its moral vision and imagination. Aldo Leopold's land ethic is one concrete way this moral vision finds expression in the form of biocentric holism—"a thing is right when it tends to preserve the integrity, stability, and beauty of the biotic community. It is wrong when it tends otherwise."[8]

Moral Values, Norms, and Principles. These sources of ethical vision and imagination find expression in various moral values, norms, and principles. Values are deeply held ideals or concepts that give meaning to the lives of individuals and societies. There are many different kinds of social, political, economic, religious, and moral values, and they are all profoundly shaped by our social location and worldview. Ethical dilemmas arise when moral values, principles, or duties come into conflict with each other in particular situations. In "Klamath Crisis" (Chapter 7), for example, societal duties to protect endangered species conflict with respect for individual property rights of farmers, and perhaps with the duty to spread burdens from environmental responsibilities fairly and equitably in society. In ethics, moral norms help us determine how to embody important values in our lives and in our societies. Norms are broad directives like *love thy neighbor* or *do no harm*. Principles, rules, and criteria are more specific *action guides* derived from general norms. For example, the *precautionary principle* warns that an action should not be taken if the consequences are uncertain and potentially dangerous. This book explores the ecological applicability of an ethic of ecological justice and its four related moral norms: sustainability, sufficiency, participation, and solidarity. Summarized earlier, these ecojustice norms help guide ethical assessment of alternatives in a case.

On the face of it, the application of these ecojustice norms to ethical issues seems fairly straightforward. Often, however, ethical issues arise because these norms can be interpreted differently. In "Hot Spot" (Chapter 10), Maggie wrestles with the norm of participation. On the one hand, she wants to support the tribal sovereignty of the Skull Valley Band of the Goshute Nation and their ability to decide whether to host a facility for the temporary storage of spent nuclear fuel rods. On the other hand, she worries the financial destitution of the tribe leaves them with no other alternatives. Can you make a free choice when you have no other options?

In other cases, ethical issues arise because at least two of the ecojustice norms come into conflict with each other. For example, the norms of sustainability and sufficiency appear to collide in "Harvesting Controversy" (Chapter 6). Crops that have been genetically modified to be resistant to pests and disease have the potential to boost food production significantly in poor, agrarian nations, but there are reasonable concerns about the ecological and social consequences of genetically modified crops. How should concerns about ecological sustainability be balanced with concerns about achieving sufficient food security for malnourished people? The answer to this question is not self-evident, but somehow the apparent conflict between sustainability and sufficiency needs to be reconciled.

There are also occasions when ecojustice norms come into conflict with other social norms. Economically, many subscribe to the maxim *growth is good*. This perspective is certainly central to the justification for mountain-top coal removal mining in "Blown Away" (Chapter 8). Economic growth via globalization is also central to "Wearing Injustice?" (Chapter 12). In both cases, key figures appeal to the norm of sustainability to challenge this normative assumption that economic growth is always beneficial. Because human development produces habitat degradation and imperils the distinctive quality of communities, a commitment to sustainability may require limits to economic growth.

Another important social norm in Western nations, and certainly within the United States, is the high value placed on individual liberty. *Don't Tread on Me* was one of the rallying cries of the American Revolution and remains a common refrain today among libertarians and members of the Tea Party. In general, Americans don't like to have their freedom constrained or to be told what to do. This emphasis on individual liberty can come into conflict with the ecojustice norms, and the tension can be found in some of the cases in this book. For example, the *right* for every couple to decide how many children to have is called into question in "Maybe One" (Chapter 4). In "Smart Growth" (Chapter 11), proponents of individual property rights oppose what they perceive as illegitimate government interference in their communities.

Legal norms can also influence ethical assessment. It is tempting in ethics to hide behind the law. Laws often reflect the ethical viewpoint of the majority, but just because something is legal does not necessarily make it moral. The laws of the nation and the decisions of a court may be binding, but they may not be ethical. For example, mountaintop coal removal mining is currently legal in the United States, but there are many reasons to view it as unethical in "Blown Away" (Chapter 8). Similarly, exploitative working conditions in global textile factories may be legal in the nations where textiles are produced but may be judged unethical from a human rights perspective, as Karla does in "Wearing Injustice?" (Chapter 12).

Finally, the ecojustice norms can come into conflict with other deeply held religious and philosophical convictions. For example, much of the religious opposition to genetic engineering is based on a concern that it violates the God-given *sanctity* of life. A smaller group of religious voices champions a limited use of genetic engineering to improve the *quality* of life, especially for human beings. Moral reflection about sustainability and sufficiency in "Harvesting Controversy" (Chapter 6) must come to terms with the way these norms may be utilized by those who wish to protect the sanctity of life or improve its quality. In all cases, ethical assessment requires careful attention to the relevance of moral norms and the way they may conflict with each other and with other norms in society.

Moral Theory. After relevant moral norms have been identified and considered, another important step is to reflect on the role moral theory plays in ethical assessment. Whereas key stories or concepts provide ethical vision, spark moral imagination, and ground moral norms, moral theories help people decide how they will use these norms imaginatively to make decisions consistent with their ethical vision. There are three main types of moral theory that are relevant to the cases in this volume.

(1) Deontology (Duty-Based Ethics). In Greek, δεῖ (dei) means duty or obligation. Those who take a deontological approach to ethics believe that we have a duty to act according to principles or rules that reveal the morality of the action itself, rather than based on the consequences of the action. Hence deontologists often defer to an extrinsic authority, whether it is Kant's duty to follow the moral law (sometimes referred to as the *categorical imperative*) or principles and rules found in the sacred texts of a religious tradition. Deontologists feel compelled by duty and find it difficult to sacrifice related principles to expediency. Some options are beyond the pale of ethical consideration because they would transgress the moral law or violate a principle or commandment. Examples of deontology include the religious belief that killing is always wrong, even in self-defense, or an animal rights perspective that killing animals for food is morally impermissible because it violates the intrinsic value of animals. For deontologists, the means must be consistent with the ends. Consistency is one of the main advantages to a deontological approach because the source of authority is extrinsic to the person making an ethical judgment, and decisions are made based on the morality of the action itself, without regard to consequences. A weakness is that principled decisions often leave little room for compromise, and sometimes considering the consequences of our actions reveals important moral considerations.

In "Moral Eating" (Chapter 5), Peter wrestles with whether eating animals itself is morally indefensible, because it causes animal suffering and pain that is avoidable or treats domestic animals as a mere means to an end, violating their intrinsic value and dignity. In "Blown Away" (Chapter 8), we learn that some colleges and universities refuse to divest from fossil fuels because they claim they are legally and morally bound by the principle of fiduciary responsibility. In both of these cases, characters appeal to certain fundamental principles or authorities in order to determine the ethical propriety of their options.

(2) Teleology (Consequentialist Ethics). In Greek, τελοσ (telos) means end or goal. Those who take a teleological approach to ethics are interested in achieving an end or maximizing a goal as much as possible. People differ, however, about the goals they seek and the ends they pursue. Some may wish simply to amass wealth and power in life, while others may seek to maximize the welfare of others, including other species. Not all ends or goals are morally laudable, however. Fundamental norms like love and justice can guide evaluation of these ends or goals. Nevertheless, all

teleologists weigh the costs and benefits of various alternatives as they figure out how to maximize the good they seek to achieve or minimize negative consequences of actions. For teleologists, the end can justify the means. One of the strengths of this approach to moral theory is that it takes consequences seriously. A weakness is that teleological thinking can ride roughshod over others as it makes compromises or violates the rights of individuals in order to maximize the good of the majority.

In the arena of public policy, assessment of costs and benefits related to particular policy options is a type of teleological reasoning commonly employed. In "Fractured Options" (Chapter 9), the Energy and Climate Task Group is engaged in serious cost–benefit analysis of the options before them to reduce Vanguard College's greenhouse gas emissions. In "Harvesting Controversy" (Chapter 6), students in a campus hunger concerns group have to assess the various costs and benefits associated with genetically modified crops in developing countries. One of the problems with the cost–benefit approach, however, is that it can be difficult to predict positive or negative consequences. This is certainly clear in "Smart Growth" (Chapter 11) and "Klamath Crisis" (Chapter 7). In addition, cost–benefit analysis is normally done in economic terms, but there are some things that are hard to measure financially. For example, it is hard to put a value on the identity of a community, the aesthetic beauty of a river basin, or the variety of services an ecosystem provides. Nevertheless, good ethics requires the consideration of specific circumstances and should include reflection about the consequences of alternatives for resolving a moral problem.

(3) Areteology (Virtue Ethics). In Greek, *ἀρετε* (arête) refers to excellence of moral character. Individuals or communities that take an areteological approach to ethics are primarily concerned about the way an ethical decision will reflect or affect their moral character. Actions that detract from or malform moral character should be avoided, whereas actions that reflect or build moral character should be embraced. Just as communities provide some deontologists with authorities or principles they feel obligated to obey, or conceptions of the good that teleologists feel compelled to pursue, for areteologists communities also play a key role in shaping the moral character of individuals and their communities. Virtue ethics is far less concerned with knowing how to act in particular situations than the overall pattern of actions for how they both build and reveal character—hence, virtue ethics can make it difficult to know how to act in any particular situation. In virtue ethics, good actions are those that flow from and reflect good character, so it can take quite a bit of moral reflection to discern what constitutes a good action and why. In resolving ethical dilemmas, a weakness of virtue ethics can be less clarity about how to act in that specific situation, but a strength is looking at the long-term effects of actions, particularly when they are repeated, for how they will reflect and shape our moral character.

Issues related to moral character crop up in at least two cases in this volume. Greg's moral character is an issue in "Maybe One" (Chapter 4). Given what he knows about demography and the likelihood for future population growth, he is reluctant to have more than one child (if any children at all), and he is honest about his apprehensions with his fiancé, even though he knows she envisions them having a larger family in the future. In "Moral Eating" (Chapter 5), it is clear that respect for animals and vegetarianism have been central to Peter's moral character. Nevertheless, Peter reconsiders his opposition to all meat eating after he meets new friends with different insights at the University of Montana.

Those engaged in ethical assessment of a case should reflect on the role of moral theory for at least two reasons. First, the description of key players and stakeholders in a case will indicate to some degree whether they are approaching the case primarily from a deontological, teleological, or areteological perspective. Appropriate moral resolution of the case should take this information into account. It would be inappropriate to ignore a troubled conscience or to force a principled stance on a character that appears more inclined to maximize the good. Good ethical judgments fit the circumstances.

A second reason to focus on the role of moral theory is because it shapes the view of anyone engaged in moral deliberation. In general, all people draw on one or more of these types of moral theory when they face an ethical problem. In a case study approach to ethics, it is helpful to spend some time reflecting on which type of moral theory may be shaping ethical assessment of issues in a case and the strengths and weaknesses associated with that approach. Moral resolution of a case can prove to be difficult if the person engaged in ethical assessment is utilizing a type of moral theory different from the key decision maker in the case. This is not uncommon, and that is why it is helpful to reflect on the role that moral theory plays in shaping ethical assessment.

It is not the case, however, that persons engaged in moral deliberation can only do so exclusively as deontologists, teleologists, or areteologists. An individual can draw on all three types of moral theory to address different ethical problems. For example, in a single day, an elected official could use a teleological approach to weigh the costs and benefits of different policy options, reject a bribe to favor one of these options out of a deontological obligation to act honestly, and later reject the advice of a campaign consultant to go negative by drawing on the areteological resources of her moral character. Different circumstances create varying ethical problems that may require the use of different types of moral theory.

The method we utilize throughout this volume is a mixed or pluralistic ethical approach that finds insight in all three ethical traditions and draws on elements of each for good ethical analysis. Hence the framework for ethical decision making in the appendix to this volume asks students to reflect on the contributions of each moral theory in analyzing the case. Ethical issues are complicated, and, in our experience, are better suited to pluralistic approaches that draw on the moral insights of several ethical traditions than to singular, monist approaches to moral theory.

Ethical Assessment. The last step of the second stage of moral deliberation is to bring this reflection about moral theory into conversation with relevant moral norms in order to assess the various alternatives and consequences associated with resolving the primary moral problem. At this point, the goal is to determine which alternative is ethically preferable. This is easier to do if the various alternatives and consequences have been clearly identified during the analysis stage.

All of the commentaries that accompany the cases in this volume are designed to assist this step of ethical assessment, but they do so in various ways. The commentary for "Klamath Crisis" (Chapter 7) provides background information related to the primary alternatives in the case. The same is true for the commentary attached to the "Hot Spot" (Chapter 10) case. The commentaries in some cases, such as "Wearing Injustice?" (Chapter 12) and "Harvesting Controversy" (Chapter 6), consider how each of the ecojustice norms apply to the case. For the sake of space, however, other case commentaries leave the applicability of specific ecojustice norms to the consideration of the reader.

Readers will find that none of the commentaries take a definitive stance with regard to which alternative in a case is ethically preferable. To do so would violate the pedagogical philosophy that drives the case study approach to ethics. We leave this step up to each reader. Ethics would be easy if it simply involved adopting the views of others. Ethical reflection is hard because it requires careful analysis and assessment in order to reach one's own moral conclusions.

Stage III: Action

Ethical reflection is also hard because ultimately it requires action. A decision about a course of action must be made in all of the cases in this volume. It is tempting to delay action through painstaking and comprehensive efforts at analysis and assessment, but ultimately a choice must be made. Choosing not to decide is after all a decision—and normally not a salutary one. At this final stage of moral deliberation, there are at least four factors to consider.

Justification. Once an ethical decision has been made, and a course of action chosen, these conclusions need to be justified to others. Ethics is always a community enterprise. Reasons supporting the decision will be couched in some type of moral theory and will appeal to relevant moral norms in order to justify the ethical preference of one alternative over the others. A well-justified ethical decision will also explain why this is the best choice given the circumstances of the case. In addition, a well-crafted decision will also anticipate and respond to the most significant counterarguments others will likely have.

Viability. As a decision is formulated, one factor to consider is whether, in fact, the decision is viable. That is, do the key players or stakeholders in the case have the power they need to put this decision into action? Is the recommended course of action unrealistic or too idealistic? If it is difficult to answer either question, the decision bears reconsideration. Good ethics gives careful attention to specific circumstances.

Strategy. Another factor that deserves consideration is whether the recommended course of action requires unique strategies in order for it to be implemented. Creative strategies for resolving the primary moral problem provide an opportunity to exercise moral imagination about a case, but they must be reasonable and justifiable.

Reflection. Finally, after reaching a decision about a case, it is important to take a step back in order to assess how one feels about the decision. The method for moral deliberation about cases that has been described in this chapter relies heavily on cognitive skills and careful moral reasoning, but ethics is not only a matter of the head, it is also a matter of the heart. Each person has a moral conscience that, when well formed, may produce nagging doubts about tentative decisions. Before rendering a final judgment and submitting it to the scrutiny of others, it is important to submit the decision to the scrutiny of one's conscience. This single step may confirm the choice and allow one to bask in the glow of a good decision. On the other hand, reflection may lead to nagging doubts and a sense of guilt that signal a need to reconsider the decision.

Conclusion

There are undoubtedly other dimensions that deserve consideration in moral deliberation about issues in Earth ethics. This chapter has proposed one method, but it can always be improved or revised. Ethics has always been more of an art than a science. In addition, while each stage of ethical deliberation deserves careful attention, the depth of moral deliberation about cases in this volume will vary according to the context. For example, in adult education settings, time constraints may not permit extensive discussion of power dynamics or the role of moral theory. In an academic setting, however, students writing research papers about a case may be able to utilize this method in an exhaustive way at each stage. Others writing shorter "case briefs" will have to be more selective, but through the use of this method will be better able to identify morally relevant information as they develop a position about how the case should be resolved.

There are certainly limitations to the case study approach to ethics.

By definition, cases are specific and do not always reflect broader, macro dimensions of a problem. This can be remedied by supplementing cases with other readings and lectures that provide greater context for the case. Another reality is that those who engage in ethical reflection about cases often do so on the basis of limited experience and knowledge. This problem is unavoidable, but it points to the need for a community of moral discourse that intentionally seeks a diversity of voices. Finally, there is the danger that ethical reflection about cases can be perceived through the lens of moral relativism. That is, since there is no one *right* answer represented in the commentary, one could draw the conclusion that any decision about the case is as good as any other. This false notion is normally challenged quickly, however, when reasons have to be given to justify decisions. Ultimately, ethical decisions made by individuals and communities are always accountable to the scrutiny of others. In one fashion or another, ethics is always a group enterprise.

Notes

[1] This is the so-called Lynn White, Jr., thesis. It has received considerable critical attention. See, e.g., James A. Nash, *Loving Nature: Ecological Integrity and Christian Responsibility* (Nashville: Abingdon Press, 1991), chap. 3. See also Steven Bouma-Prediger, *For the Beauty of the Earth: A Christian Vision for Creation Care* (Grand Rapids: Baker Academic, 2010), chap. 3.

[2] This ethic has antecedents in World Council of Churches (WCC) discussions in the 1970s. The Fifth Assembly of the WCC in 1975 emphasized the need to create a "just, participatory, and sustainable society." A follow-up conference in 1979 entitled *Faith, Science, and the Future* gave explicit attention to the norms of sustainability, sufficiency, participation, and solidarity. See Paul Albrecht, ed., *Faith, Science, and the Future* (Geneva: WCC, 1978); and Roger L. Shinn, ed., *Faith and Science in an Unjust World* (Geneva: WCC, 1978). In 1983 the Sixth Assembly of the WCC challenged all of its member communities to strive for the integration of justice, peace, and the integrity of creation. This emphasis continued with the theme of the Seventh Assembly in 1990, *Come Holy Spirit—Renew Your Whole Creation*. For a fuller discussion of the history of this ethic, see James B. Martin-Schramm, *Climate Justice: Ethics, Energy, and Public Policy* (Minneapolis: Fortress Press, 2010), 23–26.

[3] The following distinctions are drawn from Larry Rasmussen, *Earth-Honoring Faith: Religious Ethics in a New Key* (New York: Oxford University Press, 2013), 128–30.

[4] Plato, *Republic*, trans. C. D. C. Reeve (Cambridge, MA: Hackett, 2004), bk. 4, 433b.

[5] Ibid., 433e.

[6] Aristotle, *Nicomachean Ethics*, trans. J. E. C. Weldon (Buffalo, NY: Prometheus Books, 1987).

[7] Ibid., bk. 5, chap. 6.

[8] Aldo Leopold, *A Sand County Almanac* (New York: Oxford University Press, 1949), 262.

Part II

CASES AND COMMENTARIES

4

Maybe One

Population Growth, Material Consumption, and Climate Change

Acronyms and Abbreviations

CO_2	carbon dioxide
EPA	Environmental Protection Agency (US)
GDP	gross domestic product
GHG	greenhouse gas
ISA	International Students Association
PPP	purchasing power parity

Case

I

Greg swirled the coffee in his cup and ignored the new e-mail alert from his laptop. He was thinking about his conversation with Samira, an international student from Nigeria. She had become a good friend of his over the past couple years. They were both pursuing a master's degree in demography and had taken a lot of courses together. Samira offered Greg new perspectives and introduced him to many things he had not experienced while growing up in New England.

Yesterday, Samira had asked Greg to participate in a forum sponsored by the International Students Association (ISA). Titled "Think Globally, Act Locally," the forum would feature a panel of five students from all over the globe. Each panel member had been asked to address both the personal and structural aspects of population growth, material consumption, and climate change during their fifteen-minute presentations. Greg was to be the only student from North America.

The ISA had put together the forum in response to a controversial letter to the editor published in the school newspaper. In the letter, the student said he was tired of all the guilt trips dumped on North Americans. He blamed most of the world's ecological problems on high rates of population growth in developing nations and emphasized how China's greenhouse gas (GHG) emissions had far surpassed US emissions several years ago and were escalating rapidly. He closed by ridiculing the university's efforts to reduce its own GHG emissions when China was opening a new coal-fired power plant every month. The student's letter touched a nerve on campus and ignited a hailstorm of comments on the newspaper's website and via social media.

Greg understood Samira's outrage over claims like these that pinned the world's ecological problems solely on people in the developing world, but he wasn't sure what he should say at the forum. He was especially stumped by the request to address population growth and consumption at a personal level. He tried to live simply, but maybe he was just making a virtue out of a necessity since he didn't have much money. He knew he was as susceptible to advertising as anyone else. All he had to do was look at the new computer that was on the table in front of him. He was a financially strapped graduate student, but he always managed to find the money to buy the things he wanted. He had been horrified when he learned that some assemblers of Apple products in China had committed suicide out of despair over the poor working conditions in their factories, but what was he supposed to do—throw away his laptop?

Greg knew he would have to make a lot of personal consumption decisions throughout his life, but the issue that was really gnawing away at him had to do with how many children he and his fiancé, Sarah, might have. Sarah was getting her master's degree in finance and was in the process of writing her thesis on a microlending project in Peru. She hoped to be involved in similar initiatives after graduation. Greg and Sarah had not talked in depth about children, but Greg felt like this was as good a time as any to start the conversation. Sarah had been on birth control as long as Greg had known her, so neither of them had feared an unplanned pregnancy. Greg was feeling some pressure from his parents to have kids because his oldest sister, Susan, had just announced her fourth pregnancy.

Later that afternoon Greg and Sarah decided to go for a walk on the nature trail that was just a short ten-minute drive from their apartment in Boston. Sarah grabbed her Ray-Bans from the holder above the dashboard of her old Subaru and caught up with Greg, who had already started down the trail. Sarah asked Greg, if he was nervous about his panel presentation that was now only days away. Greg admitted he was. "It's the personal angle that's really hard, Sarah. Knowing what I do about global population growth, I'm not sure it's responsible for people like us to have more than one child." Grabbing Greg's hand, Sarah said, "I don't get it. You grew up with three siblings and I grew up with one. I know you've loved having a brother and two sisters. You just don't get those kinds of experiences being an only child."

Greg responded, "You're right. I did love it, but I'm worried about what life is going to be like on this planet by the end of the century. Climate change is going to wreak havoc on the next generation. I'm not sure it's fair to bring a child into this mess, let alone three or four. I just don't think this planet can handle every family having more than two children. I feel obligated to have as few kids as I can because of my sister. I don't understand why Susan feels like she can have four children. As a social worker, she knows how many kids are waiting to be adopted."

Sarah stopped on the trail and looked directly at Greg. "What? You only want to adopt? Don't you want a few kids of our own? Does it really matter how many kids we have? Isn't it more important to raise them not to be mindless consumers? I thought we were going to 'Live simply so others may simply live.' I thought we were going to try to live a life together that was carbon neutral. What difference does it make if we have two or three kids if our family has a small environmental impact?"

Greg knew Sarah had a point. It certainly did matter how children were raised and what sort of lifestyle they lived. Greg replied, "I guess I'm not saying I don't want my own kids. I really do, but maybe just one. How can we justify having more than one child knowing what we do about the state of the planet?"

Sarah, slightly taken aback, starting walking again and said, "Well, it's good to hear that you do actually *want* kids. You'd be a wonderful father, Greg. I know your parents and grandparents certainly want us to have some kids. Wouldn't it be selfish not to have any children?"

Greg knew exactly what she was talking about. His grandmother had asked about children as soon as she saw the engagement ring on Sarah's finger. Greg said, "Yeah, Sarah, I know. The organizers of the panel asked us to speak on a personal level about population growth, material consumption, and climate change. In the light of those challenges, I honestly don't know if I can justify having more than one child. I'm just trying to be honest with you."

II

A few days later Greg asked for advice from a few friends in his graduate program. Beyond the personal aspects, he was also fretting about how he would address the underlying structural factors relating to population and consumption as a part of the panel.

With the five of them crammed into a corner booth at their favorite restaurant near campus, Greg began the conversation. "As I think about high rates of consumption, fertility, and climate change, there doesn't seem to be an easy solution to these problems. Sarah and I talked about our personal decisions, but it seems like our individual actions are just drops in the bucket. The sponsors of the panel want me to make recommendations regarding structural factors, too, but I'm not sure where to start."

Ingrid, Greg's longtime friend, jumped right in. "You need to tackle the main issue, Greg: Religions are the *primary* cause of overpopulation. 'Go forth and multiply'? Are you kidding me? That's the last thing we need. Human beings are crowding out all other species and destroying what little remains of true wilderness. Islam is the fastest growing religion in the world, and Christianity isn't far behind."

"Come on, Ingrid," said Greg. "There are other reasons why there are so many people on this planet. Italy is full of Catholics, but its population growth rate over the last fifteen years has been lower than Germany, which is far more secular. Iran encouraged population growth during the revolution in the 1970s, but now fertility is at or below replacement rate. Sure, there are places like Utah that have a high percentage of Mormons and also a higher fertility rate, but there is no *direct* correlation between religious affiliation and fertility."

At this point Jon joined the conversation. Jon had grown up in Burkina Faso as the son of a Christian missionary. "Yeah, Greg. There are lots of other things that impact fertility. I think the best solution to this problem is the education of girls and the empowerment of women. There are many social benefits to educating girls, empowering women, and making modern forms of family planning methods readily available. Educated women tend to have their children further apart and can choose other options besides motherhood."

"Yes, Jon, but that is easier said than done," said Samira. "Family planning threatens our traditional preference for large families, which has a lot to do with the fact that agriculture is still the largest part of Nigeria's economy. How many siblings did your grandparents have when they were growing up on farms here in the United States? Why do you white people always blame women of color for having too many children? You're the ones that have screwed things up through colonization and overconsumption!"

"I hear you, Samira," said Greg. "But what's wrong with the education of girls and the empowerment of women?"

"Nothing," said Samira. "I wouldn't be here without both. The main problem is poverty, not population growth. We need to eradicate extreme poverty and hunger. We need better health care so mothers stop dying in childbirth and more children survive infancy and childhood. We need fairer trade terms and more debt relief. Westerners come over to Africa preaching their solutions and religions, but they are not going to help. We need Nigerian solutions for our problems, not American answers."

"Exactly, Samira," said Jacob. "Global problems require local solutions, but the main issue is really consumption, not fertility rates and population growth. Even if we all had only one child, each one of our kids would consume as much as thirty-two children in the developing world. What we really need to address are the ridiculously high rates of consumption in the industrialized world. Focusing on our own rates of consumption means that Nigerians can focus on their problems without Western fingers meddling in their affairs."

"But Jacob, population growth *is* a serious problem," said Jon. "There were only three billion people on the planet when my parents were born, and now it's over seven billion, and it sounds like we are heading for ten or eleven billion by the end of the century. The planet simply can't sustain all these people!"

Jacob shot right back: "So the solution is to reduce fertility rates in developing countries? Why? Fertility rates are decreasing across the globe except in Sub-Saharan Africa. The main problem is that improved standards of living inevitably lead to higher consumption rates. Who are we to deny the rest of the world the quality of life we have enjoyed for nearly a century? We need to focus on reducing the ecological impact of our lifestyles, and we can do that. Europeans consume half the energy that North Americans do."

Jacob's position resonated with Greg. He was truly sickened by what he viewed as wasteful and conspicuous consumption all around him, but he believed the average North American would never reduce consumption voluntarily by much. He shuddered to think what would happen if people in China or India started consuming at the level of North Americans. More importantly, Greg thought endless economic growth on a planet with ecological limits was the root of the problem. Just as he was going to say something, their server arrived and their attention switched to the huge plates of food in front of them.

III

The next morning Greg was drowsy as he talked to his older sister, Ayn, through a video chat. She was doing research in China for her doctorate in economic development. While it was 6:00 p.m. in Beijing it was only 6:00 a.m. in Boston. After getting caught up on both of their lives, Ayn offered Greg some advice about his panel remarks.

"First of all, I really think you need to frame your remarks within the context of economic globalization. That student's letter to the editor in the campus newspaper emphasized China's GHG emissions are rising at a rapid rate, but he doesn't mention that a lot of those emissions are coming from the manufacturing of products that are exported and consumed by people like him in the United States and Europe. A lot of China's emissions are really due to our demand for their products. People like you and me from wealthy, industrialized nations bear far more responsibility for past and even present GHG emissions than do people in China."

"So what's the solution, Ayn? What should I say in my panel remarks?"

"Well, if it were up to me, I think I'd focus on the need for carbon pricing and poverty reduction. We keep pumping huge amounts of carbon dioxide into the atmosphere because the prices of fossil fuels do not accurately reflect their true social and ecological costs. Once those costs are more accurately reflected by higher prices, then consumption will likely decline and cleaner energy resources will become cost competitive. This isn't a moral failure about irresponsible reproduction or consumption, it's a market failure. No one sets out to harm the planet by having kids or by driving to the grocery store. We just need to reform our economic system so that more of the external costs are included in prices."

"That sounds good in theory," said Greg, "but there is no way Congress is going to pass a carbon tax!"

"Yeah, that's probably true," said Ayn, "but the Chinese are experimenting with emissions trading and have plans to implement a national cap and trade system soon. They are already kicking our butt when it comes to investing in renewables."

A bit taken aback, Greg shifted gears. "You said something about poverty reduction being key. What do you mean?"

"What if economic growth is not the problem but rather the solution? Yes, more people consume more stuff, but we have shown a remarkable ability to come up with technological solutions to these problems. Human ingenuity is a vast resource. Think about the Green Revolution in agriculture and the amazing decline in prices for wind and solar power over the past couple decades. As economies grow and wealth increases, people put a higher value on a cleaner environment. The Chinese people are putting a lot of pressure on their government right now to clean up the air and enforce environmental laws. Finally, as wealth increases, fertility rates almost always decline. This suggests population growth and rising consumption aren't the main problem—poverty is the problem."

Greg wasn't convinced, but he also felt intimidated by Ayn's knowledge about the subject. She was the one getting a doctorate in development economics, not him. What did he know? While they were wrapping up, Ayn asked about Sarah but didn't say much when Greg quietly shared his concerns about having more than one child.

When the call was over, Greg felt pretty discouraged. Sarah was still asleep, so he poured himself another cup of coffee and moved out to the little deck on the east side of their one-bedroom apartment. He had a few hours before class. He figured this was a good time to sit down and think about what he was going to recommend in his panel remarks about personal and structural responses to population growth, material consumption, and climate change.

Commentary

It is no wonder that Greg feels overwhelmed. This case is intensely personal, but it also grapples with three of the largest phenomena in human experience—global population growth, material consumption, and climate change. Like all the cases in this volume, this one is about the sustainability of life on Earth.

In many ways Greg's reflections about these issues reflect an areteo-logical, virtue-based approach to ethics. Greg's friendship with Samira is deep and loyal. His love for Sarah is strong and faithful. His interactions with his sisters reflect an interest in prudence and the common good. Greg is fully aware that his personal choices have much larger, global ramifications. As a result, his behavior and moral character are not merely a personal or private matter.

The case does not specify how old Greg, Sarah, and their friends are, but it is reasonable to assume they are in their mid-twenties. If so, they join over three billion other people in the world who are under the age of twenty-five and are in the peak reproductive years of their lives. Approximately 90 percent are living in the developing world—especially in the Middle East and Africa.[1]

Greg, Sarah, and their global peers are members of the largest generation in human history. The decisions they make about a host of things literally will shape the future of the planet. For example, collectively their choices about the number and spacing of their children will determine whether the world's population will increase from over 7.2 billion people today to a low of 8.3 billion or a high of 10.9 billion by 2050.[2] Small differences in fertility over the next few decades will have significant impacts on the size, structure, and distribution of the human population in the twenty-first century.[3] If present trends continue, population should begin to stabilize at close to 11 billion by 2100. If various measures can reduce fertility faster, the United Nations projects the human population could decline to 6.8 billion. Alternatively, if fertility reductions fall slower than expected or stall, Earth could be home to 16.6 billion people by 2100.[4] Given these widely divergent demographic projections, many experts argue the planet is poised at a pivotal moment.[5]

Samira and her colleagues in the ISA have asked Greg and the other panelists to address both the personal and structural aspects of population growth, material consumption, and climate change. Greg's reflections lead him into interesting discussions about family size, the causes of global population growth, the empowerment of women, and the linkages between poverty, poor health, and high rates of fertility. On the consumption side, Greg is particularly concerned about the disproportionate environmental impact of high consumers in developed countries, the devastating consequences of endless economic growth, and the potential that some form of carbon pricing holds to reduce GHG emissions. This commentary provides more information about all of these issues.

Population Growth

For most of human history there have been relatively few people on Earth. Experts think there were fewer than one billion people on the planet prior to the Industrial Revolution. While many children were born each year, high rates of infant and child mortality linked to disease and inadequate food supplies kept the population from growing. High birth rates were matched by high death rates. Then, with the advances of modern science in agriculture and medicine, the increased utilization of fossil fuels, as well as improved housing and sanitation, the world's population began to grow during the nineteenth century. At the outset of the twentieth century, however, there were still only 1.6 billion people on the planet. Over the next 115 years Earth's human population more than *quadrupled* to over seven billion.[6] Why?

Demographers explain this explosive population growth through two theoretical constructs—demographic transition and demographic momentum. A demographic transition takes place when an imbalance arises between birth rates and death rates (Figure 1). The improvements in human health, access to food, and better shelter during the twentieth century enabled more children to survive infancy and childhood. Fertility rates remained high, however, even while death rates declined.[7] The result was a substantial net increase in the human population due to lower rates of infant and child mortality as well as increased longevity for adults.

Over time various factors have led women and men to desire smaller families. When children are the only means of security in old age, parents need to have several children with the hope that at least one survives to look after them when they can no longer do so. Son preference in patriarchal cultures exacerbates this situation. Reduced rates of infant and child mortality help break this cycle. Another important factor that has led to lower global fertility rates has been the transition from an agricultural economy to an industrial economy or one that revolves primarily around the delivery of services. Today, more than half the human population lives in urban settings. Whereas having several children can help with duties on farms, large families are less necessary and more difficult to support in cities. One of the most important factors driving down fertility, however,

Figure 1. The classic stages of demographic transition

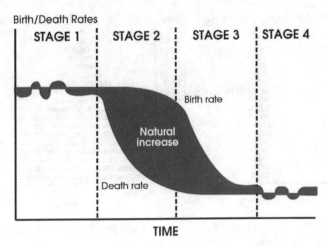

Source: Population Reference Bureau. Used with permission.

is increased opportunities for women. This begins with the education of female children, legal reforms that permit women to own property, changing social norms that embrace a wider range of vocations in addition to motherhood, and political reforms that guarantee women the right to vote. Central to increased opportunity for women has been the advent of modern methods of contraception and family planning.

These factors and others have helped most nations complete the demographic transition so that birth rates and death rates are now more in line with each other. The challenge, however, is that during this interim period when death rates decline and birth rates remain high, the children who survive grow up and have children of their own. This skews the age structure of the human population by making it younger and drives what demographers call *demographic momentum* (Figure 2). Here's how it works: Imagine a couple is fortunate to have all six of their children survive to adulthood, find a partner, and have children of their own. If each of the six couples has only three children (one-half the number of children their parents had), the total will be eighteen children—50 percent more than the sum total of their twelve parents.

This is basically what has happened over the past fifty years. The global fertility rate has declined from 4.7 children per woman in 1970 to 2.5 children per woman in 2012. In developed nations where the demographic transition is complete, 16 percent of the population is under the age of fifteen, which is similar to the 17 percent that is sixty-five and older. As a result, the population size of developed nations is projected to remain nearly the same between 2014 and 2050. The United States is actually the

Figure 2. Age and sex structure of developed and developing nations

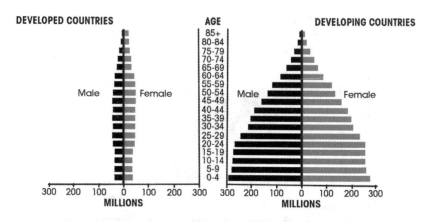

Source: United Nations Population Division, *World Population Prospects: The 2010 Revision*, medium variant (2011). Used with permission.

outlier here. Due to a slightly younger age structure compared to other developed nations, and more gains through net immigration, the population of the United States is projected to grow 20 percent from 318 million in 2014 to 395 million in 2050. By way of contrast, the population of the nations in the European Union is projected to grow from 507 million today to 517 million in 2030, and then to decline from that peak to 514 million in 2050. Remarkably, a similar pattern is projected for China, where only 16 percent of the population is under the age of fifteen. Demographers project China's population to peak in 2030 at 1.4 billion people and then to decline by 2050 to 1.3 billion.[8]

In the least developed nations in Africa and the Middle East, however, 40 to 50 percent of the population is under the age of fifteen and only 4 to 5 percent is sixty-five and older. Coupled with high rates of fertility, the populations in these regions are expected to grow considerably. For example, with a current fertility rate of 4.7, and with 41 percent under the age of fifteen, the population of the continent of Africa is projected to more than double from 1.1 billion in 2014 to over 2.4 billion in 2050. Samira's home country, Nigeria, still has a high fertility rate of 5.6, and with 44 percent of its population under the age of fifteen, the nation is projected to grow from 177 million in 2014 to 396 million in 2050.[9] Bioenvironmentalists in particular are concerned that this increase in population, combined with increasing rates of consumption through economic development of poor nations, will only exacerbate current global problems of unsustainable resource use and lead to further degradation of already fragile ecosystems.

Many war-torn nations also continue to have high fertility rates and younger age structures. For example, 48 percent of the population of Somalia is under the age of fifteen, and with a 6.6 fertility rate, the current population of 10.8 million is projected to nearly triple by 2050 to 27.1 million. Similar projections are in store for other African nations suffering civil strife, like Yemen, Chad, Mali, and South Sudan. The same is true for some nations in the Middle East. With a current fertility rate of 4.1, and with 40 percent under the age of fifteen, the number of people in Iraq and in the Palestinian Territories is projected to more than double by 2050. After more than three decades of virtually constant military conflict, the nation of Afghanistan has a 5.6 fertility rate and 46 percent of the population under the age of fifteen. As a result, the population of Afghanistan is projected to nearly double by 2050.[10]

Ingrid claims that religion is the main driver behind population growth around the world. She cites a famous text found in the sacred scriptures of Judaism and Christianity: "Be fruitful and multiply, fill the Earth and subdue it" (Genesis 1:28). This pronatalist directive made sense in a creation myth generated within the historical context of the Babylonian exile and the decimation of the Jewish people 2,600 years ago. It was a hopeful message for a people who had been defeated and whose culture was on the brink of ruin. It was never intended to be a divine command of unrestrained human reproduction. It is more accurate to view Genesis 1:28 as a blessing rather than a commandment. God utters a similar blessing to the fish of the sea and the birds of the air prior to this blessing of human reproduction (Genesis 1:22). The injunction to "be fruitful and multiply" was never intended to be a command followed blindly and without concern for its impact on the common good.

Nevertheless, Ingrid notes correctly that Islam is the world's fastest growing religion, and she claims Christianity is not far behind.[11] This does not mean these religions are the main cause of global population growth, however. Hans Rosling, a Swedish statistician and founder of Gapminder. org, demonstrates persuasively via a dynamic, graphical, online presentation that people of all religious faiths have experienced significant declines in fertility as the nations within which they live have gone through various stages of the demographic transition. Rosling demonstrates that the real causes of population growth are found in four key areas: high rates of infant and child mortality, high rates of significant poverty, lack of access to modern means of family planning, and insufficient education of women and girl children.[12] His analysis echoes institutionalists and social greens who argue we can only reduce population growth rates by addressing poverty and social inequality.

All of these factors arise in Greg's conversations with his friends. Samira notes how controversial family planning can be in patriarchal cultures. In fact, only 57 percent of married women in developing nations are using modern contraceptives, and the United Nations estimates 222 million women still lack full access to modern contraception.[13] Samira and Greg's sister Ayn both call attention to the destructive cycle of poverty and high fertility. If Greg wants to address the structural causes of global population growth, he should do further research about all four of these factors as he prepares his panel remarks.[14] While Greg has legitimate concerns about Ayn's claim that more economic development is the solution to poverty, there is no question that various forms of social development are key to ending poverty.

The more difficult thing for Greg, however, is the request to address population growth personally. He shares his concerns with his fiancé, Sarah, and floats the possibility of perhaps having only one child. Sarah seems dismayed. She seems to be thinking that two or three children would be ideal. Sarah's position is not unusual among her peers, but Greg's is. The Gallup polling firm has been asking Americans for several decades, "What do you think is the ideal number of children for a family to have?" The ideal number when the poll started in 1936 was an average of 3.6 children. Since then the ideal number has declined to around 2.6 children today. Only 2 percent of Greg and Sarah's peers want no children, another 3 percent want only one child, whereas 48 percent favor having two children, 25 percent want three children, 9 percent would like four children, and 4 percent want five or more children. Interestingly, 10 percent offered no opinion when polled.[15]

The ideal and the real often don't match, however, and this certainly is the case with regard to fertility in the United States and the European Union. While the ideal family size in both is around 2.6 children, the actual current total fertility rate in the European Union is 1.5, and in the United States it is 1.9 children per woman over the course of her reproductive life.[16] This rate of reproduction is well below the replacement level of 2.1. Bioenvironmentalists welcome this news since many countries have much higher fertility rates, and citizens of the United States and European Union consume resources at a significantly disproportionate rate. Market liberals, however, worry that declining population rates in affluent nations will jeopardize economic growth and that growing numbers of older people will become an unsustainable economic burden for decreasing numbers of younger people.

The decline in US fertility from 2.5 in 1970 to 1.9 today is primarily due to young adults postponing when to have children. Forty years ago, far more women gave birth in their twenties than in their thirties. Today, the birth rate among women ages 30 to 34 exceeds the birth rate of women ages 20 to 24. In 2010, US birth rates among teens dropped to the lowest levels ever recorded (though they are still higher than in any other industrialized nation).[17]

The decision to have children later in life is linked to several factors, including levels of educational attainment and career aspirations. In Europe, declines in fertility have been linked to high rates of unemployment and economic uncertainty. In the United States, more and more women became the primary breadwinners after their husbands lost their jobs during the recent recession. Regardless of the reason, starting childbearing at a later age means women have fewer years to achieve their ideal family size before they experience the risk of age-related infertility. If Greg and Sarah are like most of their peers, they are far more likely to have two children than three. These statistics are not likely to mollify Greg, however, because he is concerned about the disproportionate ecological impact of persons living in the developed world. His focus is typical of social greens, whereas bioenvironmentalists tend to focus on the ecological impact of population growth in the developing world and immigration that increases consumption in developed nations.

Material Consumption

"What's your consumption factor?" Jared Diamond, author of *Collapse: How Societies Choose to Fail or Succeed*,[18] posed this question in an influential editorial published in the *New York Times*.[19] A noted geographer at the University of California, Los Angeles, Diamond points out that the average person living in North America, Western Europe, Japan, and Australia consumes thirty-two times more resources like fossil fuels and metals, and produces thirty-two times as much waste like plastics and GHGs, compared to the average citizen of a developing country. Diamond illustrates his point by comparing the United States and Kenya:

> The population especially of the developing world is growing, and some people remain fixated on this. They note that populations of countries like Kenya are growing rapidly, and they say that's a big problem. Yes, it is a problem for Kenya's more than thirty million people, but it's not a burden on the whole world, because Kenyans consume so little. (Their relative per capita rate is 1.) A real problem for the world is that each of us 300 million Americans consumes as much as 32 Kenyans. With 10 times the population, the United States consumes 320 times more resources than Kenya does.[20]

Jacob alludes to Diamond's consumption factor in the case, and Greg resonates strongly with it. As social greens point out, while all citizens of developed nations have a huge ecological impact on the planet, the citizens of the United States are the elephants in the room. According to a recent article in the *Journal of Industrial Ecology*, in 2005 the United States represented 5 percent of the global population, but it used 15 percent of all extracted materials, and 20 percent of total primary energy supply, to produce 30 percent of global gross domestic product (GDP). As a consequence, the United States also produced 21 percent of all global GHGs that year.[21]

The United States leads the world's industrialized countries in terms of "real actual individual consumption" per capita, according to the World Bank's International Comparison Program.[22] Individuals in the United States consume at a rate that is about 50 percent higher than those living in the twenty-seven member states of the European Union and Japan. This is especially clear with regard to energy consumption. US citizens drive more miles each year, own the largest number of cars in relation to GDP, and have the highest fuel intensity per mile traveled. In addition, US houses are larger, and household appliances are more inefficient than in other countries, which results in high levels of residential energy use.[23]

According to the Global Footprint Network, "if everyone lived the lifestyle of the average American we would need four planets."[24] Each citizen of the United States supports his or her lifestyle by drawing upon the carrying capacity and resources of other parts of the world. This is true for citizens of other developed nations around the world, and it is also true with regard to wealthy persons within developing nations.[25] According to a recent study published in the US *Proceedings of the National Academy of Sciences*, "the United States is by far the largest importer of primary resources embodied in trade and China is the largest exporter of primary resources embodied in trade."[26] The same study emphasizes human beings around the planet are using natural resources at a level never seen before. The study claims "[t]he total amount of raw material extraction is unprecedented, and per capita levels of resource consumption are at their highest level in history."[27] While market liberals might celebrate this fact, and some institutionalists would affirm any progress in social development associated with this rate of economic development, social greens and bioenvironmentalists worry about the ecological impact of this unprecedented rate of consumption.

Greg shudders to think what would happen if the citizens of China and India were to consume at the level of citizens of the United States. China already consumes almost as much coal as the rest of the world combined.[28] It also consumes 40 to 50 percent of the world's copper, steel, nickel, aluminum, and zinc, and it raises half the world's pigs and imports half the planet's tropical logs.[29] According to *The Economist*, "China seems poised to become the next consumption superpower."[30] Its roughly $3.3 trillion in private consumption is about 8 percent of the world total, which is second only to the United States. Nevertheless, China has already become the biggest e-commerce market in the world.[31]

When the capacity to consume is measured in terms of the purchasing power parity (PPP) of gross national income, however, China's $11,850 per capita PPP is still 4.5 times less than the $53,960 per capita PPP in the United States. India's $5,350 per capita PPP is 10 times less than the US level.[32] Still, the bioenvironmentalists ask, what would happen if consumption rates in China and India were to catch up with rates in the United States? According to Jared Diamond, world consumption rates would triple. That seems hard to fathom on a planet that is already so unsustainable. While Ayn is right that environmental concerns increase as wealth rises, as market liberals maintain, Greg fears they will not rise fast enough to avoid planetary collapse.

Statistics and concerns like these recently led two prominent bioenvironmentalists, Paul Ehrlich and Michael Tobias, to recommend several measures that would better ensure planetary sustainability if they were fully embraced by most people alive today.[33] The first two measures they recommend are:

1. Have no more than one child, or none at all.
2. Try to reduce your consumption, one item and one day at a time.

One wonders whether Greg has already come across these recommendations because they appear to closely reflect his views in the case. That said, he is also concerned about poverty, inequality, and injustice as central drivers of population growth and material consumption. His fiancé, Sarah, notes that she and Greg want to live a carbon-neutral lifestyle and "live simply so others may simply live." Both of them seem motivated to reduce their ecological footprint out of a sense of solidarity with others in the world who don't enjoy their quality of life and standard of living. This is a common perspective among social greens. Given the enormous and disproportionate impact of citizens of the developed world, however, one wonders whether their lifestyles could ever be simple and frugal enough to leave a small environmental impact. That said, Greg clearly wants to do the best he can. He wants to live a life of integrity. As a result, he will want to do more research into the *simple living* and the *carbon neutral* movements as he thinks about personal measures he could take regarding consumption and climate change. But what about the structural aspects?

Carbon Pricing

The environmental problems associated with typical patterns of human reproduction, industrial production, and material consumption are "wicked problems" because they are not ordinarily the consequence of intentional malice, but rather the unintended result of our daily activities.[34] For example, no one intends to contribute to global warming by having children. Nor do people intend to harm the planet by driving to work or heating their homes or offices. We value the various services energy systems deliver (cold beer, warm spaces, reliable transportation, etc.). The reality, however, is that for most people, most of the time, engaging in these activities involves the combustion of fossil fuel and the emission of GHGs. The problem is that these emissions are externalities. The social and ecological costs associated with the combustion of fossil fuels are not reflected in the prices we pay for these fuels or goods manufactured by their use.[35] If they were, then the price would be higher, and we would think twice about driving to work, how warm to heat our homes, or whether we want to fly to visit family. The buildup of GHGs in the atmosphere is a wicked problem, in part, because it is a structural problem, and there is no social consensus on how best to deal with it. It is also a wicked problem because these *local* emissions have *global* consequences for which, institutionalists remind us, we lack global political systems or treaties to manage them.

There are a host of wicked environmental problems (loss of biodiversity, soil erosion, water pollution, fishery depletion, etc.). This case invites us to focus on climate change. Since carbon dioxide (CO_2) is the GHG having the biggest impact on global warming and future climate change, most economists argue that the introduction of some form of carbon pricing is the best way to reduce CO_2 in the future. The assumption is that once consumers have to pay a price for GHG emissions, then the volume will likely decrease.

Carbon pricing appears to be receiving growing support. Recently seventy-three nations representing more than half the world's GDP and a thousand corporations pledged support for a price on carbon emissions. The signatories included China, Russia, and the European Union, but not the United States. California, Maryland, Massachusetts, Oregon, Rhode Island, Vermont, and Washington signed separately, however. Businesses like Apple, Lockheed Martin, British Airways, Royal Dutch Shell, PepsiCo, and China Steel Corp also signed on.[36] Few specifics were offered, however, so the true test will be whether the signatories support any of the forms of carbon pricing discussed below.

Reductions in GHG emissions could not come soon enough. According to a recent study published in *Environmental Science and Technology,* GHG emissions grew at an average rate of 1.0 percent per year from 1995 to 2002, but then *accelerated* to 3.1 percent per year from 2002 to 2008. In both periods, consumption per capita and population growth were the main drivers of the increase in global emissions.[37] Greg is worried about both. The authors of the study acknowledge that economic globalization has facilitated enormous material flows between nations via international trade, but they argue economic globalization did not drive up GHG emissions. They claim GHG emissions would have increased regardless of the trade structure simply due to growing global demand for goods and services.

In the case, the author of the letter in the school paper emphasized China's GHG emissions had far surpassed US emissions several years ago and were escalating rapidly. This is true. Under the United Nations' territory-based inventory of GHG emissions, China leads the world. In fact, China's 2,626 million tons of carbon emissions in 2012 were almost twice the 1,397 million tons emitted by the United States.[38] While the United States and the European Union are cutting their emissions by about 60 million tons per year largely via fuel-switching from coal to natural gas, China is increasing its GHG emissions by over 500 million tons per year (Figure 3).[39] But Greg's sister is also right: a significant chunk of China's GHG emissions are related to the production of goods they export to the United States and other nations. *The Economist* estimates about 25 percent of China's GHG emissions are associated with export goods. According to a recent study under a consumption-based inventory, the United States would lead the world in GHG emissions, and China would come in second.[40]

Earth's atmosphere doesn't trace the source of GHG emissions, however; it merely collects these emissions, which increases their concentration and hastens global warming. Nations around the world have employed various means to reduce these emissions with only limited success thus far. There are two basic approaches—market-based measures and command and control regulations. The remainder of this commentary offers a brief summary of both.

Market liberals and institutionalists largely favor market-based solutions that seek to put a price on GHG pollution so that producers and consumers have a financial incentive to decrease emissions. Taxes and subsidies are one key approach, and various forms of cap and trade are the other primary option.[41]

Just as federal and state governments tax cigarettes to reduce consumption and to recover some of the social costs associated with smoking, a carbon tax or a series of taxes on various GHGs can be imposed to drive down emissions and reduce related social costs. Many economists favor a carbon tax as the simplest way to harness the power of the market to reduce GHG emissions. Taxes are familiar to businesses and consumers, and they provide a direct, transparent, and understandable price signal. In addition, implementation costs are typically low because tax levy and collection systems are already in place. The main advantage of a tax-based approach is a higher degree of cost certainty, but an important disadvantage is not knowing whether the tax level will be sufficient to reduce GHG emissions at the rate required. British Columbia has imposed a carbon tax on fossil fuels used for transportation, home heating, and electric power generation since 2008. The tax has been offset by reductions in personal and corporate income taxes, leaving the province of British Columbia with the lowest income tax rates in Canada. Denmark, Finland, and Sweden have modest carbon taxes as do India and Japan as well as Mexico and Chile. Australia, however, recently repealed a carbon tax that had been in force for only two

Figure 3. Top fossil fuel emitters (1960–2012) with projections to 2019

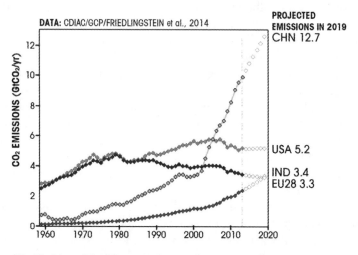

Sources: Modified from P. Friedlingstein, R. M. Andrew, and J. Rogelj, et al., "Persistent Growth of CO₂ Emissions and Implications for Reaching Climate Targets," *Nature Geoscience* (2014), provided by the Global Carbon Project. Used with permission. Historical data are from T. A. Boden, G. Marland, and R. J. Andres, *Global, Regional, and National Fossil-Fuel CO₂ Emissions,* Oak Ridge National Laboratory, U.S. Department of Energy, Oak Ridge, TN (2013). Used with permission.

years. Several bills have been introduced in Congress to establish a national carbon tax in the United States, but they have not gotten much traction because such taxes would drive up the cost of energy for homeowners and businesses and are perceived to drag down economic growth.

Subsidy programs provide a similar financial incentive to reduce GHG emissions, but they are less comprehensive in scope. Subsidies in the form of tax credits or cash payments impose a cost on all taxpayers through reduced tax revenue collection or tax receipt expenditures, but they have been more popular because they are perceived more as a carrot than as a stick. For example, no one is forcing you to buy an electric vehicle, but if you do, the federal government will give you a substantial tax credit. Certainly the federal tax credits for renewable energy have been an important factor driving investment in wind and solar power in the United States. The main advantage of a subsidy approach is that it can be more palatable politically, but it lacks the comprehensive scope that compulsory taxation offers across the economy. Many countries around the world offer various subsidy programs, including feed-in tariffs that have been the driving force behind explosive growth in renewable energy production in Germany, Spain, and Japan.

The other major market-based mechanism for carbon pricing is the cap and trade approach. In this case a government authority caps the total amount of pollution that will be allowed in a given year, or over a span of years, and then issues emission allowances. Once the allowances are distributed by auction, sale, or free allocation, then they are tradable via direct or market purchases between private parties. A well-functioning emissions trading system allows emission reductions to take place wherever it is least expensive to achieve them. In contrast to carbon taxes, a cap and trade approach offers greater certainty about the volume of GHG emission reductions but less certainty about how expensive it will be to achieve those reductions. Market liberals and many institutionalists tend to favor the cap and trade approach because it relies on market dynamics and incentives that allow businesses to decide how best to achieve GHG emission reductions.

The cap and trade approach was first employed by the United States in the 1980s to phase out leaded gasoline. Based on the success of this program, the United States employed a similar strategy to reduce ozone-depleting substances in the late 1980s and sulfur dioxide emissions in the 1990s. The United States championed a cap and trade approach during international negotiations that ultimately resulted in the Kyoto Protocol that was adopted in 1997 and went into force in 2005, despite the fact that the United States did not ratify it. The European Union Emissions Trading System was a key feature of the Kyoto Protocol, and is now in its third phase that runs from 2013 to 2030. The United States nearly adopted a comprehensive cap and trade program to reduce GHG emissions during the first year of the Obama administration. The American Clean Energy and Security Act of 2009 narrowly passed the House of Representatives but failed to garner enough votes in the Senate. Nevertheless, there are two regional cap and trade programs under way in the United States. The Regional Greenhouse Gas Initiative (RGGI) involves ten Northeastern and Mid-Atlantic States that are seeking to cut CO_2 emissions from the electric power sector 10 percent from 2015 to 2020. A similar but much more ambitious initiative in California seeks to reduce the state's GHG emissions to 1990 levels by 2020.

The devil is in the details with regard to any of these approaches, however. One of the key questions is what to do with the revenues from taxation or the sale of emission allowances. For example, should the revenues from a carbon tax be used to offset various payroll taxes and/or taxes on capital gains and dividend distributions? Many economists favor this *revenue-neutral* approach where taxes are increased in one area but reduced in another, but many social justice advocates oppose proposals that would benefit the rich more than the poor. For example, reduced taxes on investments held by the rich would cushion the impact of higher energy costs due to carbon pricing, but the poor who have few if any investments would not have a similar protection from these higher costs. Another approach would be to use the proceeds from the sale of emission allowances to reduce the federal deficit or to further subsidize renewable energy and other forms of *clean energy* like nuclear power and carbon capture and sequestration.

A third approach is to take the decision about how to use carbon pricing revenue out of the hands of the federal government and to place it in the hands of ordinary Americans. For example, the US Citizens Climate Lobby champions a national carbon fee and dividend approach that would return 100 percent of the revenue to American households in equal payments.[42]

Greg's sister Ayn points out to him that China appears to be way ahead of the United States when it comes to investments in clean energy and carbon pricing. In fact, China leads the world in investments in clean energy, and its per capita emissions are less than half compared to the United States (Figure 4). China invested $54 billion in renewables in 2013, which far surpassed the total US investment of $36.7 billion.[43] China's goal is to get 20 percent of its energy from renewables by 2020, which is the same target as the European Union.[44] In addition, China plans to introduce a national market for carbon trading in 2016 with the goal of cutting carbon emissions per unit of GDP 40 to 45 percent from 2005 levels by 2020. Seven regional cap and trade programs are already operating in different regions of China. If China's national program gets up and running, it will dwarf the European Union Emissions Trading System and become the largest in the world.[45]

Figure 4. Top fossil fuel emitters per capita (1960–2012) with projections to 2019

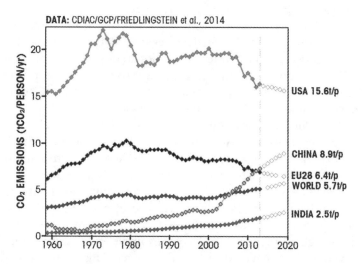

Sources: Modified from P. Friedlingstein, R. M. Andrew, and J. Rogelj, et al., "Persistent Growth of CO_2 Emissions and Implications for Reaching Climate Targets," *Nature Geoscience* (2014), provided by the Global Carbon Project. Used with permission. Historical data are from T. A. Boden, G. Marland, and R. J. Andres, *Global, Regional, and National Fossil-Fuel CO_2 Emissions,* Oak Ridge National Laboratory, U.S. Department of Energy, Oak Ridge, TN (2013). Used with permission.

Greg is skeptical about the prospects for any form of carbon pricing in the United States. After the defeat of cap and trade legislation in the Senate, the Obama administration resorted to the other primary strategy to reduce GHG emissions—command and control regulations. The US Supreme Court opened the door in a 2007 landmark decision that found the Environmental Protection Agency (EPA) does have the authority to regulate GHG emissions under the Clean Air Act.[46] The EPA is using this authority in various ways, but the most prominent (and controversial) is the Clean Power Plan that the EPA proposed in June 2014. If implemented, the plan will cut carbon pollution from the electric power sector 30 percent below 2005 levels by 2030.[47] Twelve states have already filed a lawsuit to block the proposed rule and several utilities have also expressed opposition.[48]

Conclusion

The ISA has asked Greg and all of the panelists to address both the personal and structural aspects of population growth, material consumption, and climate change. Despite what he says, Greg seems to have a firmer handle on how to address the personal aspects of population and consumption. He clearly wants to make responsible choices when it comes to having children, and he wants to live a simpler, carbon neutral-lifestyle. It's the structural aspect that is so much harder to do anything about.

It would appear that carbon pricing is a key tool to address structural aspects of climate change and perhaps to reduce material consumption. Several experts claim carbon pricing will create jobs and strengthen the economy rather than weaken it.[49] What approach should Greg recommend? Should he favor a national carbon tax or a cap and trade system? Would it be better to ramp up the subsidy approach that is the status quo? Or would it be more prudent simply to support the EPA's Clean Power Plan? Could he support some combination of these options?

The same is true for structural aspects of population growth. Greg seems to agree with institutionalists and social greens who argue we can only reduce population growth rates by addressing poverty and social inequality. Four key areas have been identified in this commentary: high rates of infant and child mortality, high rates of significant poverty, lack of access to modern means of family planning, and insufficient education of women and girl children. What is the best way to address these problems? Which policies would best accomplish them?

Greg will likely need to do more research to address the structural causes of population growth, material consumption, and climate change. He will also want to think about how the ecojustice norms can help him assess and justify the policies he favors.[50] But how much can Greg say in a brief panel presentation? The subjects raised in this case are huge, complicated, and in some cases quite personal and delicate. It is not possible to cover every nuance and detail, but it should be possible for Greg to summarize his views and sketch out preferred policies. He will want to think things through, however, because there will undoubtedly be questions from the audience after the panelists offer their remarks. The discussion will also probably continue long after the event ends. It seems clear from the case that Greg wants to do the best he can as a matter of personal integrity and global responsibility.

Notes

[1] UN Educational, Scientific and Cultural Organization (UNESCO), "Statistics on Youth," http://www.unesco.org.

[2] US Census Bureau, "U.S. and World Population Clock," http://www.census.gov/popclock.

[3] UN, *World Population Prospects: The 2012 Revision* (New York: UN Department of Economic Social Affairs, 2013), 1–2.

[4] Carl Haub, "United Nations Raises Projected World Population," Population Reference Bureau (July 2013), http://www.prb.org.

[5] Laurie Mazur, ed., *A Pivotal Moment: Population, Justice & The Environmental Challenge* (Washington, DC: Island Press, 2010).

[6] W. L. Steffen et al., *Global Change and the Earth System* (New York: Springer, 2004), 132, cited in Larry L. Rasmussen, *Earth-Honoring Faith: Religious Ethics in a New Key* (New York: Oxford University Press, 2013), 56.

[7] The term *fertility rate* refers to the average number of children born to a woman over the course of her lifetime.

[8] Population Reference Bureau, "2014 World Population Data Sheet," http://www.prb.org.

[9] Ibid.

[10] Ibid.

[11] Farzaneh Roudi-Fahimi, John F. May, and Allyson C. Lynch, "Demographic Trends in Muslim Countries," Population Reference Bureau (April 2013), http://www.prb.org.

[12] Hans Rosling, "Religions and Babies," Gapminder.org (April 2012), http://www.gapminder.org.

[13] UN Family Planning Association and the Guttmacher Institute, "Adding It Up: Costs and Benefits of Contraceptive Services—Estimates for 2012" (June 2012), http://www.guttmacher.org.

[14] For a helpful discussion of these four factors, see Al Gore, *The Future: Six Drivers of Global Change* (New York: Random House, 2013), 166–72.

[15] Frank Newport and Joy Wilke, "Desire for Children Still Norm in U.S.," Gallup Politics, September 25, 2013, http://www.gallup.com. A recent Pew Research Center study found very similar preferences among women and men living in the twenty-seven EU member states. Only 3 percent want no children, 10 percent would prefer to have only one child, but 57 percent would like to have two children, and another 30 percent prefer three or more. See Gretchen Livingston, "Birth Rates Lag in Europe and the U.S., But the Desire for Kids Does Not," Pew Research Center, April 11, 2014, http://www.pewresearch.org.

[16] Population Reference Bureau, "2014 World Population Data Sheet."

[17] Mark Mather, "The Decline in U.S. Fertility," Population Reference Bureau (July 2012), http://www.prb.org.

[18] Jared Diamond, *Collapse: How Societies Choose to Fail or Succeed* (London: Penguin Press, 2013).

[19] Jared Diamond, "What's Your Consumption Factor?" *New York Times,* January 2, 2008, http://www.nytimes.com.

[20]Ibid. The *2014 World Population Data Sheet* published by the Population Reference Bureau lists Kenya's population in mid-2014 as 43.2 million and the population of the United States of America as 317.7 million.

[21]Sylvia Gierlinger and Fridolin Krausmann, "The Physical Economy of the United States of America: Extraction, Trade, and Consumption of Materials from 1870 to 2005," *Journal of Industrial Ecology* 16, no. 3 (2011): 365.

[22]Organization for Economic Co-operation and Development (OECD), "New International Comparisons of GDP and Consumption Based on Purchasing Power Parities for the Year 2011," December 18, 2013, http://www.oecd.org.

[23]Gierlinger and Krausmann, "The Physical Economy of the United States of America," 374.

[24]Global Footprint Network, "Footprint Basics—Introduction," http://www.footprint network.org.

[25]Thomas Friedman dubs these people "Americums" in his book *Hot, Flat, and Crowded: Why We Need a Green Revolution and How It Can Renew America* (New York: Farrar, Straus and Giroux, 2008), 88.

[26]Thomas O. Wiedmann, Heinz Schandl, et al., "The Material Footprint of Nations," *Proceedings of the National Academy of Sciences of the United States of America,* 112, no. 20 (2013): 6273, http://www.pnas.org.

[27]Ibid., 6275.

[28]US Energy Information Administration, "Today in Energy," May 14, 2014, http://www.eia.gov.

[29]"The East Is Grey: China and the Environment," *The Economist*, August 10, 2013, http://www.economist.com.

[30]"Chinese Consumers: Doing It Their Way," *The Economist,* January 25, 2014, http://www.economist.com.

[31]Ibid.

[32]Population Reference Bureau, "2014 World Population Data Sheet."

[33]Paul Ehrlich and Michael Charles Tobias, *Hope on Earth: A Conversation* (Chicago: University of Chicago Press, 2014), 177.

[34]Urban planner and designer Horst Rittel coined the term *wicked problem* in 1973 while discussing limitations of a linear systems approach to urban planning and design. See "Wicked Problem," http://en.wikipedia.org.

[35]EPA, "Fact Sheet: Social Cost of Carbon" (November 2013), http://www.epa.gov.

[36]Lisa Friedman, "Global Business Leaders Back Carbon Price at N.Y. Summit," *Climate Wire,* September 23, 2014, http://www.eenews.net.

[37]Iñaki Arto and Erik Dietzenbacher, "Drivers of the Growth in Global Greenhouse Gas Emissions," *Environmental Science and Technology* 48, no. 10 (2014): 5388–94.

[38]Population Reference Bureau, "2014 World Population Data Sheet."

[39]"The East Is Grey: China and the Environment," *The Economist*.

[40]Glen P. Peters et al., "Growth in Emission Transfers via International Trade from 1990 to 2008," *Proceedings of the National Academy of Sciences of the United States of America* 48, no. 21 (2011): 8905.

[41]The following discussion draws heavily from the following publications by the Center for Climate and Energy Solutions: "Market Mechanisms: Understanding the Options," March 23, 2012, http://www.c2es.org; "Cap and Trade v. Taxes," http://www.c2es.org.

[42]Citizens Climate Lobby, http://citizensclimatelobby.org/.

[43]Bobby Magill, "World's Most-Polluting Country Leads in Clean-Energy Investment," *Bloomberg,* April 6, 2014, http://www.bloomberg.com.

[44]"The East Is Grey: China and the Environment," *The Economist*.

[45]Kathy Chen and Stian Reklev, "China's National Carbon Market to Start in 2016—Official," Reuters, August 31, 2014, http://uk.reuters.com.

[46]*Massachusetts v. Environmental Protection Agency*, 549 U.S. 497 (2007), http://www.supremecourt.gov/opinions.

[47]EPA, "Carbon Pollution Standards," http://www2.epa.gov.

[48]Andrew Zajac and Mark Drajem, "EPA Coal Plant Emissions Limits Challenged by 12 States," *Bloomberg,* August 1, 2014, http://www.bloomberg.com.

[49]Congressional Budget Office, "Effects of a Carbon Tax on the Economy and Environment" (May 2013), http://www.cbo.gov; Citizens' Climate Lobby, "The Economic, Climate, Fiscal, Power, and Demographic Impact of a National Fee-and-Dividend Carbon Tax," June 9, 2014, http://citizensclimatelobby.org.

[50]For a discussion about the relevance of these ecojustice norms and relevant ethical criteria to assess climate and energy policy options, see James B. Martin-Schramm, *Climate Justice: Ethics, Energy, and Public Policy* (Minneapolis: Fortress Press, 2010), 23–44.

5

Moral Eating

Issues around Meat, Factory Farms, and Local Food Production

Acronyms and Abbreviations

CAFOs	concentrated animal feeding operations
EPA	Environmental Protection Agency (US)
FAO	Food and Agriculture Organization (UN)
F2C	Farm to College
GHG	greenhouse gas
GM	genetically modified
PETA	People for the Ethical Treatment of Animals
SALDF	Student Animal Legal Defense Fund
SFF	Sustainable Food and Farming program
UM	University of Montana
UMCAN	University of Montana Climate Action Now
USDA	US Department of Agriculture

Case

Peter stared at the screen of his laptop in anger. He was watching a video posted recently to the Web by People for the Ethical Treatment of Animals (PETA). Titled "Meet Your Meat: How Factory Farms Work,"[1] the film showed scene after scene of hundreds of farm animals confined under appalling conditions: female hogs suckling piglets in crates too small for the mothers to stand up in, chickens with their beaks clipped off stacked ceiling high in crates barely larger than their bodies, row after row of "veal calves" standing side by side with their young heads protruding through metal bars above feeding troughs. How could anyone eat meat, he wondered, once exposed to the reality of how animals are treated in today's food system?

The images in the video were not new to Peter, but they refueled his indignation about eating meat. Peter had grown up in Des Moines, Iowa, in the heart of farm country, but as a city kid he was oblivious to the actual farm practices in his home state. Raised on nursery rhymes with bucolic farm images, like "Old MacDonald's Farm," and proud of the pioneer spirit that had converted Iowa's tallgrass prairie into some of the most productive farmland in the world, Peter had associated farming with small towns set in endless fields of corn and soybeans, carpeting Iowa's rolling landscapes. It was only through a class project in high school that Peter had learned about the environmental and animal treatment issues connected to concentrated animal feeding operations (CAFOs) or what others called factory farms. Peter learned that some of the worst problems with CAFOs were happening right in his backyard: by the time he graduated from high school Iowa had more than 8,500 factory farms, and was by far the country's biggest hog producer. Even worse, more than eighteen million of its twenty million hogs were being raised in CAFOs—most owned by or under exclusive contract to industry giants such as Smithfield, Cargill, Tyson, or Hormel.[2] After he concluded his project, Peter decided to become a vegetarian and oppose raising and killing animals for human consumption.

Peter had also become passionate about smaller-scale local agriculture as an alternative to industrial agriculture and food systems that depended on factory farms and monocrop agriculture. His interests had led to some intense debates with his best friend, Roger, whose dad, Jack, was an agronomist working overseas for Cargill. Home from one of his trips, Jack told Peter that while he was sympathetic to the goals of the localization movement, small-scale organic agriculture and farmers' markets would never feed the planet. "The real issue in agriculture is food security," Jack told him. "Here in the United States our modern agricultural system provides over three hundred million people with the cheapest and most nutritious food supply the world has ever seen, and no one goes hungry. We grow enough to export food crops all over the planet. Modern agriculture is especially important for the global poor.[3] I work at Cargill because only large companies like Cargill, Pioneer, and Archer Daniels Midland have the resources and scientists to develop and share the agrotechnology and genetically modified (GM) crops we will need to feed a growing planet. I admire your concern for animals, but I hate to see you waste your time with small-scale ag when there are so many more important issues in the world."

Despite Jack's warnings, when he finished high school Peter decided to enroll at the University of Montana (UM) where he joined UM's Sustainable Food and Farming (SFF) program to learn more about sustainable agriculture as an alternative to factory farms. When Peter arrived at UM, he was glad to find that there was a chapter of the Student Animal Legal Defense Fund (SALDF) active on campus, working on animal rights issues important to him. Peter was excited that he could address his twin passions of sustainable agriculture and animal rights while earning a college degree. SALDF was organizing a series of actions targeting meat being served in the dining halls, and Peter gladly joined their efforts. In addition to raising awareness about CAFOs and animals, they hoped to pressure UM Food Services to decrease or eliminate serving meat in UM facilities and to push for more vegetarian options instead.

Coming from Iowa, the link between vegetarianism and environmental issues seemed obvious to Peter. CAFOs not only were harmful to animals, they had numerous negative environmental effects as well. What he was not prepared for, therefore, was the number of environmentalists and local farmers he met in Montana who ate meat *and* saw animals as an important component of sustainable agriculture and ranching. He was also surprised to meet many environmentalists who hunted wild animals and who saw hunting and eating wild game as an important piece of sustainability and conservation management practices.

Now partly in response to SALDF's actions, UM's Farm to College (F2C) dining program was proposing to use local meat from Montana producers in the dining halls as an alternative to meat from CAFOs. Peter wasn't sure what to think. The F2C program had been started a decade earlier to provide local and sustainably grown food in the dining halls, while supporting local farmers and producers. It had been wildly successful, recently passing the $1 million mark for purchasing local products that year. Peter appreciated the bright posters in the dining hall buffet lines that educated students about the food they were eating and the sustainable agricultural practices that produced it. He was particularly proud of F2C's mission:

> To support agricultural and economic development statewide by purchasing Montana products to serve in our dining venues, F2C educates the campus community and others about Montana food and agriculture, thereby strengthening connections between the urban and rural areas of our state. F2C seeks to reduce our environmental impacts by shortening the physical distance that our food travels and by purchasing from ecologically responsible businesses.[4]

Jim Martinelli, the director of UM Food Services, was an enthusiastic supporter of local and sustainable agriculture and the F2C program at UM. He had become a national voice in the F2C program and recently had been granted the Silver Plate award from the International Food-service Manufacturers Association in recognition of his leadership. It was his suggestion to support local meat producers by purchasing their products for F2C.[5]

While most students at UM didn't think twice about where the meat in the dining halls came from, both the animal rights community and members of UM Climate Action Now (UMCAN) were upset at UM Food Services' decision to substitute local meat rather than reduce or eliminate meat altogether. The students in UMCAN argued that meat-based diets are a main contributor to global warming because current meat production practices produce billions of tons of greenhouse gas (GHG) emissions around the world each year. While locally raised animals addressed some environmental concerns, it still perpetuated an unsustainable meat-based diet—globally livestock produce over eighty million tons of methane a year, accounting for nearly 28 percent of global methane emissions from human-related activities.[6] Since UM had committed to reducing its carbon footprint, they thought it was wrong to include meat in the F2C program. For SALDF it was wrong to raise and kill animals under any conditions. The SALDF and UMCAN chapters asked Peter to oppose including meat in the F2C program at an upcoming rally. Several of his friends and faculty in the SFF program were strongly supportive of F2C supporting local meat producers, however, and Peter feared they would be upset with him if he led the opposition to the F2C local meat program.

Peter reflected on how his three years at UM had challenged his views about eating meat. While he was still a committed vegetarian, he had reconsidered his opposition to all meat eating in light of the different people he had met whom he respected and who had become his friends. It had seemed much clearer back in Iowa, where so much of the meat produced was tied to CAFOs and industrial agriculture. When his parents and friends had asked him why he had become a vegetarian, he replied with four main arguments: the negative effects of a meat-based diet on animal suffering, the environment, world hunger, and human health.

First was his concern for animals. CAFOs might be necessary for economies of scale in industrial agriculture, but they were inherently cruel to animals, and he wanted no part of the torture being inflicted on them unnecessarily. While not all CAFOs were as bad as the PETA videos, there was no way to raise animals in factory conditions without causing them harm and making them suffer.

Although it was animal cruelty that had first sensitized him to the issues of factory farms and eating meat, Peter soon learned there were other issues that were equally, if not more, important. Meat production has several negative environmental consequences, including pollution from concentrated animal waste "lagoons" that often spill into rivers and wipe out fish and other creatures living there. And meat-based diets were now linked to global warming, one of the concerns of UMCAN. Scientists with the UN Food and Agriculture Organization (FAO) estimated that the methane produced by cows worldwide combined with forest lands cleared for pasture and raising crops for animal feed was responsible for roughly 18 percent of all GHG emissions.[7] In addition, raising animals requires a lot of water to irrigate fields for feed, depleting aquifers, streams, and rivers.

Moreover Peter learned that meat-based diets are energy and calorie inefficient compared to diets based on vegetables and grains. It takes on average twenty-eight calories from fossil fuels to produce one calorie of meat, nearly ten times the amount needed to produce one calorie from grain.[8] There are enough grains worldwide to feed everyone with a healthy diet but not if those grains are fed to animals instead of people. Currently nearly 50 percent of the soybeans and 60 percent of the corn grown in the United States are fed to livestock.[9] With over eight hundred million people chronically hungry in the world, it seemed wrong to Peter to feed grains to animals to support meat-based diets for the affluent while the poor went hungry.   WHY?

Finally, Peter had become convinced that a vegetarian diet was healthier than eating meat, especially meat produced in the industrial food system. Growth hormones, antibiotics, intensive pesticide use—these were just some of the artificial chemicals being introduced to the food supply through raising animals for meat, and many studies indicated they were causing human health problems. It was the Centers for Disease Control, not just PETA, that listed some of the adverse health effects of CAFOs, such as groundwater contamination, air pollution, respiratory disease, and the creation and spread of antibiotic-resistant bacteria.[10] In addition, Peter was concerned about the physical and psychological problems the mostly minority workers in CAFOs experience when they must kill hundreds of animals a day and deal with their waste products.

Peter had brought these moral arguments for a vegetarian diet with him to Montana, expecting his fellow students in the SFF group to agree with him. While some of the SFF students were also vegetarians, one of the first friends he made had grown up on a cattle ranch that raised grass-fed beef. After listening to Peter talk about why he was a vegetarian, Courtney Hall invited him to spend the weekend on her family ranch to see firsthand how their cattle were raised.

Peter found himself gazing across a landscape so different from Iowa farms. Bordered to the north by one of many wilderness areas in the northern Rockies, the Hall Ranch spread for miles from the wooded Forest Service boundary across grassy slopes to the Blackfoot River below. Courtney's dad, Joel, a third-generation rancher in the Blackfoot Valley, was an active participant in the Blackfoot Challenge, a local landowner-based group that coordinated management of the Blackfoot River, its tributaries, and adjacent lands.[11] An early advocate of what he called *conservation ranching*, Joel was committed to keeping his ranch as a healthy habitat for wildlife as well as cattle. Elk, deer, and bears coexisted with cattle and called the Hall Ranch home; active restoration of the stream tributaries was returning native trout to the watershed.

"Cattle are an important part of preserving this landscape," Joel told Peter. "Ranching keeps these lands from being subdivided, which fragments the landscape and reduces habitat for wildlife. Managed well, cattle are an important part of keeping the land healthy and intact. We use holistic management practices,[12] rotating our cattle through different pastures to mimic nature's patterns, such as the grazing habits of bison and elk. This stimulates the growth of native grasses while keeping down invasive weeds that are harming Montana's native ecosystems. We raise only grass-fed cattle here. It's much healthier than grain-fed beef,[13] and we are able to market our beef locally, cutting down on transportation and fuel costs while supporting Montana's economy. All our cattle are free range from birth to slaughter—no huge feedlots for them; you won't find cattle with a higher quality of life anywhere."

Looking at the cows and heifers grazing contentedly under the big Montana sky, Peter had to admit it was a far cry from the CAFOs and huge feedlots in the PETA videos. He wasn't sure he could eat beef himself, but he could see lots of advantages to raising cattle this way. He had never considered cattle ranching to be environmentally beneficial—he knew about the years of overgrazing that had turned native grasslands into eroded and degraded wastelands throughout the West—but he could see how healthy the Hall Ranch was. He would have to learn more about holistic management and conservation ranching.

"What do you do about predators?" he asked Joel. "You mentioned there are bears here, and I've been reading all the controversy about wolves being reintroduced in Montana. Aren't they a threat to your ranch?"

"I won't lie," said Joel. "Having wolves on the land again has made ranching more difficult—you won't find many ranchers who like wolves. But we are trying to take a broader, long-term approach to see how ranching can be a part of healthy, sustainable landscapes, and large predators are also a part of that picture. We're finding ways to coexist with bears, mountain lions, and wolves, even if it means we occasionally lose some cattle. That's been one of the benefits of being part of the Blackfoot Challenge. It brings everyone together who wants to preserve this beautiful valley, so we ranchers work directly with wildlife biologists and learn together how to manage the land so that wildlife and ranching can coexist."

Peter mulled all this over as he headed to the university's organic farm to work his afternoon shift. He was looking forward to talking to Nate, the farm director who also taught the course on sustainable agriculture

Peter was taking. Nate was a real Renaissance man. After studying philosophy in college, he'd gotten a certificate in ecological horticulture—Peter had never even heard of that field before—and then spent two years in Zambia in the Peace Corps where he gained firsthand experience with local, sustainable farming. He and his wife started their own organic farm where they raised their three kids, and they were a regular presence at the Saturday morning farmers' market in town. Peter had never met anyone as busy as Nate; he was always on the go, but he seemed to have time for each of the students working with him on the farm.

When Peter got to the farm, he found Nate putting the final touches on a new hog pen. Nate had introduced hogs to the farm a few years earlier, and it had caused a rift with some of the early supporters of the farm who had helped to start it with the understanding it would only raise vegetables, not animals. The animals were a big draw for the kids at the nearby school, however, who brought over food wastes from the school cafeteria to feed the hogs. Peter admitted he was not always comfortable with what these kids were learning about how farm animals are raised, as if the college farm was anything like the CAFOs that produced most of the meat these kids were eating. But now chickens and hogs had been integrated into the farm's rhythms, and they were part of the menu at the annual fall harvest party that gathered together hundreds of people from town.

"I can understand your concerns about animals in CAFOs," Nate told Peter as he fed the pigs. "I don't want to have anything to do with industrial ag or its meat products either. That's why we're working so hard to create an alternative farming and food system, one that's rooted in local communities and local economies, one that's done sustainably and helps to keep the environment healthy. Animals have an important role to play in local food systems. They recycle food and farm waste and turn it into nutritious animal protein, while providing manure to fertilize the fields and reduce inputs. Animals are a key part of making farming a closed-loop system that works within the local ecosystem. They are important to agroecology, where we mimic ecosystem functions to make farming sustainable. Just as in nature, animals are part of the food chain. The key ethical issue for me is not whether we raise and eat animals, but *how* they are raised. Do they have a good quality of life, and have they been treated humanely? As you can see, that's what we are doing on this farm, and that is what thousands of small, sustainable farms are doing across the country now, making healthy and ethically raised meat products available to conscientious consumers."

Peter thought about his conversations with Courtney, Joel, and Nate as he headed to the coffee house to meet with Carmen, the head of UM's SALDF chapter. They had agreed to get together to help Peter outline his talk for the rally. Carmen was a philosophy major writing her senior thesis on ecofeminism and animals. When Peter told her about his visits to the Hall Ranch and the college farm, and the new perspectives on animals and eating meat he had gained, Carmen responded, "Peter, none of the points you raise get to the main issue: eating animals is morally indefensible. Meat eating hides the fact that each of those animals is a sentient being with intrinsic value and its own interests to live and to thrive—interests that must be respected and *don't* include being reduced to corpses on our plates. 'Meat' itself is simply a cultural construct we make up to make eating animals seem natural and inevitable.[14] Calling the corpses of animals 'meat' hides the actual practices of reducing individual animals to a mass category. Factory farms are the logical end to a worldview that sees animals as simply resources for our use—and using them 'sustainably' doesn't challenge this utilitarian perspective that Earth and all its creatures exist for humans. Philosophically what's relevant here is animals' capacity for suffering, their possession of their own interests that must be considered by us, and their right to be treated as ends in themselves rather than means to our ends. These are all reasons that their lives should not be taken to feed us, particularly when we have other means for obtaining nourishment that do not harm animals.[15] That's what's so disturbing about the F2C plan to include meat—animal corpses—in the dining halls. It takes the prestige and worthy goals of the F2C program to introduce local and healthy foods into the dining halls and uses F2C to make meat-eating appear acceptable—like killing animals is the same as locally grown carrots! And it takes our student fees and makes us complicit with the ongoing slaughter and suffering of innocent animals. *That's* what you need to emphasize at the rally next week!"

Peter headed home that night feeling tired and discouraged. He was not sure what he thought now about the F2C plan to support local meat producers by including their meat products in the dining halls. There were so many issues involved, and everybody had a different view on which issues were most important and why. Should he focus on animal rights and suffering, and the need to move away from a utilitarian view of animals, as Carmen insisted? But what about supporting local communities and economies, and the role that conservation ranching plays in keeping habitats healthy and sustainable? Or was the main issue developing new forms of sustainable farming where animals play a critical role in agroecological farming? And what about the really big issues, like global warming, world hunger, deforestation, and depletion of water from agriculture—would anything they did here in Montana really have impact on them? What should he say at the rally? He was glad he had another week to think about the issues, but he wasn't sure more time and information would make it any easier to decide.

Commentary

Introduction

When you look at the food on your plate, what do you see? And when that food is made from animals, what do you see? Bacon, eggs, and milk—or the individual hog, hen, or dairy cow that produced them? Do you see products of modern agricultural efficiency—or the endless acres of monocrop corn and soybean that converted sunlight into their animal feed? Or perhaps you see factory farms, feedlots, and migrant workers—the industrial means to convert animals into food products for human consumption in our modern agriculture and food systems.

Americans have long been concerned with what they were eating; whole industries have been built around shifting food tastes, diets to lose weight, and concerns about nutrition. In recent years, this focus on food has expanded to include not just *what* we eat, but *how* it is raised and processed to get to our plates. Food chains have expanded dramatically in length and complexity from earlier days when many knew their local farmers (or raised much of their own food). Today industrial food chains involve a network of production, processing, transportation, and marketing where the average supermarket product can change hands over thirty times by the time it appears in our stores or on our restaurant plates.[16]

While we purchase, prepare, and eat food on a daily basis, our diets link us to large food and agricultural systems that raise many environmental, social, and ethical issues. Who raises, processes, and transports the food we eat, and are producers and workers treated fairly? What about the *billions* of animals that are raised and slaughtered each year to provide the meat, eggs, and dairy products we consume? What are their lives like, and do they have their own interests that need to be considered? Or are they merely resources for human use like other natural resources such as timber or mining? What are the environmental impacts of industrial-scale farms that rely on vast quantities of fossil fuel and chemical inputs to produce monocrop corn and soybeans as commodities for global trade and feed for animals? What are the effects on developing nations that shift their agriculture to raise crops and animals for export to the United States and other wealthy nations under the pressure of structural adjustment programs induced by the International Monetary Fund and free trade agreements promulgated by the World Trade Organization? Is it even moral to eat animals when there are other alternatives that can meet our dietary needs?

These are just some of the questions that this case raises. While focusing on whether it is ethical to eat meat, the case exposes many other dimensions of modern industrial agriculture and food systems that raise complex and difficult ethical issues. It reveals multiple perspectives about how we view food and animals, and how food systems are both structured by and in turn help to structure the global market economy in which they are embedded.

Current concerns about food and animals arise from the intersection of many recent movements and trends. In 1962, Rachel Carson published *Silent Spring*, which helped to launch the modern environmental movement and brought particular focus to the widespread use of pesticides and chemical inputs in modern agriculture and the negative environmental impacts they cause. The rise of the animal rights movement sensitized many to the conditions in which animals are raised and slaughtered as well as animals' social needs and their abilities to experience pain. After World War II, attention to the economic and social development needs of poor nations and particularly to world hunger brought attention to the impact of global trade policies and food aid on poor nations. More recent concerns about climate change point to the various ways modern agriculture contributes to global warming, from fossil fuel and petroleum-based inputs for diesel and fertilizers, to deforestation in tropical nations to increase pasture land for cattle, to the methane produced by billions of cattle worldwide being raised for human consumption.

To understand the ethical issues in this case, we begin with an overview of the modern industrial agriculture and food systems that largely shape how food and meat arrive on our plates. We review Peter's four main areas of ethical concern for what they reveal about these systems. We then look at the rise of organic agriculture as an alternative to this movement, and the pressures it faces in trying to adapt to the market and industrial economies of scale. Finally we trace the growing local foods and agriculture movement that seeks to develop a local food economy as an alternative to *Big Ag* and ask whether this movement can address the ethical issues raised here while providing a growing global population with the food it needs. With this overview of current agriculture and food systems, we turn to moral assessment, looking at the ethical worldviews underlying each of these perspectives before reviewing philosophical arguments for vegetarianism. Readers are asked to consider all of these in deciding the best response to the case and the issues it raises.

Industrial-Scale Agriculture and Food Systems

"Eating is an ecological and political act."[17] So claims writer Michael Pollan in his influential book, *The Omnivore's Dilemma*. What and how we choose to eat inevitably has ecological and political implications, affecting the natural and social orders in which we live our lives. Like some animals, such as rats and bears, humans are omnivores who can meet our nutritional needs from a wide variety of food sources, including plants, seeds, fruits, vegetables, animals, and eggs. For all animals, eating is an ecological act—what, where, and how an animal eats affects the ecosystem that contains it. In fact predation—organisms eating other life forms—is a fundamental feature of evolution, and plants and animals coevolve to create distinct ecosystems based in part on predator–prey relationships. Unlike other animals, however, humans can reflect on the meaning of their food choices and the impacts of their actions. This is what Pollan terms the *omnivore's dilemma*. Faced with a dizzying array of food options, some that can also sicken or harm us, humans must constantly choose what and how to eat, and organize our lives around those choices. These choices inevitably have important ethical dimensions, which we highlight here.

Most of us today have chosen the default option for providing our food: the modern industrial food and agriculture system. Among its many apparent benefits are its convenience, cost, and the variety it provides. We say *apparent*, because behind each of these attractive features are troubling dimensions that bear further scrutiny. Take cost, for example. Americans on average spend about 10 percent of their disposable income on food, by far the smallest percentage of any nation, and about half of what we paid only fifty years ago. Yet we do this by paying only a fraction of the true costs that go into producing that food. The rest is externalized to the environment or society that must pay for them through taxes or government debt. Industrial-scale agriculture degrades the environment through topsoil loss and groundwater contamination. Agricultural subsidies prop up farmers, and military expenditures provide access to foreign fossil fuels needed to keep modern agriculture functioning. These and other actual costs of producing food rarely show up in the sticker price, but we are all paying these costs indirectly through higher health care costs, raised insurance premiums, and higher taxes.

Or take variety. While supermarket shelves contain a dizzying array of glitzily packaged products, the reality is that most are only variations of a few basic ingredients, increasingly corn based such as high fructose corn syrup. Actual variety in fruits, vegetables, and other products has diminished rapidly under the pressures of an industrial food system that demands standardization, efficiency, and conformity. Along with this go decreased nutritional value and genetic diversity, as well as food crops that are locally adapted to the places where they grow.

Our modern food and agricultural systems are largely products of several post–World War II developments. A rapidly growing petrochemical industry provided chemical inputs, such as artificial fertilizers and pesticides, that allowed farmers to increase productivity of harvests through monocrop agriculture that can take advantage of efficiencies of scale. New refrigeration technologies and transportation infrastructure—the rapidly developing interstate highway system and growing air travel—allowed perishable foods to be stored and transported long distances, opening up new markets traditionally served by local farmers. International trade agreements and decreasing trade barriers made food a commodity traded in a growing global market economy. Agriculture increasingly must respond to the free market dynamics of globalization, as discussed in Chapter 2. Market pressures focus on price as the bottom line, with concern for other factors such as nutritional value, how the food is grown or raised, and regional diversity squeezed out. To fit into an industrial system, food must become standardized, raised in monocrops or on factory farms that can produce a steady, reliable project—a radically simplified ecosystem that is the opposite of nature, where biodiversity and multiple ecological niches are the norm. Yet food chains are much longer and complex, with food products passing through many hands before they reach the consumer.

Advocates of the modern food and agriculture system, such as Jack in the case, argue that it is unmatched for meeting the needs of consumers, and its benefits far outweigh its costs. Proponents claim

- Industrial agriculture is more efficient and productive than traditional agriculture, and it increases food security by helping to reduce hunger and feed the world's growing population;
- Industrial food is safe, healthy, and nutritious, as well as cheap and therefore affordable to millions who would otherwise not have access to food (and conversely, organic or locally grown foods are more expensive and hence are elitist, available only to the affluent);
- The modern food system offers consumers more choices, since food products are no longer limited by geography or seasonality;
- Biotechnology will solve any problems in industrial agriculture and improve productivity and nutrition in the world food supply.[18]

Concerns about Industrial Agriculture and Animals

Critics contest each of these claims, pointing out, for example, that only extensive government subsidies to farmers and uncounted environmental externalities[19] keep food costs low, and numerous health issues have emerged with industrial foods. The Environmental Working Group, for example, documents over $256 billion in federal farm subsidies from commodity, crop insurance, and disaster programs between 1995 and 2012. In addition, just 10 percent of US farms—typically the largest and richest—collect almost three-fourths of federal farm subsidies, which further entrenches industrial-scale corporate farms at the expense of local and family farms.[20] The Union of Concerned Scientists argues that government subsidies "skewed toward commodity crops, such as corn and soybeans, help keep processed foods made from these crops cheap and plentiful. And research has linked a diet high in processed foods to our growing obesity crisis and to chronic metabolic illnesses such as diabetes and hypertension."[21] Yet many consumers find the arguments of the food industry persuasive and appreciate the efficiency and lower sticker prices of food items.

There are several implications of an industrial-model food and agriculture system for domestic animals. Two are particularly important to this case. Throughout the twentieth century, the development of high-yield hybrid corn and soybeans combined with the use of artificial fertilizers, pesticides, and larger field equipment led to a tenfold increase in crop yields. Mixed and integrated family farms across the Midwest that largely produced food and animals for human consumption gave way to larger, corporate farms growing corn and soybeans primarily as commodity crops for animal feed (and more recently biofuels). Yet because the growing glut of corn on the market lowered prices, what began as temporary government subsidies to farmers to keep the agricultural sector profitable became more or less permanent features of industrial agriculture.

At the same time, the flood of cheap corn and soybeans made it faster and more profitable to fatten cattle in feedlots than on pasture grass, and to raise chickens for meat and eggs in factories than in farmyards. The pressures of the market soon eliminated small-scale family farms with multiple crops and animals in favor of large-scale corporate farms, feedlots, and CAFOs; along with the family farms went the rural communities and towns they supported. Growing health problems from confining domestic animals in crowded factory conditions were handled through adding antibiotics to their feed rather than changing the conditions in which they were raised and slaughtered. The relentless logic of the market that demands efficiencies of scale and that all marketable products be seen as commodities requires that living animals be treated like Descartes's unfeeling machines—units of resources for human consumption. Yet the transformation of individual animals to undifferentiated meat lies largely hidden from public view or awareness, as does the wide-scale animal suffering that results.

Ethical Issues

It is this context for agriculture and food production that shapes the four main ethical concerns that Peter articulates in the case: concern for animals, negative environmental consequences of meat-based diets, the social justice of feeding grains to animals when millions of people go hungry, and health issues connected to meat-based diets. We begin by exploring objections to industrial agriculture, move on to discuss ways different characters in the case frame the issues, and conclude by examining various views regarding animal rights and defense of their interests.

The Treatment of Animals in Industrial Agriculture

The scale of suffering of animals in CAFOs is well documented;[22] worldwide an estimated seventy billion animals are raised for food, and of these nearly two-thirds are raised in confinement. For example, the vast majority of the more than eight *billion* hens raised in the United States each year for eggs and meat spend their lives in cages so small they cannot turn around.[23] "The result is extremely stressed birds, disease, high mortality rates, filthy conditions, fouled air, choking ammonia, and occasionally extreme cruelty on the part of the workers."[24] The Humane Society notes that pigs "are highly intelligent, curious animals who engage in complex tasks and form elaborate, cooperative social groups"[25] that recognize pain, suffering, and distress in others. Yet today nearly 80 percent of the more than 110 million hogs slaughtered each year in the United States are raised in large CAFOs, causing them enormous stress and suffering.[26] Similar conditions and problems are found with turkeys, cattle, sheep, and other domestic animals.

Perhaps less clear is how the need to produce meat and eggs cheaply—the only concern of the neoliberal market—produces a logic of efficiency and scale that combines government subsidies with the concentration of animal processing in the hands of a few large corporations to make CAFOs virtually inevitable. Wendell Berry, long a critic of industrial agriculture, articulates the ethical implications of this in his essay "Stupidity in Concentration":

> The principle of confinement in so-called animal science is derived from the industrial version of efficiency. The designers of animal factories appear to have had in mind the example of concentration camps or prisons, the aim of which is to house and feed the greatest numbers in the smallest space at the least expense of money, labor, and attention. To subject innocent creatures to such treatment has long been recognized as heartless. Animal factories make an economic virtue of heartlessness toward domestic animals, to which we humans owe instead a large debt of respect and gratitude.[27]

Yet the Union of Concerned Scientists notes, "The predominance of CAFOs is not the inevitable result of market forces; it has been fostered by misguided public policy. Alternative production methods can be economically efficient and technologically sophisticated, and can deliver abundant animal products while avoiding most of the problems caused by CAFOs."[28]

Environmental Consequences of Meat-Based Diets

Raising animals in industrial conditions leads to several additional concerns. The US Environmental Protection Agency (EPA) has focused its attention on the concentration of pollutants in the extensive waste lagoons produced by animal manure in CAFOs. Pollutants from CAFOs that contaminate groundwater and rivers include excessive nutrients, such as nitrogen and phosphorus; organic matter; fecal matter; pathogens, such as bacteria and viruses; trace elements, including arsenic, antibiotics, pesticides, and hormones; and volatile compounds, including carbon dioxide, methane, hydrogen sulfide, and ammonia.[29] The FAO estimates that "in the USA livestock and feed crop agriculture are responsible for 37 percent of pesticide use, 50 percent of antibiotic use, and a third of the nitrogen and phosphorus loads in freshwater resources."[30]

As the students in UMCAN argue, meat-based diets contribute to climate change in several ways. The Intergovernmental Panel on Climate Change lists livestock as a significant source of GHG emissions; the FAO estimates that livestock are responsible for nearly 18 percent of global GHG emissions through the methane they produce during digestion. The Worldwatch Institute argues, however, that when the full life cycle and supply chain of domesticated animals raised for food is factored in, this number rises to nearly *half* of all global GHG emissions.[31] For example, deforestation in the tropics is a significant factor in climate change, and much of it is driven by economic pressures to convert forest to pasture for cattle.

Raising animals for meat also contributes significantly to land degradation and water use. The United Nations notes that livestock use 30 percent of Earth's entire land surface, including 33 percent of the global arable land that is used to grow feed for animals.[32] Meat and dairy animals now account for nearly 20 percent of *all* terrestrial animal biomass, and their displacement of native animals is a significant factor in loss of biodiversity worldwide; in South America over 70 percent of the former forests of the Amazon have been converted to pasture for domestic animals. Raising livestock also requires large amounts of freshwater, often in arid areas where water already is scarce. Including water needed for forage and irrigation, producing a pound of animal protein requires nearly one hundred times more water than producing a pound of grain protein.[33] In the arid western US, agricultural irrigation to support livestock uses 85 percent of the total freshwater consumed. Hence, even much of the locally raised beef in Western states like Montana depends on diverting water from streams for irrigation, often leading to dewatered streams that threaten native species such as fish.

Social Justice Concerns around Meat-Based Diets

In addition, in a world where over eight hundred million people are chronically hungry and three billion are malnourished and food insecure,[34] meat-based diets based on feeding grain to animals divert much-needed food resources from the poor. Currently nearly 80 percent of the global soybean crop and half of the annual corn crop are fed to domestic animals, primarily to facilitate rapid weight gain and decrease the amount of time before slaughter, saving agrocorporations money. In the United States, livestock consume over seven times as much grain as the entire human population; the amount of grain the livestock consume is enough to feed 840 million people on a plant-based diet.[35] Worldwide, hungry people increasingly compete with domestic animals for food.[36] The norm of sufficiency suggests affluent people and nations should eat far more simply and reduce meat consumption and the resources it requires so that poor and hungry people have sufficient resources for their well-being.

Health Issues with Industrial Meat

Finally, numerous health issues have emerged with eating industrial meat. Looking cross-culturally, it seems that both meat-based and plant-based diets can supply our nutritional needs. Yet studies of health problems induced by industrial meat are growing. Physicians for Social Responsibility point to the overuse of antibiotics in the livestock industry as a major cause of the growing resistance to antibiotics in medicine in the United States. They estimate that nontherapeutic use of antibiotics in livestock production accounts for nearly 80 percent of all antibiotics used in the United States.[37] They observe that diets high in red and processed meat are associated with greater mortality from cardiovascular disease and cancer and are connected to higher rates of type 2 diabetes. Additionally, as Joel notes in the case, animals raised on grain-fed diets versus a more sustainable grass-fed diet show higher levels of total fat, saturated fat, cholesterol, and calories. Despite the assurances of the agricultural industry and the US Department of Agriculture (USDA) that industrial food is safe and nutritious, with the widespread use of antibiotics, growth hormones, GM grains in feed, and other chemical additives necessary to produce industrial meat, Americans are essentially participating in an uncontrolled experiment on the effects of an industrial meat-based diet on human health.

Given this host of problems, could organic agriculture provide a viable alternative to industrial agriculture? Organic agriculture began in the 1960s and 1970s as a way of farming that tried to mimic nature while reforming society from the ground up. The early organic movement sought alternative modes of production (chemical-free farms), distribution (food co-ops), and consumption (counter-cuisine) to create an alternative to industrial agriculture and a consumer society.

What began as a countercultural movement thirty years later has grown into an $11 billion industry and is the fastest-growing sector of the food economy. Yet the larger it has grown, the greater has been the pressure on organic farmers to adopt industrial means of standardization, scale, and efficiency in order to integrate into a US food system built around the supermarket. Much of the organic sector has now been captured by what Pollan calls *Big Organic*; while conforming to USDA standards of being chemical free in its production, it has largely abandoned alternative distribution systems in favor of specialty stores like Whole Foods and the organic foods sections of Walmart and large grocery store chains. Animals fare little better under this system. While they may benefit from getting organic feed, economies of scale result in cattle still being fattened in organic feedlots, and free range chickens raised in sheds that hold twenty thousand hens with small side yards that largely go unused. Pollan notes, "As in so many other realms, nature's logic has proven no match for the logic of capitalism."[38]

Disillusionment with Big Organic being co-opted by Big Ag has led many small farmers to move *beyond organic* to build a local food movement based on local agriculture. A rapidly growing network of farmers' markets, community-supported agriculture, food co-ops, and buying clubs shrink the food chain by connecting consumers directly with producers, seeking to produce both healthy food and healthy communities. As Nate observes in the case, animals form an important component of the movement, as they are an integral link in building sustainable, closed-loop small farm systems. Yet how they are integrated into farms is the antithesis of factory farming. Since domestic animals coevolved with humans in local, small-scale agricultural settings, sustainable farming builds on this symbiosis by adapting its practices to the natural predilections of the animals. When done well, it results in healthy animals and healthy animal products.

While the local foods movement is growing rapidly, it remains a tiny sliver in comparison to the industrial food system. Given the size of corporate agriculture, the structures of the market economy and government policies and regulations that favor industrial agriculture, the challenges to its success are formidable. To what extent it can provide a broad-scale alternative to Big Ag remains to be seen. For now, the vast majority of animal products, such as meat, eggs, and dairy, will be produced in concentrated feedlots and factories.

Framing the Issues

As the discussion above makes clear, there are multiple and intercon-nected ethical issues in this case, including treatment of animals and the sustainability of the industrial food and agriculture systems. How one frames issues of agriculture and animals largely shapes one's response to the issues associated with eating meat. In the case, Carmen assumes a biocentric position to argue that eating animals is morally indefensible. Her focus on animal well-being as the primary ethical concern renders other ethical issues secondary. Jack, in contrast, represents proponents of industrial agriculture who work within the anthropocentric and utilitarian framework of neoliberal capitalism. Here animals are viewed as resources to be raised efficiently for human use and maximum profit. Industrial ag-riculture aligns closely with the free market side of the continuum of per-spectives about nature. In this worldview, only humans have intrinsic value, and animals have only instrumental value. Emphasis on human interests in productivity, efficiency, economies of scale, and profit outweigh animal interests, so as Wendell Berry notes, animals are raised, housed, fed, and slaughtered under conditions that minimize expenses, labor, and attention. Proponents argue that industrial-scale animal production helps to meet critical human needs and desires while decreasing food insecurity globally.

Early organic farmers and those who practice small-scale or local farm-ing today lie closest to the critical ecology side, taking a holistic perspective that bases farming on mimicking nature's processes. Small-scale tends to mean more emphasis on egalitarian and community-oriented values, stressing cooperation with nature and viewing farm practices as intercon-nected with both nature and community. Attitudes toward animals range from purely anthropocentric to more biocentric; in most cases, however, a more holistic and ecological perspective means greater respect for animal well-being as integral members of farm ecosystems.

Practitioners of Big Organic retain a more holistic and ecological perspective in farming, insofar as they avoid chemical additives that can harm the environment. The need to work within the structures of the supermarket-based food system, however, aligns them most closely with a conservationist perspective, drawing on ecological insights to manage resources wisely. Animals in this system may have somewhat more con-sideration than in industrial agriculture, but they are still largely viewed as resources for production and profit. Raising them according to the minimal USDA organic standards may improve their treatment margin-ally, but they are still subject to the industrial conditions mandated by economies of scale.

Proponents of local food systems, such as Nate and Joel, are an eclectic bunch who tend to lie closer to the critical ecology side without necessarily embracing its more radical elements. They run the gamut from anthropocentric to ecocentric; what distinguishes them most from Big Ag and Big Organic is a strong emphasis on holistic views, both in agriculture where practices mimic nature, and in community where strong links between producer and consumer rebuild social links. Much less hierarchical than the stratified structures of the dominant economy and food system, they focus on the values of egalitarianism, cooperation, and interconnectedness in their efforts to build an alternative, locally-based series of food chains. Hence, the norms of participation, sustainability, and community are central to their moral vision. Animals are integral to this effort, and so animal well-being and welfare are stressed, without, however, a strong biocentric position that would equate animal interests and rights with those of humans.

Animal Rights and Animal Defense

It would appear that many of the ethical concerns Peter raised about eating meat are addressed by the alternatives seen in Joel's free-range grass-fed cattle ranch and Nate's integrated local organic farm. In both places, animals are treated humanely and have a quality of life that allows them to live largely in accordance with their natural characteristics. In both contexts, animals make positive contributions to the ecological health of the farms and ranches where they live. Because they feed entirely on grass and food produced within the ranch and food ecosystems rather than grain from monocrop Big Ag, they do not compete with hungry people or contribute to the environmental degradation caused by industrial agriculture.[39] And locally raised animals avoid many of the health and labor issues endemic to industrial meat and exploitative labor in food processing.

This brings us finally to Carmen's position, that eating animals itself is morally indefensible, because it causes animal suffering and pain that is avoidable. While there have been vegetarians in the Western tradition dating back several thousand years to early Greek philosophers, such as Pythagoras and Epicurus, and the later Roman writers, such as Ovid and Seneca, who refused to eat animals, it is only in recent decades that the moral case for vegetarianism has been fully developed. We look here at two of the most influential positions: animal rights based on Western utilitarian and deontological approaches, and animal defense and advocacy grounded in ecofeminism. Each seeks to extend the ecological justice norms of justice and solidarity to include animals as part of our moral community.

Moral philosophers Peter Singer and Tom Regan provided early and influential intellectual grounding for the growing animal rights movement. In his 1975 book, *Animal Liberation*, Singer takes a utilitarian approach to argue that human-inflicted suffering on animals that can experience pain is morally indefensible. Justifying these actions by arguing that animals are not human and therefore do not merit moral consideration is simply *speciesism*; like racism or sexism it uses morally irrelevant differences to justify treating some animals (domestic) differently than others (humans). Singer quotes the eighteenth-century utilitarian Jeremy Bentham to argue that the relevant criterion for treatment of animals is *sentience*—animals' ability to experience pain and pleasure. Singer says, "The question is not, Can [animals] *reason?* nor, Can they *talk?* but, *Can they suffer?*" The answer is unequivocally yes, and much of domestic animals' suffering is caused by humans. Singer argues this violates the principle of equality and our obligation to treat like individuals similarly; he thus extends the moral community to include all sentient creatures. Since many animals, like humans, are sentient individuals who experience pleasure and pain, as with humans we have the moral obligation to act so as to prevent avoidable animal pain and suffering. Since we do not need to kill and eat animals to meet our nutritional needs, we should not. Any pleasure we might derive from eating animals is outweighed by the pain and suffering we inflict on these animals.

Regan reaches a similar conclusion in his 1983 book, *The Case for Animal Rights*, but he follows a natural rights, deontological approach. Recognizing intrinsic value in all animals, Regan extends the moral community beyond humans to include other nonrational but still intelligent animals. He distinguishes between moral *agents* (individuals capable of making rational, moral judgments, such as adult humans) and moral *patients* (those incapable of making these judgments, such as children or mentally incompetent adults, who nevertheless are entitled to be treated as ends). To arbitrarily exclude intelligent nonhuman animals from moral consideration as moral patients whose intrinsic value and rights must be recognized is again to be guilty of speciesism. Hence, treating animals as ends in themselves is a moral duty, a matter of justice, not kindness.[40] Therefore it is morally indefensible to treat animals as a means to put food on our plates.

While appreciative of Singer's and Regan's influence in advancing animal rights in society, ecofeminists are critical of their Western, rationalist philosophical approach. Instead many ecofeminists ground animal defense and advocacy in the ethics of care. They note that emotions such as love, sympathy, and empathy, rather than reason, are a major basis for human–animal connections. Hence the ethics of care is explicitly relational—drawing on the centrality of caring relationships to moral society.[41] Care ethics is also contextual, focusing on the qualities of particular caring relationships, and thus it recognizes animal individuality and the experience of individual animals as critical to debates about treatment of animals. This emphasis on context means some ecofeminists recognize there may be circumstances where humans must eat animals for their survival needs, such as in hunter–gatherer groups like the Inuit who live where plant-based diets cannot sustain them. For most Americans, however, killing animals for human consumption is not necessary to meet nutritional needs and inflicts pain on animals that is unnecessary and avoidable.[42]

Like Carmen in the case, ecofeminists also frame the context of treatment of animals as one of systemic and institutionalized animal exploitation within the larger context of patriarchy. They argue that the history of patriarchy depends on the interlinked exploitation and subjugation of nature, women, and animals; therefore the liberation of women is tied to the liberation and well-being of nature and animals. It is deep care for the well-being of animals as individuals and as a class that motivates ecofeminists to link the struggle for animals to the emancipation of women and other subjugated beings.[43]

Hence, while the local foods scenarios involving animals in the case would satisfy many of Peter's initial concerns about eating meat, they are unlikely to sway animal rights and ecofeminist proponents such as Carmen and the members of SALDF.

Responding to the Case

How should Peter respond to SALDF's request that he join them in opposing F2C's proposal to bring local, grass-fed beef into the university's dining halls, and how should we respond to issues around eating meat? What is the best way to frame the complex interplay of animals, agriculture, food systems, globalization, and the environment where the future is made more uncertain by climate change? Do animals have intrinsic value with corresponding rights and moral status, or are these limited to human beings? In a world where raising livestock contributes to climate change and competes for resources with millions of hungry and malnourished people worldwide, is vegetarianism the best moral option, or can rebuilding local economies where animals play a vital role and enjoy a higher quality of life help to move us away from the many problems of industrial agriculture? In today's context of industrial agriculture where billions of animals are raised and slaughtered in inhumane conditions, do locally raised animals provide a genuine alternative, or are they simply another way for us to turn our eyes from a social context of institutionalized animal exploitation where nontransparent food and agriculture systems hide massive animal suffering from consumers? Can localized food systems and agriculture compete with industrial agriculture in today's globalized market economy and provide the food needed for a growing global population, or will it remain a small niche market whose greater expense limits it to an affluent elite? Can an ethic of ecological justice rooted in norms of justice, sustainability, sufficiency, participation, and solidarity help us to prioritize where we focus our efforts in this complex interplay, and how do we make sure the experiences and interests of animals do not get lost in the shuffle? Just what do we see when we look at the food on our plates?

Notes

[1]"Meet Your Meat: How Farm Factories Work," https://www.youtube.com.

[2]Natural Resources Defense Council, "Hog Wild: Factory Farms Are Poisoning Iowa's Drinking Water," http://www.onEarth.org.

[3]This issue is examined further in Chapter 6: "Harvesting Controversy."

[4]Adapted from UM, "UM Dining: Farm to College Program," http://life.umt.edu/dining.

[5]UM, "UM Dining Director LoParco Wins Silver Plate Award," http://news.umt.edu.

[6]EPA, "Ruminant Livestock," http://www.epa.gov.

[7]Time for Change, "Are Cows the Cause of Global Warming?" http://timeforchange.org.

[8]World Watch Institute, "Is Meat Sustainable?" *World Watch Magazine* 17, no. 4 (July/August 2004): 12–20.

[9]Grace Communications Foundation, "Animal Feed," http://www.sustainabletable.org.

[10]Centers for Disease Control and Prevention, National Center for Environmental Health, 2006 National Environmental Public Health Conference, "Factory Farming: The Impact of Animal Feeding Operations on the Environment and Health of Local Communities," http://www.cdc.gov/nceh/conference/2006.

[11]Blackfoot Challenge, http://blackfootchallenge.org.

[12]Holistic Management International, "Four Cornerstones of Holistic Management," http://holisticmanagement.org.

[13]Jo Johnson, "The Health Benefits of Grass Farming: Why Grassfed Is Best," http://www.americangrassfedbeef.com.

[14]Carol J. Adams, "The Social Construction of Edible Bodies and Humans as Predators," in "Ecofeminism and the Eating of Animals," *Hypathia* 6 (Spring 1991): 134–37.

[15]Greta Gaard, "Vegetarian Ecofeminism: A Review Essay," *Frontiers: A Journal of Women's Studies* 23, no. 3 (2002): 117–46.

[16]Barbara E. Kahn and Leigh McAlister, *Grocery Revolution: The New Focus on the Consumer* (New York: Prentice Hall, 1997), cited in Amy Guptill and Jennifer L. Wilkins, "Buying into the Food System: Trends in Food Retailing in the US and Implications for Local Foods," *Agriculture and Human Values* 19 (2002): 39.

[17]Paraphrased from Michael Pollan, *The Omnivore's Dilemma: A Natural History of Four Meals* (London: Penguin, 2006), 11. Much of this commentary draws on Pollan's analysis in *The Omnivore's Dilemma*.

[18]This list of factors is drawn from Andrew Kimball, "Corporate Lies: Busting the Myths of Industrial Agriculture," in *The Fatal Harvest Reader: The Tragedy of Industrial Agriculture*, ed. Andrew Kimball (Washington DC: Island Press, 2002), 1–36.

[19]Marcelo Ostria of the National Center for Policy Analysis notes, for example, that "Overproduction caused by subsidies also results in unintended environmental harms. In pursuit of subsidies, farmers often cultivate marginal farmland, where the thin soil is unable to replace depleted nutrients . . . Farm subsidy opponents have also criticized the overuse of fertilizers and pesticides to farm fertile croplands more intensely and to bring marginal farmland into production." Marcelo Ostria, "How U.S. Agricultural Subsidies Harm the Environment, Taxpayers and the Poor," *NCPC Issue Brief* 126, August 7, 2013, http://www.ncpa.org.

[20]See the Environmental Working Group Farm Subsidy Database at http://farm.ewg.org.

[21]Union of Concerned Scientists, "Unhealthy Food Policy," http://www.ucsusa.org.

[22]The EPA defines CAFOs as an animal feeding operation that confines animals for more than forty-five days during a growing season, in an area that does not produce vegetation, and meets certain size thresholds. See http://www.epa.gov.

[23]For annual slaughter statistics in the United States, see the Humane Society of the United States, "Farm Animal Statistics: Slaughter Totals," http://www.humanesociety.org.

[24]See http://www.factory-farming.com.

[25]The Humane Society of the United States, "More About Pigs," November 2, 2009, http://www.humanesociety.org.

[26]Doug Gurian-Sherman, *CAFOs Uncovered: The Untold Costs of Confined Animal Feeding Operations* (Cambridge, MA: UCS Publications, 2008), 11–12; Union of Concerned Scientists, http://www.ucsusa.org.

[27]Wendell Berry, *Bringing It to the Table: On Farming and Food* (Berkeley, CA: Counterpoint, 2009), 11.

[28]Gurian-Sherman, *CAFOs Uncovered*, 1.

[29]National Pollutant Discharge Elimination System Permit Regulation and Effluent Limitations Guidelines and Standards for Concentrated Animal Feeding Operations, 66 Fed. Reg. 2960, 2976–79.

[30]UN FAO, "Livestock Impacts on the Environment," *Spotlight 2006*, http://www.fao.org.

[31]Robert Goodland and Jeff Anhang, "Livestock and Climate Change," *World Watch Magazine* 22, no. 6 (November/December 2009), http://www.worldwatch.org.

[32]UN FAO, *FAO Newsroom*, November 29, 2006, "Livestock a Major Threat to Environment," http://www.fao.org.

[33]David Pimentel and Marcia Pimentel, "Sustainability of Meat-based and Plant-based Diets and the Environment," *American Journal of Clinical Nutrition* 78, no. 3 (September 2003): 660S–663S, http://ajcn.nutrition.org.

[34]Ibid.

[35]Ibid.

[36]According to the UN Environment Programme, "stabilizing the current meat production per capita by reducing meat consumption in the industrialized world and restraining it worldwide to the 2000 level of 37.4/kg/capita in 2050 would free an estimated 400 million tons of cereal per year for human consumption, enough food to satisfy the annual caloric needs for more than 1 billion people." C. Nellemann , M. MacDevette, T. Manders, et al. (eds.), *The Environmental Food Crisis* (Nairobi: UN Environment Programme, 2009), 26, cited in the Humane Society International, "The Impact of Industrialized Animal Agriculture on World Hunger," http://www.hsi.org.

[37]Physicians for Social Responsibility, "U.S. Meat Production," http://www.psr.org.

[38]Pollan, *Omnivore's Dilemma*, 184.

[39]This is not to suggest that there are no environmental problems with local agriculture or cattle grazing. But they tend to be more local and different in kind and in scale with the problems stemming from industrial agriculture.

[40]For a helpful discussion of Singer's and Regan's approaches, see Josephine Donovan, "Animal Rights and Feminist Theory," in *Beyond Animal Rights: A Feminist Caring Ethic for Treatment of Animals*, ed. Josephine Donovan and Carol Adams (New York: Continuum, 1996), 36–40.

[41]Donovan and Adams, *Beyond Animal Rights*, 15.

[42]Deane Curtin, "Toward an Ecological Ethic of Care," in Donovan and Adams, *Beyond Animal Rights*, 71–72.

[43]As noted ecofeminist Carol Adams articulates, "I value nurturing and caring because it is good, not because it constitutes women's 'difference.' Similarly, I do not value animals because women are somehow 'closer' to them, but because we experience interdependent oppressions. I support animals because they are oppressed and because I care about their experiences of harm, pain, and suffering: I wish to end their oppression." Carol Adams, "Caring About Suffering: A Feminist Exploration," in Donovan and Adams, *Beyond Animal Rights*, 171.

6

Harvesting Controversy

Genetic Engineering and Food Security in Sub-Saharan Africa

Acronyms and Abbreviations

Bt	*Bacillus thuringiensis*
CIMMYT	International Maize and Wheat Improvement Center
FAO	Food and Agricultural Organization (UN)
GHI	Global Hunger Index
GM	genetically modified
GMO	genetically modified organism
IFPRI	International Food Policy Research Institute
ISAAA	International Service for the Acquisition of Agri-Biotech Applications
KARI	Kenyan Agricultural Research Institute
USDA	US Department of Agriculture

Case

I

"It's been quite a year," thought Tom Moline. On top of their normal efforts at hunger advocacy and education on campus, the twenty students in the Hunger Concerns group were spending the entire academic year conducting a study of hunger in sub-Saharan Africa. Tom's girlfriend, Karen Lindstrom, had proposed the idea after she returned from a semester-abroad program in Tanzania last spring. Wracked by AIDS, drought, and political unrest, the nations in the region are also struggling with significant rates of hunger and malnutrition. While there have been modest gains for the more than eight hundred million people who are hungry in the world, 25 percent of the people in sub-Saharan Africa suffer from food shortages, and the number is still increasing.[1] It was not hard for Karen to persuade the group to focus attention on this problem, and so they decided to devote one of their two meetings per month to this study. In the fall, Karen and Tom led three meetings examining root causes of hunger associated with various forms of powerlessness brought about by poverty, war, and drought.

What Tom had not expected was the special attention the group would give to the potential that biotechnology poses for improving food security in the region. Adam Paulsen's participation in the Hunger Concerns group helped to educate the students about biotechnology. Majoring in economics and management, Adam had spent last summer as an intern at Monsanto. Recognized, and often vilified, as a global leader in the field of agricultural biotechnology, Monsanto has been working with agricultural researchers around the world to genetically modify crops that are planted by subsistence farmers.

In December, Adam gave a presentation to the group on efforts to develop virus-resistant cassava for Kenya. Cassava is the second-largest food crop in Kenya after maize (corn). The roots of the plant provide a staple food source and the foliage is used for animal feed. Unfortunately, cassava mosaic disease and cassava brown streak disease have had a devastating effect on cassava production in East Africa. With funding from the Monsanto Fund, the Bill and Melinda Gates Foundation, and others, the Kenyan Agricultural Research Institute (KARI) recently began field tests on nineteen varieties of genetically modified (GM) cassava.[2] Adam emphasized what an important effect this GM crop could have on food security for subsistence farmers. Even if they were able to save only half of the cassava plants, there would be a huge increase in food for people who cannot afford to buy their food elsewhere.

The group ended up learning more about the potential that biotechnology has to increase food production in Kenya because an important new member joined the group. Josephine Omondi, a first-year international student, had read an announcement about Adam's presentation on a campus flyer and knew immediately that she had to attend. She was, after all, a daughter of one of the scientists engaged in biotechnology research at the KARI laboratories in Nairobi. Struggling with homesickness, Josephine was eager to be among people who cared about her country. She was also impressed with the accuracy of Adam's presentation, and she struck up an immediate friendship with him.

Because of her father's involvement with KARI research, and her interest in hunger issues in Kenya and other East African countries, Josephine had much to offer the group. A month after Adam's presentation, she provided a summary of other biotechnology projects in Kenya. She focused on two projects that involve the development of herbicide- and insect-resistant varieties of maize. Nearly 50 percent of the food Kenyans consume is maize, but maize production is falling. Every year stem-boring insects and a weed named striga decimate up to 60 percent of Kenya's harvest.[3] As a result, Kenyan researchers have been working in partnership with the International Maize and Wheat Improvement Center (CIMMYT) to develop corn varieties that can resist striga and combat stem-borers. Josephine told the group that both projects are showing signs of success. Recently, a KARI scientist announced he had developed two different maize varieties that produce a natural chemical that suppresses the growth of striga.[4] On the other front, CIMMYT and KARI researchers have successfully engineered *Bacillus thuringiensis (Bt)* varieties of Kenyan maize that incorporate the gene that produces *Bt*, a natural insecticide.[5] Josephine closed by saying she was proud that her father was helping poor subsistence farmers in Kenya harvest the benefits of biotechnology, which had long been enjoyed only by farmers in wealthy nations.

A few days after Josephine's presentation, two members of the Hunger Concerns group asked if they could meet with Tom since he was serving as the group's coordinator. Kelly Ernst, an environmental studies major, was an ardent advocate of organic farming and a strident critic of industrial approaches to agriculture. As much as she respected Josephine, she expressed to Tom her deep concerns that Kenya might be embarking on a path that was unwise ecologically and economically. She wanted to have a chance to tell the group about the ways organic farming methods can combat the challenges posed by stem-borers and striga.

Similarly, Terra Fielding thought it was important that the Hunger Concerns group be made aware of the biosafety and human health risks associated with GM crops. Like Terra, Tom was also a biology major, so he understood her concerns about the inadvertent creation of herbicide-resistant *superweeds* and the likelihood that insects would eventually develop resistance to *Bt* through prolonged exposure. He also understood Terra's concern that it would be nearly impossible to label GM crops produced in Kenya, since most food goes directly from the field to local markets or the dinner table. As a result, few Kenyans would be able to make an informed decision about whether or not to eat genetically modified foods. Convinced that both sets of concerns were significant, Tom invited Kelly and Terra to give presentations in February and March.

The wheels came off during a heated meeting in April, however, at the end of a discussion Tom was facilitating about how the group might share with the rest of the college what they had learned about hunger in sub-Saharan Africa. Kelly brought a different matter to the attention of the group. She asked them to join an international campaign by Greenpeace to pressure the president of Mexico to ban the planting of GM corn.[6] Amidst the murmurs of assent and disapproval that followed, Kelly pressed ahead. She explained that she had learned about the campaign through her participation in the Environmental Concerns group on campus. They had decided to sign on to the campaign and were now actively encouraging other groups on campus to join the cause as well. Kelly articulated her respect for Josephine and the work of her father in Kenya but stressed that Kenya could achieve its food security through organic farming techniques rather than the *magic bullet* of GM crops, which she argued pose huge risks to the well-being of the planet as well as the welfare of Kenyans.

Before Tom could open his mouth, Josephine offered a counterproposal. She explained that similar pressures had recently led Kenya to remove all GM foods from the market and to enforce a ban on GM imports. Her father was concerned pressure like this by Greenpeace could lead to a further ban on biotechnology research at KARI. Visibly upset yet in control of her emotions, Josephine said she fully expected the group to vote down Kelly's proposal but that she would not be satisfied with that alone. She suggested that a fitting conclusion to their study this year would be for the group to submit an article for the college newspaper explaining the benefits that responsible use of agricultural biotechnology poses for achieving food security in sub-Saharan Africa, particularly in Kenya.

After a brief pause, a veritable riot of discussion ensued. The group appeared to be evenly divided over the two proposals. Since the meeting had already run well past its normal ending time, Tom suggested they think about both proposals and then come to the next meeting prepared to take a vote on both. Everybody seemed grateful for the chance to think about it for a while, especially Tom and Karen.

II

Three days later, an intense conversation was taking place at a corner table after dinner in the cafeteria.

"Come on, Adam. You're the one who told us people are hungry because they are too poor to buy the food they need," said Kelly. "I can tell you right now that there is plenty of food in the world; we just need to distribute it better. If we quit feeding almost all of the grain in this country to animals and stop using it to make biofuels for cars, there would be plenty of food for everyone."[7]

"That may be true, Kelly, but we don't live in some ideal world where we can wave a magic wand and make food land on the tables of people in Africa. A decent food distribution infrastructure doesn't exist within most African countries. Moreover, most people in sub-Saharan Africa are so poor they couldn't afford to buy our grain. And even if we just gave it away, we would undermine local markets and impoverish local farmers in Africa because there is no way they could compete with our free food. Until these countries get on their feet and can trade in the global marketplace, the best thing we can do for their economic development is to promote agricultural production in their countries. GM crops are just one part of a mix of strategies that Kenyans are adopting to increase food supplies. They have to be able to feed themselves."

"Yes, Africans need to feed themselves," said Kelly, "but I don't think they have to follow our high-tech approach to agriculture. Look at what industrial agriculture has done to our own country. We're still losing topsoil faster than we can replenish it. Pesticides and fertilizers are polluting our streams and groundwater. Massive monocultures only make crops more susceptible to plant diseases and pests and destroy biodiversity. Our industrial approach to agriculture is not sustainable. Why would we want to see others adopt it?"

"But that's not what we're talking about," Adam replied. "The vast majority of farmers in the region are farming a one-hectare plot of land that amounts to about 2.5 acres. They're not buying tractors. They're not using fertilizer. They're not buying herbicides. They can't afford those things. Instead, women and children spend most of their days weeding between rows, picking bugs off plants, or hauling precious water. The cheapest and most important technology they can afford is improved seed that can survive in poor soils and resist weeds and pests. You heard Josephine's report. Think of the positive effect those projects are going to have for poor farmers in Kenya."

Kelly shook her head. "Come on, Adam. Farmers have been fighting the weather, poor soils, and pests forever. How do you think we survived without modern farming methods? It can be done. We know how to protect soil fertility through crop rotations and letting ground rest for a fallow period. We also know how to intercrop in ways that cut down on plant diseases and pests—all without genetic engineering and the dangers that come with it."

Finally Karen broke in. "But if that knowledge is so widespread, why are there so many hungry people in Kenya? I've been to the region. Most farmers I saw already practice some form of intercropping, but they can't afford to let their land rest for a fallow period because there are too many mouths to feed. They're caught in a vicious downward spiral. Until their yields improve, the soils will continue to become more degraded and less fertile."

Adam and Kelly both nodded their heads, but for different reasons. The conversation seemed to end where it began—with more disagreement than agreement.

III

Later that night, Tom was in the library talking with Terra about their entomology exam the next day. It didn't take long for Terra to make the connections between the material they were studying and her concerns about *Bt* crops in Kenya.

"Tom, we both know what has happened with irresponsible chemical insecticide applications. Over time, the few insects that have an ability to resist the insecticide survive and reproduce. Then you end up with pests that are resistant to the insecticides you use. *Bt* crops are worse because *Bt* is expressed in every cell of the plant and thus pests are constantly exposed. While this exposure has a devastating effect on those insects that aren't naturally resistant to *Bt*, eventually those that are will reproduce and a new class of *Bt*-resistant insects will return to munch on the crop. Organic farmers in the United States are really worried about this because *Bt* is one of the few natural insecticides they can use and still claim to be organic. Insect resistance can be minimized with responsible application of *Bt*-based insecticides, but there is no way to avoid it if *Bt* is embedded in every cell of a crop."

"I hear you, Terra. But I know farmers in the United States are instructed by the *Bt* seed distributors to plant refuges around their *Bt* crops. That way some insects will not be exposed to *Bt* and will breed with the others that are exposed, thus compromising the genetic advantage that others may have."

"That's true, Tom, but some farmers aren't planting big enough refuges, and a few aren't planting any at all. If you're planting one hundred acres in corn, at least twenty acres are supposed to be left in non-*Bt* corn, but farmers don't always do that. And that's here in the United States. How reasonable is it to expect a poor, undereducated farmer in Kenya to understand the need for a refuge and also to resist the temptation to plant all of the land in *Bt* corn in order to raise the yield? Plus, the area they plant is so small, they can't afford to sacrifice any of it to a refuge."

Josephine happened to walk by just as Terra was posing her question to Tom. In response, she fired off several questions of her own. "Are you suggesting Kenyan farmers are less intelligent than US farmers, Terra? Do you think we cannot teach our farmers how to use this new technology in a wise way? Haven't farmers in this country learned from mistakes they have made?"

"Josephine, those are good questions. It's just that we're talking about two very different situations. In the United States we have less than 2 million farmers feeding over 320 million people. With a high literacy rate, a huge agricultural extension system, e-mail, and computers, it is relatively easy to provide farmers with the information they need. But you said during your presentation that 70 percent of Kenya's 43 million people are engaged in farming. Do you really think you can teach all of those people how to properly utilize *Bt* crops?"

"First of all," Josephine responded, "US farmers do not grow all of the food consumed in this country. Rich nations import food every day from developing nations. Poor nations have to grow cash crops to pay for the imports they need in order to develop, or to pay debts to rich nations. You are speaking in sweeping generalizations. Not every farmer in Kenya will start planting *Bt* corn tomorrow. My government recognizes the need to educate farmers about the responsible use of *Bt* and will equip them to do so. We care about the environment and have good policies in place to protect it. We are not fools, Terra. We are concerned about the biosafety of Kenya."

Trying to take some of the heat off Terra, Tom asked a question he knew she really wanted to ask. "What about the dangers to human health, Josephine? Many are concerned about severe allergic reactions that could be caused by foods made from GM crops. Plus, we just don't know what will happen over the long term as these genes interact or mutate. Isn't that why your own Minister of Public Health and Sanitation justified Kenya's ban on imported GM foods out of genuine concerns that adequate research had not been done on genetically modified organisms (GMOs) and that there was insufficient scientific evidence to prove the safety of these foods?[8] Isn't it wise to be more cautious and go slowly?"

There was nothing slow about Josephine's reply. "Tom, you just don't get it. We view risks related to agricultural biotechnology differently. It is reasonable to be concerned about the possible allergenicity of GM crops, and we test for these, but we are not faced primarily with concerns about allergic reactions in Kenya. We are faced with declining food supplies and growing numbers of hungry people. Virtually every scientific and nongovernmental group working on food security in Kenya has opposed the ban, and they are working to reverse it.[9] As Terra said, our situations are different. As a result, we view the possible risks and benefits differently. The people of Kenya should be able to decide these matters for themselves. We are tired of other people deciding what is best for us."

With that, Josephine left as suddenly as she had arrived.

IV

On Friday night, Karen and Tom got together for pizza. Once they settled in, they started talking about the decision the Hunger Concerns group would have to make the following week. After Karen summarized her conversation with Kelly and Adam, Tom described the exchange he and Terra had with Josephine.

Karen said, "You know, I realize that these environmental and health issues are important, but I'm surprised that no one else seems willing to step back and ask whether anyone should be doing genetic engineering in the first place. What makes us think we can improve nature?"

"But Karen," Tom replied, "human beings have been mixing genes ever since we figured out how to breed animals or graft branches onto apple trees. We didn't know we were engaged in genetic manipulation, but now we understand more about the science of genetics, and that has led to these new technologies. One of the reasons we can support over seven billion people on this planet is because scientists during the Green Revolution used their God-given intelligence to develop hybrid stocks of rice, corn, and other crops that boosted yields significantly. The first Green Revolution passed by Africa, but this second biotechnology revolution could really increase the food supply for countries in Africa."

"I understand all of that, Tom. What worries me is that genetic engineering perpetuates the myth that we are masters of the universe with some God-given mandate to transform nature in our image. We have got to stop viewing nature as a machine that we can take apart and put back together. Nature is more than the sum of its parts. This mechanistic mind-set has left us with all sorts of major ecological problems. The only reason hybrid seeds produced so much food during the Green Revolution is because farmers poured tons of fertilizer on them and kept them alive with irrigation water. And what was the result? Lots of grain but also huge amounts of water pollution and waterlogged soils. We have more imagination than foresight, and so we wind up developing another technological fix to get us out of the problem our last technological innovation produced."

"I agree that our scientific and technological abilities have outpaced our wisdom in their use, but does that mean we can't learn from our mistakes? Ultimately, aren't technologies just tools we use to achieve our goals? Why can't we use genetic engineering to end hunger? Scientists are already developing the next wave of products that will give us inexpensive ways to vaccinate people in developing nations against debilitating diseases with foods like bananas that carry the vaccine. We will also be able to make food more nutritious for those that get precious little. Aren't those good things, Karen?"

Karen, a bit defensive and edging toward the other side of the horseshoe-shaped booth, said, "Look, Tom, the way we live is just not sustainable. It scares me to see people in China, Brazil, and Kenya all following us down the same unsustainable road. There has got to be a better way. Kelly is right. Human beings lived more sustainably in the past than we do now. We need to learn from indigenous peoples how to live in harmony with the Earth. But instead, we seem to be tempting them to adopt our expensive and inappropriate technologies. It just doesn't seem right to encourage developing nations like Kenya to make huge investments in biotechnology when less expensive solutions might better address their needs. Whatever gains are achieved by biotechnology will be lost as weeds and insects become resistant, or the soils just give out entirely from overuse. But I'm really struggling with this vote next week because Josephine is my friend. I don't want to insult her, but I really do think Kenya is heading down the wrong road."

"So how are you going to vote next week, Karen?"

"I don't know, Tom. Maybe I just won't show up. How are you going to vote?"

Commentary

This commentary offers background information on global food security and agricultural biotechnology before it turns to specific ethical questions raised by the case.

Food Security

As defined by the UN Food and Agriculture Organization (FAO), "Food security exists when all people, at all times, have physical and economic access to sufficient, safe and nutritious food that meets their dietary needs and food preferences for an active and healthy life."[10]

Nations around the world have made significant gains over the last three decades in reducing hunger and increasing food security. According to the FAO, the number of human beings who are chronically hungry has declined gradually from nearly one billion people thirty years ago to around 840 million today.[11] Nevertheless, this still means that one out of every eight people in the world suffers from hunger. In addition, the International Food Policy Research Institute (IFPRI) estimates two billion people are affected by "hidden hunger," which results from deficiencies in essential micronutrients, such as iron, vitamin A, and zinc.[12]

Food security is especially tenuous in sub-Saharan Africa, where the FAO estimates one in four people are undernourished. While the percentage of hungry people in the region has declined from nearly 33 percent in the early 1990s to approximately 25 percent today, the sheer number of people who are hungry has increased from 173 million to 223 million people. Sub-Saharan African is the only region in the world where the number of hungry people has increased over the last three decades.[13]

This case revolves around the prospects for GM crops to improve the food security of Kenya, where eleven million people are hungry.[14] IFPRI's Global Hunger Index (GHI) places the country in "serious" condition, but Kenya, is marginally better off than three of its neighbors (Tanzania, Ethiopia, and Sudan) that all have an "alarming" GHI rating.[15] Over six hundred thousand refugees fleeing famine and violence in these countries have sought shelter in Kenya in recent years.[16]

This amount of migration reveals there are several factors that contribute to food insecurity in sub-Saharan Africa. Drought and crop losses to pests and disease have had devastating impacts on the amount of food that is available. Less obvious factors, however, often have a greater impact on food supply. Too frequently, governments in the region spend valuable resources on weapons, which are then used in civil or regional conflicts that displace people and reduce food production. In addition, many governments—hamstrung by international debt obligations—have pursued economic development strategies that bypass subsistence farmers and focus on the production of cash crops for export. As a result, a few countries produce significant amounts of food, but it is shipped to wealthier nations and is not available for local consumption. Storage and transportation limitations also result in inefficient distribution of surpluses when they are produced within nations in the region.[17]

Poverty is another significant cause of food insecurity. Globally, the gap between the rich and the poor is enormous. According to the World Bank, the $2,250 average annual purchasing power of a Kenyan pales in comparison with the $53,960 available to each citizen of the United States.[18] Poor people in developing nations typically spend 50 to 80 percent of their income for food, in comparison to the 10 to 15 percent that people spend in the United States or the European Union.[19] Thus, while food may be available for purchase, fluctuating market conditions often drive prices up to unaffordable levels. In addition, poverty limits the resources farmers can purchase to *improve* their land and increase yields. Instead, soils are worked without rest to produce food for people who already have too little to eat.

One way to deal with diminished food supplies or high prices is to grow your own food. Approximately 70 percent of the people living in sub-Saharan Africa are subsistence farmers, but the amount of land available per person has been declining over the last thirty years. While the concentration of land in the hands of a few who seek to export crops plays an important role in this problem, the primary problem is population growth in the region.

In 2012, the United Nations revised its projections for future global population growth. The 2015 world population of 7.2 billion is projected to reach 8.1 billion in 2025 and 9.6 billion in 2050. More than half of global population growth between now and 2050 is expected to occur in Africa—increasing from 1.1 billion today to 2.4 billion in 2050, and potentially reaching 4.2 billion by 2100.[20] Most of this growth will take place in sub-Saharan Africa. Kenya's population of 43.2 million in 2012 is projected to reach 60 million by mid-2030 and 81.3 million by mid-2050.[21]

Agricultural Biotechnology

The FAO estimates that global crop production will need to increase 70 percent by 2050 to feed another two billion people. If this is achieved, more food will need to be produced in the next thirty-five years than in the last ten thousand years combined.[22] This will be an especially daunting task in sub-Saharan Africa, where resource constraints and climate change are already having a negative impact. Given the limited financial resources of sub-Saharan nations, increasing imports is not a viable strategy for the foreseeable future. Instead, greater efforts must be made to stimulate agricultural production within the region, particularly among subsistence farmers. The main effort has been to improve the least expensive input: seeds. A great deal of public and private research is now focused on developing new crop varieties that are resistant to drought, pests, and disease, and are also hearty enough to thrive in poor soils. While the vast majority of this research utilizes traditional plant-breeding methods, several African nations are actively researching ways the appropriate use of biotechnology can also increase agricultural yields through GM crops.

Genetic engineering involves the direct transfer of genetic material between organisms. Whereas conventional cross-breeding transfers genetic material in a more indirect and less efficient manner through the traditional propagation of plants, genetic engineering enables researchers to transfer specific genes directly into the genome of a plant *in vitro*. The first GMOs were developed for industry and medicine, not agriculture. By 1996, however, the first generation of GM crops was approved for planting in six countries. These crops included varieties of corn, soybeans, cotton, and canola that had been engineered to resist insects or to tolerate some herbicides.

The United States and the European Union have taken different approaches to the regulation of GMOs. There are four important differences. First, the United States uses laws that are already in place to regulate GMOs, whereas the European Union has required passage of new laws specific to GM crops and derived foods. Second, the United States uses the same institutions (the Food and Drug Administration, the Animal and Plant Health Inspection Service, and the Environmental Protection Agency) to assess the safety of all foods and crops no matter how they are produced, whereas the European Union has required the establishment of new national biosafety committees and separate screening and approval processes for GMOs. Third, if standard tests for known risks (such as toxicity, allergenicity, and digestibility) are passed, then there is usually no regulatory barrier to commercial release of GMOs in the United States.

In the European Union, however, national biosafety committees drawing heavily on the precautionary principle have declined GMOs on grounds of uncertainty due to hypothetical risk. Finally, the United States does not currently require labeling on approved GM foods, but all products in the European Union that contain some GM content must be labeled.[23]

Given this regulatory context, farmers in the United States readily embraced GM crops after they were first commercialized in 1996. According to the US Department of Agriculture (USDA), virtually all of the corn (93 percent), soybean (94 percent), and cotton (96 percent) planted by US farmers in 2014 was planted with GM seeds that were herbicide-tolerant, insect-resistant, or possessed both qualities.[24]

Globally, approximately 25 percent of all farmland is planted in GM crops. According to the International Service for the Acquisition of Agri-Biotech Applications (ISAAA), in 2013 the United States led the world with 70.1 million hectares planted in GM varieties, which represented 40 percent of the global total of 175.2 million hectares. The other nations in the top ten were Brazil (40.3 million hectares), Argentina (24.4), India (11.0), Canada (10.8), China (4.2), Paraguay (3.6), South Africa (2.9), Pakistan (2.8), and Uruguay (1.5). Note that none of the top ten nations are in the European Union, and nine of the ten are typically regarded as developing nations. ISAAA reports eighteen million farmers planted these GM crops, and that 90 percent of them were risk-averse farmers with small landholdings in developing countries.[25] Several nations in Africa have been conducting research and field trials on GM crop varieties (Burkina Faso, Egypt, Ghana, Kenya, Mozambique, Nigeria, South Africa, Tanzania, Uganda, and Zimbabwe), but only Burkina Faso, Egypt, and South Africa have approved GM crops for commercial planting.[26]

In Kenya, KARI has been conducting field tests on insect-resistant maize and cotton as well as on varieties of cassava resistant to mosaic disease and sweet potatoes resistant to viral disease. In addition, regulatory approval is pending for field trials of drought-resistant sorghum, and contained greenhouse trials are under way on nutrition-enhanced sorghum. Funding for these research projects comes from the Kenyan government and also from a variety of external sources like the Africa Harvest Biotech Foundation, the Bill and Melinda Gates Foundation, the Howard G. Buffett Foundation, Monsanto, Syngenta Foundation, and the US Agency for International Development.[27] The case notes that the KARI is working in partnership with the CIMYYT to develop the disease- and insect-resistant varieties of maize, including *Bt* maize. A similar funding relationship with the Rockefeller Foundation is supporting research to develop varieties of maize from a mutant type that is naturally resistant to a herbicide that is highly effective against striga, the weed that devastates much of Kenya's maize crop each year.

As the case states, however, Kenya imposed a ban on GM products in

November 2012. Josephine says this action was met with dismay by many in the research community and by others concerned about Kenya's food security. Florence Wambugu, a Kenyan pioneer in the field of agricultural biotechnology, is the chief executive officer of the Africa Harvest Biotech Foundation. She explains the origins for the ban and offers her own assessment of its validity in a recent book:

> The problems in Africa can in a nutshell be traced to the politicizing of the biosafety laws regulating biotech crops. . . . The Cabinet of Kenya, at the end of 2012, temporarily put a ban on the import of GM food crops and products, following the publication of a highly controversial scientific article in a European journal, claiming that GM crops caused cancer. The ban in Kenya was championed by two ministers of the Ministry of Health, both of whom had cancer and were undergoing treatment. The experiments on which the articles were based were soon scientifically challenged by the European Biosafety Agency and many other global scientific institutions, and were found to be compromised and wrong.[28]

The ban did not pertain to existing research and development activities, however; thus GM research continues in Kenya.

Christian Concerns about Genetic Engineering

With what authority, and to what extent, should human beings intervene genetically in creation? It is clear from Genesis 2 that Adam, the first human creature, is given the task of tending and keeping the Garden of Eden. In addition, Adam is allowed to name the animals that God has made. Does that mean human beings should see their role primarily as passive stewards or caretakers of God's creation? In Genesis 1, human beings are created in the image of God (*imago dei*) and are told to subdue the Earth and have dominion over it. Does this mean human beings, like God, are also creators of life and have been given the intelligence to use this gift wisely in the exercise of human dominion?

Answers to these two questions hinge on what it means to be created in the image of God. Some argue that human beings are *substantially* like God in the sense that humans possess qualities ascribed to the divine, like the capacity for rational thought, moral action, or creative activity. These distinctive features confer a greater degree of sanctity to human life and set humans apart from other creatures—if not above them. Others argue that creation in the image of God has less to do with being substantially different from other forms of life and more to do with the *relationality* of God to creation. In contrast to substantialist views that often set human beings above other creatures, the relational conception of being created in the image of God seeks to set humanity in a proper relationship of service and devotion to other

---

creatures and to God. Modeled after the patterns of relationship exemplified in Christ, human relationships to nature are to be characterized by sacrificial love and earthly service.[29]

Proponents of genetic engineering draw on the substantialist conception when they describe the technology as simply an outgrowth of the capacities for intelligence and creativity with which God has endowed human beings. At the same time, critics draw upon the same substantialist tradition to protect the sanctity of human life from genetic manipulation. More attention, however, needs to be given to the relevance of the relational tradition to debates surrounding genetic engineering. Is it possible that human beings could wield this tool not as a means to garner wealth or wield power over others, but rather as a means to improve the lives of others? Is it possible to use genetic engineering to feed the hungry, heal the sick, and otherwise to redeem a broken world?[30] Certainly many proponents of genetic engineering in the nonprofit sector believe this very strongly.

Another issue related to genetic engineering has to do with human ignorance as well as the power of sin and evil. Many critics of genetic engineering believe all sorts of mischief and harm could result from the misuse of this new and powerful technology. There is no doubt that human technological inventions have been used intentionally to perpetrate great evil in the world, particularly in the last century. It is also abundantly clear that human foresight has not anticipated enormous problems associated, for example, with the introduction of exotic species in foreign lands or the disposal of high-level nuclear waste. The question, however, is whether human beings can learn from these mistakes and organize their societies so that these dangers are lessened and problems are averted.

Ethical Concerns about GM Crops

The significant growth of GM crops around the world has raised various concerns about threats these crops may pose to human health and the environment. In addition, many fear that large agribusiness corporations will gain even greater financial control of agriculture and limit the options of small-scale farmers. Some also raise religious concerns about genetic modification as discussed above. We will encounter many of these concerns as we explore specific ethical questions raised by the case. These questions are organized around the four ecojustice norms that have been discussed in this book.

Sufficiency

At the heart of this case is the growing problem of hunger in sub-Saharan Africa. It is clear that many people in this region simply do not have enough to eat. In the case Kelly suggests that the world produces enough food to provide everyone with an adequate diet. Is she right?

The FAO and IFPRI studies cited earlier confirm that the world does produce enough food to provide everyone in the world with a modest diet. Thus, technically, Kelly is right. Currently, there is enough food for everyone—so long as people would be satisfied by a simple vegetarian diet with very little meat consumption. The reality, however, is that meat consumption is on the rise around the world, particularly among people in developing nations that have subsisted primarily on vegetarian diets.[31] Thus, while it appears that a balanced vegetarian diet for all might be possible, and even desirable from a health standpoint, for the foreseeable future it is not a very realistic possibility.

Does that mean, however, that GM crops represent a "magic bullet" when it comes to increasing food supplies in the region? Will GM crops end hunger in sub-Saharan Africa? It is important to note that neither Adam nor Josephine make this claim in the case. Instead, Adam argues that GM crops should be part of a mix of agricultural strategies that will be employed to increase food production and reduce hunger in the region. When stem-borers and striga decimate up to 60 percent of the annual maize harvest, herbicide- and insect-resistant varieties could significantly increase the food supply.

Key to this case is the heavy pressure population growth puts on agricultural production. Until population growth declines to levels similar to those in Asia or Latin America, food insecurity will persist in sub-Saharan Africa. One of the keys to achieving this goal is reducing the rate of infant and child mortality. When so many children die in childhood due to poor diets, parents continue to have several children with the hope that some will survive to care for them in their old age. When more children survive childhood, fertility rates decline.[32] Thus, one of the keys to reducing population growth is increasing food security for children. Other keys include increasing access to a full range of reproductive health services, including modern means of family planning, increasing educational and literacy levels, and removing various cultural and legal barriers that constrain the choices of women and girl children.

A third question raised by the sufficiency norm has to do with the dangers GM crops might pose to human health. Many specific concerns have been raised over the last twenty years about the potential allergenicity, toxicity, and nutritional quality of GM-derived foods. To date, however, no serious human health problems have been attributed to food products derived from GM crops. The Board of Directors of the American Association for the Advancement of Science recently issued the following statement:

The World Health Organization, the American Medical Association, the US National Academy of Sciences, the British Royal Society, and every other respected organization that has examined the evidence has come to the same conclusion: Consuming foods containing ingredients derived from GM crops is no riskier than consuming the same foods containing ingredients from crop plants modified by conventional plant improvement techniques.[33]

A recent report by the European Commission arrived at the same conclusion.[34] Proponents of GM foods, meanwhile, are busy trumpeting the "second wave" of GM crops that actually increase the nutritional value of various foods. For example, Swiss researchers working in collaboration with the Rockefeller Foundation have produced "Golden Rice," a genetically engineered rice that is rich in beta carotene and will help to combat Vitamin A deficiency in the developing world.[35]

Nevertheless, concerns persist about GM crops and the foods derived from them. In part this is because those who champion the precautionary principle fear risks to human health that thus far have not been proven. Another reason may be that this is a case where ideological views and loyalties can affect the interpretation of facts or the lack of data. Market liberals who favor a free market approach tend to be quite supportive of GM crops and oppose making policy on the precautionary principle because it limits entrepreneurial innovation, whereas social greens and bioenvironmentalists tend to be quite suspicious. Dr. Mark Van Montagu, co-recipient of the 2013 World Food Prize, speaks for some when he concludes: "It seems to me that much of the resistance to GM foods isn't based on science, but may be ideological and political, based on fears of 'corporate profiteering' and 'Western colonialism'."[36]

Sustainability

While there appears to be plenty of evidence to allay fears about immediate dangers posed to human beings by GM crops, how well equipped is Kenya to address biosafety and protect the environment? And what about potential long-term effects that have not yet been studied or monitored?

In fact, Kenya does have serious biosafety policies on the books. Kenya's Biosafety Act was signed into law by the president of Kenya in 2009.[37] These policies were developed with substantial financial assistance furnished by the government of the Netherlands, the World Bank, the US Agency for International Development, and the UN Environment Programme. Kenya's extensive regulations reflect a very careful approach to GM products.

Another concern in the case has to do with the ecological consequences of industrial agriculture. Karen disagrees with Tom's glowing account of the Green Revolution. While it produced food to feed more than two billion people during the latter half of the twentieth century, it did so only by exacting a heavy ecological toll. Karen fears GM crops in Kenya may open the floodgates to industrial agriculture and create more problems than they solve. She thinks we need to stop viewing nature as a machine that can be taken apart and reassembled in other ways. Ecofeminists argue that such a mechanistic mind-set allows human beings to objectify and, therefore, dominate nature in the same way that women have been objectified and oppressed. Some proponents of genetic engineering acknowledge this danger but argue that the science and techniques of agricultural biotechnology can *increase* respect for nature rather than *diminish* it. As human beings learn more about the genetic foundations of life, it becomes clearer how all forms of life are interconnected. For proponents of GM crops, agricultural biotechnology is just a neutral means that can be put to the service of either good or ill ends. Critics, however, warn that those with power always use technologies to protect their privilege and increase their control. They view GMO technologies not as neutral means, but as part of a pervasive pattern of increasing commodification of nature and agricultural ways of life.

Turning from the general to the specific, Kelly and Terra express particular concern about the potential for GM crops to produce superweeds and pests. Kelly is also worried that GM crops allow farmers to continue monocropping practices (planting huge tracts of land in one crop variety), which actually exacerbate pest and disease problems and diminish biodiversity. The evidence supports Kelly's concerns. A recent article in *Nature* reveals that superweeds have been found in eighteen countries that are resistant to one of the most commonly used herbicides, glyphosate, which is marketed as Roundup by Monsanto.[38] A 2014 report issued by the USDA states "an overreliance on glyphosate and a reduction in the diversity of weed management practices adopted by crop producers have contributed to the evolution of glyphosate resistance in 14 weed species and biotypes in the United States."[39] Another article published in *Environmental Sciences Europe* found "the spread of glyphosate-resistant weeds . . . has brought about substantial increases in the number and volume of herbicides applied" as farmers utilize different herbicides to combat persistent weeds.[40]

There is also evidence to support Terra's concern that insects are developing resistance to *Bt* crops. A recent study in *Nature Biotechnology* found "reduced efficacy of *Bt* crops caused by field-evolved resistance has been reported now for some populations of 5 of 13 major pest species examined, compared with resistant populations of only one pest species in 2005."[41] In addition, while the Environmental Protection Agency requires all US farmers to plant refuges for *Bt* varieties of corn and cotton, the USDA acknowledges, "farmer compliance is not uniformly high and the required refuge percentages may not always be large enough to achieve the desired delays in evolution of resistance."[42]

This raises a third question related to the sustainability norm. Can organic farming methods achieve the same results as GM crops? Certainly Kelly believes this is the case, and there is some research to support her view. On the striga front, some farmers in East Africa have suppressed the weed by planting leguminous tree crops during the dry season from February to April. Since striga is most voracious in fields that have been consistently planted in maize and thus have depleted soil, the nitrogen-fixing trees help to replenish the soil in their brief three months of life before they are pulled up prior to maize planting. Farmers report reducing striga infestations by over 90 percent with this method of weed control.[43]

A similar organic strategy has been employed in Kenya to combat stem-borers. In this *push-pull* approach, silver leaf desmodium and molasses grass are grown amidst the maize. These plants have properties that repel stem-borers toward the edges of the field where other plants like napier grass and Sudan grass attract the bugs and then trap their larvae in sticky substances produced by the plants. When this organic method is employed, farmers have been able to reduce losses to stem-borers from 40 percent to less than 5 percent. In addition, silver leaf desmodium helps to combat striga infestation, thus further raising yields.[44]

Results like these indicate that unfamiliar agroecological methods associated with organic farming may offer a less expensive and more sustainable approach to insect and pest control than those achieved through the expensive development of GM crops and the purchase of GM seeds. Agroecology utilizes ecological principles to design and manage sustainable and resource-conserving agricultural systems. It is not clear, however, that agroecological farming techniques and GM crops need to be viewed as opposing or exclusive alternatives. Some researchers argue that these organic techniques are not as effective in different ecological niches in East Africa. Nor, in some areas, do farmers feel they have the luxury to fallow their fields during the dry season. In these contexts, GM crops might be able to raise yields where they are desperately needed. It is also not likely that the seeds for these crops will be very expensive since they are being produced through research in the public and nonprofit sectors. Still, it is certainly the case that serious ecological problems could result from the use of GM crops in Kenya, and even though donors are currently footing the bill for most of the research, agricultural biotechnology requires a more substantial financial investment than agroecological approaches.

Participation

The source of funding for GM crop research in Kenya raises an important question related to the participation norm. Are biotechnology and GM crops being forced on the people of Kenya?

Given the history of colonialism in Africa, this question is reasonable, but in this case it appears unwarranted. KARI began experimenting with tissue culture and micropropagation in the 1980s. The funding for GM crop research in Kenya has come almost entirely through public sector institutions rather than private corporate sources. Interestingly, Florence Wambugu reports that China is now the biggest foreign investor in African agriculture.[45] Thus, it does not appear that transnational biotechnology corporations are manipulating Kenya, but it is true that the country's openness to biotechnology and GM crops may open doors to the sale of privately developed GM products in the future.

Josephine, however, might turn the colonialism argument around and apply it to Greenpeace's campaign to ban GM crops in Mexico. In its online alert, Greenpeace emphasizes that "corn is an important source of food for the Mexican people, and the diversity of corn is important to the world. To lose thousands of varieties of corn, grown in diverse regions of your country, due to genetic contamination would be a serious blow to Mexico's food sovereignty."[46] Though Josephine does not pose the following question, is this well-intentioned effort to protect Mexico's unique corn heritage and the health of Mexicans a form of paternalism or neocolonialism? If a similar campaign were targeted at Kenya, would it exert undue pressure on the people of Kenya and perhaps provoke a lack of confidence in Kenyan authorities, or would it merely urge Kenyans to use the democratic powers at their disposal to express their concerns? It is not clear how these questions should be answered, but the participation norm requires reflection about them.

The concern about paternalism also arises with regard to a set of questions Karen raises about appropriate technology. Are GM crops an *appropriate* agricultural technology for the people of Kenya? Genetic engineering and other forms of agricultural biotechnology are very sophisticated and expensive. Is such a *high-tech* approach to agriculture *appropriate* given the status of a developing nation like Kenya? Is it realistic to expect undereducated and impoverished subsistence farmers to have the capacities and the resources to properly manage GM crops, for example, through the appropriate use of refuges?

In the case, Josephine responds aggressively to concerns like these when she overhears Terra's conversation with Tom. She asserts that Kenya will do what it takes to educate farmers about the proper use of GM crops. In fact, KARI is designing farmer-training strategies as a part of the insect-resistant maize project. Compared to other countries in sub-Saharan Africa, Kenya has high rates of adult literacy (72.2 percent), and about half of all boys and girls are enrolled in secondary education. In addition, almost 80 percent of Kenyans use a mobile phone, and 32 percent have access to the Internet.[47] The hunger and poverty among many Kenyans, however, may be the most significant impediment to the responsible use of GM crops. In a situation where hunger is on the rise, how likely is it that subsistence farmers will plant 20 percent of their small landholdings in non-*Bt* maize if they see that the *Bt* varieties are producing substantially higher yields?

This is a fair question. The norm of participation supports people making decisions that affect their lives, but in this case the immediate threat of hunger and malnutrition may limit the range of their choices. At the same time, GM crops have the potential to significantly reduce the amount of time women and children spend weeding, picking bugs off plants, and scaring birds away. Organic farming methods would require even larger investments of time. This is time children could use to attend more school or that women could use to increase their literacy or to engage in other activities that might increase family income and confer a slightly greater degree of security and independence. Aspects of the participation norm cut both ways.

Solidarity

Among other things, the ecojustice norm of solidarity is concerned about the equitable distribution of the burdens and benefits associated with GM crops. If problems emerge in Kenya, who will bear the costs? If GM crops are finally approved for planting, who will receive most of the benefits?

Thus far, critics argue that the benefits of GM crops in developed nations have accrued only to biotech corporations through higher sales and to large-scale farmers through lower production costs. Moreover, critics claim the dangers GM crops pose to human health and biosafety are dumped on consumers who do not fully understand the risks associated with GM crops and the food products that are derived from them. It is not clear the same could be said for the production of GM crops in Kenya where these crops are being developed through partnerships in the nonprofit and public sectors. Researchers expect to make these products available at little cost to farmers, and few corporations will earn much money off the sale of these seeds. Thus, the benefits from GM crops should accrue to a larger percentage of people in Kenya because 70 percent of the population is engaged in subsistence agriculture. Like developed nations, however, food safety problems could affect all consumers, and a case could be made that this would be more severe in a nation like Kenya where it would be very difficult to adequately label GM crop products that often move quickly from the field to the dinner table.

Another aspect of solidarity involves supporting others in their struggles. Josephine does not explicitly appeal to this norm in the case, but some members of the Hunger Concerns group are probably wondering whether they should just support Josephine's proposal as a way to show respect to her and to the self-determination of the Kenyan people. There is much to commend this stance and, ultimately, it might be ethically preferable. One of the dangers, however, is that Josephine's colleagues may squelch their moral qualms and simply *pass the buck* ethically to the Kenyans. Karen seems close to making this decision, despite her serious concerns about GM crops. Friendship requires support and respect, but it also thrives on candor.

Conclusion

Tom and Karen face a difficult choice, as do the other members of the Hunger Concerns group. Next week they will have to decide if the group should join the Greenpeace campaign to ban GM crops in Mexico or if it wants to submit an article for the campus newspaper supporting the responsible use of GM crops to bolster food security in Kenya. While convenient, skipping the meeting would just dodge the ethical issues at stake. As the students consider these two alternatives and perhaps develop others, the goods associated with solidarity need to be put into dialogue with the harms to ecological sustainability and human health that could result from the development of GM crops in Kenya. Similarly, these potential harms also need to be weighed against the real harms that are the result of an insufficient food supply. Currently, the problem of hunger in sub-Saharan Africa is only getting worse, not better.

Notes

[1]UN FAO, *The State of Food Insecurity in the World: 2013* (Rome: 2013), 2, http://www.fao.org.

[2]Otieno Owino, "Project Releases Disease-Resistant Cassava Plantlets," April 15, 2014, http://www.scidev.net.

[3]International Institute of Tropical Agriculture, "Saving Maize from Parasitic Striga in Kenya and Nigeria," July 31, 2013, http://r4dreview.org; see also International Institute of Tropical Agriculture, "About Striga," http://www.iita.org.

[4]Seed Today, "Striga-Resistant Maize Developed by Kenya Scientist," May 30, 2013, http://www.seedtoday.com.

[5]International Maize and Wheat Improvement Center (CIMMYT), "Kenya Plants Transgenic Maize to Help Farmers Rid Insect," May 14, 2012, http://www.cimmyt.org.

[6]Greenpeace International, "Demand that Mexico's President Says No to Genetically Engineered Corn," http://www.greenpeace.org.

[7]USDA, Economic Research Service, "Corn: Background," http://www.ers.usda.gov.

[8]Mike Mwaniki, "GMOs Banned as Cancer Fears Grow," *Daily Nation* (Kenya), November 21, 2012, http://www.nation.co.ke.

[9]Kate Snipes and Carol Kamau, "Kenya Bans Genetically Modified Food Imports," USDA Foreign Agricultural Service, Global Agricultural Information Network, November 27, 2012, http://gain.fas.usda.gov.

[10]UN FAO, "Food Security Statistics," http://www.fao.org.

[11]UN FAO, *The State of Food Insecurity in the World: 2013* (Rome: 2013), 2, http://www.fao.org.

[12]International Food Policy Research Institute (IFPRI), *2013 Global Food Policy Report* (Washington, DC: 2013), overview, http://www.ifpri.org.

[13]UN FAO, *The State of Food Insecurity in the World 2013*: 8.

144 CASES AND COMMENTARIES

[14]Bread for the World Institute, *2014 Hunger Report: Ending Hunger in America* (Washington, DC: Bread for the World Institute, 2014), 219, http://files.bread.org.

[15]International Food Policy Research Institute (IFPRI), *2013 Global Hunger Index* (Washington, DC: IFPRI, 2013), http://www.ifpri.org.

[16]UN International Children's Emergency Fund (UNICEF), "Humanitarian Action for Children: Kenya," http://www.unicef.org.

[17]J. DeVries and G. Toenniessen, *Securing the Harvest: Biotechnology, Breeding, and Seed Systems for African Crops* (New York: CABI, 2001), 29.

[18]World Bank, "GNI Per Capita PPP," http://data.worldbank.org.

[19]Bread for the World Institute, *2013 Hunger Report: Within Reach—Global Development Goals* (Washington, DC: Bread for the World Institute, 2013), 70, http://www.hungerreport.org.

[20]UN Department of Public Information, "World Population Projected to Reach 9.6 Billion by 2050 with Most Growth in Developing Regions, Especially Africa—Says UN Economic and Social Affairs," http://esa.un.org.

[21]Population Reference Bureau, "2014 World Population Data Sheet," http://www.prb.org.

[22]Michael Hoevel, "Food Security: Facts and Figures," http://www.scidev.net.

[23]Robert Paarlberg, "Genetically Modified Foods and Crops: Africa's Choice," in *Genetically Modified Crops in Africa: Economic and Policy Lesson from Countries South of the Sahara*, ed. José Falck-Zepeda, Gullaume Gruère, and Idah Stihole-Niang (Washington, DC: International Food Policy Research Institute, 2013), 207–8. See also Robert Paarlberg, *Food Politics: What Everyone Needs to Know* (New York: Oxford University Press, 2013).

[24]USDA, Economic Research Service, "Recent Trends in GE Adoption," http://www.ers.usda.gov.

[25]ISAAA, "Global Status of Commercialized Biotech/GM Crops," *ISAAA Brief* 46–2013, http://www.isaaa.org.

[26]José Falck-Zepeda, Gullaume Gruère, and Idah Stihole-Niang, "Introduction and Background," in *Genetically Modified Crops in Africa*, 11–13, 184.

[27]Ibid.

[28]Florence Muringi Wambugu, "The Importance of Political Will in Contributions of Agricultural Biotechnology towards Economic Growth, Food and Nutritional Security in Africa," in *Biotechnology in Africa: Emergence, Initiatives and Future*, ed. Florence Wambugu and Daniel Kamanga (London: Springer International, 2014), 6–7.

[29]See Douglas John Hall, *Imaging God: Dominion as Stewardship* (Grand Rapids: Eerdmans, 1986), 89–116; and *The Steward: A Biblical Symbol Come of Age* (Grand Rapids: Eerdmans, 1990).

[30]A recent social statement by the Evangelical Lutheran Church in America on genetics describes human beings as "innovative stewards" called "to respect and promote the community of life with justice and wisdom. This imperative should be used to direct our activity and use of genetic research and knowledge in medicine, agriculture and other areas of life." See Evangelical Lutheran Church in America, *Genetics, Faith, and Responsibility* (2011), http://www.elca.org.

[31]WorldWatch Institute, "Global Meat Production and Consumption Continue to Rise," http://www.worldwatch.org.

[32]The term *fertility rate* refers to the average number of children born to a woman over the course of her lifetime.

[33]American Association for the Advancement of Science, "Statement by the AAAS Board on Labelling of Genetically-Modified Foods," October 20, 2012, http://www.aaas.org. See also World Health Organization, "Modern Food Biotechnology, Human Health, and Development: An Evidence-Based Study," http://www.who.int; U.S. National Academy of Sciences, "Safety of Genetically Engineered Foods," http://www.nap.edu; David H. Freeman, "The Truth about Genetically Modified Food," *Scientific American* 39, no. 3, April 20, 2013, http://www.scientificamerican.com.

[34]European Commission, "A Decade of EU-Funded GMO Research: 2001–2010," ftp://ftp.cordis.europa.eu.

[35]Daniel Cressey, "Transgenics—A New Breed," *Nature* 497, May 2, 2013, 27–29, http://www.nature.com.

[36]Marc Van Montagu, "The Irrational Fear of GM Food: Billions of People Have Eaten Genetically Modified Food over the Past Two Decades. Not One Problem Has Been Found," *Wall Street Journal*, October 22, 2013, http://online.wsj.com.

[37]Kenya National Biosafety Authority, "Biosafety Act," http://www.biosafetykenya.go.ke.

[38]Natasha Gilbert, "Case Studies: A Hard Look at GM Crops," *Nature* 497, May 2, 2013, 24–26, http://www.nature.com.

[39]Jorge Fernandez-Cornejo, Seth James Wechsler, Michael Livingston, and Lorraine Mitchell, *Genetically Engineered Crops in the United States* (Washington, DC: USDA), Economic Research Report No. (ERR-162), February 2014, summary, http://www.ers.usda.gov.

[40]Charles M. Benbrook, "Impacts of Genetically Engineered Crops on Pesticide Use in the U.S.—The First Sixteen Years," *Environmental Sciences Europe* 24, no. 24 (September 2012), http://link.springer.com.

[41]Bruce E. Tabashnik, Thierry Brévault, and Yves Carriére, "Insect Resistance to Bt Crops: Lessons from the First Billion Acres," *Nature Biotechnology* 31, June 10, 2013, 510–21, http://www.nature.com.

[42]Fernandez-Cornejo, Wechsler, Livingston, and Mitchell, *Genetically Engineered Crops in the United States*, 29n28.

[43]Brian Halweil, "Biotech, African Corn, and the Vampire Weed," *WorldWatch* 14, no. 5 (September/October 2001): 28–29.

[44]Zeyaur R. Khan, Charles A. O. Midega, Jimmy O. Pittchar, Alice W. Murage, Michael A. Birkett, Toby J. A. Bruce, and John A. Pickett, "Achieving Food Security for One Million Sub-Saharan African Poor through Push–Pull Innovation by 2020," *Philosophical Transactions of the Royal Society B* 369: 20120284, February 17, 2014, http://rstb.royalsocietypublishing.org.

[45]Wambugu, "The Importance of Political Will in Contributions of Agricultural Biotechnology towards Economic Growth, Food and Nutritional Security in Africa," 14.

[46]Greenpeace International, "Demand That Mexico's President Says No to Genetically Engineered Corn," http://www.greenpeace.org.

[47]UN International Childrens Emergency Fund (UNICEF), "Kenya Statistics," http://www.unicef.org.

7

Klamath Crisis

Water Rights and Endangered Species Protection

Acronyms and Abbreviations

BOR	Bureau of Reclamation (US)
ESA	Endangered Species Act (US)
FWS	Fish and Wildlife Service (US)
KBRA	Klamath Basin Restoration Agreement
KBWRERA	Klamath Basin Water Recovery and Economic Restoration Act
KHSA	Klamath Hydroelectric Settlement Agreement
NMFS	National Marine Fisheries Service (US)
NWR	National Wildlife Refuge
WON!	Wild Oregon Now!

Case

Jennifer looked out over the blue waters of Upper Klamath Lake to the snow-capped Cascades in the west and tried to gather her thoughts after a recent conversation she'd had with her friend Kevin Andrews at the farmers' market. Recently the US senators in both Oregon and California had introduced the Klamath Basin Water Recovery and Economic Restoration Act (KBWRERA) in an effort to resolve the decades-long water wars that had engulfed the Klamath Basin in southern Oregon and northern California. The senators' news releases touted KBWRERA as a win-win solution for all stakeholders in the region, and initially Jennifer had been excited about the proposed legislation resolving an issue that had deeply divided the Klamath community.

But then her friend Kevin asked her to join a coalition to oppose KBWRERA. Kevin was a committed environmentalist and organizer from Portland, working in the Klamath Basin for Wild Oregon Now! (WON!)—a citizens' group dedicated to wilderness and restoring wild lands. WON! was particularly concerned about the management of the six national wildlife refuges in the Klamath Basin, and the impacts of dropping water levels on the native fish and birds that depend on them for habitat.

"The senators tell us that KBWRERA will resolve the water issues," Kevin told Jennifer, "but it actually does the opposite because it leaves in place agricultural use of refuge lands and waters. Farming based on irrigation is simply not sustainable in the arid Klamath Basin. Historically the Upper Klamath Basin gets around thirteen inches of rain a year, and it has been getting much less than that since the current drought began.[1] But KBWRERA keeps the Klamath Project's reclamation and irrigation framework in place, which is what exacerbated the water crisis here in the first place! And we're not alone in being worried. Just this week the elders of the Hoopa Valley Tribe reiterated their opposition to KBWRERA because they believe it will limit their tribal water and fishing rights. So we are working with the tribe and other concerned groups to oppose the bill. We know you are committed to sustainable farming and land use. That's why we are asking you to join our coalition to oppose KBWRERA."

Stirred by the site of hundreds of pelicans flying over the lake, Jennifer took a deep breath and thought about the past year. Only a year ago she had graduated from college in the Midwest where she had developed a passion for sustainable food and farming. Jennifer had joined the Ameri-Corps Food Corps program to get firsthand experience with food issues. She had been assigned to Klamath Falls, Oregon, where she was building school gardens and teaching children about local foods while helping to develop a farmers' market program.

Jennifer had grown to love the arid, wide-open landscape around Klamath Falls. But nothing in her midwestern upbringing had prepared her for how water—and particularly its scarcity—determined everything in this part of the West. It seemed that everyone here had strong views on water, who should have access to it, and why. From Native Americans who depended on free-flowing rivers for their sacred salmon, to farmers who needed to irrigate the rich basin soils to grow their crops, to environmentalists concerned for imperiled ecosystems and threatened species—everyone had a claim on the basin's limited water, and in the face of growing drought and climate change in the region, it didn't seem like there was enough to go around to satisfy everyone.

In 2010, after a decade of contentious litigation, the federal government had gotten representatives from several groups to sign off on the Klamath Basin Restoration Agreement (KBRA) and the Klamath Hydroelectric

Settlement Agreement (KHSA). The two agreements included a broad set of measures designed to create robust conditions for fisheries restoration as well as measures that would provide greater stability for the Basin's rural communities that are largely dependent on irrigated agriculture.[2] KBWRERA provided the legislation to implement them.

Yet Jennifer knew that not everyone was on board, and passions still ran high. Through her work at the weekly farmers' market in Klamath Falls, she had met folks on all sides of the issue, often getting an earful about the latest controversy. She had intentionally avoided taking sides in the debate so that she could remain friends with everyone. Now Kevin was asking her to take a stand and oppose KBWRERA. Before she could commit to that, she thought she should ask her other friends what they thought of the proposed law and then decide for herself. But once she took a side, could she really remain friends with everyone?

Jennifer started by calling Julie Thompson, a Portland-based water rights lawyer who had a cabin in the Klamath Basin and frequented the farmers' market when she was at her cabin. Julie had been working with the senators' staffs to help draft the new agreements, and Jennifer hoped she could explain some of the complex water issues to her.

"Not enough water for too many needs," Julie started the conversation. "That's the story of the West. Mark Twain hit the nail on the head when he supposedly said that in the West, 'whiskey is for drinking, water is for fighting.' Nothing illustrates that more than the water wars in the Klamath Basin. There's simply not enough water in this arid region to support all the needs people want it for.

"But the two agreements they hammered out in 2010 are an important start to resolve some of the thorniest issues, and it's amazing that both tribal leaders and many farmers and ranchers have signed off on them.

"The biggest problem is keeping enough water in the Klamath River and its tributaries to protect the two species of suckerfish and the coho salmon that have been listed as endangered under the Endangered Species Act (ESA). Once they were listed in the 1980s and 1990s, that kicked in a whole series of required government steps to keep river flows and lake levels above a required minimum. In wet years that's been possible, but when drought hits, the only way to do that is to limit the amount of water available for irrigation to farmers and ranchers. That's what happened at the end of the 1990s. Then in 2001 the drought was so bad that the US Bureau of Reclamation (BOR) allocated nearly all water in the Klamath Project for the benefit of the fish, and irrigation water was shut off completely. A group of farmers responded with a twenty thousand–strong 'bucket brigade' to symbolically pass water by bucket from the lake to the dry irrigation canals; some even forcibly opened the headgates to return water to the canals."

"But don't the salmon fishermen downstream depend on keeping water in the Klamath River to support the salmon populations?" Jennifer asked.

"That's true. A big problem is that it's not only the farmers' livelihoods that are at stake here. A year after the bucket brigade, irrigators succeeded in getting more water than had been allocated in 2001, but then thousands of salmon died on the lower part of the Klamath River, due primarily to poor fish health from reduced water levels. Commercial salmon fishermen have seen their harvests plummet as fish kills in the shrunken and overly warm rivers have reduced salmon populations to a trickle. The Klamath River was once the third-most-productive salmon river system in the United States. Today, thanks to the combination of dams, poor water quality from agricultural runoff, and especially too little water left in the river due to irrigation draw-offs, the once abundant Klamath salmon runs have now been reduced to less than 10 percent of their historic size.[3] The Pacific Coast Federation of Fishermen's Associations claims that Lower Klamath Basin communities have lost an estimated 3,780 family wage jobs, representing an annual loss of more than $75 million a year in economic benefit as a direct result of salmon losses in the Klamath River.[4] And it's not just commercial fishermen who have suffered. The Karuk, Yurok, Hoopa, and Klamath Tribes who are native to this area also depend on the salmon and the suckerfish for their subsistence and religious and cultural needs. The judge who turned off the water in 2001 cited both the tribes' treaty rights to the fish as well as the ESA to justify her decision—and that *really* polarized things in the basin."

"It sounds like the farmers felt like the rights of fish outweighed their rights," commented Jennifer.

"What these agreements do is try to help everyone get something from the limited water available. Because of past treaties, most of the senior water rights in the Upper Klamath Basin are held by the Klamath tribes. Under this agreement the tribes agree to share some of their water in dry years in exchange for riparian restoration of the rivers, economic development to create employment opportunities, and support for their cultural rights. By agreeing to resolve ongoing water litigation, farmers agree to participate in a water use program that will add some thirty thousand acre-feet of inflows to Upper Klamath Lake each year and create a stable, predictable setting for agriculture to continue in the Upper Klamath Basin.[5] And it would set in motion a process to remove four older dams on the Klamath River that impede fish and damage riparian conditions on the river."

Jennifer thought about what Julie had told her as she drove down to Tulelake, just across the border in California, to meet with her good friend Hailey Marshall. "Not everyone gets what they want completely, but KBWRERA seemed like an important way to move forward to resolve all these issues," she thought. Thirty minutes later she turned into the Marshall farm, on the edge of the Tule Lake National Wildlife Refuge (NWR). Hailey's dad, Stan, was a prominent farmer in the basin and had been active on the water issue for over a decade. A recent college graduate like herself, Hailey had a large vegetable garden on the farm and one of the larger stands at the farmers' market. Jennifer needed to talk to Hailey about the farmers' market that week but thought she could take advantage of her visit to ask Stan Marshall about his views on KBWRERA.

Standing by the garden Stan told Jennifer, "You need to know the history of farming here to understand why water is such a passionate issue for us. For thousands of years, the ash from nearby volcanoes mixed with the sediments of these lakebeds and the droppings of millions of migrating birds to give the Klamath Basin some of the richest soils anywhere in the West. White settlers started farming here in the late 1800s, and soon conflicts with the local tribes began. After the US Army defeated the Modoc Tribe in the lava beds just south of here, the land was opened to settlers.

"The BOR was formed in 1902 and the Klamath Project was one of its first undertakings. Within a few years it had drained a lot of the shallow lakes and wetlands like Tule Lake and Lower Klamath Lake to create some of the most fertile farmland anywhere in the world. Land and water rights to irrigate it were made available by lottery to veterans from the two World Wars as recompense for their service. In 1929, my grandfather, a veteran of the First World War, moved here and homesteaded our farm under the Klamath Project. We've been farming here for over eighty-five years. Hailey is the fourth generation of Marshalls to grow up here, and we hope her children and grandchildren will follow us into farming this land.

"We've always had ups and downs here with the weather—that's the nature of farming. But because we had a reliable water supply we could always irrigate our fields, and we did well. That all changed with the passage of the ESA. In the late 1980s we went through a bad drought and water levels dropped in the lakes and rivers that provide us with irrigation water. Biologists from the Fish and Wildlife Service [FWS] and the National Marine Fisheries Service [NMFS] argued more water needed to stay in the rivers and in Upper Klamath Lake to protect the fish. Then, in the early 1990s, for the first time, the BOR started to reduce the water available to us for irrigation.

"Those were really difficult years, and several of our neighbors lost their farms when they couldn't get the water they needed for their crops. You won't find many farmers here who like the federal government or the environmentalists who worked to get the fish listed. But I decided that it was better to work with the agencies to get an agreement that would protect some of the farmers' interests than to be locked into an endless cycle of lawsuits and litigation where the lawyers are the only ones who win. We've always seen ourselves as stewards of our land, and we want to coexist with the wildlife that lives here, too. We have to recognize that the context for farming has changed, and therefore we have to adapt our farming methods. The ESA is here to stay, and droughts are becoming more frequent. These agreements recognize this changed context, and everybody compromised on something to make them happen. That's why I'll support KBWRERA."

Just then Stan's neighbor, Jim Stephens, drove into the yard. "I hope you're not letting him fill your head with all this collaboration talk! What's really endangered here is not some suckerfish, but the American farmer! Environmentalists are using the ESA, Indian rights, land trusts, and a bunch of other tactics to get at what they really want: a landscape without people on it or using it. Let's call this what it really is: *rural cleansing*. These extremists argue that this area should never have had farms in the first place, and they favor birds and fish over people. Their goal is to get rid of the water reclamation and irrigation projects, and thus get rid of the farmers—make us move off the land so it can be returned to its so-called natural state. But agriculture is the economic backbone in the Klamath Basin; get rid of us and the rest of the community will shrivel up. But for environmentalists, a collapse of the rural farm economy is a good thing, because it speeds up returning farmland back to nature. These federal agreements Stan is talking up are really wolves in sheep's clothing—they're a wedge to deprive us of our property and water rights to support the environmental agenda.

"We farmers are the real American patriots here—our fathers and grandfathers fought to keep America free and homesteaded these farms, turning former wastelands into some of the best farmland in the world. As part of rewarding them for their service to their country, the federal government promised them water to irrigate their farms—and now that same federal government has turned against us and sided with the environmentalists to deprive us of our rights and our livelihoods. They even want to add fish, wildlife, and refuge purposes into the mandate of the Klamath Project—the ones who are supposed to be on our side to protect our water rights and delivery! I won't have anything to do with these so-called win-win agreements—and I won't support any politician who does!"

With her ears ringing from Jim's speech, Jennifer headed back toward Klamath Falls. Along the way she stopped at a now defunct farm that a three-generation family recently had sold to the Klamath Basin Land Trust, which was restoring both the former wetlands and hillsides to add it to the Tule Lake NWR. She'd agreed to meet Kevin there to see some of the work WON! was doing in returning farmland to a natural state.

"Look at how this land is recovering!" Kevin exclaimed, as Jennifer pulled into the restored site. It was inspiring to see the number of birds in the reclaimed wetlands, and hawks soaring over the hillside now flowering with native plants. Kevin continued, "This land illustrates WON!'s vision for the Klamath Basin better than anything I can say. The Klamath Basin—and the entire Klamath Watershed—is one of the most ecologically diverse and important bioregions in North America. It provides habitat for millions of over 350 species of birds that use the Pacific flyway through the Klamath. Tragically misguided water reclamation policies that began a century ago led to the loss of over 80 percent of the basin's wetlands. Those losses of habitat together with current pesticide runoff from agriculture threaten the amazing biodiversity of this region.

"The real issue is that this arid land is ill suited to irrigation-based agriculture—it's simply not sustainable in the long term. While I personally would love to see this entire basin restored to its natural state, WON! realizes that's not realistic—any solution to the water wars and habitat loss here needs to balance economic and conservation needs.

"We'd like to see three steps taken to move us toward a more sustainable use of resources in the Klamath Basin. First, we need a voluntary demand reduction program to work with interested farmers to buy back and retire water rights for irrigation so we can keep water in the streams and lakes where fish and wildlife need them to survive. Second, we should ban pesticides and fertilizers on NWR lands and encourage neighboring farms to reduce their use to improve water quality. Finally, refuge lands currently being leased for agriculture should be returned to their natural state as wetlands that provide habitat for wildlife and act as natural filters to maintain water quality. The bottom line is that all farming on refuge lands must stop and water for irrigation reduced.

"WON! was one of the parties working on the two Klamath Basin agreements in 2010, but we were expelled from the negotiations when we objected that the proposed agreements required all parties to support continued commercial farming on the basin's NWR lands. It became clear that the ecological needs of the basin were being compromised in favor of large agricultural interests in the basin. The agreements allow agriculture to continue indefinitely on refuge lands and are too generous to farmers' use of water for irrigation in dry years, when the lakes and rivers need them most. So while we continue to support collaborative efforts to reach a solution in the Klamath Basin, KBWRERA is the wrong way to do it—it institutionalizes a solution that simply is not sustainable within the ecological limits of the basin."

Jennifer felt torn as she listened to Kevin's vision for the Klamath Basin. Her commitments to sustainable solutions ran deep, but she flashed back to Jim's accusations of "rural cleansing" as she pondered the retirement of so much farmland back to restore preagricultural conditions. She had once hoped that KBWRERA would provide the balance of water needs that everyone claimed to support, but that now seemed elusive.

Her last stop of the day was coffee with a new friend, Frank Chiloquin of the Klamath Tribe. Before moving to Oregon, Jennifer had read all she could about the Klamath Tribe, and she was familiar with its history of displacement onto reservations at the end of the nineteenth century and the termination of its tribal status by the federal government in the 1950s. The Klamath Basin water struggles were only the most recent efforts by the Klamath to regain its homelands and restore its tribal status. She knew that Klamath tribal leaders had worked with the federal government to write KBWRERA, and she was glad that at least some of the area's tribes seemed to be on board.

"I am happy that the Klamath Tribal Council has voted to support this historic act," Frank said as he poured her coffee. "As the chairman of our tribe explained to us, 'If approved, we will see an increase in water flows, improved habitat for current and future fish populations, and economic opportunities for our tribe and tribal members. It will help us restore our homeland and honor the treaty our ancestors signed 150 years ago.'[6]

"But I am worried that the vote was closer than we expected and will increase divisions within the tribe: 564 tribal members voted in favor, and 419 against.[7] Many tribal members feel like we gave away too much in order to reach an agreement. In fact, our brothers and sisters in the Hoopa Valley Tribe have opposed the two previous Klamath Basin agreements out of concern that there will not be enough water for the fish after irrigation commitments are met.

"I worry about that, too, despite the many positive steps taken in the agreements. When the new law was announced, the drought in California was already so severe that water flows at the US Geological Survey station were below the 1977 levels that led to several fish kills. I hope that this new law will not end up being the latest effort that divides our peoples and deprives us of our rights."

On that sobering note, Jennifer headed home. When she had first heard about KBWRERA, she thought it would be the answer to end the water wars of the Klamath Basin and could serve as a model for other water conflicts throughout the West. Now she was not so sure. How should she respond to Kevin's request that she join the coalition to oppose KBWRERA? She was glad she had some time to research the issues, but she also realized more information would not resolve the very different perspectives and values in conflict here. What *would* be the best thing to do, and *why*?

Commentary

Introduction

Summer in the Klamath Basin is a study of contrasts in colors: the light blue waters of Upper Klamath Lake are framed to the west by the green pine forests of the Cascade Range; the green and blue wetlands of the

Tule Lake NWR abut the stark black lava bluffs of Lava Beds National Monument; snow-clad Mt. Shasta sits as a white sentinel to the southwest. The basin floor is a mosaic of different hues of green—a patchwork of alfalfa, potatoes, onions, and wheat, watered by the Klamath Project, one of the most extensive irrigation systems in the West. This was not the case in the summer of 2001, however. That summer, the basin fields lay brown and dusty, reflecting the high desert nature of this arid country; fertile croplands lay empty, their topsoil blowing away in the dry winds.

What happened? Most directly, the combination of a summer of se- vere drought with plunging population levels of three native fish in the Klamath River and Upper Klamath Basin, recently listed under the ESA, caused the BOR to close the headgates of the Klamath irrigation project at Klamath Falls in an effort to keep more water in Upper Klamath Lake and the Klamath River to protect the fish. For the first time in its history, the BOR—for nearly a century the provider of the irrigation water that makes possible the agricultural economy of the basin—was forced to choose between delivering water to farmers for irrigation or keeping it in the lake for species conservation. The action was taken in April 2001, just as irrigation season was to begin. It reduced irrigation deliveries by 90 percent to the roughly 1,400 farmers who depend on the Klamath Project, leaving them unable to plant or farm nearly 210,000 acres that summer.

Earlier that year two other federal agencies responsible for adminis- tering the ESA, the US FWS and the NMFS, had issued ESA-mandated biological opinions. They argued releasing water for irrigation from Up- per Klamath Lake, the main water source for the Klamath Project, would threaten the survival of the Lost River and the shortnose suckerfish and the coho salmon, all protected under the ESA. The BOR felt it had no choice but to close the headgates.

State agencies responded to farmers' pleas by pumping groundwater for irrigation. California's Department of Water Resources drilled ten deep wells in the Tulelake area to irrigate twenty thousand acres, which compensated for some of the lost water but also caused water levels in city wells in nearby Malin, Oregon, to drop forty feet. The federal government also responded with over $170 million in emergency aid to farmers over the next decade.[8] For example, in 2004–5 the BOR spent over $7.6 mil- lion to drill new wells in the basin to augment diminished water supplies for irrigation. A year later the US Geological Survey reported that water tables in the area had dropped up to twenty feet.[9]

In a larger sense, the ongoing water crisis in the Klamath Basin illus- trates the complex interplay of changing social, economic, and ecological conditions in the American West. The BOR came into being in the early twentieth century to help foster permanent settlement of the West by damming and rerouting the region's rivers to support irrigation-based agriculture and society. As legal scholars Holly Doremus and Dan Tarlock observe, rivers in this purely human-centered vision were viewed "as commodities to be allocated among individual users to promote maximum human use, including diverting the entire flow in peak irrigation seasons. The idea of such a 'working river' was that no drop of water should flow to the sea unused."[10] With the rise of the environmental movement has come a different, ecological view of rivers as integral parts of ecosystems and bioregions that provide valuable ecosystem services. Emphasis today is less on developing *working rivers* than on restoring *rivers that work* ecologically. Traditional economies rooted in resource extraction, such as water, mining, and timber, are shifting to be more amenities- and recreation-based, with high value placed on healthy and intact ecosystems that support wildlife and conserve biodiversity. Unfortunately, climate change makes a region already prone to cycles of drought hotter and drier, exacerbating competing claims for scarce water as populations grow and expand into previously rural and agricultural areas.

Water issues in the Klamath Basin are representative of clashes between the needs of farmers, ranchers, city dwellers, and endangered wildlife throughout the West. But where most western watersheds begin in steep, wet mountainous terrain and flow into broader, flatter and dryer basins, the Klamath does the opposite, bringing additional challenges. Its headwaters lie in the broad, arid Upper Klamath Basin where snowmelt historically gathered in a mosaic of shallow lakes and wetlands, creating rich habitat for the annual migrations of millions of birds on the Pacific flyway, and an abundant fishery used by the Klamath and Modoc—members of the larger Snake Paiute Tribe. The flat topography makes it difficult, however, to store water for agriculture. The Lower Klamath plunges through the steep terrain of California's coastal ranges on its way to the Pacific, and historically teemed with coho and chinook salmon, sustaining the local Yurok, Hoopa, and Karuk peoples. Taking water from the Upper Basin for agriculture deprives downstream fisheries of needed flow levels (Figure 1).

The Klamath Project: Providing Water for Agriculture

The Upper Basin wetlands and marshes proved an obstacle to the ranching and agricultural aspirations of white settlers in the late 1800s. Following the 1872–73 Modoc War, the US Army removed the Klamaths and Modocs from their twenty-two-million-acre homeland of what is now central Oregon and northern California, forcing these former enemies to share a reservation. Ranchers began to drain the wetlands to plant them with hay for cattle, and ditch companies formed to develop private irrigation projects to support incipient agriculture. With the passage of the Reclamation Act in 1902, the federal BOR became the lead actor in developing a reclamation economy in the basin, authorizing the Klamath Project in 1905 (Figure 2).

Figure 1. Klamath River watershed

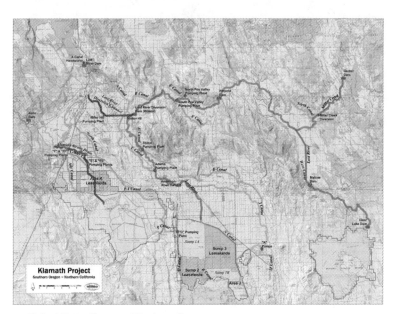

Source: United States Bureau of Reclamation.

Figure 2.The Klamath Project

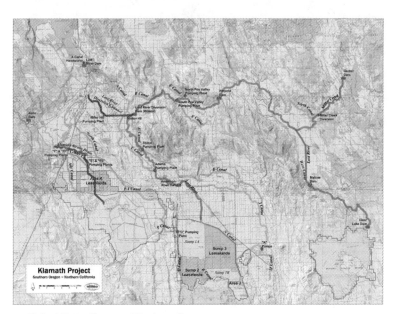

Source: United States Bureau of Reclamation.

Completed in 1960, the Klamath Project draws about 1,345,000 acre-feet of water out of Upper Klamath Lake and the Klamath River to irrigate 240,000 acres in the Upper Klamath Basin. Virtually all of Lower Klamath Lake and nearly 90 percent of Tule Lake were drained and converted to farmland. A series of dams between the California border and Upper Klamath Lake retains some water in reservoirs and provides cheap hydroelectric power to farmers and basin residents. At the same time as the Klamath Project was diverting the basin's waters for agriculture, several national wildlife refuges were established to protect the abundant waterfowl inhabiting the many lakes and wetlands in the basin. The 1964 Kuchel Act mandated that in addition to protecting habitat for waterfowl, agriculture also continue on refuge lands.[11] As Doremus and Tarlock note, "The Klamath Basin refuges were the first to be superimposed on 'a watershed being revamped by the Reclamation Service for irrigation-based agriculture.'" While the Kuchel Act mandates both conservation of waterfowl habitat and continued use of refuge lands for agriculture, when these interests collided, "farming has always had the upper hand" (Figure 3).[12]

Figure 3. Agricultural lease lands in the Lower Klamath and Tule Lake National Wildlife Refuges

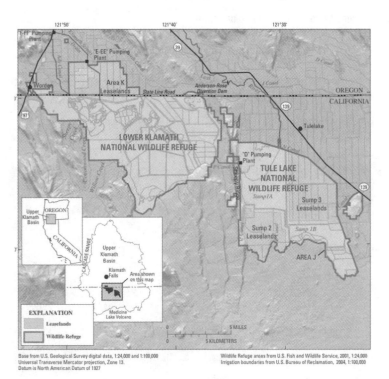

Source: United States Geological Survey.

Agriculture was not the only resource-based industry in the basin. Timber, ranching, and fishing all thrived. The now-threatened Lost River and shortnose suckerfish, once "the most highly prized food fish in the basin,"[13] supported recreational and tribal fishing into the 1980s. The once prevalent old-growth ponderosa pine forests were largely depleted by the 1990s when Weyerhauser closed its Klamath Falls sawmill. Ranching and agriculture persist, dependent on increasingly contested water from the Klamath Project. Each of these activities has had an impact on the ecological health of the watershed and the survivability of endangered fish, but due to the ESA's particular focus on federal actions that impair endangered species, most attention has focused on the BOR's water diversions for agriculture.

In the Tule Lake region of Northern California, the Klamath Project was paired with homesteading. The BOR distributed lands through the 1940s to expand agricultural settlement as well as reward veterans from both world wars. Stan Marshall's grandfather was a veteran of the First World War and received the original Marshall homestead by lottery as reward for his service. Many Tule Lake farmers look with pride at the origins of their farms in military service, and remember the promises the federal government made to their forbears to provide land and water for irrigation in exchange for them creating productive farmland from former lakebeds and wetlands. Many feel a profound sense of betrayal that the federal government has now abrogated or reduced their rights to water for the sake of fish conservation, and popular media has portrayed the struggle as *farmers vs. fish* (Figure 4).

Figure 4. Aerial photo of leased agricultural lands in the Tule Lake National Wildlife Refuge

Photo credit: Brett Cole, courtesy of Oregon Wild. Used with permission.

Indeed, at one level, the crisis reveals a conflict between government duties and responsibilities that reflects the changing legal and social panorama in the nation. Like much of the West, water rights in the Klamath Basin are rooted in the doctrine of prior appropriation, where early settlers who first put the water to *beneficial use*—withdrawing it from its source and using it for human use—could claim a right to that water over any subsequent users. While technically water rights in the West are vested in the federal government, they are adjudicated by the states, and the federal government has largely recognized and respected state-issued rights.[14] For most of the twentieth century, the noncommercial water needs of stakeholders, such as Native Americans and wildlife, were simply ignored in favor of the needs of farmers and ranchers who claimed and felt entitled to water as a perpetual property right dating back to white settlement.

An aggravating factor is that the Klamath Basin is *overallocated*. Claims to water exceed the amount available in most years, leading to contentious disputes and litigation over who has rights to the scarce water. In 2013, the state of Oregon concluded a decades-long process of adjudicating conflicting claims to water rights in the Klamath Basin, but dissatisfied parties pursuing judicial appeals means it may be many more years before these water rights disputes are resolved.[15]

Changing Views of Water in the American West

That status quo began to change, however, with the passage of environmental legislation in the 1970s such as the National Environmental Policy Act, the Clean Water Act, and the ESA. These laws recognized the public interest in a clean and healthy environment and, in the case of the ESA, implied rights for other species to survive, even if this means limiting the exercise of property rights. The ESA in particular can restrict or prohibit actions, including water projects that threaten the survival of species listed as endangered.

The ESA delegates responsibility for its implementation to two federal agencies. The US FWS oversees terrestrial species and freshwater fish, such as the two species of suckerfish in the Upper Klamath Basin. The NMFS oversees marine species and anadromous fish—fish that spend their life cycle in both fresh- and saltwater environments, such as the chinook and coho salmon. The ESA specifies that only scientific criteria be used in determining whether to list a species as endangered; other factors, such as likely economic impacts, are not supposed to be considered.

Once a species is listed, the ESA acts in two ways to protect it. Section 9 of the ESA prohibits the "take" of a listed species, defined as capturing or killing a protected animal as well as altering its habitat in such a way as to cause it injury. Diverting water for irrigation can harm fish both through depletion of water in streams, rivers, and lakes, which can degrade their habitat, as well as *entrainment* where fish are trapped in project facilities such as irrigation ditches or dam turbines. The second ESA requirement applies only to federal actors. "Under Section 7, actions taken, authorized, or funded by federal agencies must not be likely to jeopardize the continued existence of any listed species or modify any formally designated critical habitat."[16]

In practice, it is difficult to apply the Section 9 prohibitions against takings to the protection of aquatic species. It is far easier to detect and sanction the taking of terrestrial animals, such as the illegal collection of desert tortoises or shooting of wolves, than plunging fish numbers due to habitat deterioration stemming from multiple actors and multiple causes—many of them carried out for socially valuable reasons such as agriculture or logging. In the Klamath case it made far more sense to address the Section 7 restrictions on federal actions because the large majority of water diverted for irrigation comes through the federal Klamath Project.

Although the ESA gives agencies legal authority to limit or curtail the use of both state and federal water rights, holders of valid water rights and water delivery contracts often see any limits as unfair and an unwarranted deprivation of their rights. Some have sought relief through appeal to the *takings* clause of the Fifth Amendment to the US Constitution, which requires the government to compensate property owners if it deprives them of their property for public use. Through a series of legal cases, the Supreme Court has established three situations where the government must compensate property owners: (1) when it permanently physically occupies property; (2) if its restrictions or regulations deny all economically viable use of property; or (3) if some are singled out to bear burdens that should be shared by the whole public. Klamath Basin irrigators filed suit under the takings clause in October 2001, seeking compensation of nearly $1 billion for breach of their water rights and federal water delivery contracts due to enforcement of the ESA. In 2005 the US Court of Federal Claims rejected their takings suit, noting that the vast majority of federal water contracts in the basin expressly absolve the federal government for shortages due to drought. Subsequent efforts to gain compensation for their loss of water have also been unsuccessful, though irrigators continue to insist that their senior water rights be recognized and given the protection of full property rights.[17]

The other factor that has challenged the status quo of water distribution in the Klamath River has been the reemergence of the tribes and their demands that water rights embedded in early treaties that predate white settlement be recognized. The Upper Basin Klamath Tribe not only lost most of its lands to white settlers in the nineteenth century, in 1954 Congress went further, passing the Klamath Termination Act that ended its status as a legally recognized tribe. The stated goals of the legislation were to end Indian dependency on the federal government as wards of the state and to help them assimilate into white society,[18] but the results were disastrous. Tribal lands were sold off, the Klamath reservation disestablished, and its valuable timberlands sold either to large timber interests or folded into the federal Fremont-Winema National Forest.[19]

After decades of struggle and recourse to legal guarantees in treaties and Indian law, the Klamath Tribe regained its tribal status in 1986, although not its tribal lands. Now the tribe is reasserting its water rights in the Klamath watershed, based on the 1908 *Winters v. United States* Supreme Court decision that recognized tribal *reserved* water rights as holding priority over all other water rights. In the Lower Klamath Basin, the Yurok and Hoopa Tribes hold federally recognized fishing rights that include water rights necessary to maintain the fisheries. Until recently, these tribal rights have existed more on paper than in actuality, but in 2013 the state of Oregon reaffirmed "time immemorial" tribal water rights in the Upper Klamath Basin.[20] This decision gives the tribes an increasingly powerful voice in the multiple stakeholder discussions of the Klamath crisis.

Collaborative Efforts to Resolve the Klamath Basin Water Crisis

A potential breakthrough in the Klamath water crisis took place in 2010, when representatives of forty-five organizations, including federal and state agencies and most of the stakeholders in the water disputes, signed the KBRA and KHSA. Requiring some compromise from all stakeholders, these agreements are discussed further in the final section of this commentary. It is worth quoting the documents' summaries here to show their intent:

> The Restoration Agreement is intended to result in effective and durable solutions which will: 1) restore and sustain natural fish production and provide for full participation in ocean and river harvest opportunities of fish species throughout the Klamath Basin; 2) establish reliable water and power supplies which sustain agricultural uses, communities, and National Wildlife Refuges; and 3) contribute to the public welfare and the sustainability of all Klamath Basin communities.

> The Hydroelectric Settlement lays out the process for additional studies, environmental review, and a decision by the Secretary of the Interior regarding whether removal of four dams owned by Pacifi-Corp: 1) will advance restoration of the salmonid fisheries of the

Klamath Basin; and 2) is in the public interest, which includes but is not limited to consideration of potential impacts on affected local communities and tribes. . . . The Hydroelectric Settlement includes provisions for the interim operation of the dams and the process to transfer, decommission, and remove the dams.[21]

Implementing the agreements will be costly. Estimates in 2013 for the federal government to implement the Klamath settlements top $920 million over fifteen years, including $250 million of new appropriations. If the four dams are removed under the KHSA, it would be one of the largest and most complex dam removal projects in US history. Bond issues and costs to ratepayers in California and Oregon to pay for it would likely exceed $450 million.[22] The KBWRERA was introduced into the US Senate in May 2014 to provide federal legislation to implement and fund these historic agreements.[23]

Differing Stakeholder Perspectives, Visions, and Values

How do we assess the conflicting visions and values of each of the multiple stakeholders in this dispute? While it is an oversimplification to think each stakeholder group has one set of values and beliefs, we can sketch in broad outline some of the common elements represented in the case to clarify and inform our ethical analysis.

Farmers. In addition to forming the economic base of the Klamath Basin, farmers see themselves representing an important way of life that deserves protection, based on stewardship of the land that has made the basin productive. They strongly value individualism, property rights, hard work, and self-sufficiency, and see themselves living out the Jeffersonian vision of a nation of yeoman farmers who, through local reliance and independence from government interference, take care of their families and provide food for a growing world. In the continuum of perspectives about nature, most of the basin farmers take a utilitarian view of nature. While farming should include good stewardship of the land, nature is there to provide the resources—water, soil, and inputs—that farmers need to grow crops.

Most farmers view water as a renewable resource that should be put to beneficial use in agriculture. When there is a conflict between farmers and other water users, farmers' prior water rights should be respected and their irrigation needs met first. When government limits their water rights, farmers believe they should be compensated for the economic harm, as whenever the government takes physical property for some public good. Some, like Stan Marshall in the case, acknowledge that farmers must share limited water resources with other groups, such as wildlife and Native Americans, and are working proactively to integrate better conservation practices into their farming. Marshall, for example, participates in an innovative *walking wetlands* program that returns leased refuge farmland to temporary wetlands for one to four years for wildlife habitat. Others, such as Jim Stephens, see a conspiracy of actors including environmentalists, Native Americans, federal agencies, and the courts working against rural interests in the basin. They argue that proposals like KBWRERA exemplify a pattern of federal overreach that threatens their rural way of life. They see themselves as the true endangered *species* in this struggle—what Stephens refers to as *rural cleansing*. They fiercely defend individual liberty in the face of what they see as government overreach and overregulation. Many invoke the Bible and the Genesis teachings on dominion together with the Constitution's protection of property and individual rights to argue that they have a sacred constitutional right to the basin's water and their way of life. Many farmers in the Klamath Basin are skeptical of precautionary approaches to science, which they see as *junk science* that favors fish over farmers. Instead they demand hard evidence of environmental harm *before* government actions that curtail their activities can be implemented.

Tribes. The Native American tribes frame current water struggles as the most recent manifestation of a long history of conquest and racism that has deprived them of their historical lands and way of life. Tribes view the issues holistically: the native fishes, plants, waters, and lands all are critical to maintaining an entire way of life that integrates spiritual and material needs. Animals are not simply resources, but rather relatives in a holistic fabric and way of living. While the tribes are focused on the critical economic and social development needs of their impoverished peoples, they link these to their spiritual needs and take a long-term perspective of having inhabited these lands for millennia. Hence, the tribes' views of nature are closer to the position of critical ecology, emphasizing a holistic, ecocentric perspective. We see this in the Klamath Tribal Council's affirmation of KBWRERA both for restoring a healthy ecosystem that can support fish as well as increasing economic opportunities for tribal members. It has learned to work within a western legal framework that emphasizes rights and property in order to advance its interests, even while recognizing that this framework cannot fully accommodate its more holistic worldviews. It is acutely aware of the history of laws and legal opinions that have worked against the tribe and divided its peoples, and so it approaches current legislation with some caution.

Environmentalists. Environmental watchdog organizations in the basin, represented here by Kevin Andrews, take an explicitly ecocentric, bioregional perspective, locating themselves toward the preservationist and critical ecology side of the continuum. Many give priority to the needs of wildlife, viewing all forms of life as having intrinsic value. They lament the loss of critical habitat through the draining of the once extensive lakes and wetlands in the region in favor of agriculture. Some environmentalists argue that the reclamation vision of an irrigation-based farm economy is inappropriate and ecologically unsustainable in arid regions like the Klamath Basin. They are concerned that commitments of already overallocated water to farmers will compromise full implementation of the ESA to protect endangered fish populations. They argue that we need to shift our views of water and wildlife as resources for human consumption to seeing ourselves as interdependent members of the ecosystems where we live.

Many environmentalists favor using the precautionary principle to guide policy. Instead of waiting for conclusive evidence that environmental harms result from a particular set of actions—by then the harms may be irreversible, such as species extinction—policy makers should act on the best available science that indicates likely sources of harm. In fact, the ESA directs that when there are gaps in scientific information, the benefit of the doubt should go to the species. Some environmental groups advocate for ecological restoration, returning *working rivers* like the Klamath to *rivers that work* ecologically. They see the region's rivers as vital to anchor healthy ecosystems that provide critical services, such as clean water, while maintaining the critical biodiversity of the bioregions they traverse. Environmentalists in the Klamath conflict vary in their views as to how much, if any, agriculture the basin can sustain long term and whether refuge lands set aside to protect wildlife habitat should continue to be leased for farming, as KBWRERA allows. Hence, some support KBWRERA as an important collaboration to balance environmental, social, and economic needs, while others oppose it for compromising vital ecological needs. All agree, however, that farming cannot come at the cost of long-term ecological sustainability or exceed the carrying capacity of the region.

Salmon Fishermen. Largely absent from direct participation in the intense conflicts of the Upper Klamath Basin, the voices and interests of the Lower Basin salmon fishermen have been important to recognizing the impacts of actions in the Upper Basin on the fish and fishing interests downstream. The perspectives of the commercial salmon fishermen span the continuum of views of nature in interesting ways. Like farmers, most fishermen view salmon primarily as a renewable resource that supports their livelihoods and a way of living they wish to continue and protect. In that sense, their views align largely with the free market side of the spectrum, and indeed, in early years the largely unregulated salmon industry overfished many salmon runs along the Pacific coast. But in this legal struggle, they have built important alliances with the tribes and environmental groups, recognizing that without a healthy river ecosystem, salmon cannot thrive, and their industry and way of living are imperiled. Therefore many salmon fishermen fit most closely into the conservationist perspective: still largely anthropocentric, they view fish as a resource but stress the need for good science and management policies to protect the ecological well-being of salmon habitat in the Lower Klamath Basin. The fishermen also draw attention to the conflicting economic interests in this case. The economic returns from the Klamath salmon fishery and the losses the fishermen have incurred are both greater than the Klamath Basin agricultural sector, but due to the widespread publicity of the 2001 protests of the cutoff of irrigation waters, most attention has focused on the farmers' plights from restricting water to aid the salmon.

Federal Agencies. The Klamath Basin crisis illustrates the conflicts that can occur between government agencies when the interests of their primary constituencies conflict. Though the BOR, FWS, and NMFS are all federal agencies expected to act in the public interest, how each views that interest is shaped largely by the constituencies they serve. The BOR administers the Klamath Project and sees itself serving the interests of farmers and their irrigation needs, even when these conflict with other public interests, such as species conservation. The wildlife agencies are mandated by the ESA to focus on the needs of wildlife, but even the different needs of fish can lead to conflicts between the agencies. At one point FWS called for more water to be retained in Upper Klamath Lake to protect the suckerfish while NMFS was calling for more water to be released into the Klamath River to serve the needs of downstream salmon. In addition, individuals working within these agencies may not share all of the agencies' values and perspective, but they are obligated to implement them—yet individuals can strongly affect how actions are implemented.

Elected Officials. Whether elected officials with a stake in the Klamath Crisis support or oppose KBWRERA reflects differing national, state, and local interests and perspectives. The Obama administration and the states of California and Oregon support the legislation, seeing in it a potential solution to the protracted resource conflicts in the Klamath Basin. State and federal government representatives seek an end to the high costs that resulted from previous conflicts in the basin, including supplemental aid, crop insurance, mitigation actions, and litigation costs. In contrast, local elected officials in Klamath County in Oregon and Siskiyou County in California are on record opposing KBWRERA. They express concerns that the Klamath agreements will damage the region's resource-based economy, cause economic damages to farmers from water rights retirement and restoration requirements, and result in the loss of the PacifiCorp dams that provide flood protection and economic benefits for downstream areas.[24]

Each of these stakeholder perspectives raises important ethical issues. Perhaps most central are issues of justice, fairness, and equity. Farmers believe they are being treated unfairly, asked to bear the lion's share of the burden of a problem that many sectors helped to create, without fair compensation. Native Americans and salmon fishermen believe they have been treated unfairly for many years now, and are demanding that their rights be recognized and compensated. Environmentalists want to shift ethical consideration away from human impacts because they believe ecosystems have been harmed most—to the point that some species within them are on the brink of extinction. For environmentalists the interests of these species are paramount.

A second set of issues is how best to frame the conflict. Farmers insist on framing the issue anthropocentrically, focusing on individual human rights they believe are protected in the US Constitution. All other matters are secondary. The fishermen also frame the issue anthropocentrically and in terms of rights but broaden the scope to argue for a healthy river ecosystem to maintain needed salmon habitat. Both the tribes and environmentalists argue for an ecocentric, holistic framing, where humans are merely one member of a much larger ecological whole. The tribes frame this largely within their long history on the land, while environmentalists emphasize bioregional parameters. Both argue that humans need to better adapt to the ecological constraints of the Klamath watershed. Differing positions among elected officials raise challenging questions about whose interests are primary in this conflict: local, state, or federal?

Insight from the Norms of Ecological Justice

The five norms of ecological justice further clarify differences. As noted above, the norm of *justice* draws particular attention to fairness and equity, with a special concern for the disadvantaged. Interestingly, each stakeholder sees itself largely as a victim of unfair actions, and as a culture and way of life threatened by government or lack of government actions. How one frames the debate largely shapes how one sees justice applying.

Sustainability and the lack thereof in a region of chronic drought and overcommitted water lies at the heart of this case. Sustainability implies respect for the carrying capacity of a region and adapting human behaviors to it, but what that capacity is in the Klamath is hotly debated. Carrying capacity also raises the question, capacity *for whom*? We can increase the capacity for human population and consumption to a certain point by overriding the interests of other members of the ecosystem, but an ethic of ecological justice refuses to sacrifice the interest of other species or the planet as a whole. Yet extinction of species is a naturally occurring part of evolution. How do we decide the appropriate balance between human and other-than-human interests, particularly when there is little agreement within human communities where our interests lie?

Sufficiency acknowledges that all forms of life are entitled to share in Earth's goods, not only humans. While market mechanisms may be important for distributing scarce resources, they are not enough to assure the well-being of other forms of life. One of the positive outcomes of the Klamath crisis is the generation of initiatives to share resources and to be more efficient in our use of resources such as the walking wetlands program that farmers like Stan Marshall now participate in on refuge lands. Integrating the interests of wildlife and the refuges into the purposes of the Klamath Project is another step in this direction, though it remains to be seen how effective this will be in fostering restraint and frugality to leave more for other species. Others argue that continuing to lease refuge lands for agriculture violates the norm of sufficiency.

One of the most challenging dimensions of the Klamath crisis has been to honor the norm of *participation* when there are so many affected stakeholders, and actions have been triggered at the federal level by the ESA. In that regard, the 2010 agreements are a remarkable achievement, bringing together forty-five stakeholder groups and agencies. Not all chose to participate or sign the agreements, but the large majority did. A key challenge will be to integrate authentic participation in the implementation of the agreements.

Since all stakeholders in this dispute have legitimate concerns that they are not being treated fairly, *solidarity* suggests an empathetic listening to each stakeholder and a genuine effort to address the issues each sees as most central. History, however, suggests that Native Americans and endangered species have been most discriminated against and placed at risk—even of extinction—in the Klamath Basin disputes. A special concern for their well-being in any settlement therefore is particularly warranted.

The Future of the Klamath River Watershed

What is the best future for the Klamath River watershed, and who should decide it? The Klamath crisis is a good example of a "wicked problem" that can only be resolved by first articulating a vision for a desirable future community.[25] Finding a consensus vision for the Klamath has to this point proved elusive, but the 2010 agreements and KBWRERA may be an important start. They envision a future of restored fisheries, sustainable communities, a vibrant agricultural sector resilient in the face of drought and climate change, and ongoing economic and social development for the tribes.

Legal scholars Doremus and Tarlock argue for a bioregional approach to the Klamath. "Bioregionalism begins by defining the appropriate geographic scale of management for nature systems such as river basins. Next, the stresses to the system are identified and ways to relieve those stresses are detailed. The final, and most difficult, step is to devise institutions capable of implementing needed management steps at the appropriate scale."[26] They suggest the following principles to resolve the Klamath and similar conflicts:

1. There must be articulation of a vision of a sustainable landscape that rejects either extreme of the ideal of pristine nature or the nineteenth-century irrigation society.
2. The vision must be based on the region's carrying capacity to balance biodiversity conservation and human use, recognizing that the Klamath is both a unique and valuable ecosystem and a working landscape.
3. The vision must be science based while recognizing the need for sound judgment of scientific data.
4. The process should begin in the Klamath watershed, including both Upper and Lower Basin stakeholders, but be integrated with regional, state, and federal agencies.

Whether the 2010 agreements and KBWRERA can be implemented to meet all these criteria and resolve the decades-old water crisis in the Klamath watershed remains to be seen.[27] Additional challenges loom, including climate change with the potential for longer and drier droughts, and increasing competition for agriculture through global free trade agreements. The ethical questions remain, however: What are the most important issues in this case, and why? How should the case itself be framed? Whose interests should get preference? If you think the Klamath crisis is best resolved by a bioregional approach, how will you justify this to farmers or commercial fishermen who may lose their livelihoods? Do those who champion species preservation have any financial obligations to those whose economic interests are sacrificed for the benefit of these species? To what extent should these financial obligations extend to all US taxpayers since it is federal legislation that pertains? What do you think should be done?

Notes

[1]Oregon State University Extension, Table 1: Annual Precipitation at Klamath Falls, OR, http://extension.oregonstate.edu; Klamath Basin Rangeland Trust, http://www.kbrt.org.

[2]Klamath Restoration Agreements, "Frequently Asked Questions," http://www.klamathrestoration.org.

[3]Pacific Coast Federation of Fishermen's Associations, "The Struggle to Save Salmon in the Klamath Basin," http://www.pcffa.org.

[4]Pacific Coast Federation of Fishermen's Associations, News Release, April 30, 2001, http://www.pcffa.org.

[5]Steve Rothert, "Historic Agreement Reached on Upper Klamath Basin Water," American Rivers: The River Blog, March 6, 2014, http://www.americanrivers.org.

[6]State of Oregon, Press Release: "Historic Agreement Reached on Upper Klamath Basin", March 5, 2014, http://www.oregon.gov.

[7]Klamath Tribes of Oregon, Press Release, "Klamath Tribal Members Vote to Approve Upper Klamath Basin Comprehensive Agreement," April 9, 2014, http://klamathtribes.org/news.

[8]Klamath Basin Settlement Agreements, *Congressional Research Service Report* R42158, September 9, 2014, 3, http://www.crs.gov.

[9]Holly Doremus and Dan Tarlock, *Water War in the Klamath Basin: Macho Law, Combat Biology, and Dirty Politics* (Washington, DC: Island Press, 2008), 164.

[10]Ibid., 57. Much of this commentary is based on their excellent analysis of the Klamath Basin water crisis.

[11]"Such lands shall be administered by the Secretary of the Interior for the major purpose of waterfowl management, but with full consideration to optimum agricultural use that is consistent therewith." Kuchel Act of September 2, 1964, Public Law No. 88–567, 78 Stat. 850.

[12]Doremus and Tarlock, *Water War in the Klamath Basin*, 81.

[13]Ibid., 27.

[14]US Department of Justice, "Federal Reserved Water Rights and State Law Claims," http://www.justice.gov.

[15]Klamath Basin Settlement Agreements, *Congressional Research Service Report* R42158, September 9, 2014, 4, http://www.crs.gov.

[16]Doremus and Tarlock, *Water War in the Klamath Basin*, 92.

[17]For an excellent discussion of the legal issues around takings claims, water rights, and the ESA, see Doremus and Tarlock, *Water War in the Klamath Basin*, 100–103.

[18]"Whereas it is the policy of Congress, as rapidly as possible, to make the Indians within the territorial limits of the United States subject to the same laws and entitled to the same privileges and responsibilities as are applicable to other citizens of the United States, to end their status as wards of the United States, and to grant them all of the rights and prerogatives pertaining to American citizenship." House Concurrent Resolution of the Eighty-third Congress, First Session, 1953, Indians, August 1, 1953 [H. Con. Res. 108], 67 Stat. B122, 108.

[19]For the perspective of the Klamath Tribes on Termination, see http://www.klamathtribes.org/background/termination.

[20]Klamath Basin Settlement Agreements, *Congressional Research Service Report* R42158, September 9, 2014, 5, http://www.crs.gov.

[21]Klamath Basin Coordinating Council, "Summary of the Klamath Basin Settlement Agreements," May 2010, http://www.edsheets.com/Klamathdocs.html.

[22]Klamath Basin Settlement Agreements, *Congressional Research Service Report* R42158, September 9, 2014, 7, http://www.crs.gov.

[23]The KBWRERA of 2014 is covered in two related bills introduced to the 113th Congress, S. 2379 and S. 2727. "The only difference between the two bills is that S. 2727 includes a section at the end of the legislation, Section 10, which would alter the requirements for a mutual ditch or irrigation company to be exempt from certain income taxes under Section 501(c) of the Internal Revenue Code. This potential change was not addressed in the KBRA or KHSA. . . . Both bills would provide new federal authority for actions envisioned under the agreements, in particular elements that many argue were key for obtaining widespread support for the agreements. This includes approximately $250 million for new activities envisioned under the KBRA and the Upper Basin Settlement for various actions in the on-project plan. Some of the most prominent activities include a drought response plan, water rights retirement for certain junior water rights holders, and low-cost power for project and off-project irrigators, among other things. Both bills would also provide congressional authorization for a secretarial determination on dam removal under the KHSA, which is key to the dam removal process moving forward as currently envisioned. Many elements of the KBRA and KHSA could hypothetically go forward under existing authorities, but parties have agreed to support authorization for the full agreements." Klamath Basin Settlement Agreements, *Congressional Research Service Report* R42158, September 9, 2014, 8–9, http://www.crs.gov.

[24]Klamath Basin Settlement Agreements, *Congressional Research Service Report* R42158, September 9, 2014, 15, http://www.crs.gov.

[25]See Horst W. Rittel and Melvin M. Webber, "Dilemmas in a General Theory of Planning," *Policy Sciences* 4 (1973): 155, 160–67, cited in Doremus and Tarlock, *Water War in the Klamath Basin*, 117.

[26]Doremus and Tarlock, *Water War in the Klamath Basin*, 199.

[27]As this book goes to press, KBWRERA has been introduced to Congress but not yet passed. For the full text of the act, see http://www.gpo.gov.

8

Blown Away

Mountaintop Coal Removal Mining and Fossil Fuel Divestment

Acronyms and Abbreviations

CCS	carbon capture and storage
CO_2	carbon dioxide
EPA	˙Environmental Protection Agency (US)
GHG	greenhouse gas
GW	gigawatts
MTR	mountaintop removal

Case

Daniela was convinced by Reverend Malena Rodriquez, her pastor in Charlotte, North Carolina, to attend Goldsboro University, a Methodist school in the middle of soybean fields in a rural area of the state. El Salvadoran by birth, Pastor Malena had moved to Charlotte to start a new Hispanic church for the burgeoning immigrant population in the state. Daniela's parents were from Mexico, but she was born in the United States. She was very involved in the church's youth group and helped run the children's church summer camp for several years. Her deep relationships with immigrant children also led her to community organizing on immigrant rights. From these experiences Daniela had a strong interest in both youth ministry and social justice. Pastor Malena knew Goldsboro had a strong Religion Department and a thriving college ministry program, and thought the school would be a perfect fit for Daniela's vocational goals and keen intellect.

In her second year at Goldsboro, Daniela decided to take a course entitled Christian Environmental Ethics to fulfill the ethics requirement for her major. She grudgingly signed up for the course, thinking that environmental issues were of little concern compared to the social injustice and poverty experienced by so many around the world. At the first session, her professor, Dr. Susan Thompson, announced an opportunity to go on a three-day field trip to West Virginia to learn about mountaintop removal (MTR) coal mining, which was a strongly encouraged part of the course. Subsidized by a grant, the trip was an affordable option for Daniela. While, at first, the idea of sleeping in a tent wasn't so appealing, she decided she could at least give it a try.

Mountaintop Coal Removal Mining Field Trip to West Virginia

A couple of weeks later, Daniela and ten other students crammed into the van for the three-hour drive to West Virginia. Dr. Thompson gave them a rundown of their schedule for the three days. They would arrive on Thursday afternoon and, after setting up their tents, help the staff of Coal River Mountain Watch, an environmental organization addressing the problems of MTR. That afternoon, they would prepare food for the Friday arrival of sixty to seventy students from different universities coming for workshops on environmental activism. Then on Friday they would work on a service project, painting the home of an elderly woman who was trying to raise three grandchildren on her own. Dr. Thompson told her students that while they would not be attending the environmental activism workshops with the other students, they would get a chance to get to know them on Friday and Saturday evenings and learn what they were doing on their campuses to address the issue of MTR and coal as an energy source. Instead of the workshops, Dr. Thompson had arranged with Reverend Robin Bleckmann, a Presbyterian minister who worked with environmental organizations in the area, for them to participate in a walking prayer vigil to be held at Kayford Mountain on Saturday.

The whole weekend was eye-opening for Daniela. While she had done plenty of service with Hispanic immigrant families in urban Charlotte, she had not experienced rural poverty in white communities. The house they painted was in a beautiful mountain setting surrounded by colorful fall foliage, yet it was in a complete state of disrepair. The grandmother, looking much older than her forty-something years, was caring for her three grandchildren ranging in age from three to ten by relying on monthly welfare checks and food stamps. Her daughter was in jail on drug charges, and it wasn't clear where the father was. On the way back to the campsite after a long day of house painting, Daniela and her fellow classmates stopped at the local school—Marsh Fork Elementary—that two of the grandchildren attended. They wanted to see for themselves what they had heard, that the school sat 400 yards from a massive toxic waste storage facility (or *sludge dam*), 150 feet from a coal silo next to the railroad tracks, and was surrounded by a 1,849-acre surface strip mining operation.[1] Daniela was appalled when she brushed her hand on the front of the school door and noticed it was covered completely in coal dust.

Before the trip, Dr. Thompson had presented a lecture about MTR coal mining. First, land is deforested, with the trees often not even sold commercially, but burned or dumped into valleys nearby. Second, explosives are set off to get down to the seams of coal that can sometimes be five hundred to eight hundred feet below the surface. Third, a twenty-two-story-high excavator called a dragline removes the coal and debris, dumping the leftover waste in nearby valleys, burying streams. Fourth, the coal is processed before being loaded on trains. The remaining sludge, containing toxic chemicals, is stored in nearby valleys behind huge earthen dams. These toxic *lakes* are called open coal impoundments and can contain more than a billion gallons of sludge. Last of all, companies reclaim the removal sites because they are required to do so by federal law. Reclamation entails the spread of grass seed, fertilizer, and mulch to cover the immediate aesthetic damage to the site but does nothing to address the deeper environmental and humanitarian injuries. There is no recompense to the families whose drinking water is polluted and whose homes are threatened by mudslides and, of course, no replacement or restoration of the lost mountain, trees, and filled-in streams (Figure 1).[2]

Figure 1. Mountaintop coal removal mining operation, Kayford Mountain, West Virginia

Photo credit: Laura Stivers.

While MTR started in the 1960s, the method was widely adopted in the 1990s because it is more efficient, profitable, and safer than underground coal mining. The MTR method reduces the number of workers as underground miners are no longer needed, and many workers are replaced by machinery. Furthermore, many of the environmental costs are externalized to the surrounding environment and communities. If coal companies were forced to pay the full costs of the polluting side effects of MTR, profitability would be greatly reduced. In the last three decades, total coal output remained steady in West Virginia and Kentucky, yet 38,000 coal mining jobs were lost.[3] While coal fuels about 40 percent of US electricity generation, MTR only accounted for 4.5 percent of US coal production in 2009. In West Virginia, however, 95 percent of the coal was mined that year through MTR.[4]

On Saturday evening, Daniela and her fellow classmates joined the student activists around a huge bonfire. Not being actively involved in the environmental movement, she and the students from her university felt a little out of place. Clearly the other students knew each other from other environmental events they had attended before. Daniela noticed that nearly all the students were white. She put aside her shyness, however, and listened to what they had to say about environmental activism on their campuses, especially the fossil fuel divestment campaigns many of them were involved with. Students from one campus had already been successful at getting their university administration to invest the school's endowment fund in companies not related to fossil fuel extraction and development, while others were in various stages of conversation with their administrations and boards of directors. Daniela didn't stay up for the late-night discussions, knowing she needed to get up early for the harrowing drive up Kayford Mountain to help set up the walking prayer vigil.

Arriving at the mountain ahead of the other college students, Dr. Thompson's students got to hear the history of famed Larry Gibson, self-dubbed Keeper of the Mountains, who had fought until his death to stop MTR and save Kayford Mountain.[5] Larry's family had lived on or near Kayford Mountain since the late 1700s and he had more than three hundred relatives buried in the cemetery on the mountain that now stands as an inaccessible island surrounded by blasted areas.[6] The Gibson family used to look up to the mountain peak, but the destruction of the mountain since 1986 left Larry's home at the highest point of land around. Each house in the Kayford Mountain community has a family name posted on it, yet the inhabitants all moved off the mountain because of the deafening noise from constant blasting and the polluted air filled with coal dust. Larry was the only one who stayed on the mountain as a protest to the destruction. Daniela wondered why she didn't hear any noise that morning until Robin told her that the coal company had gotten wind of the number of people coming for the prayer vigil and had cut production for the day to avoid bad press.

The prayer vigil began with a welcome by staff of Coal River Mountain Watch and a short music performance. Then Dr. Thompson's students shared what they were going to do in their own personal lives to consume less energy. They encouraged the other vigil participants—local community members, environmental activists, and out-of-town church members concerned about MTR—to write on a piece of paper what they were willing to change and put it in a basket they passed around. Daniela shared her decision to shorten her long hot showers since the energy on campus used to heat the water at Goldsboro University relied, in part, on coal. With stops along the way to hear different stories, the participants began the vigil. At one stop, Daniela was horrified to see the brown water in a bottle that came from one resident's tap. Another resident, who had a shirt that said "Save the Endangered Hillbilly," shared her troubles with asthma from breathing coal dust. At another stop, Daniela found out how being an environmentalist can be dangerous when she listened to Shari, a resident turned activist, recount her experience of getting death threats and having to pay former miners to guard her house. Shari became involved in fighting MTR when a sludge dam was installed above her home and the homes of her neighbors. Not willing to wait for a wall of sludge to storm into her hollow, Shari started organizing community meetings to address the problems. She told of one meeting where Massey Energy filled the meeting hall with their workers, leaving no room for residents of the community to get in the meeting hall.

After hearing these stories, the real sobering part of the vigil took place when the students arrived at the precipice where the mountain had been blown away. There were no trees for miles and on one cut-away mountain wall the students could see the veins of coal that would be mined. Daniela could see how the coal was much easier to access this way than through traditional tunnel mining and how it required fewer workers. Also visible were the tall dragline and huge dump trucks with wheels the size of large cars that hauled all the unusable blasted mountain dirt and rock to the adjacent valley. The view was utterly devastating; the only greenery in view was the island of land left where the cemetery stood and yet was completely inaccessible to community residents.

Fossil Fuel Divestment Conversation

Back in class after the trip, some of the students proposed creating a campus environmental club to launch a campaign to get Goldsboro University to divest its endowment from fossil fuel companies. Dr. Thompson thought this sounded like a great idea but reminded them that divestment is only one way to address the issue of MTR coal mining. "Perhaps your newly formed environmental club might start by having an educational session for the campus community. First you might host a slideshow to share your experiences and images from the trip. Then you could sponsor a panel, inviting some people to present possible strategies for addressing environmental problems associated with using coal as an energy source."

Jonathan, who had spent a lot of time talking to the students from other universities the past weekend said, "I can e-mail one of the students from Swarthmore College to be on the panel. Its student group has had quite a battle with its administration, which has refused to divest on the basis that divestment would drastically hurt the financial return on its endowment."

Daniela added, "It would be great to have Reverend Bleckmann come speak about her firsthand experience living near MTR and her organizing efforts to change public policy. She gave me her phone number, so I can call her."

Dr. Thompson thought both of these panelists would be good and added, "Dr. Jim Shorne here at Goldsboro teaches Environmental Science and has written a book on energy policy. He would also have some important insights. Plus, what about having one of Goldsboro's top administrators share the financial implications of divestment?"

Environmental Science major Valerie said, "Dr. Shorne is my advisor. I'll see if he can be on the panel."

Dr. Thompson nodded and said, "I'm willing to ask our vice president of finance to present and to find a room if you all can promote the event."

The panel discussion took place on campus a month later. After the panelists were seated, Aaron, the founder of Swarthmore's Mountain Justice environmental student organization, presented first. Daniela was most impressed with his passion and idealism. She hadn't realized that he and the Swarthmore students were part of a handful of college groups that started the divestment movement, sponsoring the first student-led Fossil Fuel Divestment Convergence in 2013 with more than seventy-five schools attending. When the Mountain Justice group started, there were only twenty to thirty campaigns on college campuses,[7] and now there were several hundred divestment campaigns in universities and church denominations. Environmental activist Bill McKibben was instrumental in promoting fossil fuel divestment campaigns with his organization 350.org and national speaking tour in 2012.[8] The biggest success thus far came when Stanford University, with an $18.7 billion endowment, voted to divest from publicly traded companies whose primary business is mining coal.[9]

One of Aaron's comments made Daniela think of her own university. He said, "It is hypocritical that a college like Swarthmore, which honors its Quaker roots and prides itself on social justice, insists that the financial return on its investment endowment, which is substantial, matters more than the future health of our planet." While Daniela knew the endowment of Goldsboro was much smaller, she agreed that her university similarly should be investing in ways that reflect its mission of service and justice. As Aaron pointed out, in the 1980s divestment was a powerful tool to get the South African government to end apartheid. The next presenters gave Daniela other options to consider, however.

Vice President of Finance Michele Hargood said she believed Goldsboro should be true to its mission but that the situation wasn't as simple as the divestment proponents suggest. "While we want to respect socially responsible investing, how do we determine what to invest in? There are many worthy causes, but can we champion them all? Furthermore, another part of our university mission is to educate first-generation college students by offering scholarships so their education is affordable. Our ability to do this requires the best return on our investment." Daniela, who received one of those scholarships, was glad that they were part of the university's mission. Vice President Hargood ended her presentation by saying that she would at least commit to researching what fossil fuel divestment would mean for Goldsboro financially.

Professor Shorne, who teaches courses on energy policy at Goldsboro, made Daniela think seriously about whether divestment was the best strategy. He said, "It is not clear to me how fossil fuel divestment will produce changes in US energy or climate policy. The form of divestment proposed by 350.org and GreenFaith.org, as near as I can tell, does not engage in shareholder activism and instead seeks simply to wash one's hands of fossil fuel stocks. I don't see how selling one's stock to another party (in China, perhaps) leads to any change in US dependency on fossil fuels or any decline in greenhouse gases [GHGs]." He went on to say, "While I don't want to defend large corporations per se, a few of the big fossil fuel companies are some of the biggest investors in alternative and renewable fuels. For example, Exxon Mobil is the largest investor in algae-based biofuel research.[10] When one divests, one has lost any voice as a shareholder to urge the corporation to make different business decisions." Daniela wondered whether Goldsboro University engaged in any form of shareholder activism. Dr. Shorne concluded his comments by saying, "Finally, I find it hard to divest from companies that are delivering the energy I use on a daily basis to visit my family, travel to conferences, or heat the office at Goldsboro University. While I certainly agree that we need to abandon fossil fuels, I am more complicit in fossil fuel dependency than I was in propping up apartheid in South Africa."

Reverend Bleckmann brought the conversation back to the reality of environmental and social injustice. She shared her own family's history with coal mining. Both of her grandparents worked in the mines, and her family had always been a strong proponent of coal mining until the advent of MTR. The decrease in jobs and the pollution of their communities changed their perspective. Reverend Bleckmann pointed out that the issue is not just about the devastating environmental and social destruction in West Virginia, but also about the looming fact of global warming. "While I'm working on a local level in my own state to stop MTR, we need to be thinking about national and global public policy as well. We've got to regulate GHGs more strictly and, as much as I hate to say it, charge more for fossil fuels so that people are forced to conserve."

While Daniela agreed that stiffer environmental regulations are important, she couldn't help but worry that raising the price of fossil fuels would hurt the poor immigrant families she worked with and the families like the one she met in West Virginia. She felt better when Reverend Bleckmann said, "Poverty alleviation must go hand-in-hand with environmental justice efforts. It is no coincidence that my state, one of the poorest in the nation, is the home to such destructive coal mining that hurts the Earth and human communities. Poor communities, especially communities of color, bear the brunt of environmental pollution and destruction."

Daniela wanted to be a member of the new environmental club on campus, but she wasn't yet clear in her own mind which aspects of energy policy and sustainability were most important. Should divestment from fossil fuels or at least from companies who do coal mining be the primary focus? Should changes to local, state, national, and/or international energy policy instead be central? Perhaps the starting place should simply be for students at her university to live more sustainably. Every weekend Daniela saw tons of beer bottles and soda cans in the garbage, lights were always being left on in the classrooms and dorms, and students routinely took twenty-minute hot showers. Before the environmental class and field trip, Daniela hadn't given a thought to her own unsustainable practices.

Daniela was also concerned that the environmental club would be composed primarily of middle-class white students who might not be ready to address the racial and class aspects of environmental issues. She'd prefer to recruit a more diverse membership, but would her friends of color be interested? The environmental club was meeting the following week to debrief the panel presentations and plan next steps. Daniela wanted to be prepared to share what she thought were the primary issues to be addressed. Clearly coal as an energy source is unsustainable and environmentally destructive, but she wondered how college students could most effectively address energy issues and climate change.

Commentary

The substitution of coal for wood was foundational to the success of the Industrial Revolution. Steamships and railroads, the chief forms of transportation, used coal to fuel their boilers; factories burned coal to heat their furnaces; and, by the 1880s, most homes and factories relied on coal for electricity. Thus, at the start of the twentieth century, coal was the main energy source in the United States. Today 39 percent of US electricity still comes from coal,[11] and 40 percent of the world's energy demand is met by coal.[12] As a result of cheaper natural gas, and pending carbon pollution regulations, the demand for coal has recently lessened in the United States, but coal consumption has surged in several countries and globally. China's use of coal rose from 1.5 billion tons in 2000 to 3.8 billion in 2011, with world coal consumption increasing during that time period by 54 percent.[13] China relies on coal for 80 percent of its electricity.[14] While China now has the highest carbon dioxide (CO_2) emissions, the United States continues to be much higher in emissions per capita.[15] Currently coal is behind oil in terms of global energy demand, but the International Energy Agency predicts that by 2017, coal could be the top source of energy in the world.[16] Others argue that if governments pass policies to curb their CO_2 emissions, global coal production and consumption will decrease.[17]

While coal is one of the cheapest sources of energy to produce, it is also one of the dirtiest and thus most expensive in the long run, when social and environmental costs are factored in. From destruction of mountains and pollution of streams in West Virginia, to mining deaths and smog-filled cities in China, the mining and burning of coal are destroying local environments and human health. Most critical is the effect on climate change. Globally, eight million tons of coal are burned each year, making coal the largest contributor to the 45.5 billion metric tons of CO_2 emitted in 2012.[18] In 2013, the Intergovernmental Panel on Climate Change reported that we have already emitted more than half our carbon budget, if we want to limit global warming to 2° Celsius over preindustrial levels, and we will use the rest in the next thirty years, if we continue at current fossil fuel consumption rates.[19]

More than one-third of the coal produced in the United States comes from the Appalachian area, with West Virginia the largest coal-producing state in the region.[20] While coal mining is a large part of the economy in the southeastern region of the United States, 40 percent of the nation's coal actually comes from the Powder River Basin in Wyoming (with 20 percent of the coal coming from two mines).[21] Increasingly this coal is being exported, and citizens in the Pacific Northwest are dealing with open coal trains traveling through their towns to ports along the coast. Coal that isn't exported is purchased by coal-fired power plants in the United States. Due to low natural gas prices and more stringent Environmental Protection Agency (EPA) emission standards, however, a number of plants are being retired. In 2012 there were 1,308 coal-fired generating units in the United States with a total of 310 gigawatts (GW) of capacity. The US Energy Information Administration projects that by 2020, 60 GW of capacity will be retired.[22]

Environmental Destruction

Mountaintop Removal Mining

MTR has been practiced since the 1960s, but not on a large scale until the 1990s. MTR was considered safer for miners and cheaper for coal companies, and was therefore increasingly used to replace underground mining in the Appalachian Mountain regions of Kentucky, West Virginia, Virginia, and Tennessee. A look at the history of coal companies in the area highlights how MTR became possible. Beginning in the late 1800s coal companies bought up subsurface mineral rights through *broad form deeds*. In effect, many Appalachian landowners sold the rights to extract the subsurface coal to mining companies, while retaining the right to live and farm on their land. These deeds were signed when underground mining, not surface mining was practiced; hence, landowners never expected their homesteads would be turned into strip mines. Many of the deeds absolved the mineral rights holder from any liability for damage to the land, even surface damage, leaving landowners powerless to fight the damages wrought by MTR.[23]

The process of MTR destroys whole ecosystems. After clearing trees and other vegetation, explosives are used to remove rock and reach coal seams. Coal and debris are removed with huge machines called draglines, and the unwanted debris or *overburden* is dumped into adjacent valleys. The coal is then washed and treated before being shipped to power plants. The processing of the coal creates a sludge that contains toxic chemicals, and this mixture is kept in open impoundments or *slurry ponds*. Federal law requires that mining areas be reclaimed—but not restored—so merely planting grass seed has been deemed sufficient.

In addition to the destruction of whole mountains and the loss of habitat for numerous animal species, there are many other negative impacts from MTR. When debris is dumped into valleys, streams are destroyed, and water is polluted. From 1985 to 2001 alone, federal and state agencies approved 6,700 valley fills in central Appalachia. Coal slurry has also leached into groundwater supplies, causing many residents to have toxic drinking water, as illustrated by the brown water one resident showed the students on the vigil. In addition, the coal dust–polluted air and the ongoing noise of the blasting forced the majority of Kayford Mountain's residents to move to different locations.

Deforested mountains cause flash flooding. For example, Mingo County, near the southern West Virginia coalfields, had nineteen floods in eleven years.[24] If impoundments fail, entire communities can be wiped out, which is exactly what got Shari involved in organizing to stop MTR. In 2000, more than three hundred million gallons of toxic sludge spilled into the Big Sandy River in Kentucky (thirty times larger than the 1989 Exxon Valdez spill in Alaska), killing all aquatic life for seventy miles downriver.[25] Marsh Fork Elementary School, which the Goldsboro students visited, is located four hundred yards downslope from a massive impoundment that holds 2.8 billion gallons of toxic coal sludge.[26] Appalachian communities near MTR sites are some of the unhealthiest in the United States.[27] Poverty, increased cancer rates, and a higher number of birth defects all correlate with a form of mining that destroys both the environment and human communities. Yet while most residents are struggling to pay rent, the CEOs of coal companies make out like bandits, getting paid over $10 million per year.[28]

Burning of Coal

The emissions from burning coal cause air, soil, and water pollution. Coal particulates coated with heavy metals are toxic to wildlife and human life. An American Lung Association study found that over 386,000 tons of 84 separate hazardous air pollutants are emitted from over 400 plants in 46 states.[29] In particular, over 40 percent of US mercury emissions and 76 percent of acid gas emissions come from coal-fired plants.[30] These toxins contaminate soil and water, affecting plants, animals, and other microorganisms. Acid rain is also created, changing the acidity of lakes and streams and damaging trees and crops.

After coal is burned, an ash remains that contains heavy metals like arsenic, cadmium, and mercury. Coal plants in the United States create nearly 140 million tons of coal ash each year, constituting the second-largest industrial waste stream after mining.[31] For decades there were no federal regulations and minimal state regulations on where and how coal ash could be dumped, despite the over two thousand coal ash disposal sites across the country.[32] Coal ash is commonly disposed of in landfills, surface impoundment ponds, and sometimes in abandoned mines. A 2011 study done by Earth Justice and Appalachian Mountain Advocates found:

> of nearly 700 coal ash dams in the 37 states examined, only three states require composite liners for all new coal ash ponds; only five states require composite liners for all new coal ash landfills; only two states require groundwater monitoring of all coal ash ponds; only four states require groundwater monitoring of all coal ash landfills; only six states prohibit siting of coal ash ponds into the water table; and only seventeen states require regulatory inspections of the structural integrity of coal ash ponds.[33]

There have been numerous breaks in coal ash ponds,[34] but even more insidious are the pollutants that seep from improperly lined dumps, exposing people and wildlife to toxins. The states with the most lax regulation are those where the dumps are likely to impact low-income communities and communities of color (overwhelmingly southern states).[35] Due to lobbying efforts of coal companies, coal ash was officially designated by the EPA as "nonhazardous" in May 2000, giving states the leeway to do with it what they want.[36] A subsequent 2010 EPA study proved that there are extremely high cancer risks from coal ash.[37] As part of a settlement from a lawsuit filed by environmental groups, the EPA began to regulate the disposal of coal ash in 2015.[38]

At the global level, far and away the most dangerous problem with the burning of coal, however, is the effect of GHG emissions on climate change. The coal industry has consistently pressured politicians to deny global warming and accused anyone who critiques coal's contribution to global warming as being part of a *war on coal*. In 2014, the EPA proposed a Clean Power Plan that aims by 2030 to cut carbon pollution from the power sector by 30 percent from 2005 levels.[39] One way for the coal industry to minimize GHG emissions is to replace older coal-firing plants with more efficient plants. Another is carbon capture and storage (CCS) where the CO_2 emitted is captured and injected and stored in deep geological formations. Still another is to recover the methane released during mining.[40] While the technology exists for CCS, gathering and storing the two to three billion tons of carbon each year from hundreds of coal power plants would require an enormous infrastructure of pipelines, compressors, and pumps. The cost would likely make coal less competitive with other energy sources. Furthermore, at least 30 percent of the energy produced from burning coal would be needed to capture and bury the CO_2.[41] As of 2014, there are only twelve active commercial-scale CCS projects around the world (eight of them in the United States).[42] The Goldsboro students would be right to be skeptical about the prospects of *clean coal*.

Preservation of Biodiversity

The Appalachian Mountains are among the oldest mountains on Earth, with rocks at their core formed over one billion years ago. The region is also known for its great beauty and biological diversity. The southern and central Appalachian Mountains are one of the most biologically diverse regions in the temperate world. Animal species include 255 birds, 78 mammals, 58 reptiles, and 76 amphibians. Of fifty-five salamander species, twenty-one are not found anywhere else. In addition there are over 6,374 plant species, 1,722 of which are exotic, and 76 native endemics. And the southern Appalachians are a hotspot for aquatic species. Tennessee alone has 290 fish species (more than all of Europe).[43]

According to the EPA, over 470 of Appalachia's largest mountains have been destroyed, with the overburden filling whole valleys. As much as two thousand miles of Appalachian streams were buried between 1992 and 2010.[44] Destruction of trees, plant species, and topsoil decreases plant and animal diversity. Burying of headwater streams destroys aquatic organisms as well as the nutrient cycling and production of organic matter for downstream food webs.[45] Companies are only required to reclaim mining sites. Environmentalists believe "land reclamation"—making mining sites accessible for development uses—is inadequate. They believe "land restoration"—ecological restoration of sites to their natural landscape and habitat—should be the norm. The latter, however, is impossible since mining companies cannot replace the lost mountains, nor remove the valley fill. Even reclaimed soils at the sites have lower organic content as well as low water-infiltration rates and nutrient content.[46] The ecosystems of the Appalachian region formed over millions of years yet were destroyed in a couple of decades. Coal advocates argue that nature regenerates, but these areas will not do so within a human time frame and may never regenerate the original ecosystems that are now destroyed.

Globally we are experiencing the greatest rate of species extinction since the loss of the dinosaurs sixty-five million years ago. Natural rates of species extinction are about one to five species per year, whereas we are losing one thousand to ten thousand times that currently.[47] Clearly, wholesale destruction of ecosystems contributes to "biological meltdown."[48] Global warming from burning coal and other fossil fuels has drastic effects on both plant and animal species. Rising temperatures change vegetation patterns and cause animal species to migrate to cooler areas. If temperatures continue to rise at the current rate, experts predict that one-fourth of Earth's species will be headed for extinction by 2050.[49] Distressed ecosystems can rapidly deteriorate—as species go extinct, there is a ripple effect to all other species—much like strings of a web being severed.

The Appalachian area was central to the conservation movement that started at the turn of the twentieth century. By 1890, deforestation was large scale, facilitated by sawmills and railroads. Gifford Pinchot began the modern forestry movement and, through the creation of the US Forest Service in 1905, worked to regulate more sustainable use of environmental resources. While Pinchot supported sustainable use, he certainly could not have foreseen the wholesale destruction of mountaintops and massive species extinction. Clearly more than a conservation ethic is required today. Aldo Leopold's holistic ecocentric perspective is more apt to promote biodiversity. His land ethic—"A thing is right when it tends to preserve the integrity, stability, and beauty of the biotic community"—can guide our assessment of MTR.[50]

In the 1990s, a number of environmentalists created the Wildlands Project to stem the tide of species extinction and promote ecological integrity. They adopted four fundamental goals:

1. Represent, in a system of protected areas, all native ecosystem types and real stages across their natural range of variation.
2. Maintain viable populations of all native species in natural patterns of abundance and distribution.
3. Maintain ecological and evolutionary processes such as disturbances regime, hydrological processes, nutrient cycles, and biotic interactions, including predation.
4. Design and manage the system to be responsive to short-term and long-term environmental change and to maintain the evolutionary potential of lineages.[51]

These principles, while primarily applied to larger landscapes in the West, can also be useful in assessing MTR. Proponents of ecocentrism have advocated for extensive wilderness corridors and the reintroduction of large predators in the West, as both play a critical role in ecosystem health. In West Virginia, the destruction of mountains, streams, and vegetation for coal clearly does not support the integrity, stability, and beauty of the biotic community but causes species extinction and loss of whole ecosystems instead. An emphasis on ecosystem integrity and health, following these four principles, would be a radical shift from both the free market emphasis on more efficient and profitable coal mining as well as the conservation focus on sustainable human use of resources. An ecocentric approach, with priority on protection of species and ecosystems, would advocate elimination of MTR mining and the burning of coal, despite growing human energy needs.

Adherence to the Clean Water Act of 1972, passed to protect all waters of the United States, is one way to promote the integrity and stability of Appalachian ecosystems. Section 404 of the act requires that mining companies get a permit from the Army Corps of Engineers, but until the creation of more stringent requirements in 2009, permits were easily accessible. Environmental groups have filed lawsuits since 2003, trying to stop the issuing of permits based on violation of the Clean Water Act. The EPA can also veto permits issued by the corps, but did not do so until recently. In 2011, the EPA vetoed a permit given to the Spruce No. 1 Mine in West Virginia, on the basis that the mining waste dump of over two thousand acres of land would have buried more than six miles of pristine mountain streams that sustain local communities and wildlife. In 2014 the Supreme Court defended the EPA decision, signaling a shift in tide in favor of ecological protection, albeit a bit late for already devastated areas.[52]

Poverty, Environmental Destruction, and Justice

"As goes coal so goes West Virginia," argues the senior vice president of the West Virginia Coal Association. Coal has been one of West Virginia's leading industries and historically provided many jobs, albeit dangerous and low paying. Residents with a family background in mining often still support the coal industry. Yet jobs are no longer readily available due to the move from underground to MTR mining. In a state reeling from poverty, however, it is understandable that many residents are wary of any more jobs being lost. Less than 20 percent of West Virginia's residents have a college degree, and almost 20 percent of families live below the poverty line.[53] The state also has the highest rates of obesity, smoking, and prescription drug abuse.[54] Despite the natural beauty of the state, there is deep suffering connected to coal mining. One study found that "in the 14 counties where the biggest coal mining operations are located residents reported higher rates of cardiopulmonary disease, chronic obstructive pulmonary disease, hypertension, diabetes, and lung and kidney disease."[55]

Despite these alarming statistics, state officials generally support the coal industry and resist federal oversight of mining operations. In January 2014, just hours before a coal-washing plant leaked nearly thirty thousand liters of toxic chemicals into the Elk River, West Virginia Governor Earl Ray Tomblin said in his annual State of the State address that he "will never back down from the EPA because of its misguided policies on coal."[56] Proponents of coal see regulation from the EPA or environmental organizing against MTR mining as a "War on Coal."[57]

The environmental justice movement that started in the 1980s has worked tirelessly to address the disproportionate dumping of toxic waste on poor communities and communities of color. The movement widened the concept of environmentalism in the United States from a focus primarily on wilderness preservation and conservation to encompass all environments where people live, work, and play. Furthermore, it encouraged more diverse leadership in the environmental movement, an issue Daniela is concerned about. While environmental racism is not at issue for the 94 percent white population of West Virginia, classism clearly plays a role. Poverty, low education, health issues, and the fear of being unemployed deter many residents from confronting the power of coal companies. Furthermore, many elected state and local politicians receive campaign contributions from the coal industry, ensuring a larger voice for corporations over residents and environmentalists critical of MTR. Those who do resist, like Shari, often get harassed or even receive death threats. Despite these obstacles, many environmental organizations, like Coal River Mountain Watch, have been organizing to stop MTR.[58]

Environmental justice advocate Robert Bullard offers five principles of environmental justice to guide environmental decision making: (1) right to protection from environmental degradation, (2) prevention of harm, (3) shifting the burden of proof, (4) obviating proof of intent, and (5) redressing inequities. Bullard notes that while the harm and destruction of the poor and communities of color might not always be a result of intentional racism or classism, the actual outcome is what counts. Most important to the environmental justice movement is prevention of harm before it occurs. The burden of proof for harm should be on the companies. They ought to be required to show *before* mining is allowed that their operations will not decimate the environment, be harmful to human health, or disproportionately affect the poor and communities of color.[59] There are already laws, like the Clean Water Act, that, if properly enforced, would shift the burden of proof to coal companies. Even if West Virginia residents support coal mining for the jobs, they certainly do not want to live in poverty, have polluted water and air, or be subject to flash flooding.

The ethic of ecological justice outlined in Chapter 3 includes the norm of solidarity, that is, for the powerful to share the plight of the powerless and recognize our interdependence with one another and nature. The principle of commensurate burdens and benefits holds that those who derive the benefits (the middle and upper class who consume the most energy and goods) should sustain the commensurate burdens (toxic waste and pollution).[60] Since the mountains where coal resides cannot be moved, and the residents who suffer the burdens are rooted in their beautiful Appalachian surroundings, the question is how to shift the commensurate burdens. Switching to a different type of mining and employing new technologies like carbon capture and storage might lessen environmental damage. Such changes would also make coal more expensive, thereby shifting the burden to the consumer. Yet, rising costs could also make coal less competitive as an energy source. West Virginians do not want to lose avenues for economic development, but they also cannot rely indefinitely on jobs based on a nonrenewable and unsustainable energy source, nor can they flourish in environmentally devastated areas. Solidarity with the residents and nature requires attention to both social and environmental justice.

Sustainability and Sufficiency

Clearly mountaintop mining and the burning of coal are unsustainable, especially in relation to global warming. Coal is also nonrenewable—at least on any meaningful time frame. Some researchers believe that we have hit global "peak coal" production: when maximum coal production is reached, after which there will be a decline.[61] Others believe we are still decades away. Coal supplies will not run out, but the remaining deposits are often buried too deep and not economically feasible to mine.

Despite the availability of coal, continuing on a path of endless economic growth is not feasible. There simply are not enough resources on Earth to support the high-tech modern lifestyle of residents in developed countries and extending this lifestyle to developing nations, nor can we survive global warming in the long term. Currently coal is popular because it is cheap and subsidized. More sustainable energy sources have not been promoted on a large scale in part due to their expense. If the destruction of the environment and societal health costs were figured into the *full cost* of mining and burning of coal and not treated as externalities, the price of coal would soar, thus making more sustainable alternative energy options attractive. Opponents of coal, however, are skeptical that coal can ever be sufficiently clean, and they realize the difficulty of overcoming the political hurdles to put full-cost pricing into practice. Therefore, they advocate other strategies.

One strategy is for individuals to live more sustainably, especially those of us who overconsume. Without public policy changes that promote radical social change, however, this strategy, while noble and important, is limited. For example, in the United States, people would be more likely to live sustainably if there were policies that limit energy use, promote public transportation, regulate the fuel economy of cars, and require green architecture and energy-efficient appliances, among other changes. Public policies and infrastructure can do a lot to shape our understanding of needs. For example, if gas prices were high, bike lanes were plentiful, and public transportation inexpensive and efficient, many families might see they don't need more than one car (if any). A large-scale paradigm shift toward sustainability requires infrastructure for people to live more sustainably and a change of cultural expectations from overconsumption to sufficiency.

Public policies directly related to the mining and burning of coal can also be promoted. For example, organizers in the Sierra Club's "Beyond Coal" campaign are advocating for stricter environmental regulation and the end of MTR mining, and are lobbying for the retirement of old coal plants and the prevention of new plants opening.[62] Environmental groups have had some success as illustrated by a 2014 federal court ruling that allows the EPA, along with the Army Corps of Engineers, to more carefully scrutinize applications for mountaintop coal mining sites to ensure they meet requirements of the Clean Water Act.[63]

The strategy that has caught fire on college campuses across the nation, and was proposed by Goldsboro students, is divestment from fossil fuels. Daniela wonders whether divestment is the most useful strategy for change. Divestment advocates argue that it sets a positive example. If a college or church embraces social and environmental justice, then they ought to practice what they preach. Divestment is a way for individuals and groups to be part of a movement toward sustainability by publicly withdrawing their investments in the mining and production of fossil fuels. While advocates realize that divestment might not hurt a company's bottom line, it makes a statement that they are deeply concerned about environmental destruction from use of dirty energy sources and that these investments must be replaced with clean sources of energy. Last of all, divestment advocates argue that it will not hurt college endowments, despite the fact that some college administrations, like Swarthmore, claim otherwise.

One of the most historically prominent divestment campaigns was in resistance to apartheid in South Africa. In 1962, the UN General Assembly passed a resolution calling for economic sanctions on South Africa, but the anti-apartheid divestment campaign did not gain critical momentum until the 1980s. Michigan State University was the first university in 1978 to divest from bonds and financial institutions directly involved with the South African regime. By the mid-1980s, many students erected shantytowns on college campuses that had not divested. By 1986, there was an international campaign against Royal Dutch Shell. The divestment movement led Congress to pass the Comprehensive Anti-Apartheid Act of 1986, overriding President Reagan's veto.[64] While it is not clear that the anti-apartheid divestment campaign had substantial financial impact, the campaign fostered worldwide popular opposition, which led to the decline of apartheid.[65]

Critics of the divestment strategy argue that it doesn't actually hurt companies but simply transfers ownership of shares to a party that cares less about the issue. Second, divestment leaves educational institutions voiceless within energy companies, whereas ownership of shares gives institutions the ability to elect boards of directors and vote on shareholder proposals. Fossil fuel companies pour big money into fighting energy and climate policy proposals. Thus, there is something to be said for engaging in shareholder activism. Third, as Professor Shorne points out, many of the fossil fuel companies are also the biggest investors in alternative energy sources. Last of all, critics argue that divestment from fossil fuels is more complex than divesting from tobacco or companies doing business in South Africa. Our economy is heavily dependent on fossil fuels, and we are all complicit in their use. Divestment from fossil fuels, critics argue, is simply the easy way out and does not reduce our impact on the environment.

The Interfaith Center on Corporate Responsibility is an example of shareholder advocacy. They are a coalition of faith organizations that engage hundreds of corporations to promote more sustainable and just practices. They initiate in-person dialogue with companies and also sponsor roundtables on industry-wide issues of moral concern. In addition, they send statements and letters from large groups of institutional investors. As a last resort, if investor concerns are not met, they file proxy resolutions that are voted on by all shareholders.[66] For example, they have filed resolutions on energy policy and climate change with a number of energy companies, such as Consol Energy, American Electric Power Company, and Devon Energy, and with several fossil fuel corporations, like Exxon Mobil and Chevron. They believe the shareholder advocacy approach is more effective than divestment because it preserves an active voice within energy and fossil fuel companies, and reaches a broader array of companies that create greenhouse emissions through use of fossil fuels.

Writer and environmentalist Wendell Berry, a supporter of divestment, counters that "fossil-fuel energy must be replaced not just by clean energy, but also by *less* energy."[67] In other words, Berry contends that individual behavior and public policy changes to conserve energy, as well as institutional divestment from fossil fuels, are strategies that should simultaneously be employed to promote both sustainability and sufficiency. If Goldsboro does pursue fossil fuel divestment, it should also invest heavily in energy conservation, energy efficiency, and renewable energy production.

Daniela has a lot to ponder before the next meeting of the environmental club. The trip to West Virginia opened her eyes to the destructive coal mining practices and the overwhelming issue of climate change from the burning of coal and other fossil fuels. Listening to the stories of residents who were negatively impacted by MTR made her even more aware of the interconnections between social and environmental injustice. The torn-apart mountains and buried river valleys were a stark contrast to the heavily wooded mountains she viewed on their drive into West Virginia. While she can take seriously her vow to use less energy by taking shorter showers, she must decide what other strategies she and her fellow classmates ought to pursue if they want to address effectively the environmental and social problems associated with coal use.

Notes

[1]Coal River Mountain Watch, "Marsh Fork Elementary," http://crmw.net.

[2]See http://ilovemountains.org.

[3]Patrick Reis and Stephanie Stamm, "Who Killed All the Coal Jobs?" *National Journal*, November 4, 2013, http://www.nationaljournal.com.

[4]Appalachian Voices, "Mountaintop Removal 101," http://appvoices.org.

[5]Larry Gibson has since passed away (2012). See tributes to him on the Keeper of the Mountains Foundation website, http://mountainkeeper.blogspot.com.

[6]Keeper of the Mountains Foundation, http://mountainkeeper.blogspot.com/p/about.html.

[7]James B. Stewart, "A Clash of Ideals and Investments at Swarthmore," *New York Times*, May 16, 2014, http://www.nytimes.com.

[8]See http://350.org for more information.

[9]Stewart, "A Clash of Ideals and Investments at Swarthmore."

[10]Andrew Herndon, "Exxon Refocusing Algae Biofuels Program after $100 Million Spend," *Bloomberg News*, May 20, 2013, http://www.bloomberg.com.

[11]US Energy Information Administration, "Frequently Asked Questions," http://www.eia.gov.

[12]Michelle Nijhuis, "Can Coal Ever Be Clean?" *National Geographic* (April 2014), 29.

[13]Ibid., 34.

[14]Ibid., 39.

[15]Ibid.

[16]Nick Cunningham, "What Green Revolution? Coal Use Highest in 44 Years," *Oilprice.com*, June 19, 2014, http://www.nasdaq.com.

[17]Julia Pyper, "COAL: S&P Predicts 'King Coal' Will Lose Its Crown," *Climate Wire*, July 24, 2014.

[18]Nijhuis "Can Coal Ever Be Clean?" 29–33.

[19]Ibid., 40.

[20]West Virginia Coal Association, "Mining 101," http://www.wvcoal.com.

[21]"Idea of the Day: Powder River Basic Coal Leasing," Center for American Progress, July 24, 2014, http://www.americanprogress.org.

[22]US Energy Information Administration, "AEO2014 Projects More Coal-Fired Power Plant Retirements by 2016 Than Have Been Scheduled," http://www.eia.gov.

[23]Blakely Elizabeth Whilden, "Mineral Rights in Central Appalachia: A Brief History of the Broad Form Deed in Kentucky and Tennessee," http://studentorgs.law.unc.edu.

[24]Appalachian Voices, "Community Impacts of Mountaintop Removal," http://appvoices.org.

[25]Ibid.

[26]Ibid.

[27]See Coal River Mountain Watch, "Health Impacts," http://crmw.net.

[28]Darren Epps and Neil Powell, "Most Major Coal Company CEOs Received Sizable Compensation Increases in 2013," http://www.snl.com.

[29]American Lung Association, *Toxic Air: The Case for Cleaning Up Coal-Fired Power Plants* (March 2011), http://www.lung.org.

[30]Ibid., 2.

[31]Jeff Goodell, "Coal's Toxic Sludge," *Rolling Stone*, April 1, 2010, 46.

[32]Sierra Club, "Coal Ash Map," http://action.sierraclub.org.

[33]Lisa Evans, Michael Becher and Bridget Lee, "State of Failure: How States Fail to Protect our Health and Drinking Water from Toxic Coal Ash," *Earth Justice and Appalachian Mountain Advocates* (August 2011), 3.

[34]The largest industrial disaster occurred in December 2008 when a pond of coal waste broke near Kingston, Tennessee, spilling a billion gallons of sludge into the Emory River.

[35]Robert Bullard, "Environment and Morality: Confronting Environmental Racism in the United States," October 1, 2004, http://www.unrisd.org.

[36]Jeff Goodell, "Coal's Toxic Sludge," 46–49.

[37]Physicians for Social Responsibility, "Coal Ash the Toxic Threat to Our Health and Environment" (August 2010), http://www.psr.org.

[38]Kristen Lombardi, "EPA to Regulate Coal Ash Amid Court Settlement," January 30, 2014, http://www.publicintegrity.org.

[39]EPA, "Clean Power Plan Proposed Rule," http://www2.epa.gov.

[40]World Coal Association, "Climate Change," http://www.worldcoal.org.

[41]Roman Espejo, ed., *Coal: Opposing Viewpoints* (Farmington Hills, MI: Greenhaven Press, 2011), 34–35.

[42]Center for Climate and Energy Solutions, "Carbon Capture and Storage: Quick Facts," http://www.c2es.org. See also Global CCS Institute, "Large CCS Projects," http://www.globalccsinstitute.com.

[43]John Pickering et al. in *Wilderness—Earth's Last Wild Places*, ed. P. R. Gil et al. (Arlington, VA: Conservational International, 2003), 458–67, http://www.discoverlife.org/co/.

[44]Claudia Copeland, "Mountaintop Mining: Background on Current Controversies," Congressional Research Service, 1, April 12, 2010, http://congressionalresearch.com.

[45]Joshua R. Purtle, "Mingo Logan Coal Co. v. EPA." *Harvard Environmental Law Review* 37, no. 1 (2013): 282, http://www3.law.harvard.edu.

[46]Ibid., 284.

[47]Center for Biological Diversity, "Extinction Crisis," http://www.biologicaldiversity.org.

[48]Dave Foreman, "Wilderness: From Scenery to Nature (1995)," in *The Great New Wilderness Debate*, ed. J. Baird Callicott and Michal P. Nelson (Athens: University of Georgia Press, 1998), 573.

[49]The Nature Conservancy, "Climate Change Impacts," http://www.nature.org.

[50]Aldo Leopold, *A Sand County Almanac* (Oxford: Oxford University Press, 1966), 262.

[51]Ibid., 578.

[52]Claudia Copeland, "Mountaintop Mining: Background on Current Controversies," Congressional Research Service, July 16, 2014, http://congressionalresearch.com.

[53]"America's Best (and Worst) Educated States," Fox Business, October 15, 2012, http://www.foxbusiness.com.

[54]Omar Ghabra, "How the Coal Industry Impoverishes West Virginia, *The Nation*, January 24, 2014, http://www.thenation.com.

[55]Don Hopey, "W.Va. Study Unearths Higher Health Risks in Coal Mining Communities," *Pittsburgh Post Gazette*, April 2, 2008, http://www.post-gazette.com.

[56]Omar Ghabra, "How the Coal Industry Impoverishes West Virginia.

[57]Chris Hamilton, "As Coal Goes, So Goes West Virginia," in West Virginia Coal Association, *Coal Facts 2013*, http://www.wvcoal.com.

[58]See also Ohio Valley Environmental Coalition, Keepers of the Mountain Foundation, Appalachian Voices, Kentuckians for the Commonwealth, the Alliance for Appalachia, United Mountain Defense, Statewide Organizing for Community Empowerment, Southern Appalachian Mountain Stewards, Mountain Justice, Rainforest Action Network, and RAMPS (Radical Action for Mountain People's Survival).

[59]Robert Bullard, "Justice and Environmental Decision Making," in *Environmental Ethics: Concepts, Policy, Theory*, ed. Joseph DesJardins (Mountain View, CA: Mayfield, 1999), 438–48.

[60]Peter Wenz, "Just Garbage," in Joseph DesJardins, ed., *Environmental Ethics*, 450–51.

[61]Patrick Reis, "Study: World's 'Peak Coal' Moment Has Arrived," *New York Times*, September 29, 2010, http://www.nytimes.com.

[62]See http://content.sierraclub.org/coal/.

[63]Jeremy P. Jacobs and Manuel Quiñones, "COAL: Appeals Court Upholds Obama's Crackdown on Mountaintop Mining," *Greenwire*, July 11, 2014.

[64]Cecelie Counts, "Divestment Was Just One Weapon in Battle against Apartheid," *New York Times*, January 27, 2013, http://www.nytimes.com.

[65]Eric Hendey, "Does Divestment Work?" *Harvard Institute of Politics* (2014), http://www.iop.harvard.edu. Others are making similar claims for the fossil fuel divestment campaign—that it is helping to shift public opinion about climate change. See Marc Gunther, "Why the Fossil Fuel Divestment Movement May Ultimately Win," *Yale 360*, July 27, 2015, http://e360.yale.edu/.

[66]Interfaith Center on Corporate Responsibility, http://www.iccr.org.

[67]Wendell Berry, "Less Energy, More Life," *The Progressive*, September 4, 2013, http://progressive.org.

9

Fractured Options

Combined Heat and Power, Hydraulic Fracturing, and Greenhouse Gas Reductions

Acronyms and Abbreviations

ACUPCC	American College and University Presidents Climate Commitment
CAP	climate action plan
CHP	combined heat and power
eCO_2	carbon dioxide equivalent
EIA	Energy Information Administration (US)
EPA	Environmental Protection Agency (US)
GHG	greenhouse gas
IPCC	Intergovernmental Panel on Climate Change (UN)
kW	kilowatt
MROW	Midwest Reliability Organization–West
MT	metric tons
PV	photovoltaic
SDWA	Safe Drinking Water Act
USGCRP	US Global Change Research Program

Case

"Vanguard College Reduces Carbon Footprint 40 Percent." Megan Peters beamed as she read the headline of the campus paper. She was proud of her college. While members of Congress insisted that significant greenhouse gas (GHG) reductions were impossible and would cripple the US economy, Vanguard College had already managed to reduce its emissions 40 percent without driving up the cost of tuition.

Megan remembered how she happened to be visiting Vanguard the day the college installed its 1,600 kilowatt (kW) wind turbine on the western edge of campus. She had admired the college's visible commitment to environmental stewardship and decided that day this was where she wanted to go to college.

The wind project had cost $3.2 million, but the college had defrayed about half that expense with federal grants. Since then the turbine had been generating about 30 percent of the electricity consumed on campus. One year later Vanguard signed a lease agreement for a 300 kW solar photovoltaic (PV) array to power a housing complex that utilizes geothermal energy for heating and cooling. Megan was one of 112 senior students living in the facility this year.

Megan became further interested in issues related to global warming when she took a January seminar for first-year students on climate change. She learned that Vanguard College was a charter signatory of the American College and University Presidents Climate Commitment (ACUPCC). This required the college to make sustainability a part of every student's learning experience and to achieve climate neutrality (net zero GHG emissions) at some point in the future.[1]

When Vanguard's Board of Regents formally adopted a climate action plan (CAP), it challenged the college to cut its carbon footprint in half by 2015, to achieve a 70 percent reduction in emissions by 2020, and to reach the goal of climate neutrality by 2030. The Energy and Climate Task Group of the college's Campus Sustainability Council was entrusted with developing strategies to meet the goals in Vanguard's CAP. Megan joined this group of students, faculty, and staff at the start of her junior year.

It was a steep learning curve at first, but she loved the monthly meetings. This was where the rubber hit the road, since 85 percent of the college's GHG emissions were related to its energy consumption. She learned that 50 percent of the campus carbon footprint was due to electricity purchases because two-thirds of all power in the Upper Midwest was generated by coal-fired power plants. Another 35 percent of Vanguard's emissions were due to the college's central heating plant, which burned natural gas to produce steam heat for the campus.

Megan was pleased to learn Vanguard had made big investments in energy efficiency. An initial investment of $1.5 million a decade ago had reduced electricity consumption by about 23 percent and heating fuel consumption by approximately 5 percent. The college had borrowed the money to install more efficient lights, fans, motors, and several other measures, and then paid the loan back with energy cost savings over seven years. Now that the loan was paid off, the college was using the $250,000 annual savings to help finance the refurbishing of two of the oldest dorms on campus. Most students had no idea the college had taken these prudent measures and that the vast majority of Vanguard's emission reductions were due to energy efficiency. All they saw was the wind turbine and the solar PV field, which visibly reflected Vanguard's commitments to sustainability.

Megan was also impressed last year when Vanguard's vice president for finance and administration, Ann Simpson, accepted the task group's recommendation to pay for a high-level study from an engineering firm to identify significant GHG emission reduction strategies. The study was completed by the end of Megan's junior year, and the firm presented its findings in a joint session to members of the task group and the college's administration.

Megan remembered the meeting very well. She had felt a little intimidated sitting between Ann Simpson and the president of Vanguard, but she felt welcome and valued nonetheless. The firm had explored a host of technological options, including more widespread use of geothermal heat pumps, a second wind turbine, a larger solar PV array, and the prospects for solar water heating on building rooftops. In the end, the two most cost-effective options to reduce emissions were a biomass heating plant and a natural gas-fired combined heat and power (CHP) plant (Table 1).

Table 1. Vanguard College Emission Reduction Options

	Capital Cost	Service Life	MT eCO$_2$ Reduction		Life Cost
		(Years)	Annual	Cumulative Service Life	($/MT eCO$_2$)
Cogeneration/CHP					
Reciprocating Engine 1,420 kW; 4,500 PPH	$3,200,000	20	2,654	53,080	$60.28
Renewables					
Biomass Boiler 34,500 PPH	$7,250,000	40	3,672	146,880	$49.36
Wind Turbine 2,000 kW	$4,000,000	20	2,016	40,320	$99.20
Solar PV Array 500 kW	$1,000,000	20	340	6,800	$147.06
Geothermal Heat Pump 600 Tons	$2,020,000	20	299	5,980	$337.79
Solar HW System 6,500 SF Collector	$1,250,000	20	74	1,480	$844.59

The biomass boiler would burn wood chips to produce about 75 percent of the steam needed to heat the campus, and the existing natural gas-fired boiler would provide the rest. While this option was the most expensive, it would reduce the most GHG emissions each year as well as cumulatively over the forty-year life of the boiler plant. As a result, it was the lowest-cost option per ton of emission reductions. Due to currently low natural gas prices, however, the biomass heating plant would only offset about $285,000 of natural gas heating fuel purchases each year, which left the $7.25 million project with a very long payback of twenty-five years.

By way of comparison, the CHP option featured a sixteen-cylinder reciprocating engine fueled by natural gas that would generate about 60 percent of the college's annual electricity consumption. The residual heat from the internal combustion engine would be used to heat the campus via the existing steam distribution system. This CHP option was less than half as expensive as the biomass option but it would still reduce a lot of emissions each year since natural gas-fired power production is less carbon-intensive than coal-fired electricity. The engine's shorter equipment life of twenty years, however, resulted in two-thirds fewer cumulative emission reductions compared to the biomass boiler and a 20 percent higher emission reduction cost per ton. Due to higher electricity prices compared to heating fuel prices, however, the $3.2 million CHP system was projected to save the college $355,000 each year, which resulted in a payback of nine years. Annual operating costs had been accounted for in each of these two payback estimates.

It was not hard at the end of the presentation to see which GHG reduction option most attracted the administration. With a much smaller capital cost and a shorter payback, the CHP project required a much smaller and shorter debt burden than the biomass project. With the college gearing up for a big remodel of the old main building that would also make it more energy efficient, Megan knew Vanguard needed to borrow a lot of money to tackle this long-needed project. After a brief conversation with the president, Ann Simpson asked Vanguard's director of facilities, Ray Upland, to investigate the CHP option more thoroughly over the summer.

Megan now found herself sitting in the first meeting of the fall semester of the Energy and Water Task Group. Shania Jefferson, the faculty chair, began promptly at 8:00 a.m. The sole item on the agenda was to receive, discuss, and take action on a proposal to invest in the CHP option that emerged last spring. They had gathered in their usual meeting place—a small conference room in the environmental studies suite. Megan was seated next to another student, Phil Johnson, and across from the other faculty member, Greg Stimby. Ann Simpson was seated next to Ray Upland, and across from them sat Arlene Holland, a staff member in information technology. Arlene was seated next to Bill Hewitt, a retired Vanguard alumnus and the owner of the 300 kW solar PV array the college was leasing.

Shania explained that she and Ray had spent a considerable chunk of the summer doing more research on the CHP option. They had visited a hospital sixty miles away that had installed such a system a few years ago, and it was working very well. They had also consulted an energy resources center at the state university, which confirmed Vanguard was a good candidate for a CHP system. The center also confirmed the expected reduction in GHG emissions.

Ray remained seated and said, "Okay, I've come up with four reasons why Vanguard should invest in this 1,400 kW CHP system. The first is that it seems like a logical next step given the major investments we have made in energy efficiency over the past decade or so. CHP is the poster child for energy efficiency. We burn natural gas every day of the year to heat and make hot water for buildings across the campus. Why not use it to generate electricity first and then put that waste heat to work on campus?"

"But it's pretty expensive and there are lots of moving parts in that engine," said Arlene. "Aren't there aggressive forms of energy efficiency we could invest in instead? We only spent $1.5 million to cut our energy consumption by over 20 percent a few years ago. This project has smaller annual emission reductions and costs twice as much."

Ray replied, "That's true, Arlene, but we've been picking all the low-hanging fruit. We keep investing in energy efficiency projects that pay back in seven years or less. This CHP project pushes that payback out to nine years, but that's a lot less than our wind project at thirteen years, which got a lot of federal subsidies that are no longer available."

Ray continued by pointing to a graph on the wall, "A second reason to invest in this CHP system is because it represents a significant GHG reduction wedge. I think we should be able to hit our 50 percent GHG reduction goal with the new energy efficiency projects we started last year. But there is no way we are going to meet our 70 percent goal or achieve climate neutrality without major investments in projects like this CHP system and more renewable energy systems" (Figure 1).

Figure 1. Vanguard College greenhouse gas reduction goals

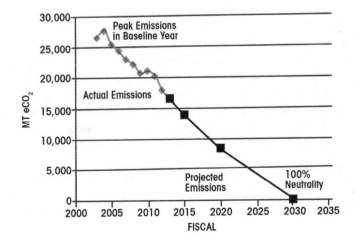

Phil jumped into the discussion at this point. "What about the huge amount of methane that is being released into the atmosphere through increases in natural gas production and distribution due to fracking? Are those emissions factored into the projected GHG reductions for the CHP project? Dr. Jefferson, you had us read a study last year in your energy policy class that claimed there is actually a net *increase* of GHG emissions if natural gas is used to fuel power plants instead of coal."

Shania replied, "That's right, Phil. Since then other studies have challenged that claim, but others have reconfirmed it."

Megan found herself thinking that *every* option has some environmental consequences. Apparently some bald eagle advocates had raised concerns at a public hearing when the college requested a conditional use permit from the county for the wind turbine project, and some members of the student environmental group had pointed to the toxic chemicals used to produce solar panels. There was certainly going to be a lot of noise to muffle with this CHP system. The main component was a huge, sixteen-cylinder internal combustion engine as big as a dorm room. Still, if the whole point of the CHP project was to reduce emissions, Megan thought Phil's question was pretty important.

Ray went on, "A third reason to invest in this CHP system is because it provides a prudent way to manage our electricity costs. I think most of you know that Vanguard purchases about 60 percent of the natural gas we consume each year on a fixed price contract. We purchase the rest of our heating fuel at market prices. This fixed price contract protects us from some of the variability in natural gas prices. We could do something similar with this CHP system because it would produce about 60 percent of the electricity we consume. Given our wind turbine's production, we would only have to purchase the remaining 10 percent of our electricity from the utility, which is a lot less than we are purchasing now. With natural gas prices at record lows, and forecast to remain low for many years to come, this seems like a good time to invest in a natural gas-fired CHP system."

Greg interjected, "Can we really trust those pricing forecasts? There has been a lot more variability in natural gas pricing over the years than there has been in electricity pricing. Plus, if the Environmental Protection Agency (EPA) is able to implement and enforce its carbon regulations for existing power plants, our utility isn't the only one that's going to switch to gas-fired power generation. They all are, and as a result, demand will soar, prices will increase, and this project's nine-year payback could take a lot longer."

Nodding his head, Ray replied, "You're right, Greg. Our utility is going to build a new gas-fired power plant to replace some old coal-fired units, and it got approval from the public utility commission to pass those costs on to ratepayers like us. Those EPA regulations are going to drive up our electricity costs because we have been getting cheap coal-fired power for a long time. The reality, however, is that we are going to get hit by the economic impact of these regulations one way or another. They are going to drive up our operating costs with or without CHP." Megan noted Ann quietly nodding her head.

At this point Phil jumped back into the discussion. "Yes, the college's operating costs are going to go up, but isn't our utility going to be able to generate power cheaper than we could with this CHP system? In addition, won't our emissions also actually go up once the EPA figures out just how much methane is actually leaking into the atmosphere?"

Professor Jefferson replied, "Those are good points, Phil, but like Ray said, our costs are going to go up either way. In addition, the leakage rate is still a matter of scientific dispute. Based on the tool we use to calculate our emissions, a CHP system will reduce our emissions by 15 to 20 percent. Plus it has other benefits."

Ray continued, "Yes, that leads me to the fourth reason Vanguard should invest in this CHP system and that is its compatibility with our wind and solar facilities. As you probably recall, most of the year, the campus consumes around 2,000 kW of power at any given time. When the wind is blowing twenty-five miles per hour and the sun is shining, we can generate 1,900 kW and thus meet almost all of the power demand on campus. In situations like these we could back off our 1,400 kW CHP system so as not to produce more power than we consume. Alternatively, and this would be true most of the time, we could turn up our CHP system to replace the power lost when the sun sets or the wind calms down. The same is true all over the country. Gas-fired power plants are ideal sources of base load power when you have an increasing number of intermittent wind and solar generators on the electrical grid."

Greg said, "Yes, that's all true, but we haven't really talked yet about the elephant in the room—hydraulic fracturing. As I understand it, at least 70 percent of the US natural gas supply is now produced this way. You've all seen the movies and those crazy Internet videos of people lighting the water from their kitchen faucets on fire. The process of drilling these fracking wells is very water intensive and winds up polluting a lot of groundwater and streams. It's also linked to earthquakes that have caused property damage. And then there's the mining for sand that is mixed with water and a bunch of chemicals and then injected at high pressure to fracture the shale and release the gas. I took the students in my environmental sociology class on a field trip to my hometown over in southwestern Wisconsin. They couldn't believe what they saw. The sand mining has changed the whole topography of the region."

"We ought to drive over to where I'm from in western North Dakota," said Phil. "It's like the state's been invaded. Towns have grown to three times their original size with all of the workers coming from out of state to work on drilling projects. Rents are out of control, roads are being ruined, and crime rates are skyrocketing. There is so much natural gas being flared that this part of the state looks as bright as Chicago on night-time satellite pictures."

"I know," said Ray. "My brother is a pharmacist in Williston. My wife and I saw the growth firsthand when we visited him last summer. But he emphasizes that fracking is reducing US dependence on foreign oil, reducing energy prices, creating jobs, raising tax revenues, and stimulating rural economies. North Dakota now has the lowest unemployment rate in the nation and a rapidly growing economy. I also don't want to think how cold we all would have been this past winter had we not had natural gas to heat the campus and our homes."

"But the whole thing is completely unsustainable," said Phil. "It's a classic boom that will soon be followed by a bust, and North Dakotans are going to be left holding the bag. I'm all for Vanguard reducing its GHG emissions, but at what cost to others? I really think we should be looking hard at the biomass heating plant instead of burning even more natural gas. We could include a CHP system in that facility, couldn't we?"

"Yes," said Shania, "but CHP is not included in the biomass boiler cost estimate because it would add another $2 million to the project. We looked hard at the biomass option five years ago and backed away over major concerns about material handling, wood chip pricing, the adequacy of sustainably harvested supplies, and air pollution. We'd need about five thousand metric tons (MT) of wood chips each year to supply 75 percent of our steam requirements. That's about five hundred truckloads of wood chips—two truckloads a day during the heating season. The study said there was nine times that much supply within seventy-five miles of campus, but when Ray and I called one of the six big sources in the state, we got a disconnected number because it had gone bankrupt. When Ray picks up the phone to order wood chips in the middle of winter, he needs to have someone who can deliver. We also have to make sure the wood we get has been harvested sustainably. As near as we can tell, none of the sources we have for wood chips offer any kind of certification in this regard. Finally, we also got really concerned about air quality since we're located in this valley. We can't afford to antagonize the town the way the University of Montana did with its biomass heating project a few years ago.[2] These are all major issues. In my view the biomass option needs a lot more study before we can even think about moving forward."

Bill asked, "What about more wind and solar? According to the report, two new wind turbines would offset more emissions than the biomass plant and a lot more than the CHP system."

Ray replied, "That's true on paper, but the problem is we don't have two more sites close to campus. We have potential sites that are three to four miles away, but it would cost a lot to bring the power back to campus, and we would have to negotiate land leases and transmission right of way with all of the property owners. On top of that, there would be many times when all three turbines would produce more electricity than we can consume. That extra power would have to be sold to our utility at very low rates. Energy storage would be a great solution, but that's just getting off the ground. The economics just don't pencil out very well for more wind turbines right now, especially since some of the federal incentives have dried up. You all have the engineering firm's report in front of you. You can see that the wind option is twice as expensive per ton of emissions reduction as the biomass boiler and 50 percent more expensive than the CHP system. Solar PV is more than twice as expensive as CHP, and we don't have nearly enough space on campus for as much as we would need."

By the end of the meeting Megan's head hurt from all the numbers swirling around in her head. Still, she was excited and determined to take her role as one of the student representatives on the committee seriously and weigh carefully all the options in front of her. She knew Dr. Jefferson would soon ask the task group to vote on Ray's proposal to invest in a CHP system. She knew, based on prior votes, that her vote counted just as much as the others on the task group, but she couldn't recall a vote where the group had lacked consensus. In the end, they would not have the final word anyway. That was up to the administration and the Board of Regents. Still, her voice counted. Her responsibility mattered. How should the competing goals of cost effectiveness and substantial emission reductions be attained? Which option had the least adverse social and environmental consequences? If they were burning natural gas anyway, why not maximize efficiency by investing in the CHP system? Wouldn't it buy them time to study the other options and get the problems figured out? What was the best decision—and how would she be able to justify or defend it to her peers?

Megan found her gaze lingering on a poster on the wall next to the chart showing Vanguard's GHG reductions. The poster featured a beautiful picture of a mature forest. Beneath was a provocative Native American quote: "We do not inherit the Earth from our ancestors, we borrow it from our children."

Commentary

It is no wonder Megan's head hurts. This case is filled with numbers, unfamiliar terms, and contested facts. It also involves a certain amount of cost–benefit analysis that some might dismiss as unnecessary or that others might find too technical and dry. Vanguard College's goal to eliminate its GHG emissions is morally laudable, but achieving that goal is not going to be easy or inexpensive. The devil is in the details. This commentary provides additional information about key aspects of the case and concludes with some comments about the relevance of the ecojustice norms.

Global Warming and Climate Change

The overarching context of this case is global warming and climate change. Two recent assessments by the UN Intergovernmental Panel on Climate Change (IPCC) and the US Global Change Research Program (USGCRP) paint a dire picture. This commentary will focus on the latter since Vanguard College is located in the Upper Midwest region of the United States.[3]

The Global Change Research Act of 1990 requires that, every four years, the USGCRP prepare and submit to the president and Congress an assessment of the effects of global climate change in the United States. The 841-page Third Assessment Report was issued in May 2014.[4]

The report reveals widespread evidence of climate change and claims human activities are the primary cause of global warming over the past fifty years. Globally, the combustion of fossil fuels (coal, oil, and natural gas), combined with the release of methane from agriculture and deforestation, has increased the concentration of GHGs in Earth's atmosphere. As a result, the average temperature in different regions of the United States has increased by 1.3° Fahrenheit (F) to 1.9°F since 1895, with most of this increase occurring since 1970. The report projects US temperatures will rise another 2°F to 4°F in most areas of the nation over the next few decades, but the report then offers the following very sobering comment:

> The amount of warming projected beyond the next few decades is directly linked to the cumulative global emissions of heat-trapping gases and particles. By the end of this century, a roughly 3°F to 5°F rise is projected under a lower emissions scenario, which would require substantial reductions in emissions . . . , and a 5°F to 10°F rise for a higher emissions scenario assuming continued increases in emissions, predominantly from fossil fuel combustion.[5]

While Earth has been much warmer in the past, this rate of warming would be much faster than any of the climate changes on the planet over the past ten thousand years.[6] If present trends continue, global warming will rapidly increase more than 3.6°F (2° Celsius) above the preindustrial level, which many scientists believe is a key threshold to preserve the relatively stable climate that has led to human flourishing and remarkable biodiversity. According to the USGCRP report, to hold warming to this level "would require rapid emissions reductions (more than 70% reduction in human-related emissions by 2050, and net negative emissions by 2100)."[7]

ACUPCC

Similar findings by the IPCC led twelve US college presidents and university chancellors to issue a "Call for Climate Leadership" in October 2006:

> With global warming, society faces a crisis that threatens its very viability. Reversing global warming is the defining challenge of the 21st century. Addressing this threat successfully will mean transforming our economy, our institutions, our daily lives—and doing so within a generation. This is a challenge of massive proportions, one that desperately calls for the vision and leadership of higher education.[8]

By March 31, 2007, 152 presidents and chancellors representing a wide range of schools in higher education had answered the call to become charter signatories of the ACUPCC. Vanguard's president was one of these signatories.

Today there are nearly 700 active signatory institutions representing over 6.5 million students, which is approximately one-third of all college and university students in the United States.[9] As part of their commitment, each of these schools has accepted the following obligations:

- Complete a GHG emissions inventory.
- Within two years, set a target date and interim milestones for becoming climate neutral.
- Take immediate steps to reduce GHG emissions by choosing from a list of seven short-term actions.
- Integrate sustainability into the curriculum and make it part of the educational experience.
- Make the action plan, emission inventories, and progress reports publicly available.

Vanguard College has taken these obligations seriously and has already reduced its GHG emissions 40 percent via investments in energy efficiency and renewable energy. In addition, the college has an aggressive timetable to achieve climate neutrality (net-zero GHG emissions). It appears from the graph in the case that the college's peak emissions totaled approximately 28,000 MT of carbon dioxide equivalent (MT eCO_2) in 2004.[10] That yields the emission reduction targets as shown in Table 2.

Table 2. Vanguard College Emission Reduction Targets

Year	MT eCO2	Reduction Target
2004	28,000	Peak Emissions
2015	14,000	50% Goal
2020	8,400	70% Goal
2030	0	Climate Neutrality

Vanguard College's GHG Emission Reduction Options

One of the reasons Vanguard's GHG emissions are so high is because it is located in the Upper Midwest region of the United States. Vanguard College is in the Midwest Reliability Organization–West (MROW) region of the US electrical grid. This region includes all of Iowa, Minnesota, and North Dakota, most of South Dakota and Nebraska, a small portion of eastern Montana, and about one-third of Wisconsin. Approximately 65 percent of the power in this region is generated by coal-fired power plants. The rest comes from nuclear reactors (14 percent), wind farms (10 percent), hydroelectric dams (6 percent), natural gas peak power plants (3 percent), biomass facilities (1 percent), and a few small solar arrays and diesel power plants. Out of twenty-six subregions in the US electrical grid, MROW is the eighth dirtiest in terms of the hourly rate of GHG emissions from electrical power production.[11]

Professor Greg Stimby notes correctly that the EPA has proposed to reduce carbon pollution from existing power plants nationwide. In fact, the EPA's Clean Power Plan seeks to reduce GHG emissions from the power sector 30 percent from 2005 levels by 2030.[12] This plan will impact the MROW region in a significant way, but the power generated in the region will still be carbon intensive in 2030, even if the plan is fully implemented. Thus, Vanguard may get some help from the federal government as it seeks to achieve its goals, but most of the work will still fall on the college's shoulders.

Based on Ray Upland's comments in the case, it appears Vanguard is on track to meet its 50 percent GHG reduction goal primarily because of its investments in energy efficiency. This is no minor accomplishment and deserves much praise and celebration. It has long been the case that citizens of the United States use twice the amount of energy on a per capita basis compared to citizens of the European Union, yet most Europeans enjoy a standard of living that is as good or better than most Americans.[13] Vanguard College has demonstrated that Americans can be just as efficient as Europeans and maintain their standard of living.

Nevertheless, two questions arise. The first is how the college will reduce another 5,600 MT eCO_2 by 2020 to reach its 70 percent goal. The second is how Vanguard will achieve climate neutrality by shedding the remaining 8,400 MT eCO_2 no later than 2030. Table 1 in the case provides a lot of very important information about Vanguard's various GHG reduction options, but the simplified Table 3 reveals there is no single *silver bullet* that will help the college achieve either goal. In fact, it would appear that in order to meet its goals, Vanguard might need an *all of the above* strategy to reach climate neutrality by 2030.

Table 3. Vanguard College Emission Reduction Options (Simplified)

GHG Reduction Options	Capital Cost	Annual GHG Reduction (MT eCO2)	Simple Payback (Years)
CHP Reciprocating Engine 1,420 kW; 4,500 PPH	$3,200,000	2,654	9
Biomass Boiler 34,500 PPH	$7,250,000	3,672	25
Wind Turbine 2,000 kW	$4,000,000	2,016	22

Ray Upland and Professor Shania Jefferson in the case are aware that Vanguard will need multiple GHG reduction strategies. Based on their comments, it is clear Vanguard has already done some pretty extensive investigation of the wind and biomass options. While it appears the fundamental problem with both is economic (high capital costs and long paybacks), there also appear to be some important environmental, legal, and operational issues that need to be resolved.

Professor Jefferson identifies several issues associated with the biomass heating plant that Phil champions as an alternative to the natural gas-fired CHP plant. Both seem to assume that a biomass-fueled heating plant would, in fact, reduce Vanguard's carbon footprint. This is not certain. A lot depends on the source of the fuel stock. The only way the use of biomass achieves carbon neutrality is if growing biomass is able to absorb the carbon dioxide released into the atmosphere via combustion or gasification. If trees are cut down and not replaced, the use of biomass increases global GHG emissions. In addition, even if one tree is planted for every tree burned, it will take decades for the newly planted tree to absorb the carbon dioxide that was released through the combustion of another tree in a matter of minutes.[14] Concerned that the EPA's proposed Clean Power Plan could result in unsustainable forestry practices, a group of prominent US forest scientists has urged the EPA to jettison "the flawed assumption that bioenergy is inherently carbon neutral" and to develop "a scientifically sound methodology for determining the carbon emissions impact to the atmosphere from burning long-recovery woody biomass feedstocks—most notably, whole trees."[15] The emerging consensus is that the only acceptable sources of biomass for carbon reduction will be dedicated crops that don't replace food production, wood residues from paper and timber mills, and woody waste associated with various forestry practices. Professor Jefferson is aware of this issue and is concerned Vanguard can't currently secure a sufficient volume of sustainably harvested biomass.

Professor Jefferson also raises some legitimate concerns about operating a biomass-fueled heating plant. These concerns include operational safety, environmental concerns, and public relations. In 2009, the University of South Carolina shut down a brand-new $20 million facility after an explosion hurled metal parts sixty feet in all directions, endangering nearby workers and students. This was the last straw for the poorly designed facility that had been shut down over three dozen times and had only been operational for 98 out of 534 days.[16] Professor Jefferson refers specifically to a biomass project at the University of Montana that failed even to get off the drawing boards due to public concerns about environmental impacts on human health. Like Vanguard, this $16 million state-of-the-art biomass gasification facility was prompted by the university's desire to reduce its carbon footprint. Even though gasification offers far more ability to control emissions than direct combustion, the facility would nevertheless have increased emissions of some toxic emissions and particulate matter above levels currently produced by the natural gas-fired boilers on campus. This alarmed and angered many residents of Missoula because the city often experiences atmospheric inversions that produce poor air quality during the winter.[17] A much smaller school, Goddard College, has experienced similar public opposition to its plans to install a small biomass combustion facility on its campus in Plainfield, Vermont. Local residents are concerned about the health impacts from particulate emissions near their homes.[18] Given these examples, there are good reasons for Vanguard College to assess carefully the biomass heating plant option. But there are also plenty of examples of successful biomass heating plants at Middlebury College,[19] Bennington College,[20] Colby College,[21] and at various schools and hospitals elsewhere around the United States.

Given that it will take multiple GHG reduction strategies to achieve its goals, it would be wise for Vanguard to commence further study of the biomass heating plant option and also begin negotiating land leases and easements for at least one more wind turbine. It also may want to explore the benefits of leasing a biomass heating plant and/or a small wind farm so that investor alums like Bill Hewitt can harvest the various tax incentives associated with owning such facilities since the college is not eligible for them as a nonprofit entity. This would eliminate the need for upfront capital by the college, but the lease payments would increase annual operating costs. Alternatively, the college might consider forming a for-profit corporation to tap these incentives, but then the college will need to raise some of the capital through an investment of its own funds. Another possibility worth exploring would be the viability of a third-party power purchase agreement by which the college would contract to purchase power from a nearby wind farm for a set price over an extended period of time.[22] Unfortunately, none of the states in the MROW region currently allow such agreements, though a recent ruling by the Iowa Supreme Court has opened the door in that state for third-party power purchase agreements with nonprofits.[23] Finally, Vanguard may want to study the feasibility of combusting biogas from any nearby wastewater treatment plants or landfills in its heating plant. Biogas is rich in methane and would offer a significant GHG reduction opportunity. The University of New Hampshire[24] and five colleges in Virginia[25] are all tapping landfill gas for various purposes.

The one option that appears ready to implement now, however, is the CHP project. It would bring Vanguard about halfway to its 70 percent reduction goal while offering other benefits. We turn now to look closely at the strengths and weaknesses of this option.

CHP

Few realize that approximately two-thirds of all energy expended in a typical coal-fired or nuclear power plant is lost as waste heat that is discharged into the atmosphere and water sources. CHP systems put this wasted heat to work by generating electricity and useful thermal energy in one integrated system. While the conventional method of producing usable heat and power separately has a typical combined efficiency of 45 percent, CHP systems can operate at levels as high as 80 percent.[26]

There are several benefits associated with CHP systems. One, of course, is that the reduced energy consumption results in lower overall energy costs for the system owner. Another benefit is that CHP systems enable owners to generate their own power at a more fixed cost than what they can likely purchase from their electric utility. Ray Upland points out both of these benefits in the case. For the next twenty years, Vanguard College would be able to generate 60 percent of its annual electricity consumption, which would be especially helpful in the summer when the college pays higher prices for power during the air conditioning season. A third benefit Ray does not mention is that CHP systems enable the user to generate power when the electrical grid goes down. After Hurricane Sandy decimated large swaths of New Jersey and New York in 2012, several hospitals and large institutions decided to install CHP systems to provide greater energy security. Vanguard's CHP system would enable the college to offer a portion of its campus as an emergency public shelter during a grid outage in the area. Finally, another advantage Ray Upland does note is that natural gas-fired CHP systems work well with intermittent power generators like wind turbines and PV arrays. While it takes a long time to adjust power production at a coal-fired plant or a nuclear reactor, many natural gas-fired CHP systems can be ramped up or down rapidly to generate the desired amount of power. Thus, Vanguard could *step on the gas* or *hit the brakes*, as necessary, based on the production from its wind turbine and solar array.

The main benefit driving Vanguard's interest in a CHP system is environmental—reduced GHG emissions. Nationally, the EPA claims CHP systems reduce GHG emissions and other air pollutants by as much as 40 percent compared to conventional fossil fuel power plants. In addition, CHP systems consume virtually no water resources, whereas a typical coal-fired or nuclear power plant consumes 0.2 to 0.6 gallons of water per kW hour of electricity generated.[27] In the case, Phil Johnson and Professor Greg Stimby dispute the environmental benefits of a natural gas-fired CHP system. They also identify several social problems associated with current means of natural gas production. We turn now to address these concerns in more detail.

Issues Related to US Natural Gas Production

The United States has recently experienced a boom in oil and natural gas production. In fact, the United States has led the world in natural gas production since 2010, and the Energy Information Agency (EIA) projects gas production will grow over 40 percent by 2040. In 2014, US production of crude oil, along with liquids separated from natural gas, surpassed the world's largest producers—Saudi Arabia and Russia. The EIA projects US oil production will increase until 2020 when it will plateau and then likely decline. There is considerable uncertainty in these projections, however, because the increases in US oil and gas production are associated with drilling in shale rock formations made possible by recent innovations in drilling technologies.[28] Most oil and gas production has been derived from large pools of oil and gas that are easily recoverable via vertically drilled wells. Over time the amount of oil and gas that could be recovered in this conventional way has declined, but it is now being replaced and increased with unconventional supplies of oil and gas trapped in various shale formations in the United States.

This boom in oil and gas production has been made possible by horizontal drilling and hydraulic fracturing. Since shale formations often extend for many miles at the same depth below the surface of the Earth, the ability to drill down and then horizontally has been a game changer. Now one vertical well platform can contain several horizontal wells that recover the oil and gas for five thousand to ten thousand feet in all directions from the shale formation below. The vertical section of the well is cased with a steel lining and secured by concrete to prevent leakage from the well into surrounding rock. The horizontal section of the well is perforated with many holes so that the second key technology, hydraulic fracturing, can fracture the shale and release the oil and gas that is trapped in microscopic pores in the rock.[29]

Hydraulic fracturing (*fracking*) involves the injection of millions of gallons of water, a dozen different chemicals, and thousands of tons of silica sand under high pressure into the horizontal sections of the well. Each well requires up to 1,500 truckloads to deliver the water, sand, and well-drilling equipment to the site. The high pressure of the fracking fluid causes narrow fractures in the shale rock. The silica sand flows into these fissures to prop them open so that the oil and gas can flow through them into the well.[30] Water trapped in the shale also flows into the well along with some of the fracking fluid. As a result, dissolved salts, metal ions, and radioactive compounds end up in the well and are pumped back up to the surface as long as the well is in production. This drilling wastewater can be highly toxic and must be disposed of properly. During the drilling period, any recovered wastewater is often held in lined ponds for reuse in other wells. Other wastewater is disposed of by injecting it under high pressure into rock layers deep underground.[31]

According to a recent report by the Union of Concerned Scientists, the productivity of fracked wells can decline by up to 75 percent over their first three years. As a result, many wells are *refracked* at least once and often twice. When a well ceases to be productive economically, it is typically plugged to prevent oil and gas leaks, but some abandoned wells have not been plugged.[32] This leads us to the most important issue in terms of climate change and natural gas production.

Methane Leakage

The EIA reports that the number of producing natural gas wells has nearly doubled in the United States since 1990.[33] As a result, the amount of natural gas has grown by 31 percent,[34] and the price has declined to levels not seen since the 1990s.[35] Due to these low prices, many utilities have found they can now generate electrical power at a lower cost at natural gas-fired power plants than at coal-fired plants. As a result, natural gas-fired power production is growing, and coal-fired production is declining. The EPA attributes some of the recent decline in US GHG emissions to this switch from coal to natural gas for power production because natural gas is about half as carbon intensive as coal.[36]

As Phil points out in the case, however, some scientists are disputing the EPA's claims. The primary component of natural gas is methane

(CH_4), which is a much more potent GHG in the short term compared to carbon dioxide. For example, if the same mass of methane and carbon dioxide were introduced into the atmosphere, the methane would trap eighty-six times more heat than the carbon dioxide over the next twenty years or thirty-four times as much heat over one hundred years.[37] Thus, it is vital to reduce the emission of methane into the atmosphere now and in the future. The question is how much methane is leaking into the atmosphere from approximately 500,000 wells, 305,000 miles of pipelines, and hundreds of natural gas transfer facilities around the United States. The EPA estimates that 1.5 percent of annual natural gas extractions are lost via leakage at various points throughout this massive production and distribution system.[38] According to a study published in the *Proceedings of the National Academy of Sciences*, natural gas-fired power plants emit fewer GHG emissions compared with coal-fired plants, if the leakage rate from the natural gas wells to the power plants is less than 3.2 percent.[39]

The EPA arrives at its 1.5 percent estimate via a *bottom-up* accounting-based approach that assumes a certain amount of methane leakage from each well, pipeline, and transfer station. Some *top-down* studies have found much higher rates of methane leakage at specific points in the US natural gas system. For example, a study conducted in the Uintah Basin in Utah used aircraft and a network of towers to find that the natural gas fields in the basin leaked 6 to 12 percent of the methane produced, on average, each day during one month.[40] Another study used satellite data to discover that oil and gas basins in North Dakota and East Texas leaked 9 to 10 percent of the natural gas they produced to the atmosphere between 2006 and 2011.[41] Obviously the leakage rates reported in these studies far surpass the 3.2 percent rate noted above and are almost an order of magnitude higher than the rate estimated by the EPA.

The question is whether the leakage rates found via these top-down studies are representative of the nation as a whole. Recently a study conducted by scientists at Stanford University, the Massachusetts Institute of Technology, and the National Renewable Energy Laboratory analyzed more than two hundred technical publications that looked into methane leakage from oil and gas operations. The study concluded "recent regional atmospheric studies with very high emissions rates are unlikely to be representative of typical natural gas system leakage rates." The study also found "system-wide leakage is unlikely to be large enough to negate climate benefits of coal-to-natural gas substitution."[42]

Nevertheless, the Obama administration announced in January 2015 that the EPA would issue new regulations under section 111(b) of the Clean Air Act regarding methane emissions from oil and gas production and distribution facilities. These regulations would require the oil and gas industry to reduce emissions 40 to 45 percent below 2012 levels by

2025, but they would only apply to new or modified pieces of equipment. Studies estimate as much as 90 percent of methane emissions from the oil and gas production sector in 2018 would come from sources installed prior to 2012.[43]

Given this information, it is clear there is genuine debate among scientists about the amount of methane leakage and whether shale gas-generated electricity reduces net GHG emissions in the United States. The latter is the main motivation for Vanguard College as it considers a natural gas-fired CHP system for its campus. Given the fact that it is already entirely dependent on natural gas to heat its campus, it is understandable why it would also like to generate electricity as well as steam heat and thus save money and reduce GHG emissions over time. But what about the other environmental and social concerns raised in the case about hydraulic fracturing?

Water Quality and Use

As noted above, hydraulic fracturing involves the injection of millions of gallons of water, sand, and chemicals deep underground. Remarkably, most hydraulic fracturing operations are exempt from federal regulation under the Safe Drinking Water Act (SDWA) because of a provision inserted in the Energy Policy Act of 2005 commonly known as the Halliburton loophole. The provision prevents the EPA from applying the SDWA to fracking unless diesel fuel is used in the fracking fluid. A patchwork of varying laws and regulations constrained the activity, to some extent, in most of the twenty-eight states in 2014 where fracking was taking place, but nine states still did not have any laws regarding the disclosure of the chemicals in the fracking solution.[44]

This lack of stringent regulation is a serious problem because there have been many documented cases of groundwater being contaminated with fracking fluids. In addition, methane and volatile organic compounds have been found in groundwater supplies that furnish potable water supplies for homes and businesses.[45] While most wastewater that is not reused is disposed of by injections into deep wells, some of this water is either dumped in nearby streams or sent to public or private wastewater treatments that are often ill equipped to treat the water before it is released to surface waters.[46]

There are also legitimate concerns that the huge amount of water withdrawals required for fracking will strain local ground and surface water supplies, especially in more arid regions of the United States like the Southwest. While studies show that water use for oil and gas development is smaller than residential and industrial uses in most states, this relatively new and substantial use of water could have serious impacts at a localized level.[47]

Air Quality

The boom in US oil and gas production has also led to a significant increase of truck traffic in affected states. As noted above, each well requires up to 1,500 truckloads of water and materials. Diesel trucks emit particulate matter that is linked to asthma and other respiratory ailments and diseases. Trucks also churn up huge amounts of dust when they traverse unpaved roads, which can also cause breathing problems.[48]

Other air pollutants like ozone, methane, and volatile organic compounds are often found near drilling sites—especially near oil wells that flare natural gas that cannot be piped economically to the market. Prolonged exposure to these elements can also cause asthma and other respiratory ailments as well as cardiovascular disease and cancer. Here the EPA has been more proactive. The EPA required that *green completion* technologies—those that capture volatile organic compounds and methane from flowback water and fractured wells—be installed by January 2015.[49]

Land Use Impacts

In some areas with high rates of fracking, the construction of roads and well drilling sites can harm local ecosystems by fragmenting wildlife habitats and migration patterns (Figure 2). This construction also often results in erosion that leads to increased rates of sedimentation in surface waters, which stresses fish and other aquatic species by clouding the water, altering habitats, and reducing photosynthesis.[50] In addition, the injection of fracking wastewater under high pressure in deep wells has been linked to a rise in the number and severity of earthquakes in some parts of the United States.[51]

Socioeconomic Concerns

As Phil points out in the case, states experiencing a boom in oil and gas production due to hydraulic fracturing also typically experience a local population boom in the cities near the drilling locations. On the one hand, this amount of growth can pump a lot of money into the economy. For example, in 2011, Williston, North Dakota, experienced a 76.2 percent increase in local sales tax revenue, which surpassed every other city in the state.[52] In 2013, Williston reported an unemployment rate of 0 percent. In 2015, North Dakota led the nation with the lowest unemployment rate—2.8 percent.[53] Other significant economic benefits are land lease and royalty payments to landowners. This unexpected source of revenue has proven vital for some poor, rural families.

On the other hand, the population boom in fracking areas causes enormous strains on local roads and a wide range of public services like police and emergency services, public utilities, public schools, and vari-

Figure 2. Jonah Field in Wyoming

Photo credit: Bruce Gordon at EcoFlight. Used with permission.
Source: Flickr/Creative Commons. Used with permission.

ous social services. In addition, the increased demand for housing often drives up the cost of rental housing to levels that are no longer affordable for poor households. Increases in crime rates have also been reported in boomtowns—especially in relationship to prostitution, alcohol, and drug abuse.[54]

In the case, Professor Stimby also points out the negative impacts of *frac-sand* mining in his home state of Wisconsin. In fact, the majority of this mining takes place in the Upper Midwest through surface strip mining, and it now constitutes 41 percent of all silica sand mining in the nation. The state of Wisconsin has over one hundred mining sites alone. Reasonable health concerns have been raised about exposure to harmful silica dust by mine workers and local residents. Recently, the Occupational Safety and Health Administration issued a Hazard Alert after finding hazardous airborne silica concentrations at several sites in five different states.[55]

Conclusion

What conclusions can be drawn from all of this information? How do the ecojustice norms pertain to this case and the options before Megan and the Energy and Water Task Group at Vanguard College? Can the CHP option be justified by these norms? Would other options satisfy the norms better, or will every option include important trade-offs and some negative consequences?

Clearly this whole case revolves around the norm of sustainability.

Global warming and climate change are revealing that our current way of life is simply not sustainable. The unprecedented rate of warming ahead will have calamitous effects on the habitats and food supplies of human beings and most of Earth's other species, which is a clear violation of the sufficiency norm. We clearly need to change how we do things—including how we heat and power our homes, businesses, and institutions of higher education. We also need to change our highly consumptive lifestyles that are fueled by *cheap* fossil fuels that, in fact, are producing huge social and economic costs. As we have seen, there are a host of concerns about hydraulic fracturing that call into question continued reliance on natural gas. Nevertheless, could a CHP system at Vanguard be a bridge to a more sustainable future that would eventually be marked by greater reliance on renewable energy through a biomass heating plant and more wind turbines and solar arrays? Or would a CHP system be a *bridge to nowhere* and, in fact, a road to even more climate change due to methane leakage?

The ecojustice norms of solidarity and participation are also relevant. Should present generations be responsible for the impacts of generations that preceded them, when we have enjoyed many of the benefits fossil fuels have provided? What sacrifices should present generations have to make to better ensure the welfare of future generations? Do we actually have moral obligations to future generations? If so, what are they and why do we have them? While Vanguard's investments in energy efficiency have actually helped to keep a lid on the rising cost of an education at the college, it is likely that implementation of any of the options before the Energy and Water Task Group will probably drive up costs to some extent in the future. Most schools spend about 2 percent of their budget on energy costs. What if achieving carbon neutrality required doubling or even tripling these energy costs? Would it be fair for future students to have to pay more than those who preceded them? More specifically, given the concerns discussed above about hydraulic fracturing, would Vanguard be violating the norms of solidarity and participation if it installed a CHP system? Vanguard's current purchases of electricity produce about 50 percent of its GHG emissions, which impose a burden on future generations. A CHP system would reduce these emissions in a significant way, but it would maintain Vanguard's reliance on natural gas. Most of this gas is derived via hydraulic fracturing, and many in present and future generations are or will be burdened by these consequences. The norm of solidarity cuts both ways.

There are no easy answers in this case. The sheer inertia and pervasiveness of a fossil-fuel-based economy makes change very hard. Nevertheless, higher education institutions have an opportunity, and some would say a responsibility, to be a model for society rather than a mirror of it. Someone has to lead. Someone has to show that reducing GHG emissions at the rate required can be done. Someone has to demonstrate the potential of energy efficiency and renewable energy to power a sustainable future. The question is how that can best be done. How should Megan decide this issue? What should the Energy and Water Task Group recommend to the administration of Vanguard College?

Notes

[1]For more information on the ACUPCC, see http://acupcc.org/.

[2]Chelsea Moy, "UM Scraps Biomass Heating Plant, Apologizes for 'Eco-Terrorism' Remark," *The Missoulian*, December 3, 2011, http://missoulian.com.

[3]The commentary for the case "Maybe One" (Chapter 4) draws extensively on the Fifth Assessment Report of the Intergovernmental Panel on Climate Change issued in four volumes released in 2013 and 2014. See http://www.ipcc.ch/report/ar5/.

[4]Jerry M. Melillo, Terese (T. C.) Richmond, and Gary W. Yohe (eds.), *Climate Change Impacts in the United States: The Third National Climate Assessment* (2014), http://nca2014.globalchange.gov/.

[5]Ibid., 8.

[6]EPA, "Frequently Asked Questions about Global Warming and Climate Change," 6 (April 2009), http://www.epa.gov.

[7]Melillo, Richmond, and Yohe, *Climate Change Impacts in the United States: The Third National Climate Assessment*, 25.

[8]ACUPCC, "A Call for Climate Leadership: Progress and Opportunities in Addressing the Defining Challenge of Our Time," http://www2.presidentsclimatecommitment.org.

[9]ACUPCC, "ACUPCC Network Progress Summaries: March 2014," http://www.presidentsclimatecommitment.org.

[10]Carbon dioxide equivalent is a measure used to compare the emissions from various greenhouse gases based upon their global warming potential.

[11]EPA, "eGrid Summary Tables: Sub-Region Resource Mix" (February 2014), http://www.epa.gov.

[12]EPA, "Carbon Pollution Standards," http://www2.epa.gov.

[13]International Energy Agency, "Energy Consumption per Capita and Energy Intensity for Selected Countries, 1990–2012," http://www.iea.org.

[14]For an excellent overview of issues related to biomass as an energy source, see Union of Concerned Scientists, "How Biomass Works," http://www.ucsusa.org. See also Association for the Advancement of Sustainability in Higher Education, "Appropriate Heating or Power Plant Fuel Choices," http://www.aashe.org.

[15]Elizabeth Harball, "Scientists Urge EPA to Tread Carefully on Upcoming Biomass Emissions Rule," *ClimateWire*, June 19, 2014, http://www.eenews.net/climatewire.

[16]Wayne Washington, "USC's Biomass Plant Debacle," *The State*, October 9, 2011, http://www.thestate.com.

[17]Chelsea Moy, "UM Scraps Biomass Heating Plant, Apologizes for 'Eco-Terrorism' Remark," *The Missoulian*, December 3, 2011, http://missoulian.com.

[18]Kathryn Flagg, "Plainfield, Vermont Residents Near Goddard College Oppose Biomass Plant," *Seven Days*, January 16, 2013, http://www.sevendaysvt.com.

[19]Middlebury College, "A Milestone toward Carbon Neutrality," http://www.middlebury.edu.

[20]Joan Wickersham, "How to Boil Water—And Heat a College Campus," *Boston Globe*, January 23, 2014, http://www.bostonglobe.com.

[21]Colby College, "Biomass Plant Goes Online," January 17, 2012, https://www.colby.edu.

[22]Second Nature, "Financing Renewable Energy," http://www.secondnature.org.

[23]US Department of Energy, "On-Site Renewable Energy: Third Party Solar Financing," http://apps3.eere.energy.gov.

[24]University of New Hampshire, "Cogeneration & Ecoline (Landfill Gas)," http://www.sustainableunh.unh.edu.

[25]Lynchburg College, "LC to Get Electricity from Landfill Gas," January 23, 2014, http://www.lynchburg.edu.

[26]American Council for an Energy-Efficient Economy, "Combined Heat and Power (CHP)," http://www.aceee.org.

[27]EPA, "Combined Heat and Power: Frequently Asked Questions," http://www.epa.gov.

[28]EIA, *Annual Energy Outlook 2014—With Projections to 2040*, 25–27, http://www.eia.gov. See also Grant Smith, "U.S. Seen as Biggest Oil Producer after Overtaking Saudi Arabia," *Bloomberg News*, July 4, 2014, http://www.bloomberg.com.

[29]Gretchen Goldin, Deborah Bailin, et al., *Toward an Evidence-Based Fracking Debate: Science, Democracy, and Community Right to Know in Unconventional Oil and Gas Development*, 3–4 (October 2013), http://www.ucsusa.org.

[30]Ibid., 4–5.

[31]Ibid., 5.

[32]Ibid.

[33]EIA, "U.S. Natural Gas: Number of Gas and Gas Condensate Wells," http://www.eia.gov.

[34]EIA, "U.S. Natural Gas: Gross Withdrawals," http://www.eia.gov.

[35]EIA, "U.S. Natural Gas: Wellhead Price," http://www.eia.gov.

[36]EPA, "National Greenhouse Gas Emissions Data," http://www.epa.gov. A recent study published in *Nature*, however, says increased supplies of natural gas will not only displace coal-fired power, but also other low-carbon but more expensive sources like nuclear power and renewable energy. While low-cost power from natural gas-fired power plants will improve air quality and energy security, it will also spur economic growth and thus increase the consumption of energy overall. The study concludes that without new climate policies, abundant supplies of natural gas will have little impact on global warming and climate change. See H. McJeon et al., "Limited Impact on Decadal-Scale Climate Change from Increased Use of Natural Gas," *Nature*, October 23, 2014.

[37]IPCC, *Climate Change 2013: The Physical Science Basis*, Contribution of Working Group I to the Fifth Assessment Report of the Intergovernmental Panel on Climate Change, 714, tbl. 8.7, http://www.climatechange2013.org.

[38]Eric D. Larson, "Natural Gas and Climate Change," *Climate Central* 20 (May 2013), http://assets.climatecentral.org.

[39]Ramón A. Alvarez, Stephen Pacala, et al., "Greater Focus Needed on Methane Leakage from Natural Gas Infrastructure," *Proceedings of the National Academy of Sciences* 109, no. 17 (2012), http://www.pnas.org.

[40]Anna Karion et al., "Methane Emissions Estimate from Airborne Measurements over a Western United States Natural Gas Field," *Geophysical Research Letters*, August 28, 2013, http://onlinelibrary.wiley.com.

[41]O. Schneising et al., "Remote Sensing of Fugitive Methane Emissions from Oil and Gas Production in North American Tight Geologic Formations," *Earth's Future*, October 6, 2014.

[42]A. R. Brandt et al., "Methane Leaks from North American Natural Gas Systems," *Science* 343, no. 6172 (2014): 733, http://www.sciencemag.org. A subsequent study conducted a meta-analysis of nearly one hundred life cycle assessments of GHG emissions from the production and use of shale gas. The study concluded, "[W]e find that per unit electrical output, the central tendency of current estimates of GHG emissions from shale gas-generated electricity indicates life cycle emissions less than half those from coal and roughly equivalent to those from conventional natural gas." See Garvin A. Heath et al., "Harmonization of Initial Estimates of Shale Gas Life Cycle Greenhouse Gas Emissions for Electric Power Generation," *Proceedings of the National Academy of Sciences* 111, no. 31 (2014), http://www.pnas.org.

[43]Gayathre Vaidyanathan, "White House Announces Plan to Slash Industry's Methane Emissions," *ClimateWire*, January 14, 2015, http://www.eenews.net.

[44]Goldin, Bailin, et al., *Toward an Evidence-Based Fracking Debate*, 28.

[45]Ibid., 8.

[46]Ibid., 10.
[47]Ibid., 11.
[48]Ibid., 12.
[49]Ibid., 13.
[50]Ibid., 15.
[51]Ibid., 13.
[52]Ibid., 14.
[53]US Department of Labor, Bureau of Labor Statistics, "Unemployment Rates for States," http://www.bls.gov.
[54]Goldin, Bailin, et al., *Toward an Evidence-Based Fracking Debate*, 14. Another health and public safety issue revolves around the transfer of crude oil from fracked wells via rail to refineries. An increasing volume of oil is being shipped in this fashion, which has resulted in some dramatic and fiery accidents as well as significant delays for other passenger and freight rail service.
[55]Ibid., 16.

10

Hot Spot

Nuclear Waste, Public Responsibility, and Environmental Racism

Acronyms and Abbreviations

BIA	Bureau of Indian Affairs (US)
BLM	Bureau of Land Management (US)
DOE	Department of Energy (US)
DOI	Department of the Interior (US)
GAO	General Accounting Office (US)
MT	metric tons
NIMBY	not in my backyard (syndrome)
NRC	Nuclear Regulatory Commission (US)
PFS	Private Fuel Storage
SNF	spent nuclear fuel

Case

Maggie had a love/hate relationship with her environmental ethics class. She loved how interesting it was, but she hated how tough the problems were. Their current topic, nuclear waste storage, was really making her think hard. The topic hit close to home because the leadership of the Skull Valley Band of the Goshute Indians had wanted to host an interim storage facility for spent nuclear fuel (SNF) on their reservation about fifty miles southwest from her classroom in Salt Lake City.[1]

The Skull Valley reservation is ringed by toxic and hazardous waste facilities (Figure 1). To the south lies the Dugway Proving Grounds, where the US Army tests chemical, biological, radiological, nuclear, and other weapons and trains elite members of the US armed forces in their use. To the west is the Utah Test and Training Range, a vast swath of desert the US Air Force uses for target practice by bombers, the testing of cruise missiles, and air-to-air combat training for fighter jets. North and west of the reservation a private company, Enviro Care, landfills 93 percent of the nation's Class A, low-level nuclear waste. East of the reservation sit the Tooele Army Depot, one of the largest weapons depots in the world, and the Deseret Chemical Depot, which until recently was home to nearly 50 percent of the nation's aging stockpile of chemical weapons. From 1996 to 2012 the US Army worked around the clock to incinerate over a million rockets, missiles, and mortars packed with sarin, mustard gas, and other deadly agents. Maggie could see how a nuclear waste storage facility would fit right in.

Figure 1. Regional location of Skull Valley Indian Reservation in Utah

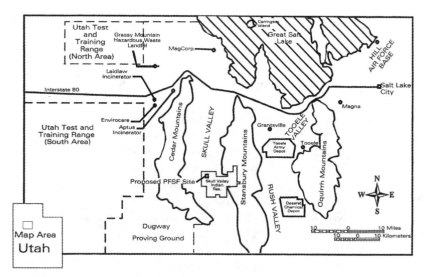

Source: US Nuclear Regulatory Commission, Office of Nuclear Material Safety and Safeguards et al., *Final Environmental Impact Statement for the Construction and Operation of an Independent Spent Fuel Storage Installation on the Reservation of the Skull Valley Band of Goshute Indians and the Related Transportation Facility in Tooele County, Utah*, NUREG-1714, Vol. 1, December 2001, Section 1, p. 2.

Professor Springs had assigned a great deal of reading about the history of nuclear power in the United States. Maggie understood why the electric utilities were frustrated. They had built nuclear reactors back in the 1960s and 1970s with the expectation that the federal government would take legal responsibility for the disposal of the waste, but that had not happened. Intentions to reprocess most of the waste had been abandoned early on, and the plan to bury the waste at a proposed repository in

Nevada's Yucca Mountain had stalled due to partisan politics in Congress. As a result, the SNF assemblies were piling up at reactor facilities around the nation, and the utilities were saddled with the expense of maintaining and providing security for their storage in cooling ponds or dry casks.

Fed up with shouldering these expenses, the utilities that own the reactors started suing the federal government to recover these costs. After the courts ruled in favor of the utilities, the Department of Energy (DOE) began settling the lawsuits. At the end of 2013, the DOE reported the US Treasury had already shelled out $3.7 billion to reimburse utilities for storage expenses and that they were on the hook for an additional $21.4 billion because the utilities can sue to recover their costs every three to four years. The costs will climb even higher if the DOE does not take legal possession of the waste and start storing it on an interim basis by 2021.[2] Given the persistent gridlock in Congress, Maggie thought this was very unlikely.

In an effort to overcome this impasse, President Barack Obama had commissioned a panel of experts to propose a way forward with regard to the management and disposal of the nation's used nuclear fuel and other high-level radioactive waste. Professor Springs had assigned as required reading the executive summary of the 180-page final report by the Blue Ribbon Commission on America's Nuclear Future.[3] While the content was clearly important, Maggie found the prose dull and bureaucratic. At the heart of the commission's recommendations were proposals for who should take responsibility for the nation's nuclear waste and how sites should be selected. The commission recommended this responsibility be shifted from the DOE to "a new, independent, government-chartered corporation" that would be focused solely on that mission. The commission also recommended that Congress amend the Nuclear Waste Policy Act (NWPA) to authorize a new "consent-based process" to select, evaluate, and license sites for interim consolidated storage and long-term disposal facilities in the future. They also recommended that Congress amend NWPA to permit one or more interim consolidated storage facilities be established independent of any schedule to construct a permanent nuclear waste repository. Professor Springs noted that Senator Lamar Alexander (R-TN) and Senator Dianne Feinstein (D-CA) had introduced the "Nuclear Waste Administration Act of 2013" to enact the commission's recommendations, but Congress had not yet taken any action on the bill.[4] Maggie wondered if they ever would.

The whole issue really came alive for Maggie, however, when the former director of Indian affairs for the state of Utah, John Chee, gave a guest lecture about the Skull Valley Goshute project. He explained that back in the late 1980s and early 1990s the Skull Valley Band of Goshute Indians was one of sixteen Native American groups that had, upon invitation by the federal government, expressed interest in serving as the host for an interim storage facility for SNF from commercial nuclear reactors. When

Congress defunded the Office of the Nuclear Waste Negotiator that had issued the invitation, a consortium of utilities that own and operate thirty-three nuclear reactors continued discussion with parties that had expressed interest in storing waste on an interim basis. In 1997, after considerable research and heated debate within the tribe, the leaders of the Skull Valley Goshutes signed a lease agreement with this consortium, Private Fuel Storage (PFS), to store up to four thousand casks of SNF on a relatively small portion of their eighteen-thousand-acre reservation for up to forty years (Figure 2). Each one of the sixteen-foot-tall steel and concrete casks would store ten metric tons (MT) of SNF with a radioactive half-life of at least ten thousand years. The casks would be stored upright on pads of reinforced concrete three feet thick. At the time, this forty thousand MT was nearly equivalent to all of the SNF that had been produced to date. By 2015, about seventy thousand MT of SNF was being stored at seventy-five sites around the nation.[5]

Figure 2. Artist's rendering of PFS storage facility on Skull Valley Goshute Reservation

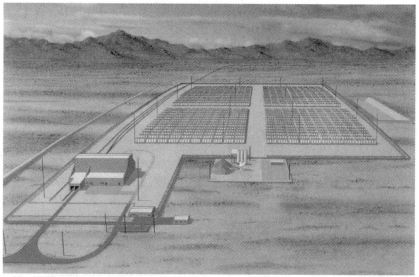

Source: Private Fuel Storage, *Response to Questions about the Operation of the Private Fuel Storage Facility: A Report to Citizens of Utah* (Salt Lake City, UT: Private Fuel Storage), February 2001. Used with permission.

Faced with this unprecedented project, some Utah citizens and Native American leaders accused PFS of engaging in environmental racism. They argued that PFS was taking advantage of a destitute tribe in a desperate economic situation. They claimed the tribe had been targeted to store the waste no one else wanted. It sure looked that way to Maggie, but John

Chee emphasized that the tribe's leadership had studied the risks very carefully. While the tribe had not been consulted when the federal government built several dangerous facilities all around their reservation, and thus had been victims of environmental racism in the past, Chee implied the tribe was not the victim of environmental racism today because it was informed and had the power to enter into the lease agreement with PFS or not. Maggie wasn't sure what to think.

Utah's legislature and governor were very opposed to the deal from the outset, and they worked tirelessly over ten years to scuttle it. They accused PFS of circumventing the will of Utah's two million citizens by hiding behind the skirt of tribal sovereignty offered by the 127 members of the Skull Valley Band. The tribe's status as a quasi-independent nation left the state of Utah with no ability to deny the project legally. State officials raised dozens of concerns in a series of multiyear public hearings and other meetings convened by the Nuclear Regulatory Commission (NRC). The Utah State Legislature funneled $1.6 million to lawyers fighting the project and left unfunded a bill promising $2 million to help the Goshutes and other tribes with economic development on their reservations. The governor of Utah, Michael Leavitt, was adamantly opposed to the Skull Valley project. He argued that Utah did not have any nuclear reactors and did not want to become the dumping ground for states that did. He seized the only county road that leads into the Skull Valley reservation and erected a sign along the highway prohibiting the transport of high-level nuclear waste. When it became clear the NRC might license the facility, the Utah congressional delegation attached a rider to a defense authorization bill that established the Cedar Mountain Wilderness Area in late 2005. Up to this point Utah's political leaders had opposed this and other proposals for new wilderness areas in Utah, but they quickly changed their stance once it became clear this new wilderness area would make it impossible for PFS to build a rail spur to the reservation to transport the SNF.

Maggie just shook her head when John Chee noted that one of the seven special provisions in the bill stipulated that "nothing . . . shall preclude low-level overflights and operations of military aircraft, helicopters, missiles, or unmanned aerial vehicles over the covered wilderness, including military overflights and operations that can be seen or heard within the covered wilderness."[6] Maggie laughed out loud when Chee put up a PowerPoint slide with the following warning from the Bureau of Land Management (BLM): "Because of the proximity of military test and training ranges to the wilderness area, always be on the lookout for unexploded military ordnance. Do not touch or move any suspicious objects you may find."[7] Some wilderness area, she thought.

Despite all this opposition by the state of Utah, the NRC issued a license to PFS for the Skull Valley facility in February 2006—about ten years after the lease agreement had been signed between PFS and the Goshutes. The

NRC had studied a host of issues over the decade, including the potential for a terrorist attack on the site, fighter jets colliding and crashing into the site, and the potential for the release of radioactivity during transportation of waste to the facility. The NRC had concluded the threats were small and that the waste could be stored in casks for up to forty years at the reservation without jeopardizing the health and safety of those on the reservation or in the area nearby. Two other federal agencies had to weigh in on the project, however, and they both entered negative decisions in 2007 at the end of the George W. Bush administration.[8] The tribe and PFS challenged these decisions in court, and a federal district court judge ruled in 2010 that the reasons given by the BLM and the Bureau of Indian Affairs (BIA) were arbitrary and capricious.[9] The judge kicked the case back to these federal agencies to come up with better reasons to oppose the project.

About the same time, the utilities that were members of PFS were being awarded financial settlements by the US Treasury to reimburse them for the cost of storing SNF at their reactor sites. In addition, the NRC decided SNF could remain stored in wet cooling ponds and in dry steel and concrete casks at reactor sites for an indefinite period.[10] Both of these developments took some of the urgency out of the Skull Valley project and led some of the utilities in PFS to decide it was time to "cut their losses" and walk away. They had spent $70 million to $80 million on the project over about fifteen years, and they would have to spend even more to work through the issues that had been raised by the BIA and the BLM and to pay the annual $250,000 licensing fee to the NRC. Much to the dismay of the tribe, PFS informed the NRC in late 2012 that they wanted to relinquish their license. The NRC offered to waive their fees, however, and later changed their rules so that fees only have to be paid for facilities that are up and operating.

Given these changes, PFS decided to retain their license and resumed conversations with the tribe about moving forward with the project. Their new goal was to have the DOE take legal responsibility for the waste and lease the Skull Valley facility to the federal government as the nation's first consolidated interim storage site for SNF. At this point, however, both parties realized the clock had run out on their lease agreement. John Chee reported that confidential negotiations took place between the tribe and PFS during 2014, but in early 2015 PFS informed the tribe, once again, that they had decided to abandon the project and relinquish their license to the NRC. Nearly twenty years after the project began, the tribe was left high and dry.

When the class was over, Maggie pulled out her course syllabus and reread the prompt for the paper she had to write on the subject of nuclear waste storage:

> Should the United States leave spent nuclear fuel stored in place at over seventy locations around the United States until Congress passes

legislation to implement the Blue Ribbon Commission's recommendations for the management and disposal of nuclear waste, or would
it have been better for the PFS project at the Skull Valley Goshute
Indian Reservation to move ahead while we wait for Congress to pass
legislation that takes a consent-based approach to the management
and disposal of nuclear waste? In either case justify your decision
by appealing to the ecojustice norms and explain whether you think
the Goshutes have been the victims of environmental racism or not.

The paper was due in a week.

Commentary

This case raises important ethical questions about the fairest way for
present generations to share the burden of storing high-level nuclear waste
that poses great dangers to current and future generations. It also raises
questions about the responsible use of tribal sovereignty and the threat
of environmental racism.[11] From the perspective of ecological justice, the
sustainability and sufficiency norms are certainly relevant, but the major
ethical issues revolve around participation and solidarity.

The participation norm emphasizes that all forms of life are important,
and their interests must be heard and respected in the decisions that affect
their lives. The norm is concerned with empowerment and seeks to remove
obstacles to participation constructed by various social, economic, and
political forces and institutions. The norm puts importance on open debate
and dialogue and seeks to hear the voices or perspective of all concerned.

The solidarity norm emphasizes the kinship and interdependence of
all forms of life and encourages extra support and assistance for the
most vulnerable, particularly those who suffer. The norm highlights the
fundamental communal nature of life in contrast to individualism and
encourages individuals and groups to join together in common cause and
stand with those who are the victims of discrimination, abuse, and oppression. Underscoring the reciprocal relationship of individual welfare
and the common good, solidarity calls for the powerful to share the plight
of the powerless, for the rich to listen to the poor, and for humanity to
recognize its fundamental interdependence with the rest of nature.

Both norms are highly relevant to the following saga regarding the
storage and disposal of high-level nuclear waste in the United States.

Sharing the Burden of Nuclear Waste Disposal

The United States has more nuclear reactors than any other nation
in the world.[12] In 2015, there were sixty-one commercial nuclear power

plants with ninety-nine nuclear reactors operating in thirty states. These facilities produce almost 20 percent of the nation's electricity and serve approximately fifty million people. Over 90 percent of these reactors are located east of Utah.[13] There are also seventeen reactors at fourteen sites that are no longer in service and are now undergoing decommissioning.[14]

Each nuclear reactor is fueled with enriched uranium oxide that is approximately 4 percent fissile uranium-235 and 96 percent nonfissile uranium-238. The uranium is cast into hard pellets and stacked inside long metal tubes called fuel rods. The rods are bundled into fuel assemblies that are twelve to fourteen feet long. Once the rods are in close proximity to each other, the neutrons from the fission of the U-235 become dense enough to sustain a chain reaction that releases enormous heat. This heat is used to produce steam to run an electrical generator. Depending on the reactor's design, a typical commercial nuclear power reactor in the United States contains two hundred to five hundred fuel assemblies, totaling approximately one hundred MT of uranium oxide. Each assembly will power a reactor for four to six years, after which it can no longer efficiently produce energy and is considered used or spent.[15]

The SNF that has been removed from a reactor is thermally hot and highly radioactive. Each spent fuel assembly can deliver a fatal radiation dose in minutes to anyone nearby who is not adequately protected. To protect workers, and to dissipate the heat from the fuel rods, the fuel assemblies are placed in steel racks in deep pools filled with water. The SNF is stored in these cooling ponds for at least five years, but many US reactor sites have had fuel rod assemblies in "wet" storage for several decades. "According to the DOE, through 2012 approximately 50,000 MT of SNF fuel was being stored in 'wet' pools in the United States and another 15,000 MT was being stored in 'dry' steel and concrete casks outside or nearby reactor facilities at 75 sites in 33 states"[16] (Figure 3).

US commercial nuclear reactors produce an additional 2,000 to 2,400 MT of SNF on an annual basis. If the industry does not expand significantly in the years ahead, the total inventory of SNF by 2050 is projected to be below 150,000 MT. Under a high-growth scenario, however, the inventory of SNF would significantly exceed 200,000 MT by midcentury. Even if all commercial reactors in the United States were shut down tomorrow, about 75,000 MT would require short-term storage and long-term disposal.[17]

The amount of SNF produced to date is fairly small when measured by volume. It could be stored in an area the size of a football field to a height of approximately twenty feet. The problem is that the waste is highly radioactive and toxic for thousands of years. A recent report by the US General Accounting Office (GAO), the nonpartisan, investigative arm of Congress, summarizes the danger:

Figure 3. Commercial spent nuclear fuel stored in wet, dry, and shutdown storage sites

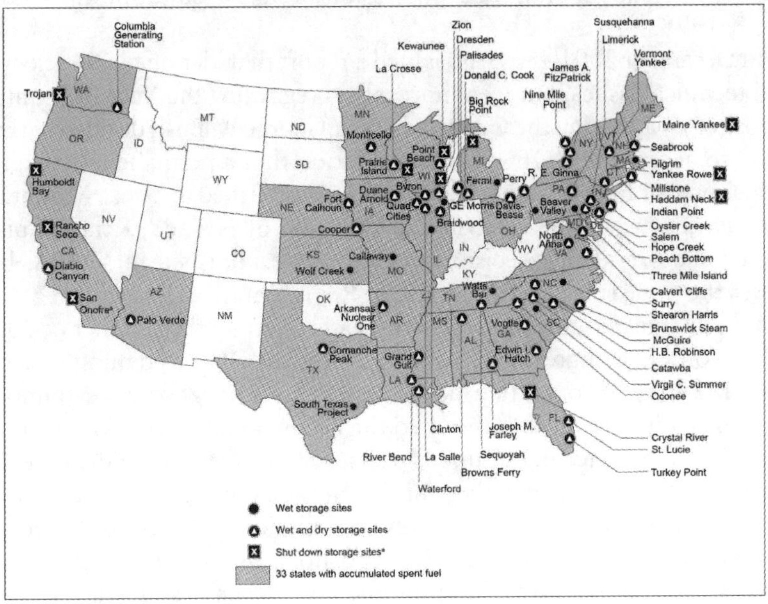

Source: U.S. Government Accountability Office, *Spent Nuclear Fuel Management: Outreach Needed to Help Gain Public Acceptance for Federal Activities That Address Liability,* October 2014, GAO-15-141, 13, http://www.gao.gov/assets/670/666454.pdf.

Spent nuclear fuel is considered one of the most hazardous substances on Earth. Without protective shielding, its intense radioactivity can kill a person exposed directly to it within minutes or cause cancer in those who receive smaller doses. Although some elements of spent nuclear fuel cool and decay quickly, becoming less radiologically dangerous, others remain dangerous to human health and the environment for tens of thousands of years.[18]

This danger for future generations is a certain violation of the solidarity norm if the waste is not stored safely. It also threatens the sustainability norm. Passing along tons of highly radioactive waste for future generations hardly seems a fair and sustainable way to live.

In 1957 a report by the US National Academy of Sciences concluded a geologic repository would be the safest and most secure method of isolating SNF and other types of nuclear waste from humans and the environment. In 1982, Congress passed the NWPA, which directed the DOE to begin studying sites for an underground geological repository. In 1987, responding to constituents who were concerned that nuclear waste might be stored permanently in their state, Congress amended the

NWPA to require the DOE to focus on developing Yucca Mountain in Nevada as the site for the permanent repository. Congress also required the DOE to start taking legal possession of SNF from utilities by January 1, 1998.[19]

In December 2001, the GAO issued a report that identified 293 scientific and technical issues that were unresolved regarding the Yucca Mountain repository.[20] Ignoring the GAO, President George W. Bush decided early in 2002 to accept the DOE's recommendation that a permanent geological repository for high-level nuclear waste be established at Yucca Mountain. Shortly afterward, the governor of the state of Nevada, Kenny Guinn, vetoed the president's decision under rules established in NWPA, but, under the same rules, the US House of Representatives and the US Senate voted by large margins to override Nevada's veto in the summer of 2002. These votes in Congress cleared the way for the DOE to request a license from the NRC to operate a permanent repository at Yucca Mountain. The Bush administration submitted the license application in 2008 at the end of its second term, but under pressure from Senate Majority Leader Harry Reid and other members of the Nevada congressional delegation, the Obama administration withdrew the application in 2010 and vowed never to open the Yucca Mountain repository. In 2013, a federal appeals court ruled the NRC was "flouting the law" when it stopped reviewing the proposed nuclear waste dump at the request of the Obama administration.[21] While the Obama administration will likely remain opposed to Yucca Mountain through the end of 2016, there is far more support for the project among Republicans.

To date, the federal government has spent over $15 billion studying the scientific feasibility of establishing a permanent repository for high-level nuclear waste and SNF at Yucca Mountain in Nevada.[22] If and when Yucca Mountain does open, however, it will be too small to accommodate the amount of SNF produced to date. In 2008, the DOE notified the president and Congress that the United States needs a second underground geological repository to store the increasing amount of commercially produced SNF and other high-level radioactive waste.[23]

Until the federal government takes legal possession of the SNF, however, the generators and owners of this waste have the responsibility both to provide and pay for the interim storage of it. This is what led the eight utilities that are members of the PFS consortium to explore the possibility of operating an interim storage facility on the Skull Valley Goshute Indian Reservation in Utah. As the case notes, this project was highly controversial and was uniformly opposed by Utah's governor, legislature, and congressional delegation. The state felt it had no say in the matter. It argued that the interests of millions of Utah citizens were not being considered and respected—a clear violation of the participation norm.

President Obama announced the formation of a Blue Ribbon Commission on America's Nuclear Future in January 2010. The commission met more than two dozen times between March 2010 and January 2012 to hear testimony from experts and stakeholders, and to visit nuclear waste management facilities in the United States and abroad. The commission's 180-page report is an invaluable resource that is hard to summarize in this short commentary. It is possible, however, to list the eight key elements in the strategy they recommended:

1. A new, consent-based approach to siting future nuclear waste management facilities.
2. A new organization dedicated solely to implementing the waste management program and empowered with the authority and resources to succeed.
3. Access to the funds nuclear utility ratepayers are providing for the purpose of nuclear waste management.
4. Prompt efforts to develop one or more geologic disposal facilities.
5. Prompt efforts to develop one or more consolidated storage facilities.
6. Prompt efforts to prepare for the eventual large-scale transport of SNF and high-level waste to consolidated storage and disposal facilities when such facilities become available.
7. Support for continued US innovation in nuclear energy technology and for workforce development.
8. Active US leadership in international efforts to address safety, waste management, nonproliferation, and security concerns.

Based on these recommendations, the DOE announced one year later in January 2013 that it was adopting "a new phased, adaptive, and consent-based" strategy for the management and disposal of used nuclear fuel and high-level radioactive waste. Assuming Congress passes the appropriate enabling legislation, the DOE plans to implement a program over the next ten years that:

- Sites, designs and licenses, constructs and begins operations of a pilot interim storage facility by 2021 with an initial focus on accepting used nuclear fuel from shut-down reactor sites;
- Advances toward the siting and licensing of a larger interim storage facility to be available by 2025 that will have sufficient capacity to provide flexibility in the waste management system and allows for acceptance of enough used nuclear fuel to reduce expected government liabilities;
- Makes demonstrable progress on the siting and characterization of repository sites to facilitate the availability of a geologic repository by 2048.[24]

It is interesting to compare the Blue Ribbon Commission's recommendations for a consent-based approach and a new federal organization focused solely on the management and disposal of nuclear waste with a similar though short-lived initiative in the late 1980s and early 1990s. In 1987, Congress amended NWPA to create the Office of the Nuclear Waste Negotiator. The office was created as "an independent establishment in the executive branch" and the nuclear waste negotiator was appointed by the president with the advice and consent of the Senate. The sole mission of the negotiator was "to attempt to find a State or Indian tribe willing to host a repository or monitored retrievable storage facility at a technically qualified site on reasonable terms" and to "negotiate with any State or Indian tribe which expresses an interest in hosting a repository or monitored retrievable storage facility."[25]

In May 1991, the Office of the Nuclear Waste Negotiator sent letters to every state, county, and federally recognized tribe in the country inviting interest in hosting an interim nuclear storage facility and offering grants for further study. Only four US counties responded and submitted applications for Phase I study grants: Grant County (ND), Apache County (NM), San Juan County (UT), and Fremont County (WY). Objections by state governors and widespread public opposition prevented the four counties from moving forward. At the same time, sixteen Native American tribes applied for the Phase I study grants, and four also received Phase II grants. When members of the public learned about these possibilities, they complained to their legislators. As a result, Congress ceased funding for the Office of the Nuclear Waste Negotiator in October 1993.[26]

Given this history, Maggie, in the case, legitimately wonders whether Congress will pass the enabling legislation to implement the Blue Ribbon Commission's recommendations and DOE's new nuclear waste strategy. Even if legislation is passed, will public outcry over the prospect of nuclear waste stored or buried nearby result again in the elimination of funding for this work? Given the dysfunctional way Americans have dealt with nuclear waste thus far, this seems a fair question to ask. This brings us back to the Skull Valley Goshute/PFS project in the case. Would this have been an ethically acceptable way to achieve the goal of establishing an interim storage facility for SNF? How would the ecojustice norms apply?

As noted above, the solidarity norm encourages individuals and groups to join together in common cause and stand with those who are the victims of discrimination, abuse, and oppression. The participation norm is concerned with empowerment and seeks to remove all obstacles to participation constructed by various social, economic, and political forces and institutions. On the basis of these two norms, was the PFS proposal to store SNF temporarily on the Skull Valley Goshute Indian Reservation a violation of solidarity and an example of environmental racism and environmental injustice, or were the Goshutes simply exercising their legitimate right of tribal sovereignty?

The Skull Valley Goshute/PFS Project

The Skull Valley Band of the Goshute Indians is one of 554 Indian nations within the boundaries of the United States. Today, the lands of these native peoples comprise only 56 million acres on 314 reservations and amount to less than 2 percent of the nation's land mass.[27] The Skull Valley Band of the Goshute Indians traces its claim to tribal sovereignty back to the peace treaty they signed with Abraham Lincoln in 1863 and the executive orders that Woodrow Wilson signed fifty years later establishing their reservation. Like other tribes, the Goshutes had to give up vast swaths of land and other concessions in order to gain the right of self-governance on tribal homelands and reservations. Anthropologists think that originally there may have been as many as ten thousand Goshutes roaming the Great Basin between Nevada's Ruby Mountains and Utah's Wasatch Range. After the first settlers arrived in 1847, the Goshute population dropped to less than one thousand as it was besieged by hunger and sickness. Today the Skull Valley Band has dwindled to 127 adult members, with less than 30 living on its reservation.[28]

As the case points out, the Skull Valley Goshute Indian Reservation is ringed by toxic and hazardous waste facilities. Trapped in this desolate and degraded landscape, the financial situation of the Goshutes is dire. The tribe looked into selling bottled water from springs on the reservation but concluded few will want to buy water they fear may be laced with toxic substances released over nearly two decades by the nearby chemical weapons incinerator. The tribe also considered vegetable farming, but it feared the land was still polluted by a nerve gas experiment at the Dugway Proving Grounds that went awry in the 1960s and killed many sheep. Faced with few options, the tribe explored the costs and benefits associated with storing high-level nuclear waste on its reservation.

The Skull Valley Goshutes are one of the sixteen Native American tribes that expressed interest when the federal government's short-lived Office of the Nuclear Waste Negotiator invited communities around the United States to consider hosting a facility for the interim storage of SNF. In 1992 the office awarded the tribe a $100,000 grant to do a preliminary study. Upon completion of that study, the tribe's executive committee concluded it was in the best interests of the tribe to pursue the matter further. Shortly thereafter, the federal agency awarded the tribe a $200,000 grant to study the possibility in greater detail. These funds were used primarily to tour nuclear storage facilities in the United States, France, Sweden, England, and Japan. The tribe also used grant funds to visit with environmental groups like Greenpeace that oppose interim nuclear waste storage facilities.[29]

Upon conclusion of the second phase of the study process, the General Council of the Skull Valley Band met to receive a report from the leadership. The General Council consists of the members of the tribe who are age eighteen and older. A majority agreed at this meeting that the tribe should offer its reservation as an interim storage site. Then Congress eliminated funding for the Office of the Nuclear Waste Negotiator.

Cut off now from a federal contract, yet still convinced that interim nuclear waste storage was in their best interests, the Goshutes decided to pursue a relationship directly with the electric utilities. Over the course of six months in 1996–97, the Goshutes negotiated a lease agreement with PFS, a consortium of eight utility companies that own and operate thirty-three nuclear reactors around the United States[30] (Figure 4). In December 1996, more than two-thirds of the tribe's General Council signed a resolution authorizing the tribe's executive committee to sign the lease agreement with PFS.[31]

Figure 4. Locations of PFS reactors in the United States

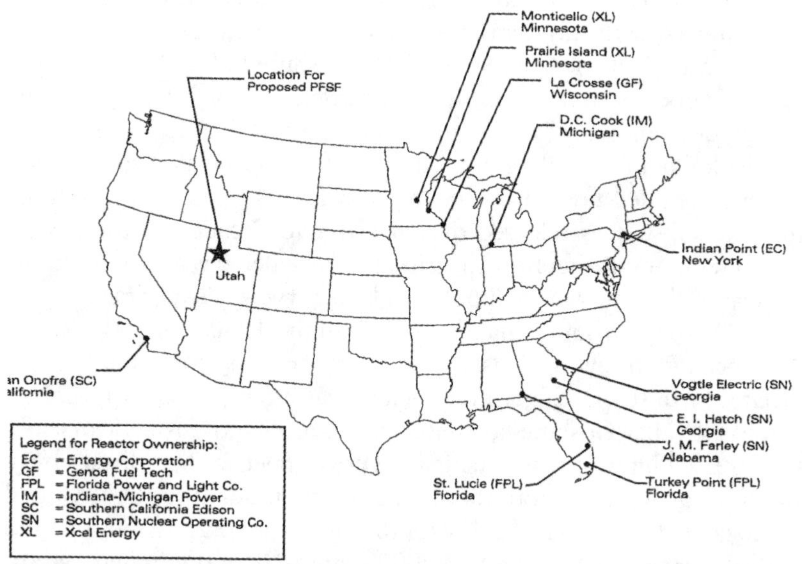

Source: US Nuclear Regulatory Commission, Office of Nuclear Material Safety and Safeguards et al., *Final Environmental Impact Statement for the Construction and Operation of an Independent Spent Fuel Storage Installation on the Reservation of the Skull Valley Band of Goshute Indians and the Related Transportation Facility in Tooele County, Utah,* NUREG-1714, Vol. 1, December 2001, Section 1, p. 4.

Shortly after the NRC commenced its review of the lease agreement in 1997, several members of the tribe publicly expressed their opposition to the plan. Some sued the BIA for supporting the lease agreement but lost in federal district court. Others complained the tribe's leadership distributed "dividends" from PFS only to members of the tribe who supported the proposal. In September 2001, thirty-eight dissident members gathered to elect new leadership for the tribe. The BIA later deemed the election illegitimate because it did not include a majority of the adult members.[32] More recently, a YouTube video surfaced that featured two members of the tribe who held opposing views about signing a new lease agreement for the project.[33] What this reveals is that there has been significant disagreement and discord among members of the tribe about the terms of the original lease agreement and the wisdom of the project. However, few major policy decisions at any level of government lack serious and substantial opposition. It should come as no surprise that the Goshutes were not fully united about the nuclear waste storage plan. Undoubtedly they are not fully united today. Nevertheless, the tribe's leadership was ready to negotiate a new lease agreement with PFS.

After nine years of review that explored a wide range of health, safety, and legal issues, the NRC issued a license to PFS for the Skull Valley facility on February 21, 2006. The NRC concluded that the facility could be operated safely and posed no significant danger to the Goshutes and the surrounding area.[34] As the case notes, however, the NRC was not the only federal agency that needed to approve key aspects of the project. The BLM and the BIA both issued negative decisions in September 2006.

The BLM offered two main arguments to justify its decision.[35] It argued first that the newly established Cedar Mountain Wilderness Area precluded BLM approval of PFS's application to build a rail spur to the Skull Valley facility because a portion of this railway would be constructed within the new federal wilderness area. The BLM also rejected the alternative of transporting SNF to the facility by heavy trucks. The BLM argued this option would impede traffic on the two-lane road leading to the reservation, which served as one of only three emergency evacuation routes for the chemical weapons incinerator then operating in Tooele Valley. The BLM noted also that traffic on this twenty-foot-wide county road had increased significantly since the tribe signed an agreement in 2005 to landfill baled municipal waste generated in and around Salt Lake City on a portion of the reservation. Each day 130 to 160 garbage trucks haul baled waste to the reservation. The BLM thought these garbage trucks would jeopardize the safety of the two trucks per week that would be hauling SNF to the storage facility during daylight hours at speeds below ten miles per hour.[36]

The BIA based its decision in part on the transportation issues in the BLM ruling, but it also offered additional reasons for not approving the final draft of the lease agreement. The BIA emphasized that the NRC had concluded that SNF "is safely stored at the locations where it is currently located."[37] It also emphasized that the local BIA official "acted outside the scope of his delegated authority, and in violation of BIA policy when he conditionally approved the 1997 lease."[38] Finally, the BIA said it lacked confidence that the SNF would ever be removed from the Skull Valley Goshute Indian Reservation despite the assurances regarding this matter in the lease agreement and the legal conditions in the NRC license.

In 2007, the tribe and PFS filed an appeal against these two decisions in the Tenth US District Court of Appeals. In the summer of 2010, the court ruled in favor of the tribe and PFS when it vacated the decisions by the BLM and BIA and remanded the right-of-way application and the Goshute-PFS lease agreement to the Department of the Interior (DOI) for further consideration. The judge was scathing in his criticism of the two agencies.[39]

What are we to make of these developments? Did the BIA and BLM protect the Skull Valley Band from becoming victims of environmental racism, or did they vitiate the band's tribal sovereignty with their decisions?

Environmental Racism and the Skull Valley Goshutes

Grace Thorpe, a Native American activist and ardent opponent of nuclear power, complained in the 1990s that tribes like the Skull Valley Goshutes were "selling our sovereignty" to utilities that will benefit from it in order to store their nuclear waste on their reservation. Thorpe said, "The issue is not [tribal] sovereignty. The issue is Mother Earth's preservation and survival. The issue is environmental racism."[40] It would be false, however, to give the impression that all Native Americans share Thorpe's views. In fact, several tribes have refused to take a stand on the issue and have also affirmed the sovereign right of the Goshutes to make decisions with which they might disagree.

Clearly some Native Americans inside and outside of the tribe have thought storing high-level nuclear waste on the reservation is a misuse of tribal sovereignty, but a majority of the Skull Valley Goshutes have thought locating a temporary storage facility for SNF on their reservation is in the best interests of the tribe. On the one hand, the participation norm requires respect for the moral agency and tribal sovereignty of the Skull Valley Goshutes. On the other hand, the justice norm asks whether the destitution of the tribe left it with no real choice. If the latter was true, was this a case of environmental racism?

The term *environmental racism* was coined in 1982 by the Reverend Benjamin Chavez, the future director of the National Association for the Advancement of Colored People, while protesting the dumping of highly toxic polychlorinated biphenyls in Warren County, North Carolina. Evidence of environmental racism can be found in the disproportionate number of waste facilities and polluting industries located in or near communities of people of color. Evidence of environmental racism can also be found in the way environmental laws have been enforced, or not enforced, in white communities and communities of people of color. Environmental racism pertains not only to actions that have a racist *intent*, but also to actions that have a racist *impact*. It occurs when people of color are either targeted or bear a disproportionate level of the burden created by the disposal of toxic wastes or the pollution produced by industry. *Environmental justice* broadens the scope of this concern to include people of any race, class, or income level.[41]

President Bill Clinton signed an executive order in February 1994 establishing environmental justice as a national priority.[42] Under this order, the BIA is required to conduct an environmental justice review of contracts involving the lease of Indian trust lands that may adversely impact Native American tribes. NRC staff worked together with staff from the BIA and other cooperating federal agencies to review the PFS-Goshute project. This environmental justice review featured "an analysis of the human health and environmental impacts on low-income and minority populations" resulting from activities related to the PFS-Goshute facility. Following NRC policy, the staff focused their impact assessment primarily within a four-mile radius around the Skull Valley Indian reservation, though a fifty-mile radius was utilized to examine the impact of transportation of SNF casks on low-income and minority populations in the area. The study concluded "the cumulative effect of the proposed [storage facility] and other activities on environmental justice concerns . . . is small."[43]

Despite this official finding with regard to environmental justice, some would argue the PFS storage agreement nevertheless constitutes a case of environmental racism. In many respects, storage of SNF rods on the reservation of a Native American tribe could be viewed as the completion of a painful circle of death and exploitation. The vast majority of the mining and milling of uranium in the United States since 1950 has taken place on or adjacent to Indian reservations. Approximately 25 percent of the fifteen thousand workers employed in these activities were members of various tribes, especially Navajos. A large number of these workers eventually were diagnosed with diseases and other health problems caused by exposure to radiation.[44] In addition, Native Americans not directly engaged in uranium extraction and processing have been subjected to dangers posed by groundwater contamination, radon exposure, and pollution of the air via tailings dust. Studies indicate that Indians living near uranium mines face the same health risks as those engaged in mining.[45]

This brief history reveals that Native Americans have borne a disproportionate share of the burdens associated with mining fuel for nuclear reactors, and the Skull Valley Goshutes would have borne higher risks associated with storing the spent fuel. At the same time, Native Americans are by far the nation's most underserved constituency when it comes to receiving the benefits of nuclear energy (or any form of electricity generation). Many reservations lack basic electricity infrastructure even though they are adjacent to uranium and coal mining areas and coal-fired power plants. For some, this lack of access to electricity is clear evidence of environmental racism and injustice.

Conclusion

It is clear that the storage, transportation, and ultimate disposal of high-level nuclear waste is a major public policy issue on the verge of becoming a national crisis. From California to New York, people all around the nation are saying, "Not in my backyard!" (NIMBY). This NIMBY syndrome led Congress to focus solely on Yucca Mountain as a permanent repository in the first place. All citizens of the United States must shoulder some of the blame for failing to muster the political will to deal with this problem in an effective way. In many respects, US citizens driven by the NIMBY syndrome helped to drop this issue in the laps of the Goshutes. Over fifty million people in the nation enjoy the benefits of nuclear power, but most refuse to accept the burdens associated with its waste.

Some environmentalists see this waste bottleneck as the most effective way to bring an end to the nuclear energy industry in the United States. When utilities run out of places to store SNF on an interim basis, federal law requires them to shut down the reactors. Over time, this means the United States would have to find other ways to either produce or conserve 20 percent of the nation's current electricity supply. Investments in renewable energy production and energy efficiency, together with changes in patterns of energy consumption, could meet this challenge, but none of these measures resolve the issue of what to do with the nuclear waste.

Even if nuclear waste is not produced in the future, the United States is still faced with the challenge of storing temporarily or disposing permanently the high-level nuclear waste that has been produced to date. This raises the question of whether it would be better to store existing stockpiles at over seventy locations around the country or to consolidate these stockpiles in one place. PFS contended that it would be more cost effective and easier to provide a high level of security if much of the nation's SNF was stored in one place. The state of Utah, however, argued that if it is safe to store SNF where it is now, then it should remain where it is—possibly in perpetuity.

There lies the rub. The radioactivity of some elements in SNF has a half-life of at least ten thousand years, and a few have a half-life that extends for hundreds of thousands of years.[46] Is it ethically responsible to store thousands of steel and concrete casks containing this waste above ground at over seventy locations around the nation for up to and perhaps beyond the one-hundred-year rated life of these casks? Is it safer to entomb such highly radioactive waste in a geological repository deep underground? Like it or not, and absent any new alternative strategies, disposal underground still appears to be the best option. But Yucca Mountain is not open and the DOE's new strategy doesn't plan to open a permanent repository until 2048—fifty years after Yucca Mountain was supposed to open.

So, who should bear the burden (and reap the benefits) from storing the nation's high-level nuclear waste, either on an interim or a permanent basis? On the face, it seems clear that those who benefit the most from nuclear energy should also shoulder most of the waste burden. But how realistic is it to expect that millions of people in thirty-one states will abandon the NIMBY syndrome in order to muster the courage and political will to address this problem in a responsible manner?[47] Isn't it more likely that they will still try to externalize their costs by dumping the problem on others?

This brings us back to the PFS-Goshute interim storage plan. Whereas most US residents live a middle-class lifestyle or better, virtually all Goshutes on and off the reservation live below the poverty line. In addition, while most people in the United States are members of the white, dominant culture, the Goshutes are members of a tribe that now constitutes a tiny fraction of its former glory. The tribe hoped some members would qualify for jobs building and operating the storage facility. Once operational, revenues from the lease agreement would have provided private health care for tribal members on the reservation who now have to travel over two hundred miles to the closest office of the Indian Health Services. In addition, lease revenues would have been utilized to build a religious and cultural center on the reservation to help the band preserve their disappearing heritage. Finally, funds would have been used to encourage members of the band to return to the reservation through subsidized housing construction and other infrastructure improvements.[48]

Examining the proposal from these financial and health perspectives, it is clear that there would have been significant benefits for the Skull Valley Goshutes. But what about cultural concerns? Was the tribe selling its soul to accept the waste? Would the storage facility have been an insult or betrayal of Mother Earth? Were the Goshutes threatening the foundations of their very culture through this *misuse* of tribal sovereignty? These are troubling questions, but why do many who do not lose sleep over the invention and use of nuclear energy expect Native Americans to maintain a principled opposition to storing nuclear waste on religious terms? Is it possible for Indian cultures to embrace the costs and benefits of certain technologies just as other cultures have done around the world? Are Native Americans put on a pedestal and expected to live up to some environmental ideal that most people conveniently do not apply to themselves?

In the end, it is clear that those who have produced the waste should bear the burden of dealing with it. Both the nuclear utilities and their customers have benefited greatly from nuclear power, but the burdens, costs, and externalities associated with its waste are being displaced onto future generations. At the very least, the norm of solidarity requires us to bear some of the burden that is carried by others. The Blue Ribbon Commission and the DOE strategy seek to accept this national responsibility, but the political headwinds are strong. Is it completely out of the question, therefore, to see the limited good (and harm) this project could have done for the Skull Valley Goshutes while the United States strives yet again to build a political consensus to deal with nuclear waste? Would it have been beyond the pale of ethical respectability for the Goshutes to store temporarily most of the SNF produced in the United States? Or was this, truly, one of the most egregious cases of environmental racism to date? Maggie has a lot to think about.

Notes

[1]This case continues to explore issues raised in "Skull Valley: Nuclear Waste, Environmental Racism, and Tribal Sovereignty," which was published in *Christian Environmental Ethics* (Maryknoll, NY: Orbis Books, 2003), 218–52. Two high-level, confidential sources associated with the Skull Valley Goshutes and PFS provided valuable information about recent developments.

[2]GAO, "Disposal of High-Level Nuclear Waste," http://www.gao.gov. Originally the utilities asked to be reimbursed from the federal Nuclear Waste Fund that was established by the Nuclear Waste Policy Act of 1982 as a way to fund the research and construction of a permanent geological repository. Per the terms of the law, the utilities that operate nuclear power plants have been charging ratepayers $0.001 per kilowatt hour and transferring these funds to the Nuclear Waste Fund. More than $30 billion had been collected by the end of 2014. On November 19, 2013, the US Court of Appeals for the District of Columbia Circuit ruled the federal government could no longer collect fees for nuclear waste storage until it finds a way to store the waste permanently. The fees that have been collected cannot be used to pay the settlement fees to utilities that are recovering interim storage costs in the federal courts. The settlement fees are paid out of a special fund in the US Treasury Department. See Keith Johnson, "Court Orders Government to Stop Collecting Nuclear-Waste Fees," *Wall Street Journal*, November 19, 2013, http://online.wsj.com.

[3]DOE, *Blue Ribbon Commission's Nuclear Future Report to the Secretary of Energy* (December 2012), http://www.energy.gov.

[4]US Senate Committee on Energy and Natural Resources, "Senators Introduce Bipartisan, Comprehensive Nuclear Waste Legislation," http://www.energy.senate.gov.

[5]GAO, "Disposal of High-Level Nuclear Waste."

[6]Wilderness.net, "Wilderness Special Provisions, Cedar Mountains Wilderness," http://www.wilderness.net.

[7]BLM, "Cedar Mountains Wilderness FAQs," http://www.blm.gov.

[8]DOI, BLM, "Record of Decision Addressing Right-of-Way Applications U76985 and U76986 to Transport Spent Nuclear Fuel to the Reservation of the Skull Valley Band of Goshute Indians," *Federal Register* 71, no. 188, September 28, 2006, http://www.gpo.gov; DOI, BIA, "Record of Decision for the Construction and Operation of an Independent Spent Fuel Storage Installation (ISFSI) on the Reservation of the Skull Valley Band of Goshute Indians (Band) in Tooele County, Utah," *Federal Register*, 71, no. 192, October 4, 2006, http://www.gpo.gov.

[9]Skull Valley Band of Goshute Indians v. Davis, 728 F.Supp. 2d 1287 (D. Utah 2010), http://www.ecases.us.

[10]NRC, "Continued Storage of Spent Nuclear Fuel," *Federal Register*, 79, no. 182, September 19, 2014. See also David McIntyre, "'Continued Storage'—What It Means and What It Doesn't," September 4, 2014, http://public-blog.nrc-gateway.gov. In October 2014, three states (Vermont, New York, and Connecticut) and nine environmental organizations filed a petition in the US Court of Appeals for the District of Columbia seeking a rehearing of the NRC "waste confidence decision." At issue is the NRC's conclusion that SNF can be stored safely for up to sixty years after a plant is closed, or indefinitely if a permanent repository isn't built. The parties argue the latter violates the National Environmental Policy Act. See Hannah Northey, "Three Northeastern States Vow to Fight NRC Waste Rule," *E&E News PM*, October 27, 2014; "Green Groups Join States' Fight Against Waste Policy Rule," *E&E News PM*, October 29, 2014, http://www.eenews.net/pm.

[11]This commentary expands and updates information presented in the commentary for "Skull Valley: Nuclear Waste, Environmental Racism, and Tribal Sovereignty," which was published in *Christian Environmental Ethics*, 218–52.

[12]Mycle Schneider, Antony Froggatt, et al., *World Nuclear Industry Status Report 2014*, 98, http://www.worldnuclearreport.org. At the end of 2014, there were 388 nuclear reactors in operation around the world.

[13]US Energy Information Administration, "FAQs: How Many Nuclear Power Plants Are There in the U.S. and Where Are They Located?" February 12, 2015, http://www.eia.gov.

[14]NRC, "Location of Power Reactor Sites Undergoing Decommissioning," February 12, 2015, http://www.nrc.gov.

[15]US Department of Energy, *Blue Ribbon Commission's Nuclear Future Report to the Secretary of Energy*, December 2012, 10, http://www.energy.gov.

[16]Ibid., 11.

[17]Ibid., 14.

[18]GAO, *Commercial Nuclear Waste: Effects of a Termination of the Yucca Mountain Repository Program and Lessons Learned*, GAO-11-229, April 2011, 6, http://www.gao.gov.

[19]Ibid., 2.

[20]Government Accountability Office, *Nuclear Waste: Technical, Schedule, and Cost Uncertainties of the Yucca Mountain Repository Project*, GAO-02-191, December 2001, http://www.gao.gov.

[21]Matthew L. Wald, "Government Must Continue Review of Nevada Nuclear Waste Site, Court Says," *New York Times*, August 13, 2013, http://www.nytimes.com. See endnote #2 in the case for more information.

[22]Hannah Northey, "Yucca Mountain: DOE Temporarily Saved Money by Closing Repository," *Greenwire*, April 21, 2014, http://www.eenews.net.

[23]DOE, *The Report to the President and the Congress by the Secretary of Energy on the Need for a Second Repository*, DOE/RW-0595 (December 2008), http://energy.gov. The report explains: "In addition to commercial used nuclear fuel, high-level radioactive wastes that are the by-products of the production of the nation's nuclear weapons and used fuel from the Navy's nuclear powered combat vessels also require a defined disposal path. These wastes are currently stored at sites in Idaho, South Carolina, and Washington. Also, significant quantities of weapons-capable plutonium and highly enriched uranium have become surplus to our national security needs, and in some form will be destined for disposal in a repository" (ibid., 3).

[24]DOE, *Strategy for the Management and Disposal of Used Nuclear Fuel and High-Level Radioactive Waste*, January 11, 2013, http://www.energy.gov.

[25]42 USC § 10242—Office of Nuclear Waste Negotiator, http://www.law.cornell.edu. For an interesting Public Broadcasting System interview of Richard Stallings, the second nuclear waste negotiator, see http://www.pbs.org.

[26]Public Citizen, "Radioactive Racism: The History of Targeting Native American Communities with High-Level Atomic Waste Dumps," https://www.citizen.org; Sierra M. Jefferies, "Environmental Justice and the Skull Valley Goshute Indians' Proposal to Store Nuclear Waste," *Journal of Land, Resources, and Environmental Law* 27, no. 2 (2007): 415.

[27]Timothy Eagan, "New Prosperity Brings New Conflict to Indian Country," *New York Times*, March 8, 1998, http://www.nytimes.com.

[28]Utah American Indian Digital Archive, "Goshute," http://www.utahindians.org.

[29]Peggy Connolly, David R. Keller, et al., *Ethics in Action: A Case-Based Approach* (New York: Wiley-Blackwell, 2008), 134.

[30]The following companies are members of PFS: Entergy Corporation, First Energy, Genoa Fuel Technology, Florida Power and Light (Next Energy), Indiana-Michigan Power (American Electric Power), Southern California Edison, Southern Nuclear Operating Company, and Northern States Power (Xcel Energy).

[31]PFS, *Response to Questions about the Operation of the Private Fuel Storage Facility: A Report to Citizens of Utah* (Salt Lake City: PFS, 2001), 6.

[32]Kevin Fedorko, "In the Valley of the Shadow," *Outside*, 25, no. 5 (May 2000): 166–67. See also Jerry Johnstone, "Goshutes Players in New Game," *Deseret News*, September 28, 2001, http://www.deseretnews.com.

[33]Citizen Media, "Skull Valley Goshute Reservations," https://www.youtube.com. The Skull Valley/PFS segment runs from 4:35 to 9:04. The Salt Lake City affiliate of the Public Broadcasting System produced a ninety-minute documentary in 2001 that provides a comprehensive history of the project and includes diverse perspectives from members of the Skull Valley Band of the Goshute Indians: *Skull Valley: Radioactive Waste and the American West*, KUED-TV, 2001.

[34]Nuclear Regulatory Commission, "NRC Issues License to Private Fuel Storage for Spent Nuclear Fuel Storage Facility in Utah," No. 06-028, February 22, 2006, http://www.nrc.gov. The final environmental impact statement released in 2001 is available online. See NRC, Office of Nuclear Material Safety and Safeguards et al., *Final Environmental Impact Statement for the Construction and Operation of an Independent Spent Fuel Storage Installation on the Reservation of the Skull Valley Band of Goshute Indians and the Related Transportation Facility in Tooele County, Utah*, NUREG-1714, vol. 1 (December 2001), http://pbadupws.nrc.gov.

[35]DOI BLM, "Record of Decision Addressing Right-of-Way Applications U76985 and U76986 to Transport Spent Nuclear Fuel to the Reservation Of the Skull Valley Band of Goshute Indians," *Federal Register* 71, no. 188, September 28, 2006, http://www.gpo.gov/.

[36]Ibid.

[37]DOI, BIA, "Record of Decision for the Construction and Operation of an Independent Spent Fuel Storage Installation (ISFSI) on the Reservation of the Skull Valley Band of Goshute Indians (Band) in Tooele County, Utah," *Federal Register* 71, no. 192, October 4, 2006, http://www.gpo.gov.

[38]Ibid.

[39]*Skull Valley Band of Goshute Indians v. Davis*, 728 F. Supp. 2d 1287 (D. Utah 2010), http://www.ecases.us.

[40]Grace Thorpe, "Our Homes Are Not Dumps: Creating Nuclear-Free Zones," in *Defending Mother Earth: Native American Perspectives on Environmental Justice*, Jace Weaver, ed. (Maryknoll, NY: Orbis Books, 1996), 54.

[41]J. Timmons Roberts and Melissa M. Toffolon-Weiss, *Chronicles from the Environmental Justice Frontline* (New York: Cambridge University Press, 2001), 9–11.

[42]President William J. Clinton, Executive Order 12898, *Federal Actions to Address Environmental Justice in Minority Populations and Low-Income Populations*, sec. 2–2, http://www.epa.gov.

[43]NRC, Office of Nuclear Material Safety and Safeguards et al., *Final Environmental Impact Statement for the Construction and Operation of an Independent Spent Fuel Storage Installation on the Reservation of the Skull Valley Band of Goshute Indians and the Related Transportation Facility in Tooele County, Utah*, 6–28.

[44]Jace Weaver, introduction to Grace Thorpe, "Our Homes Are Not Dumps," 49.

[45]Grace Thorpe, "Our Homes Are Not Dumps: Creating Nuclear Free Zones," 50.

[46]Jonathan Fahey and Ray Henry, "AP Impact: U.S. Spent-Fuel Storage Sites Are Packed," *Washington Post*, March 22, 2011, http://www.washingtonpost.com. According to Fahey and Henry, "[s]pent nuclear fuel is about 95 percent uranium. About 1 percent are other heavy elements such as curium, americium and plutonium-239, best known as fuel for

nuclear weapons. Each has an extremely long half-life—some take hundreds of thousands of years to lose all of their radioactive potency. The rest, about 4 percent, is a cocktail of byproducts of fission that break down over much shorter time periods, such as cesium-137 and strontium-90, which break down completely in about 300 years."

[47]Recently, Waste Control Specialists, LLC announced they intend to ask the NRC for permission to build an interim storage facility for SNF on 1,000 acres of land in Andrews County, which is about 350 miles west of Dallas, Texas. See Hannah Northey, "Texas Company Rolls Out Plan for Private Spent-Fuel Storage Site," *Greenwire*, February 9, 2015, http://greenwire.com. Two other counties in western Texas and southeastern New Mexico have also expressed interest in serving as hosts for an interim storage facility for SNF. See Matthew L. Wald, "County of 95 Sees Opportunity in Toxic Waste," *New York Times*, August 7, 2014, http://www.nytimes.com; Charles Taylor, "N.M. Counties Hope to Store Nuclear Fuel Waste," *NACo County News*, October 22, 2012, http://www.naco.org/.

[48]These were all conditions and expectations in the original lease agreement. See Jerry D. Spangler and Donna Kemp Spangler, "Toxic Utah: Goshutes Divided over N-Storage," *Deseret News*, February 15, 2001, http://www.deseretnews.com.

11

Smart Growth

Affordable Housing, Public Transportation, and Open Space

Acronyms and Abbreviations

ABAG	Association of Bay Area Governments
EPA	Environmental Protection Agency (US)
FHA	Federal Housing Administration (US)
MTC	Metropolitan Transportation Commission
OBAG	One Bay Area Grant
PCA	priority conservation area
PDA	priority development area
SCS	sustainable communities strategy
TAM	Transportation Authority of Marin
TOD	transit-oriented development

Case

Nancy Ross felt lucky to be living in the Strawberry neighborhood north of the Tiburon Peninsula in Marin County. The area was safe, the neighbors were friendly, and the geography of open hills and the San Francisco Bay nearby was stunning (Figure 1). Despite this suburban serenity, a new sign appeared in the yard next door that said "No Strawberry PDA." When she asked her neighbor Bill Diers about it, she got an earful about their neighborhood being designated a priority development area (PDA). He was worried that the PDA designation would encourage the city to permit high-density development that would bring increased traffic, crime, and other problems. Bill shared enough of his reasons for

245

resistance that Nancy decided to attend the community forum on the proposed Strawberry PDA to be held at the Marin Civic Center.

Figure 1. Map of San Francisco Bay Area

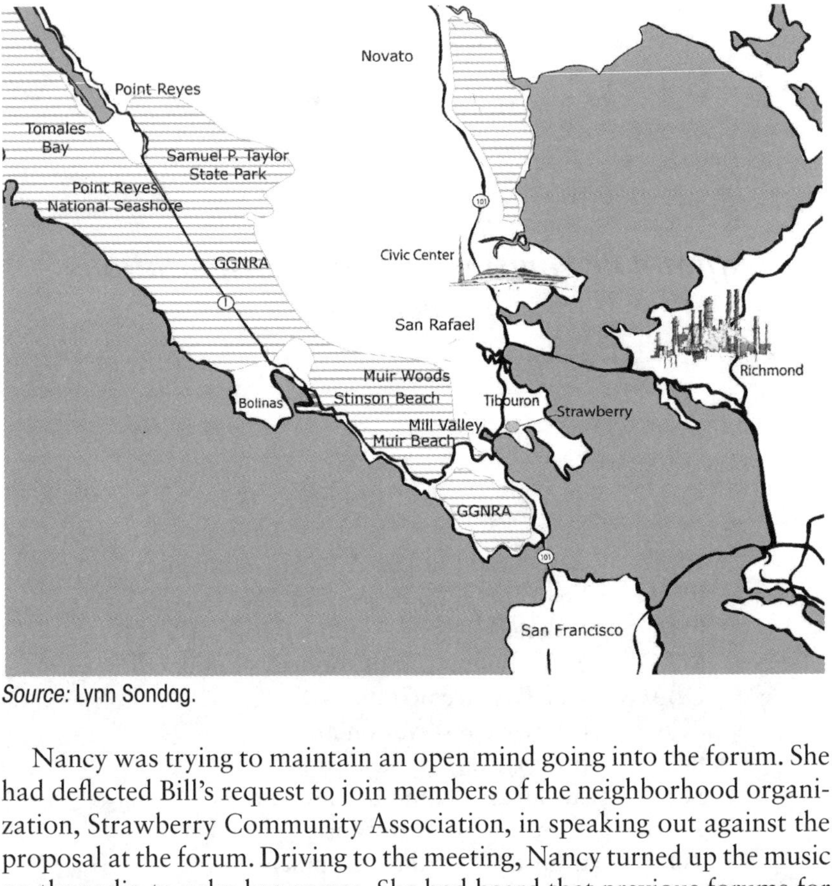

Source: Lynn Sondag.

Nancy was trying to maintain an open mind going into the forum. She had deflected Bill's request to join members of the neighborhood organization, Strawberry Community Association, in speaking out against the proposal at the forum. Driving to the meeting, Nancy turned up the music on the radio to calm her nerves. She had heard that previous forums for public comment on the issue of regional smart growth and PDAs had been quite contentious and heated. She would much rather be curled up on her couch with the cat watching a movie, but Bill had scared her with his predictions of what would become of their neighborhood if the PDA was approved.

In preparation for this forum, Nancy had gone online and tried to make sense of the "Plan Bay Area: Strategy for a Sustainable Region,"[1] a smart growth development plan for the entire San Francisco Bay Area that was jointly approved in July 2013 by the Association of Bay Area Governments (ABAG) Executive Board and by the Metropolitan Transportation Commission (MTC). The plan grew out of "The California Sustainable Communities and Climate Protection Act of 2008" (SB 375), which requires each of the state's metropolitan areas to reduce greenhouse gas emissions from cars and light trucks. The law had been signed by Republican Governor Arnold Schwarzenegger and required each metropolitan area to develop a sustainable communities strategy (SCS) that encourages future development to be in areas that are accessible via walking and biking and close to public transit, jobs, schools, and other amenities. Nancy was impressed that the plan addressed both environmental issues (e.g., reduction of greenhouse gases and the preservation of open space and agriculture) as well as social equity (housing and transportation affordability, potential for displacement, healthy communities, and access to jobs).

Equitable land use distribution and public transportation upgrades are central to the plan. One goal is for accessible, affordable, and diverse housing in neighborhoods where transit, jobs, schools, and services are located near people's homes. Another goal is protection of the region's unique natural environment that includes both agriculture and open space. PDAs would be in existing neighborhoods nominated by local jurisdictions as places to concentrate future growth. Priority conservation areas (PCAs), also nominated by local jurisdictions, are regionally significant open spaces and agricultural areas. Nancy saw that the proposed PDAs in Marin County were intentionally located along the Highway 101 corridor where people could more easily access jobs and transportation, and so the open spaces for which Marin is famous could be preserved. Nancy routinely sat in traffic jams in the morning rush hour. She would have more incentive to stop driving everywhere if alternative forms of transportation were readily accessible.

The incentive for counties to approve housing growth in PDAs through planning and zoning policies is access to transportation grants through the One Bay Area Grant (OBAG) program that provides funding for bicycle and pedestrian paths, preservation of local streets and roads, and even specific funding for safe routes to schools and PCAs.[2] Nancy liked the idea of safe paths because her two kids would soon be biking to middle school, especially since there were no school buses to transport them due to state budget cuts. She also thought concentrating growth in the highway corridor near jobs, transportation, and other services was important for preserving the beautiful surrounding hills that are currently public lands. Her house was near the highway, however, and she was worried about what a PDA designation would mean for development and density in her neighborhood.

While Nancy lived in one of the richest counties in the nation, she herself, despite a professional salary as a regional bank manager, was living paycheck to paycheck. She became sole owner of her 1950s three-bedroom home after her recent divorce settlement, but the mortgage payments were high and something always needed to be repaired. Unlike most of the Strawberry neighborhood, her street was not far off the freeway and comprised modest single-family homes. She only had to drive five minutes east or west, however, to ogle million-dollar homes. Nancy wasn't sure how other single moms survived in Marin. She had thought of selling her home and renting a place, but she couldn't find a three-bedroom place to rent for under $3,500/month. Receiving little child support from her ex-husband and having to shoulder the cost of braces for her teenager, afterschool sports, and counseling, Nancy felt fortunate that she had a decent job.

In fact, Nancy had learned how precarious life is for single moms in Marin when she was invited to volunteer once a month at Homeward Bound, the transitional housing program for homeless families, where her good friend Kate Pagett works. As the clinical director who works closely with formerly homeless individuals and families, Kate was very aware of the obstacles these families face. Nancy found out that some of the moms living at Homeward Bound were working, but the pay from minimum-wage jobs was not sufficient to cover housing costs, and for many, childcare costs for small kids. Many of the moms did not have cars, and Marin is known for having very little public transportation. Years ago, residents of Marin kept the Bay Area Rapid Transit (BART) subway system from crossing over the bay, and buses in Marin are only efficient if one is commuting straight to downtown San Francisco. Nancy was influenced by Kate's passion and dedication to helping poor families succeed and her views on the necessity of providing structural supports like affordable housing, livable wages, and public transportation.

While Nancy realized the need for more affordable housing in Marin County, her neighbor Bill and others had been telling her that any such development would make her property value go down, increase traffic, and lead to the deterioration of the public schools. It was going to be hard to stay open-minded when the changes might negatively affect her children, but she also wondered whether these assertions were supported by facts. Entering the conference room at the Civic Center, Nancy chose to sit near the back and politely declined the offer of a sticker that would advocate which position she was taking on the issue. She also chose not to submit a comment card. The meeting began with the chair of the Transportation Authority of Marin (TAM), Alice Phillips, giving a short introduction about the development designation and its implications.

Alice explained that PDAs are part of a regional plan to accommodate future expected population growth and that in fact the growth projections for Marin County were much lower than other counties in the Bay Area.[3] Alice also laid to rest the fear that a PDA designation would change the zoning of existing properties. She said, "All single-family residential neighborhoods located within the Corridor PDA will remain that way under existing zoning rules, and any new development will be subject to review by the county. The primary benefit of a PDA designation is access to federal transportation dollars, creating opportunities for safer, walkable, bikeable communities with more transit options and less dependence on automobiles."[4] Nancy hadn't realized that a PDA designation did not give rubber-stamp approval for affordable housing, something she thought was sorely needed in Marin County. Alice concluded, "While mixed-income housing is not mandated by a PDA designation, smart growth advocates will likely propose such development for the mixed-use zoning areas that already exist in Strawberry, in conjunction with well-designed paths and parks funded by the grants we would receive as a PDA."

After the introduction, the floor was opened up for public comment. Each person with a card had up to three minutes to speak. The first people who came up to the microphone spoke quite favorably of the PDA, some of their points shedding more light on the perspectives Nancy had already heard. At times, however, Nancy was hearing conflicting views of the facts. For example, there was wide disagreement on whether a PDA designation entailed new development, and if so, how much density any new development would have. Similarly, there were different views on the expected impacts of increased development, especially on the schools.

Nancy was impressed with comments made by Carl Metzger, the director of Sustainable Mill Valley, who asked everyone to think about what would happen if they didn't consider smart growth with higher-density affordable housing and convenient transportation. "If all the housing in Marin is market rate, how many more people will have to commute? Almost 62,000 people already commute into Marin every day for work, many of whom cannot afford to live where they work."[5] He also noted that the water use and the number of cars per household are lower in multifamily versus single-family households, thus putting less pressure on the natural environment. "If we take seriously the threat of global warming, we must rethink how we live and utilize 'best practices,' like walkable development, green buildings, and conservation measures. We have a responsibility to live sustainably and more simply for both environmental and social justice reasons. How we treat the Earth and all of its species today will also have implications for future generations." Another speaker asked if new development would be required to use solar photovoltaic panels or have electric vehicle charging stations, and he advocated that any development should not be based on natural gas in light of Marin's recent call for a moratorium on hydraulic fracturing in the state.[6]

A woman from the League of Women Voters named Kim Hsu pointed out that only with regional planning like the Plan Bay Area could they actually promote diversity and equity within and between communities. She explained that the League of Women Voters is very concerned about promoting sustainable and inclusive communities where all people can flourish. "Rich neighborhoods like Strawberry will choose to keep out affordable housing and public transportation based on fear of who might move in. California is one of the most diverse states in the country. Are we going to create pristine gated communities where only upper-income people can afford to live, while twenty minutes across the Richmond Bridge people live in poverty near oil refineries? There are environmental, economic, and social benefits to having neighborhoods with race and class diversity. But even more important are the principles of inclusion and social justice."

"I second the principles of inclusivity and diversity. I drove over the bridge to be here for this meeting today because there are many of us who work here in San Rafael yet cannot afford to live here," said André Herrera. "I have worked as a janitor here at the civic center for five years, and although I get health benefits, my salary is not high enough to afford the over $3,500-per-month rental rates. The only place my wife, two kids, and I could find affordable rentals was in Richmond where we live by one of those oil refineries as well as a truck depot. One of my children suffers from asthma and other health problems, so my wife needs to be home to care for her. If I didn't have to commute so far each day, I'd have more time to help out with the kids." André ended by adding, "Furthermore, the segregation of neighborhoods by race and class means not only poorer health for my children, but also inferior schools and exposure to neighborhood violence. All I and many of the other families in my neighborhood want is to live in healthy and stable communities so that our children can do well."

Next a man in a wheelchair asked whether new housing would accommodate people with disabilities. Another person noted that there are plenty of residents in Marin who need affordable housing. "I'm retired and am not sure if I'll be able to stay in Marin where I've always lived. My grandchildren have already had to move farther north where housing is cheaper." An affordable housing developer from the Ecumenical Association for Housing argued that while their housing developments are higher density than single housing, their projects in Marin have been around twenty-three units per acre, much lower than the California Housing and Community Development default density of thirty units per acre for metropolitan areas.[7] He said, "Our developments are modern and aesthetically pleasing, and we were just certified as a Bay Area Green Business."

Nancy was happy that someone finally spoke up about the bike and walking paths that might be created if Strawberry were designated a PDA. A lead advocate from the Marin County Bicycle Coalition said that OBAG funds could pay for a safe route to Mill Valley Middle School across the busy and dangerous Highway 101. "Our goal is for 20 percent of all trips in Marin to be made by walking or bicycling by 2020. We want our kids to be bike riders and we want them to have a future without road congestion and global warming. Last of all, we believe transportation equity for our low-income neighbors is important."[8] Nancy liked this vision but wondered whether the PDA designation was the only way to access state funds for paths. It appeared that all the advocates for PDA status had gotten the first speaker cards, but now opponents were beginning to line up.

A number of Strawberry Community Association members spoke up next. One resident began by asking about the traffic impact of higher-density development. "We already have issues with the highway on-ramps. We don't want lots of traffic lights and roundabouts in our suburban community. Current residents should not have to pay a penny for increased development that we don't want." A second Strawberry resident said, "Why do we have to be the housing and transit center for Marin, one of only a handful of land-use areas designated? If we accept this development, what will be next? Is it really worth any money we'd get?" A third opponent passionately said, "Tall structures with high density are 'out of character' for our community. We pay a lot to live in a low-density neighborhood, and we earned it; we did not get a government giveaway. If you increase density tenfold, you increase everything—litter, noise, traffic, and crime."

Nancy wondered about the fears that Strawberry would end up with high-density apartment buildings. In Larkspur, two exits north off Highway 101, there did seem to be a lot of new apartment buildings going up, but Alice Philips did say that new development would be subject to review. Nancy certainly didn't want to have a higher tax bill to pay for new services needed for higher density in her community, nor did she want to live in a crowded, crime-ridden area.

Next a mother of school-age children argued, "We have excellent schools in Mill Valley. More students mean increased services and I've heard that affordable housing developments don't pay property taxes.[9] Plus renters are more transient which negatively affects schools."[10] Nancy's neighbor Bill argued, "Communities in Marin are already models of sustainability for other communities to follow. Marin has a history of environmental advocacy to preserve open space and habitat connectivity. We could do more to support public transportation, but new development will have negative environmental effects, especially on our watersheds. And do we really want to consign all low-income people to living near the freeway noise and pollution?" Nancy agreed that Marin had a long history of environmental advocacy and preserving open land. Many residents shopped at farmers' markets and recycled. She would prefer to live farther from the freeway if she could afford to do so.

One gentleman named Kevin Williams spoke up, arguing that while he was not a Strawberry resident, he was concerned about there being an open democratic process. He argued that the regional focus of smart growth plans leaves no room for communities to determine what works best for them. "Why are state and regional organizations like ABAG and MTC determining what happens in local communities? Who benefits from these projects?" He went on to say, "Strawberry residents want a voice in their own community—to have local control and not have their neighborhood changed by special interests, regional planners, and laws from Sacramento. Surveys show that over 90 percent of residents do not support the development. We need genuine community participation." Another person pursued this point even more adamantly: "Legislators in Sacramento are heavy-handed 'social engineers,' determined to remake our cities in their own image. We ought to be able to preserve the good things about our small communities and still encourage sustainability, diversity, and social equity. The 'Smart Growth' vision of retailing and apartment living is only something a highly paid consultant who doesn't live here could love."[11] Nancy agreed that people should have a voice in their own community, but she wondered how social equity, diversity, and sustainability would be encouraged if communities could keep out affordable housing and if residents were all commuting everywhere by car.

More comments followed from both sides. Nancy was impressed that the TAM facilitators managed to keep the forum civil and orderly. She felt much more at ease than she had before the meeting. Perhaps tensions were not as high because a decision wasn't being made on the designation yet. That would happen later at a Marin County Board of Supervisors meeting.

Nancy felt quite divided about this whole issue of smart growth. Both sustainability and social equity are important goals, but she wondered whether regional planning is necessary to achieve these goals. Will residents in her neighborhood voluntarily choose to have mixed-income housing and adequate public transportation in their area or even give up their incessant car driving? And what will her children's future be like if we don't make a concerted effort to curb greenhouse gas emissions and slow down climate change?

The next afternoon was Nancy's day to help at Homeward Bound. She decided to go a little early to ask Kate her thoughts on smart growth. Kate only had ten minutes before seeing a client, but in that little time she tried to convince Nancy to join Sustainable San Rafael and advocate for the Strawberry PDA. "Just like my Marin neighbors, I like the quality of life in my neighborhood, but we need to think strategically about sustainable development and transportation in the region as a whole. Too many people are trying to hold on to what they have by excluding and disparaging families like those I work with, rather than envisioning progressive strategies to address global warming and population growth in our area."

Then, while walking her dog that evening, Nancy ran into Bill. He asked what she thought of the community forum, and then, like Kate, urged Nancy to join his group: "Your voice as a single mom concerned about neighborhood safety and good schools would really go a long way toward defeating the PDA proposal. Would you be willing to join the Strawberry Community Association and attend the upcoming Board of Supervisors meeting to argue against the PDA designation?" Nancy felt torn between the various implications of this proposal, but said she would think about it. In light of global warming it seemed imperative that communities have strategies to promote sustainability, she thought. But what strategies make a difference, and which are politically feasible? She understood and shared some of her neighbors' fears that higher-density housing developments might change the suburban feel of the community, but she also realized the inevitability of population growth in the Bay Area, and with it a need to think regionally about development. She was glad she had some time to think about the issue before the Board of Supervisors meeting. Hopefully Kate and Bill would give her some leeway to make up her mind.

Commentary

Owning a home in the suburbs has been central to the American Dream for more than half a century, but unsustainable urban sprawl and automobile use has been the result. Both contribute to global warming and the destruction of farms and open space. Models of sustainable development are plenty, but garnering the public will to put them in place is difficult, especially in affluent neighborhoods where residents have privilege and access to all that the dream entails. The threat of global warming, however, has prompted some states to pass legislation supporting sustainable development strategies.

In September 2006, the California State Legislature passed AB 32, the Global Warming Solutions Act of 2006, with the goal of reducing greenhouse gas emissions back to 1990 emission levels by 2020. Then in 2008, SB 375 required each of the state's eighteen metropolitan areas to develop an SCS to accommodate future population growth and reduce greenhouse gas emissions. The Plan Bay Area, approved in 2013, is a long-range integrated transportation and land-use/housing strategy for nine counties. It draws on best practices from the "smart growth" movement. The Bay Area's population is expected to grow from seven million today to nine million by 2040. The plan proposes to meet 80 percent of the region's future housing needs in PDAs, which are neighborhoods within walking distance of frequent transit service, with mixed-income housing options, bike paths, and amenities such as grocery stores, restaurants, schools, and community centers.[12]

The plan aims to steer development along the highway corridors to stem suburban sprawl and support the preservation of open space and agriculture. The goal of reducing greenhouse gas emissions is achieved by transit-oriented development (TOD) with higher-density affordable housing. The plan does not require that any particular actions be taken in local areas but does offer incentives, including grants for affordable and higher-density housing and priority in receiving transportation funds not already committed for other uses. It has been a hard sell, however, in affluent, predominately white communities like Marin County as many residents believe smart growth development will eliminate the suburban lifestyle they enjoy. Yet there are negative impacts on traffic and the environment when, as the director of Sustainable Mill Valley points out in the case, almost 62,000 people commute into the county for work each day because they cannot afford to live there.[13] Fifty-four percent of people who work in Marin make less than $40,000 and thus commute from outside the county.[14]

Urban Sprawl

Defined by the National Trust for Historic Preservation as "poorly planned, low-density, auto-oriented development that spreads out from the center of communities," *urban sprawl* is the direct or indirect result of various federal policies. The most significant of these policies was the creation of the Federal Housing Administration (FHA) during the Great Depression of the 1930s. After millions defaulted on mortgages and the construction of new homes fell by 95 percent, the FHA changed the way home loans were structured. Instead of a 50 percent down payment and a ten-year loan on the balance, homebuyers now had to come up with only a 10 percent down payment and could finance the rest with a thirty-year mortgage. These changes put homeownership within the reach of millions of Americans and resulted in a boom in new housing construction on the edges of urban centers, especially after the Veterans Administration offered similar loan terms after World War II.

At the same time, the federal government subsidized the construction of a 41,000-mile interstate highway system. Large arterial highways were built to enable workers to drive from their homes in the suburbs to their jobs in the cities. Many of these highways also bisected formerly intact urban neighborhoods, fostering urban blight. The flip side of urban sprawl has been the deterioration of inner cities and increasing inner-ring suburbs. Density-efficient trolleys and buses for urban mass transit were quickly replaced by the automobile as far-flung suburbanites discovered they needed a car to get just about anywhere in their new communities. In addition, low federal tax rates on fossil fuels encourage the use of private automobiles and the trucking of goods around the nation. Not surprisingly, then, traffic is growing at a significant rate. Studies indicate that in the United States each passenger vehicle travels around 12,500 miles annually, up from 9,000 miles in 1980,[15] and despite the development of more fuel-efficient cars, the emission of carbon dioxide—the largest contributor to global warming—more than doubled in the United States between 1950 and 2010.[16]

A significant amount of urban sprawl has taken place through the purchase and conversions of farmland. The American Farmland Trust reports that from 1982 to 2007 the United States lost 41,324,800 acres of rural land to development, which is the size of Illinois and New Jersey combined. Of that land, 56 percent, or twenty-three million acres of it, was active agricultural land.[17]

The development of wetland, woodland, and other wild tracts of land has destroyed life-sustaining wildlife habitats for many species. Even though patches of green exist in residential subdivisions and around shopping plazas, these developments create habitat fragmentation that disrupts migratory corridors and breeding patterns. In Marin County, wetlands are extensive and very important to species preservation. One-half of all bird species and one-third of other species in the United States depend on wetlands.[18] Furthermore, Marin County has a concentration of diverse plant habitats from marine to coastal to higher-elevation plant communities and is home to some rare and endangered endemic plants that do not grow anywhere else. A 2013 study documented fifty-one rare plants on Marin open space lands and eleven special status wildlife species.[19]

Of concern to social justice advocates is inequitable development between communities in metropolitan areas. In the San Francisco Bay Area, the inequities are stark: the city of Mill Valley where the Strawberry neighborhood resides is almost 89 percent white with a median household income of almost $117,000,[20] while the city of Richmond across the bridge is only 17 percent white with a median income around $54,500.[21] As André points out in the case, concentrated poverty and wealth also means differential access to quality schools, crime-free neighborhoods, green space, and more. Organizers in the environmental justice movement also note that poor neighborhoods often bear the brunt of environmental pollution from industry, toxic waste dumps and landfills, and dilapidated housing with lead paint or other environmental hazards. For example, the Environmental Protection Agency (EPA) notes that Richmond is "surrounded by more than 350 industrial facilities, including waste incinerators, oil refineries, pesticides and other toxic hazards, which produce tens to hundreds of pounds of toxic air contaminates, toxic pollutants and wastewater, and hundreds of tons of hazardous waste."[22] The health problems that Andre's daughter faces could be the result of this reality.

Smart Growth and Sustainability

The smart growth movement, which emphasizes TOD, began in the 1990s in the United States as a way to curb the negative effects of sprawl.

Smart growth advocates seek to revitalize central cities and older suburbs, support public transit and pedestrian options, preserve open spaces and agricultural lands, and have a greater mix of uses for housing, commercial, and retail purposes. The idea is to focus on the already-built environment with the goal of creating more livable communities with sufficient housing and public transportation for the region's workforce. Smart growth is not meant to be gentrification that displaces low-income residents, but if done right includes social equity so "that people of all income levels have access to housing that they can afford, good schools, reliable transportation, various types of employment, and toxic-free communities."[23] The EPA offers the following smart growth principles:

1. Mix land uses
2. Take advantage of compact building design
3. Create a range of housing opportunities and choices
4. Create walkable neighborhoods
5. Foster distinctive, attractive communities with a strong sense of place
6. Preserve open space, farmland, natural beauty, and critical environmental areas
7. Strengthen and direct development towards existing communities
8. Provide a variety of transportation choices
9. Make development decisions predictable, fair, and cost effective
10. Encourage community and stakeholder collaboration in development decisions[24]

Smart growth promotes the ecological justice norm of sustainability. Concentrating higher-density housing in Marin County along the Highway 101 transportation corridor, providing easily accessible transit centers with frequent and quality public transportation, building paths for biking and walking, and placing housing near services and jobs allow residents to use their cars less. Smart growth fosters community since people can live, work, and play in the same place and not spend hours of isolation in their cars. Building affordable housing, especially for people in the service industry (e.g., teachers, police, janitors, restaurant workers), cuts down on the number of people commuting to work. The time residents save can mean increased community involvement, and a larger number of people walking and biking promotes social interaction and healthy lifestyles.

Compact housing, especially with energy-efficient design, uses less energy and water than single-family development. Furthermore, development in cooler areas near the bay requires less water for landscaping and air conditioning than in hotter areas inland. Compact housing also allows open space preserves, one of the distinctive features of Marin County, to remain. Without smart growth to accommodate projected population increase, it is estimated that 83,000 acres of currently undeveloped land in the San Francisco Bay Area region could be converted to urban use by 2020. That acreage is more than twice the area of San Francisco, and development will erode the open space, greenbelts, and farmland that are the hallmark of the area.[25] In addition to the anthropocentric benefits of open space for recreation, property values, and aesthetic enjoyment, there are multiple ecological reasons to support its preservation. Open space is crucial to the diversity of plant species, serves as habitat for fish and wildlife, enhances air and water quality, filters and absorbs runoff, and reduces the carbon dioxide footprint.

Smart growth faces some real obstacles, however. First, most zoning in the United States has been modeled on the Standard Zoning Enabling Act of 1922, which emphasizes density prevention and the separation of uses. This zoning hinders the development of compact communities with stores, services, housing, and jobs mixed in close proximity to each other. Second, land use planning is primarily controlled by local governments, many of which are not keen on state and regional control. Many local governments use land use regulations for exclusionary purposes.[26] One of the most common is the stipulation that lots must be a certain size, which makes the creation of affordable housing nearly impossible due to the cost of large plots of land. Smart growth requires regional planning to identify transportation corridors, urban areas for intended growth, and open space to be protected. A regional focus is also necessary for improving the well-being of low-income neighborhoods and promoting social equity.

Livable Communities for All

A regional focus on urban development that aims for environmental health and social equity is connected to the ecological justice norms of justice, sufficiency, and solidarity. The early American preservationists' goal of keeping wilderness areas intact was beneficial for curbing overdevelopment in the United States, but many environmentalists from the preservationist movement had a negative view of cities (despite the fact that most of them lived in cities). They failed to realize that environmentalism also encompasses the areas where we live, work, and play. The environmental justice movement reframed the definition of environmentalism to include urban areas and argued that how we live in cities is intricately connected to the conservation of the natural environment. The ecological norms of justice and sufficiency entail that basic needs be met and equity realized. Unlimited consumption and inequitable distribution of goods violates these norms. In Marin County, there are multimillion-dollar homes while just across the bridge in Richmond, communities of color lack access to basic needs, suffer from failing schools, and are exposed to toxic waste from oil refineries, truck depots, and other industries.

The norm of justice can be differently framed, however. Critics of regional equity plans argue that they unfairly penalize people who have worked hard and achieved the American Dream. They believe that they should be able to enjoy the fruits of their labor and that policies of redistribution hinder their individual freedom and are therefore unjust. Environmental justice organizers argue that leaving development and land use up to local jurisdictions allows affluent communities with power and privilege to keep their neighborhoods "pristine" from unwanted land uses (e.g., landfills, industry, ports, prisons) and particular groups of people (the poor and people of color). This phenomenon of exclusion is often referred to as not in my backyard syndrome (NIMBY), and reinforces race- and class-segregated neighborhoods. The status quo of poverty versus privilege is kept intact. Thus, critics argue that a regional focus with an emphasis on solidarity with low-income communities is necessary to address inequity and the injustice of unwanted land uses being located disproportionately in poor communities of color.

Carl Anthony, former director of the Bay Area environmental justice organization Urban Habitat, offers a vision of urban environmental and social flourishing:

> Imagine cities as places where working people can afford to live and raise their families, where there is concern for clean air, water, and land. Imagine vital exchanges across generations and beautiful places where people gather. Urban life is at its most vibrant when people from various parts of the world bring together their music, food, cultural systems, and religious expressions. All of these make for cities that manifest the strength and brilliance of the human garden.[27]

Urban Habitat supports the smart growth strategy in the Bay Area but is adamant that it must include solidarity with and support for low-income communities and communities of color. Proponents of the environmental justice movement are wary of calls for sustainability that do not emphasize regional equity and are aware that communities of privilege will often tout sustainability (e.g., bike paths, green buildings, organic agriculture, open space) while ignoring the norms of sufficiency and solidarity. One of Urban Habitat's project areas is *transportation justice*. Organizers advocate that transportation funding be shifted from massive freeway development toward basic transit (buses and subways) that low-income people and people of color rely on every day. Transportation justice embraces the ethical norm of solidarity and promotes sustainability.

In the case, Kim Hsu from the League of Women Voters supported inclusion and social justice, and argued that neighborhoods with race and class diversity benefit us all. She agreed with Carl Anthony that diversity makes urban/suburban life more vibrant and enriching. Yet others, without explicitly alluding to race, were clearly worried that people of color would move into their neighborhoods and bring violence and crime and lower the quality of the schools. These residents wanted to keep certain people and land uses out of their neighborhoods. They were more concerned about preserving the *suburban character* of their neighborhood, which presumably meant affluent residents with big homes and yards and multiple cars.

Nancy is struggling to understand the implications of a PDA status and the adoption of a smart growth strategy. While solidarity with low-income people is important to her, she also wants to make sure her community remains livable and that her children grow up in safe neighborhoods with good schools. She is supportive of more walking and biking paths but is not sure about higher-density housing and increased public transportation.

There are two direct benefits of having a PDA status: "a) a greater opportunity for funds and grants to implement transportation and land use projects to address the local impact of a regional transit project; and b) the potential for development projects within the PDA to qualify for a more streamlined environmental review process."[28] Funding would bring transit infrastructure, especially paths for walking and biking. The environmental review process for development projects would be streamlined, but the projects would still need to be approved by the county, and residents could have a voice in the process. Accepting transportation funds does not change zoning, nor does it commit residents to accept affordable housing plans. PDAs are part of incentive-based approaches to smart growth that still leave a lot of autonomy in local communities.

If residents did accept affordable housing plans, the density figure of twenty-three units per acre for new housing development in Marin would not be high-rise apartment buildings as many argue but would more likely be two-story attached homes or apartments.[29] While nonprofit housing developments are exempt from property taxes, developers do have to pay special assessments and parcel taxes to fund schools, public safety, and other community services.[30] The idea that the quality of the schools will be affected by low-income renters who are more likely to be transient than homeowners could be alleviated if the neighborhoods were vibrant, safe, and clean, and renters were welcomed as part of the community.

The smart growth goal of less people in cars would help alleviate traffic congestion, but creating affordable housing so people do not have to commute and getting people out of their cars will not happen overnight. Mixed-income neighborhoods will also help lower car use because low-income residents have fewer cars and use public transit more often. Smart growth advocates believe that the smart growth results of increased diversity, housing and transportation options, and nearby amenities, not to mention preservation of open space, will only make Nancy's community more livable and dynamic. They argue that we will all have a better ability to flourish and thrive if we live sustainably on Earth and ensure everyone has access to livable neighborhoods.

Perspectives on Participation

The norm of participation is concerned with empowerment and seeks to remove the obstacles to participating in decisions that affect lives. People in this case disagree over whose participation counts, however. Critics of the Plan Bay Area and regional planning argue that it robs communities of local control. Some even view what they call smart growth communism as a "global conspiracy to trample American liberties and force citizens into Orwellian 'human habitation zones.'"[31] These critics of smart growth believe that community voices are not being given a proper seat at the decision-making table. They are adamantly opposed to regional planning and feel that decision making should happen at the local level. While the Plan Bay Area only encourages and does not enforce any particular policies, its critics nevertheless associate it with policies from the California state legislative body, most notably mandated county affordable housing quotas. State law requires that each city and county submit a housing element plan that shows how they will address affordable housing needs. Residents were especially bothered that Marin was characterized as metropolitan, not suburban, making the default density requirement thirty units per acre (as opposed to twenty). As a result of community activism a new law was passed in September 2014 designating Marin as suburban.[32]

Advocates of regional planning to promote equitable development and sustainable practices argue that rich neighborhoods in counties like Marin have a much larger political voice, which is why they have good schools, few unwanted land uses, lots of green space, and other desirable amenities. In fact, Marin environmentalists in the 1960s and 1970s were very successful in protecting open lands. And recently, many Marin citizen groups have also been successful at thwarting efforts to build affordable housing in the county, the most notable being George Lucas's proposal in 2012 to turn a failed studio site into affordable housing.[33] Communities with concentrated poverty have not had much political sway to gain access to livable wage jobs, quality education, adequate health services, or protection from violence and crime. Regional planning based on smart growth principles aims to remedy these inequities and promote sustainability. The Plan Bay Area promotes the principle of subsidiarity, which holds that social problems should be addressed at the most local level consistent with their solution. The plan advocates local decision making but also contends that without some regional planning and solidarity between communities, the status quo of inequity and unsustainable practices will continue unabated.

How then should we frame the norm of participation? Decentralization and local control based on the principle of subsidiarity sound appealing until we note the stark inequity between communities. Can people adequately participate in social life if they suffer from poverty and all that it entails? And are the interests of other species and particular ecosystems of concern? Who will speak up for the needs of the environment? Human population growth continues apace yet Americans continue to live unsustainably, destroying and polluting the habitat and air that sustains other species. Nancy must decide how to adjudicate the different claims to participation, in light of her definition of justice.

Conclusion

How should Nancy respond to the proposed PDA designation for her neighborhood? While clearly the problem of global warming requires that communities adopt sustainable practices, what is the best strategy for promoting long-term sustainability? Regional planning has created significant dissent in her community, but would she think differently if she lived in Richmond instead? How should we balance local community autonomy with regional and state policies that seek to ensure other moral ends such as equity and sustainability? Does sustainability require equity? Environmental justice and social justice are linked in this case, but how accountable must Nancy be if she is simply trying to get by and provide for her children? The smart growth strategy could make her neighborhood more vibrant, but it would also entail higher-density development and more public transportation. How should we envision the American Dream? Is it about owning a single-family home in the suburbs and driving everywhere, or does the dream need to be revised? Whose interests are important to consider, and what is just? Nancy gets to voice her opinion and participate in the process of PDA designations, but how does her perspective and how do her actions impinge on the ability of others to participate fully in life? While this case has its own particular factors, regional equity planning and smart growth strategies have hit roadblocks in communities across the nation. Nancy must decide what her perspective on these issues will be.

Notes

[1]See ABAG and MTC, "Plan Bay Area: Strategy for a Sustainable Region" (adopted July 18, 2013), http://files.mtc.ca.gov/.

[2]There is also a PCA grant program that seeks to "protect or enhance resource areas or habitats, provide or enhance bicycle and pedestrian access to open space/parkland resources, or support the agricultural economy of the region." See State of California Coastal Conservancy, "Plan Bay Area Priority Conservation Area Grant Program," http://scc.ca.gov.

[3]The plan projects lower growth rates for Marin than for any of the other nine Bay Area counties: 9 percent household growth is projected from 2010 to 2040 and 17 percent for jobs

over that period, as compared to 27 percent household growth and 33 percent job growth for the Bay Area in that time period. League of Women Voters of Marin County, "Dispelling the Myths around Affordable Housing" (August 2013), http://www.marinlwv.org/.

[4]Marin Supervisor Kate Sears website, http://www.marincounty.org.

[5]Measure of America, *Portrait of Marin 2012* (January 2012), http://www.measureofamerica.org/marin.

[6]Jessica Mullins, "Marin Supervisors Back Resolution Calling for Statewide Fracking Ban," *San Rafael Patch,* August 23, 2013, http://sanrafael.patch.com.

[7]California Department of Housing and Community Development, "Analysis of Sites and Zoning: Realistic Development Capacity," http://www.hcd.ca.gov.

[8]Marin County Bicycle Coalition, "About MCBC," http://www.marinbike.org.

[9]"Under California state law, nonprofit institutions that provide a public good (such as churches/schools/nonprofit housing developments) are exempt from the basic 1% *ad valorem* property taxes (the portion based on assessed value). In most cases, however, affordable housing developers are subject to special assessments and parcel taxes that are in place to fund schools, libraries, paramedics, parks, public safety, water supply, hazardous waste and other community services. In addition, affordable housing developments are subject to one-time impact fees, including school impact fees." League of Women Voters of Marin County, "Dispelling the Myths around Affordable Housing," 9 (August 2013), http://www.marinlwv.org.

[10]Ibid.

[11]Bob Silvestri, *The Best Laid Plans: Our Planning and Affordable Housing Challenges in Marin* (Mill Valley, CA: Robert J. Silvestri, 2012), 1–3.

[12]ABAG and MTC, "Plan Bay Area: Strategy for a Sustainable Region" (adopted July 18, 2013), http://onebayarea.org.

[13]Measure of America, *Portrait of Marin 2012* (January 2012), 7, http://www.measureofamerica.org/marin/.

[14]"Marinwood: Affordable Housing," http://marinwoodvillage.com.

[15]Worldwatch, "The Geography of Transport Systems," cited by Dr. Jean-Paul Rodrigue, Department of Global Studies & Geography, Hofstra University, New York, USA, https://people.hofstra.edu.

[16]World Resources SIMS Center, "US Energy-Related CO_2 Emissions, 1950–2009," http://www.wrsc.org.

[17]American Farmland Trust, "America Has Lost More Than Twenty-three Million Acres of Agricultural Land," April 17, 2010, http://www.farmland.org.

[18]US Department of Agriculture, "Restoring America's Wetlands: A Private Lands Conservation Success Story," http://www.nrcs.usda.gov.

[19]Samantha Kimmey, "County Releases First Draft Trail Plan," *Point Reyes Light*, October 3, 2013, http://www.ptreyeslight.com.

[20]US Census, "State and County Quick Facts: Mill Valley (city), California" (2014), http://quickfacts.census.gov.

[21]Ibid.

[22]EPA, "Environmental Justice Community Success Stories: Asian Pacific Environmental Network," http://epa.gov.

[23]Smart Growth America, "Smart Growth Strategy Builder," 4 (December 1, 2007), http://www.smartgrowthamerica.org.

[24]"About Smart Growth," Environmental Protection Agency, http://www.epa.gov.

[25]ABAG, "Smart Growth Strategy: Regional Livability Footprint Project: Shaping the Future of the Nine-County Bay Area" (October 2002), 20, http://www.abag.ca.gov.

[26]Through zoning codes, suburban areas can set minimum lot sizes, effectively making property unaffordable for low-income families. They can also require special permits or fees for affordable housing development, or even ban multi-family developments.

[27]Carl Anthony, "Livable Communities," *Race, Poverty, and the Environment* 15, no. 1 (Spring 2008): 9.

[28]City of San Rafael, CA, "Civic Center Priority Development Area (PDA) Responses to Community Questions," 6, August 29, 2013, http://docs.cityofsanrafael.org.

[29]In California thirty units per acre is standard for metropolitan jurisdictions (any city or county over 25,000 population in a Metropolitan Statistical Area (MSA) with a population of 2 million persons or greater and any city or county over 100,000 population in any size MSA). Twenty units per acre is standard for suburban jurisdictions, although there are cities in Marin County that have regularly allowed densities up to forty units per acre. Information from Mark Stivers, "Analysis of Bill NO AB 1537—Housing Element Default Densities," Senate Transportation and Housing Committee, State of California (hearing date June 24, 2014), http://www.leginfo.ca.gov.

[30]League of Women Voters of Marin County, "Dispelling the Myths Surrounding Affordable Housing," 9 (August 2013), http://www.marinlwv.org.

[31]Stephanie Mencimer, "We Don't Need None of That Smart-Growth Communism," *Mother Jones*, 1, November 18, 2010, 1, http://www.motherjones.com. See also Silvestri, *The Best Laid Plans*. These critics see the UN document *Agenda 21* as fueling regional smart growth movements that will curtail private property rights and deprive Americans of constitutional freedoms.

[32]Renee Schiavone, "New Law Designates Marin as Suburban County," *San Rafael Patch* (20 September 2014), http://patch.com.

[33]Aaron Sankin, "Grady Ranch in Marin: George Lucas Proposes Turning Failed Studio Site into Affordable Housing," *Huff Post San Francisco*, May 8, 2012, http://www.huffingtonpost.com.

12

Wearing Injustice?

Free Trade, Worker Rights, and Consumption

Acronyms and Abbreviations

DSP	Designated Suppliers Program
FTZ	free trade zone
GATT	General Agreement on Tariffs and Trade
GHG	greenhouse gas
IMF	International Monetary Fund
MDGs	UN Millennium Development Goals
MEC	Movement of Working and Unemployed Women "María Elena Cuadra"
NGO	nongovernmental organization
SAPs	structural adjustment policies
SSEJ	Students for Social and Economic Justice
TNC	transnational corporation
USAS	United Students against Sweatshops
WRC	Worker Rights Consortium
WTO	World Trade Organization

Case

Karla Jeffries rummaged through her closet, checking out the labels on her shirts to see where they were made. Thailand, Indonesia, Bangladesh, Sri Lanka. Honduras, Mexico, El Salvador, Nicaragua. Her Columbia winter coat had been made in Vietnam—did they even have winter in Vietnam? Some countries she had never heard of—where was Mauritius, anyway? Weren't *any* clothes made in the United States these days? She wasn't sure—it seemed every single item of clothing she owned was made somewhere far away in Asia or Latin America.

A year ago Karla wouldn't have noticed or cared where her clothes were made. When she shopped, she paid attention to two things: style and price. She enjoyed window shopping at the high-priced boutiques downtown, but growing up in a rural farm community had conditioned her to pay attention to the bottom line. Karla was glad that stores like Target and Walmart carried a lot of the name brand clothes she liked at a cheaper price.

Everything had changed when she took a travel seminar to Nicaragua last summer. A double major in English and Environmental Studies at the state university, Karla knew this trip would open her eyes to harsh realities she had only read about, but she wasn't prepared for the emotional effect of walking through the textile factory. Formally known as textile assembly factories, Karla thought the name *sweatshop* was more accurate: in row after row, over a thousand young women her own age labored over sewing machines in the hot, un-air-conditioned factory. She walked with her classmates through the aisles under the watchful eye of the manager who had just told them about the economic opportunities his factory provided for unskilled Nicaraguans. Most of the workers seemed unwilling to meet their eyes and only reluctantly answered their questions. It wasn't just the unbearable heat of the factory that made her uncomfortable. She thought about the clothes she had on that she had recently bought for this trip—she had gone excitedly to REI to pick out backpacking shirts and pants designed especially for travelers in tropical countries. It had never crossed her mind to think about *who* had made those clothes and under what conditions (Figure 1).

Figure 1. Textile factory in the Las Mercedes Free Trade Zone, Managua, Nicaragua

Photo credit: Daniel Spencer.

The biggest shock for Karla, however, came at the end of the aisle where a large box held a pile of recently completed North Face jackets for export to the United States. Karla picked one up and noticed the price tag was already attached to it. $229.00! How much of that actually went to the workers who made it? She had read that the average textile worker in Nicaragua earned less than $200 *a month*, and the factory manager had just boasted to them that Nicaragua's low wages made it one of the best places for US companies to invest. The combination of low wages and proximity to US markets meant a good return on profits to shareholders. The women who made these jackets—and the clothes she was wearing— would never be able to afford the very things they made!

Karla was relieved to leave the assembly plant and noticed that the heat of the Managua afternoon that had seemed so oppressive to her only hours before now seemed cool in comparison to the factory. As they drove out through the guarded gated, she noticed the sign: Las Mercedes Free Trade Zone (FTZ). From her Spanish class, she knew that *mercedes* meant mercies, and *las Mercedes* was a shortened form of *María de las Mercedes*—the Virgin Mary of the Mercies. How ironic, she thought, as they passed through the slums that surrounded the FTZ. Some mercies! She thought about all the women her own age who lived there and worked in the factories day after day, making the clothes that she and her classmates mindlessly wore. Were these factory conditions typical of the textile industry everywhere? And why did the women working there put up with them?

Karla began to get some answers to her questions at their next stop. Driving along the dusty streets of one of Managua's working-class neighborhoods, they pulled up to an unassuming house, set off from its neighbors by a brightly painted mural showing a woman's face with multicolored hair inside a map of Nicaragua. Below the mural it read, *Movimiento de Mujeres Trabajadoras y Desempleadas "María Elena Cuadra"* (the Movement of Working and Unemployed Women "María Elena Cuadra" [MEC]) (Figure 2).

Inside, Karla's class met with María Zelaya, Marta Gómez, and Roberta Zúniga, three members of the MEC workers movement in Managua. These women worked in one of the many textile assembly plants that operate in Managua's FTZs. These special areas, set up by the government, focus on making products for export where transnational corporations (TNCs) pay no taxes and receive other financial incentives in exchange for providing employment for chronically unemployed poor Nicaraguans. The women of MEC organize other women workers, who typically earn $40 to $50/week—less than a dollar an hour, and less than half a livable wage in Nicaragua.[1] The women explained that transnational clothing corporations set up shop in Nicaragua's FTZs to take advantage of its tax-free status and cheap labor.

**Figure 2. Women leaders of the María Elena Cuadra
Women's Workers Movement, Managua, Nicaragua**

Photo credit: Daniel Spencer.

Roberta described the difficult labor conditions in the factories, especially the long hours, low pay, and lack of benefits such as access to health care. While the right to unionize is guaranteed by the Nicaraguan constitution, efforts to organize the women in the sweatshops were typically met by workers being fired or retaliated against. As a result, less than 10 percent of the workforce in the FTZs is made up of union members, and there is virtually no collective bargaining power in the zones.[2] Eighty to 90 percent of the labor force is made up of young women, usually unmarried, between the ages of eighteen and twenty-five. The companies prefer to hire young women for their manual dexterity with textiles and because they are perceived as more submissive and compliant then male workers.

Karla found her anger rising as she listened to the women's stories. She couldn't believe that women were forced to take pregnancy tests before being hired and would be fired if they got pregnant! These women faced forced overtime and long hours with few breaks, injuries from repetitive motions, lack of access to health care, and sexual harassment by male supervisors. If the women protested, they were let go.[3] And the air and water pollution from the factories often contaminated the very neighborhoods where the workers lived, leading to many incidences of illness and health-related issues. But the women in MEC had also been successful in negotiating better working conditions and recently had pressured the government to pass a much-needed comprehensive law prohibiting violence against women. In response to a student's suggestion that they organize a boycott of the companies who contract with the garment factories in the FTZ, Marta cautioned about protesting directly against the corporations. The women fear too much pressure would cause the companies to pull out of Nicaragua, leaving them with no employment at all. Karla now understood MEC's motto better: *Empleo Sí, pero con Dignidad!* (Employment Yes, but with Dignity!). Karla wondered how she could help them improve their work conditions without jeopardizing the jobs they needed to support their families.

Unsure about how anyone could justify the textile factories in the FTZs, Karla was glad they were meeting with PRONicaragua, the official Investment and Export Promotion Agency of the Government of Nicaragua. She certainly had questions she wanted to ask them. Located in one of Managua's upscale neighborhoods, Karla noticed the marked contrast with the MEC offices and that Lourdes Montenegro, the PRO-Nicaragua spokesperson who received them, spoke flawless English. In an air-conditioned conference room, they were treated to coffee and bottled water before Ms. Montenegro began her PowerPoint presentation.

"PRONicaragua was started by the Nicaraguan government in 2002 in conjunction with the United Nations Development Programme," Montenegro told them. "Since then we have become central to implementing the Nicaraguan government's national strategy to reduce poverty and foster sustainable development, promoting Nicaragua as a safe and stable destination for foreign investment. We help to improve the business climate in Nicaragua to encourage investors to choose Nicaragua and, ultimately, generate employment opportunities, technology transfer, and improve the population's quality of life."[4]

"Why should international corporations invest in Nicaragua?" asked Lourdes Montenegro. "Our workforce is young and dynamic, with three-quarters of our workers under age thirty-nine. We have developed a strong legal framework to protect international investments, and have generous investment incentives, especially the FTZs where companies enjoy 100 percent exemption from payment of income tax during the first ten years of operation and 60 percent from the eleventh year onward. We have the lowest minimum wage in Central America, with typical wages ranging from $0.51 to $1.55 per hour. Our proximity to the US market means lower transportation costs and a quick turnaround time on orders."

Thinking back to what the women at MEC had told them, Karla blurted out, "But what about the working conditions and low wages for those workers? How can the women working in the textile plants even support their families with what they earn?"

Lourdes Montenegro looked at Karla sympathetically, and answered, "I realize that compared to wages in the United States, our wages are much lower—but you need to compare what these women are earning in the

FTZs with what they would earn elsewhere in Nicaragua. TNCs typically pay their workers significantly more than domestic factories do, and the working conditions are better, too. Nicaragua's lower wages are important for attracting foreign investment, which we need in order to grow our economy and gain resources for development. As our workforce gains experience and skills, wages will rise and all will benefit—but we have to attract investors who will create jobs first. As US economist Jeffrey Sachs has argued, the most important thing for poor countries to do is to get on the first rung of the global economy ladder by opening themselves up to foreign investment and free trade. Do that, and economic growth and development will follow. That's what we are about at PRONicaragua— helping our poor people to get out of poverty by attracting foreign investment to provide jobs. While well intentioned, protesting the behavior of international corporations will only make them move elsewhere, leaving our country poor and people without jobs."

Karla thought about her experiences in Nicaragua on the long plane ride back to the United States. Some of her friends had organized a campus group called Students for Social and Economic Justice (SSEJ). She vaguely remembered that they had started a campaign about the university's logo clothing and sweatshops, and she now felt a little guilty that she had dismissed their efforts as just another college fad. She would have to attend an SSEJ meeting when she got back to campus in a few weeks.

When she returned to campus, Karla joined SSEJ, which she learned was a chapter of United Students against Sweatshops (USAS). USAS was a national movement of college students working together on over 150 campuses to protect workers' rights—especially textile workers in the sweatshops around the world. Pete Samuels, co-president of SSEJ, explained to Karla that SSEJ was working on USAS's Garment Worker Solidarity project to get the university administration to guarantee that any clothing carrying the university's logo would be made in factories that respected workers' rights.

"First," Pete explained, "we asked that the university administration tell the companies that make our collegiate apparel to disclose the locations of the factories that produce them so we could examine the worker conditions there. Then we pushed our university to adopt labor codes of conduct that set minimum standards for any collegiate apparel production that bears the university logo. We did this by demanding that our school affiliate with the Worker Rights Consortium (WRC), the only independent apparel monitoring organization in the United States. Now that we are affiliated with the WRC, we want our university to adopt a comprehensive sweatshop-free solution, called the Designated Suppliers Program (DSP)."[5]

"We made a lot of progress last year, meeting with University President Stevenson and his vice president for financial administration, Jack Stiles. We've also been educating the campus about the issues—you might remember the teach-ins we held. We got a lot of resistance from the administration at first, but eventually they agreed to have the university sign onto the WRC and begin monitoring the factories. The administration, however, has refused to sign onto the DSP, the program that would actually ensure that state university clothing isn't made in sweatshops, but rather factories where worker rights are being respected. That's going to be our focus this year—it would be great if you would join us."

And that's what Karla had done. Fueled by the memory of the textile workers in Nicaragua, and especially by the stories of María, Marta, and Roberta, she plunged into SSEJ's efforts to get the administration to change its mind about the DSP. They had tried everything. SSEJ held a mock funeral for a mistreated factory worker, a mock wedding marrying the university to the DSP, and a sweat-free fashion show where several sympathetic faculty members modeled sweat-free clothing. But the administration refused to budge. Finally as the end of the school year neared, SSEJ felt they had no choice but to plan a sit-in in the president's office. They would refuse to leave until he signed onto the program or they were forcibly removed from his office.

Karla was particularly discouraged by SSEJ's meetings with Vice President Stiles, President Stevenson's point person on the worker rights issue. Initially Karla had been optimistic because Jack Stiles had come out of a labor background, and they had assumed he would be sympathetic to their cause. But he had stonewalled them for a year on the proposed affiliation with the WRC, only changing his mind after months of student protests. Now he insisted that the university had fulfilled its commitment to protecting workers' rights when they affiliated with the WRC and that signing on to the DSP could violate US antitrust laws and bring the university into legal controversy. "Any collective activity with actual or potential market impact is vulnerable to a costly antitrust investigation," Stiles told them. "The marketing of university brand clothing definitely falls in that category. We must be cautious about signing onto the DSP, because when all is said and done, it's a movement to provide collective decision making by the largest possible group of universities that choose to join. That's an antitrust issue, plain and simple."

Stiles's arguments just seemed like further stonewalling to Karla. Already more than forty other schools had signed on to the DSP, including prestigious universities like Duke, Georgetown, and UCLA. "I'm so disappointed in my university and in you," she told Stiles. "It seems hypocritical that the issues and values I am learning about in my classes and that are embedded in the university's mission are not being carried out on campus. This is a human rights issue and our participation in the DSP can make a big difference in real people's lives, like the women I met in Nicaragua. Why shouldn't the university sign on to this letter? It's not legally binding. It would say a lot for the university to say they agree with it."

When Stiles still refused to sign, a dozen members of SSEJ, including Karla, prepared for an occupation of the president's office. Karla had never done anything like this before, and the thought made her nervous, but she would not walk away from the commitment she had made to the women workers in Nicaragua. She had to make a stand on their behalf. She and her SSEJ colleagues organized a workshop on nonviolent civil disobedience modeled on Martin Luther King Jr.'s civil rights movement that helped her to envision how the occupation would unfold.

She was caught off guard, however, by a meeting they had with Barbara Williams, the dean of students. Karla had always admired Dean Williams and although she didn't know her well, her previous interactions with the dean had been positive. This time, however, Dean Williams struck her as formal and impersonal. She warned the students that they would be violating several sections of the student code and breaking the law if they staged a sit-in, and refused to leave when asked. She emphasized that there would be serious academic repercussions for any student who participated, adding, "What we learned from the civil rights movement in the 1960s is every action has to have a consequence. If it doesn't, it has no moral value. Please think carefully about the consequences for each of you before you decide to go through with this action."

Now Karla found herself facing one of the most important decisions during her time in college. Her fellow SSEJ members asked Karla to draft a position statement that could be read to the president and distributed to the press. After their meeting with Dean Williams, Karla felt conflicted about whether she should participate in the sit-in. On the one hand, remembering the women she had met in Nicaragua, she felt deeply committed to justice and fair working conditions for textile workers, and she believed that the university had a moral obligation to change its purchasing policies. On the other hand, she was only one semester away from graduation, and the dean's threat of academic suspension for any student who participated in the occupation would jeopardize her financial aid. The day of the occupation was approaching rapidly, and she knew she needed to make a decision. Perhaps she could at least draft the position statement for the students that would be read at the demonstration, though she needed to think about what to say in it. But should she also participate in the sit-in?

Commentary

Introduction

Take a moment to look at the labels on your clothes. Where were they made? Chances are that, like Karla, most of your clothing was made outside the United States, in China or countries in Latin America or Southeast Asia. Yet thirty or forty years ago, most of your clothing would have had "Made in USA" on the label. Why? What has happened in the intervening decades?

The pattern of finding poor and developing nations on our clothing labels is not coincidental. It reflects broad changes in the global economy that in turn have led to profound transformation of societies worldwide and the lives of their citizens—especially the poor. Some see these changes as bringing hope for better lives for poor people; others say they simply continue centuries of colonial exploitation by the wealthy nations of the North.

From either perspective evolving dynamics in the global economy raise many challenging ethical issues and questions:

- How are societies changing in response to the global economy, and what say, if any, do citizens have in these transformations?
- How are wealth and incomes being distributed, and how does this affect access to resources, wealth, and power, within and between nations?
- What are the environmental effects of globalization, both on local ecosystems and the planet? Does globalization affect climate change?
- What responsibilities, if any, do consumers and citizens of affluent nations have in response to issues of injustice, inequity, and environmental degradation in the countries that make our clothing, electronic devices, and a whole host of other consumer goods?

This case reflects these and other issues related to globalization, labor, and consumption. It shows how broad dynamics of the global economy discussed in Chapter 2 bear on the individual lives of two groups who are connected through complicated global chains of production and consumption: textile workers in a garment factory in Nicaragua and consumers in the United States. Does Karla have any moral responsibility to respond to what she perceives as the unjust situation of the women she met working in the textile factory in Nicaragua, and, if so, how should she best respond? The case in turn asks each of us to reflect on what responsibilities we as consumers in the affluent world have for the work conditions, societies, and environments of poor people in the developing world who increasingly make the consumer goods we buy.

To understand the historical dynamics behind Karla's encounter with the Nicaraguan textile workers, we begin with background on the global economy to examine how and why the textile manufacturing industry, once a mainstay of the US economy, has shifted almost entirely overseas. We trace the concerns about worker conditions in garment factories that have led to international monitoring efforts to assure minimum standards of worker rights. We then explore the moral dimensions of these issues through two lenses: (1) how the issues are viewed from the four global perspectives discussed in Chapter 2 and (2) how the five norms of the ethic of ecological justice discussed in Chapter 3 inform our ethical analysis. We end by returning to Karla's situation in the case to ask what she should do and in turn how we should respond to issues raised by globalization.

Rise of the Global Garments Industry

All of us wear clothing and shoes, and we make decisions about what to buy based on several factors such as style, price, quality, and availability. These individual decisions enter into a marketplace where they cumulatively shape and are shaped by a garment industry that is now global in extent. Yet unlike perishable food items that can only be grown or raised in certain locations or may not travel well, clothing and shoes have no similar restrictions. This means that in the neoliberal context of decreased barriers to international trade, they can be produced wherever conditions are most profitable. Poor nations often have two advantages over developed nations that are attractive to businesses concerned about profits: large quantities of poor people who will work for very low wages and lax environmental regulations that keep production costs low. Producing clothing and shoes requires low-skill labor and relatively low levels of technology, giving poor nations a clear economic advantage in attracting clothing manufacturers. Lack of transparency and access to the factories that produce our clothing often hides abusive and unsafe conditions and makes monitoring them difficult.

Gaps between wealthy and poor nations are not new, though they have grown dramatically in recent decades. Historically, more developed nations protected their domestic industries from foreign competition through tariffs on imports: cost advantages from producing textiles overseas were erased by imposing tariffs that made imported goods more expensive than locally produced items. High transportation costs and poor international communications systems added to the expense of producing goods internationally, helping to favor domestic production and national economies.

These conditions began to change following World War II, as shipping costs fell and international communications became faster and cheaper with the rise of satellite communications and the Internet. Perhaps most important, however, has been the shift to a neoliberal market economy grounded in the principles of trade liberalization and free trade.

Near the end of World War II, representatives of the Allied nations gathered in Bretton Woods, New Hampshire, to discuss rebuilding the global economy after the war. They laid the groundwork for three international institutions to oversee the global capitalist economy. Faced with a war-torn Europe, they created the World Bank to fund Europe's redevelopment and reconstruction. A decade later the World Bank shifted this mission to the "Third World,"[6] focusing on economic and social development to reduce poverty. Needing to revitalize trade between nations, the Allied nations created the International Monetary Fund (IMF) to address monetary issues. Its primary mission was to stabilize and regulate currency exchange rates to facilitate trade and to make loans during financial crises to help nations with balance of payment problems. Finally, they created the General Agreement on Tariffs and Trade (GATT), as an interim institution to facilitate international trade in goods and services by decreasing trade barriers. The GATT was replaced by the World Trade Organization (WTO) in 1995.

Trade liberalization is the freeing of trade from state-imposed restrictions by reducing tariffs and other trade barriers (such as customs requirements or regulations on how goods are produced) in the belief that government interventions disrupt the natural efficiency of the market.[7] The GATT organized eight rounds of multilateral trade negotiations to reduce barriers between member nations from 1947 until 1995 when the newly organized WTO took over its mission.

In the decades following World War II, the United States protected its large domestic textile industry by limiting imports to preset quotas rather than include textiles in GATT negotiations. This began to change with the rise of neoliberalism under the Reagan and Bush administrations in the 1980s, and the Clinton administration's embrace of free trade in the 1990s. In 1994, the GATT passed the Agreement on Textiles and Clothing. This treaty sought to reduce trade barriers on textiles by phasing out the fixed quotas on the amount of textiles that could be exported from the Third World over a ten-year period. The goal was to give domestic textile producers in affluent nations time to adjust to increased competition from Third World countries. In reality, this made little difference, given the far cheaper labor costs in poor nations. Today virtually all textile production has shifted to developing nations.

Advocates of neoliberal globalization see this shift as critical to integrating poor nations into the global economy and facilitating their economic growth and development. Critics see it as devastating an important sector of the manufacturing industry in the United States, leading to loss of good-paying jobs and downward pressure on wages while exploiting poor people in the Global South. They argue it leads to a global *race to the bottom* where poor nations compete with each other to attract investment by TNCs. These nations face pressure to lower wages and eliminate regulations that protect workers and the environment. Many of them have also implemented structural adjustment policies (SAPs),[8] resulting in a shift of their domestic economies away from meeting local needs in favor of exports.

The shift of jobs overseas was accelerated by the *Walmart effect*. Although Walmart had long prided itself in featuring products *Made in the USA*, by the 1990s it began to import less expensive products from China to gain a competitive edge over its retail rivals. Walmart also demanded that its US-based suppliers lower the costs of their products each year if they wanted to retain their contracts with Walmart. The result was a mass exodus of production from the United States since manufacturers now reliant on the large retail chains for selling their products could no longer compete with lower production and manufacturing costs overseas.

This led to buyer-driven global production chains that now propel global manufacturing. In the garment industry, global production and trade are controlled by relatively few TNCs, large retailers like Walmart and branded merchandisers like Nike. In buyer-driven commodity chains, these corporations set up decentralized production networks in a variety of exporting countries throughout the developing world. Rather than producing goods themselves, corporate retailers or marketers order the goods and supply all the specifications from tiered networks of contractors who produce the actual products. New information technologies allow transnational manufacturing companies to send product design and specifications instantly throughout their global networks.[9]

FTZs and Worker Rights

Poor nations with high unemployment rates, such as Nicaragua, compete for these TNC investments and contracts by creating FTZs, which are designated areas exempt from national tax laws to attract foreign companies and provide jobs. Just outside Managua, Las Mercedes FTZ houses factories owned by companies based mostly in Taiwan, Korea, and the United States that employ over thirty thousand workers who make clothing for export to the United States.

Worldwide over 80 percent of textile and garment workers are women between eighteen and twenty-five years of age, usually employed in the lowest skilled and lowest wage sectors. Often migrants from rural areas, they send some of their paychecks home in the form of remittances to support their families, making rural communities increasingly dependent on the export sector. As the women from the MEC detailed in the case, export factories prefer to hire women who are single and often dismiss them if they marry or become pregnant. They frequently are denied bathroom breaks and forced to undergo pregnancy tests or take birth control so the companies do not have to pay maternity leave costs.[10] Many are hired under so-called flexible contracts, which mean they are brought in during times of peak demand and forced to work long hours and overtime, but then they are let go when demand slackens.[11] Male supervisors often inflict verbal and physical abuse on the women, who are forced to complete high quotas each day.

While FTZs provide jobs for workers, they generate very little additional local economic activity because wages are usually below subsistence level, and governments collect no tax revenue to support infrastructure and social programs. There are few economic ripple effects as the raw materials assembled into clothing are rarely made in the host country but instead are brought in duty free from other poor nations, assembled in the factories, and exported duty free again. Though the label on the finished garment may say *Made in Nicaragua*, in actuality it is typically assembled in the final country from components made all over the world: fabric from India, buttons from Indonesia, zippers from El Salvador. FTZs have proliferated throughout the Global South as nations desperate to provide jobs for their chronically underemployed populations forgo tax revenues in favor of employment for some.

The rush to outsource clothing and other manufacturing to the Global South led to widespread human rights concerns, as hard-fought labor gains and regulations in developed countries did not accompany the shift to poor nations. Concerns about worker conditions in textile assembly plants accelerated in 1996 when labor activists revealed that clothing endorsed by actress Kathie Lee Gifford was being made in Honduran factories by underage workers under exploitative conditions. In another high-profile case, activists accused Nike of contracting with sweatshop factories in countries like Indonesia, Vietnam, and China that prohibited union organizing. When workers gained some rights or increases in income in countries where Nike products were made, Nike moved their contracts to countries with fewer rights and cheaper production costs. Consumer pressure on clothing companies like Nike and the Gap led to increased international monitoring efforts by independent groups such as the International Labor Organization and the WRC, as portrayed in the case.

Some US-based companies tried to address concerns about the working conditions of contract workers, achieving mixed results. For example, in 1991 Levi-Strauss was the first TNC to develop a comprehensive code of conduct with its Global Sourcing Guidelines, and two years later Levi's cited its guidelines as the reason for pulling out of China due to ongoing human rights violations there. Yet by 1998 Levi's had softened its standards and reentered China, citing market pressures that required it to use low-cost Chinese factories to remain competitive.

Student Activism on Sweatshop Conditions

In 1997, college students concerned with labor abuses in sweatshops organized USAS to put pressure on their university administrations that earn revenue by contracting with clothing companies to sell apparel with university logos. The market for university logo apparel is estimated at nearly $4 billion a year, providing significant potential leverage for universities to pressure clothing retailers. Because a single garment might combine parts, labor, fabric, and other elements from many countries, it is difficult to create a fair trade labeling standard, and so efforts have focused on creating codes of conduct to monitor factories where logo clothing is produced. A coalition of students, labor experts, and workers created the WRC as a nonprofit organization in 2001 "to investigate worker rights abuses in factories producing college-logoed apparel to ensure that the Codes of Conduct adopted by colleges, universities, high schools, and school districts are enforced. These codes are designed to ensure that factories producing clothing and other goods bearing school logos respect the basic rights of workers, such as the freedom to organize a union and dignified wages and working conditions."[12]

USAS and the WRC began the DSP so that universities can acquire logo apparel from suppliers that commit to worker rights, including the right to a living wage,[13] the right to organize, and collective bargaining. Universities that join the DSP commit to long-term contracts with suppliers that cover the actual costs of producing apparel under applicable labor standards and provide workers with a living wage. Antitrust concerns led the US Department of Justice in 2011 to issue a *business review letter* stating that the DSP did not violate antitrust standards and was unlikely to lessen competition in the university apparel market. As of 2015, 185 colleges and universities have affiliated with the DSP.

An incident in Honduras shows the potential of collective consumer pressure to help factory workers. After years of organizing efforts, workers in a clothing factory in Choloma, Honduras, succeeded in forming a union in 2009. Shortly thereafter, Russell Athletic closed the factory and relocated to another country with lower labor costs, eliminating jobs for 1,200 Honduran workers. USAS and the WRC issued a report declaring the action to be a flagrant violation of the code of conduct many universities had signed to cover factories that produce licensed apparel, since the codes include the right to unionize. Student activists sprang into action to pressure their administrations, and more than a hundred DSP-affiliated schools threatened to end their licensing agreement with Russell. A year later Russell announced it was opening a new factory in Choloma and rehiring all 1,200 workers. The new workers union in turn negotiated a 26 percent pay increase and the right to hold independent freedom of association trainings at all Russell plants.[14]

Despite some successes with these efforts, conditions in many garment factories remain appalling, with long hours, forced overtime, and unsafe and unsanitary conditions. Major brands subcontract production to local and foreign-owned factories and then try to absolve themselves of responsibility for conditions in the plants, claiming that is the responsibility of local authorities and governments. Sometime results are dire. In April 2013, for example, the shoddily built Rana Plaza building in Bangladesh that housed five garment factories producing clothing for 29 major brands collapsed, killing over 1,125 workers and injuring another 2,500. Shortly after the tragedy, a group of nongovernmental organizations (NGOs) and retailers created the Accord on Fire and Building Safety in Bangladesh.[15] This was a five-year legally binding agreement between international labor organizations, NGOs, and retailers involved in the textile industry to maintain minimum safety standards in Bangladeshi textile factories. Citing liability concerns, several US-based retail giants, including Walmart and the Gap, refused to sign the accord. Instead they created a parallel, but nonbinding proposal, the Alliance for Bangladesh Worker Safety.[16] The same retailers also refused to help compensate family members of the workers who were killed or injured in the collapse.[17]

Yet as seen in the case, workers desperate for employment of any kind generally do not support consumer boycotts of factories or the TNCs that contract with them for fear that the companies will simply move their operations to another country, and they will be left without jobs. These are not empty threats. In 2010, for example, when Honduras raised its minimum wage 6.5 percent, sixteen textile factories moved next door to Nicaragua, whose minimum wage was half that of Honduras.[18]

This case focuses on the textile industry to expose and analyze broader dynamics in the global economy. The concerns discussed here are not unique to textiles, however. Similar worker safety and environmental problems are reported in the electronics industry, where Apple and other retailers of devices from smart phones to tablets have been dogged by accusations of abuses by the manufacturers with whom they contract. These repeated abuses raise questions about whether exploitative practices are endemic to the neoliberal global economy where profit, decreased regulation, and reduced production costs are the bottom line, or whether they can be reformed and changed through greater transparency and consumer pressure. How one views this debate is largely shaped by one's social location in the global economy and how one frames the issues. This in turn shapes moral assessment, to which we now turn.

Ethical Issues in the Global Garment Industry

Each of the four global perspectives discussed in Chapter 2 frames this case differently. Market liberals see textile factories in FTZs as key to stimulating economic growth that reduces poverty. FTZ factories provide income and job skills to millions of otherwise unemployed poor people, helping to break cycles of poverty that trap rural people, especially rural women, in destitute conditions. In a global economy where affluent nations have abundant wealth, technology, education, and job skills, one of the few comparative advantages poor nations have is a workforce willing to work for low wages. FTZs allow them to attract the international investment they need to get on the first rung of the ladder of the international economy. Once there, poor nations can gain the resources, technology, and job skills to begin to lift their populations out of poverty.

Lourdes Montenegro represents this position in the case. PRONicaragua's purpose is to attract foreign investment by promoting the cost savings available in Nicaragua, particularly its low wages and proximity to US markets. What looks like exploitation to Karla, Lourdes sees as economic opportunity for young women, allowing them to earn their own income and break out of traditional patriarchal rural social patterns, building autonomy through increased prosperity. Interference from the outside, either from government regulations or protests from well-meaning but misinformed international activists, threatens the few opportunities poor workers in Nicaragua have to gain employment and work their way out of poverty.

Institutionalists largely agree with the market liberal view of the benefits of the textile industry for poor countries like Nicaragua. FTZs can be important initial strategies to attract foreign investment, though their tax-free status should be temporary. Phasing out businesses' tax-free status over time allows governments to gain needed revenue to carry out social development programs that lead to greater equity in the population.

Institutionalists see economic growth from foreign investment as critical to achieving the UN Millennium Development Goals (MDGs) for social development.[19] Progress toward meeting the goals is apparent already. Whether reducing extreme poverty by 50 percent, lowering the number of people without safe water or sanitation by half, reducing hunger by 50 percent, or lowering child mortality by two-thirds, several of the MDGs were reached well before 2015.[20] This is an enormous global achievement, brought about in large part by an unprecedented period of economic growth. Institutionalists argue that even though conditions in the sweatshops can be harsh and should be improved, virtually every poor country that has developed successfully began with similar factories in their early stages of industrialization. Depriving poor nations of much-needed international investment leaves them mired in poverty. As economist Jeffrey Sachs argues, "rich-world protesters should support increased numbers of [sweatshop] jobs, albeit under safer working conditions, by protesting trade protectionism in their own countries that keeps out garment exports from countries such as Bangladesh."[21]

While not insensitive to the economic needs and factory conditions of workers in global manufacturing, bioenvironmentalists focus on the environmental unsustainability of the global economy. The shift of manufacturing to the Global South only further fuels ever-increasing levels of human consumption of resources that already exceed the carrying capacity of Earth. While the economic empowerment of women is important to slowing population growth, tying women's advancement to global capitalism only exacerbates unsustainable consumption patterns. Long production chains distance consumers in the Global North not only from exploitative work conditions in sweatshops, but also from the negative environmental effects of free trade. These include increased pollution in poor countries and the unsustainable use of their natural resources.

Trade in essence allows countries to mask their true "ecological footprint."[22] By shifting the production and environmental impact of the goods they consume to developing nations, people in affluent countries can live well beyond their nation's carrying capacity while poor nations live below theirs. In addition, the globalized manufacturing industry from textiles to electronics to food exports is dependent on fossil fuel–based transportation systems that contribute significantly to GHG emissions as well as externalize many other environmental and social costs.[23] For bioenvironmentalists, therefore, focusing on the sweatshop conditions in textile factories only treats the symptoms of a much larger and unsustainable globalization disease.

Like their bioenvironmentalist allies, social greens critique globalization for spreading large-scale industrialism that exploits both people and the environment in poor nations. With their deep concern for economic justice, however, social greens focus most on workers and examine the systemic issues in the global economy that foster a manufacturing system they see as inherently exploitative of its workers and destructive of local communities. Contrary to the market liberal claim that globalization is a rising tide that lifts all ships, social greens argue that free trade does not benefit all trading partners equally. The disproportionate and growing power of TNCs under IMF- and WTO-imposed conditions makes poor countries like Nicaragua vulnerable to the *race to the bottom* effect where they compete against each other to attract investment without TNCs paying their fair share of revenues and costs. FTZs starve governments of needed revenue, and the income workers earn is usually well below a livable wage.

In Nicaragua, for example, since passage of the Central America Free Trade Agreement, textiles and apparel make up roughly half of exports to the United States, and over 99 percent are produced in FTZs. Yet the average wage in textile factories is only 37 to 52 percent of a Nicaraguan living wage.[24] In the case, social green perspectives are most closely reflected in the women of the MEC movement. They seek better working conditions in the textile factories and are concerned with the negative impacts of the FTZs on their communities, but fear too much pressure might lead to companies relocating the factories and leaving them without work. They seek long-term transformation of textile manufacturing in favor of more just conditions for workers and yet recognize the importance of textile jobs for Nicaragua's development in the current configuration of the global economy.

Insights from the Norms of Ecological Justice

What insights might we gain from applying the five norms of the ethic of ecological justice to this case? Drawing from the discussion in Chapter 3, we remember that moral norms are broad directives that help us determine how to embody important values in the actions we take. The following norms each suggest ways to frame and respond to the case in order to embody particular values important to ecological justice.

Justice is the central norm from which the other four are derived. It is also the central ethical issue in this case. Justice demands fairness and equity in how others are treated, and in ecological justice it requires a special concern for the poor and marginalized, including all species, not just humans. Here, framing is key to how we apply this norm. Do FTZs and their clothing factories represent an expansion of opportunity and freedom for poor people by providing jobs and incomes that typically exceed what they could earn in rural communities or domestic factories? Or are they simply the latest form of exploitation that takes advantage of the legacy of poverty from centuries of colonialism and oppression to add to the wealth of the Global North at the expense of the Global South? And what of the effects on other forms of life and ecosystems?

Justice also demands an equitable distribution of burdens and costs. How equitable is the current global economy that provides an abundance of cheap goods and services to affluent nations, allowing them to live well beyond their local carrying capacities, while poor nations are left with the social and environmental costs of production? At the very least, justice would demand a better global balance of burdens and benefits, starting with better conditions for factory workers. It may also require going beyond particular cases to address structural injustices that underlie the global economy in order to address pervasive economic, social, and environmental inequities.

Issues of sustainability arise at many levels in this case. Most immediate is the unsustainability of the work itself in textile factories. Difficult conditions force many women to leave sweatshops before the end of their twenties; others are simply let go once they reach a certain age, get married, or become pregnant. Critics also question the sustainability of the global economy itself, arguing that ongoing economic growth and consumption threaten planetary well-being on several fronts, from excessive resource use and species extinction to rising pollution and climate change. Advocates counter that allowing the market to act free of government interference allows for the most efficient use of resources and contributes long term to sustainability.

Sustainability raises the question of how to meet the demands of current generations without compromising the anticipated needs of future generations (both human and other kind). Advocates argue that the global economy is the best way to stimulate economic and social development in poor nations. This in turn lowers birth rates, moving populations more quickly toward sustainable levels. Critics counter that increasing rates of social and economic inequality both between and within nations combined with poverty contribute to population growth and other unsustainable social dynamics such as massive immigration by poor people in search of jobs.

Directly related to debates about sustainability is the norm of sufficiency that stresses all forms of life are entitled to a share of the goods of Earth. Critics argue that human consumption levels stimulated by the global economy already threaten the survival of many species and call for a radical decrease in consumption to move toward environmental sustainability. There is a tension, however, between embodying frugality and moderation in our consumption habits and the demands of the global economy for ever-greater levels of consumption to keep poor people employed. Indeed, the fall in demand for consumer goods in affluent nations during the 2008 global recession led to the loss of jobs and increased poverty for millions of poor people throughout the Global South, illustrating how dependent poor nations have become on the global economy for economic development.[25] In addition, pervasive and growing inequities between affluent and poor nations and increasingly within nations make even visualizing sufficiency a challenge, as the wealthy have more than enough to meet their basic needs while the poor do not. Yet meeting the needs of the poor seems dependent on producing ever-greater amounts of consumer goods for the already wealthy and the growing global middle class. The norm of sufficiency calls each of us to evaluate how much is enough while addressing the longer-term structural dynamics of the global economy that maintains there is no ceiling on what is enough.

The norm of participation also raises difficult issues at multiple levels in this case. Most workers in the textile industry have very little opportunity for genuine participation in the political and economic decisions that affect them, especially with pervasive pressures against unionizing or speaking out, as the women of the MEC movement remind us. How much moral agency can desperate people exercise in contexts of economic poverty and political repression when their families' survival is on the line? Proponents of globalization argue that over time free trade increases democracy and worker rights, pointing to previously authoritarian regimes in nations, such as South Korea and Taiwan, that now enjoy high levels of income and political democracy. Others question how inevitable this transition is, arguing that communist countries, such as China and Vietnam, that have embraced free trade and market economies show little evidence of greater respect for human rights or democracy. The concern for empowerment at the center of the norm of participation highlights the importance of consumer pressure to improve factory conditions and guarantee worker rights without, however, jeopardizing their jobs. Bioenvironmentalists remind us that we need to recognize the cumulative impacts of sweatshops and global manufacturing on both local environments and planetary systems.

Together with justice, solidarity is perhaps the central norm in this case, and the one Karla in the case wrestles with most directly. Solidarity acknowledges the kinship and interdependence of all forms of life, suggesting that we do have moral responsibility for the actions we take that affect others' well-being—in particular the most marginalized. Even though the producer–consumer chain in globalization is often long and complex, the actions affluent consumers in the Global North take or refrain from taking can have profound effects on marginalized others, both human and other kind. For example, the decisions that millions of middle-class persons make each day about purchasing and driving automobiles fuels the emission of GHGs that cause global warming. Conversely, consumer pressures on companies like Nike led it to become a leader in corporate social responsibility, lowering the ecological footprint of the production of its shoes while monitoring conditions in the factories where they are produced. How can Karla best embody the solidarity virtues of humility, compassion, courage, and generosity in this case? Humility suggests listening directly to the voices of the marginalized and responding to their pleas. Compassion means *suffering with others* and implies active empathy for their plight. Courage suggests we share the risks and costs of addressing the situation and working for change. And generosity demands that we share our resources of time, money, and energy.

Responding to the Case

How then should Karla embody these norms and virtues in her particular situation? In the case, Karla is faced with drafting a statement outlining the concerns of the students to be read at the demonstration. She also has to decide whether she should also participate in the sit-in to pressure the administration,[26] knowing that possible arrest and academic suspension could prevent her from graduating. How should she frame the issues in the statement she writes? What are the most relevant ethical issues and facts in the case, and why? Is the university wise to avoid possible costly legal liabilities by refusing to sign the DSP? Or does it have a moral responsibility to avoid benefiting from exploitation of workers in the factories that produce its logo clothing? Would Karla's participation in the sit-in be an act of moral courage and responsibility, fulfilling the commitment she made to the women of the MEC movement, or would it be prudent to avoid arrest and suspension so that she can graduate and focus her efforts elsewhere? What would you counsel Karla to do, and what might you do if you were in her shoes? Where should citizens in affluent nations concerned about sweatshops focus their efforts?

Notes

[1]Witness for Peace, "Fact Sheet: The Winners and Losers of DR-CAFTA in Nicaragua's Free Trade Zones," http://www.witnessforpeace.org.

[2]International Confederation of Free Trade Unions, "ICFTU Annual Survey of Violations of Trade Union Rights 2006," http://www.newunionism.net.

[3]War on Want, "Women Factory Workers in Honduras," http://www.waronwant.org.

[4]PRONicaragua, "About PRONicaragua," http://www.pronicaragua.org.

[5]United Students Against Sweatshops, "Garment Worker Solidarity," http://usas.org.

[6]The term *Third World* came out of the post–World War II Cold War era to refer to the former colonies of the Global South. *First World* referred to the capitalist democracies of Europe, the United States, Japan, Australia, and New Zealand; *Second World* referred to the communist countries in the Soviet Bloc (see note 8 in Chapter 2). Elsewhere in the book we use the term *Global South*; because much of the literature analyzing globalization drawn on in this commentary uses *Third World*, we retain that usage here.

[7]Richard Peet, *Unholy Trinity: The IMF, World Bank and WTO*, 2nd ed. (London: Zed Books, 2009), 182.

[8]According to the World Health Association, "Structural Adjustment Programmes (SAPs) are economic policies for developing countries that have been promoted by the World Bank and International Monetary Fund (IMF) since the early 1980s by the provision of loans conditional on the adoption of such policies. . . . They are designed to encourage the structural adjustment of an economy by, for example, removing 'excess' government controls and promoting market competition as part of the neo-liberal agenda followed by the Bank. . . . SAP policies reflect the neo-liberal ideology that drives globalization. They aim to achieve long-term or accelerated economic growth in poorer countries by restructuring the economy and reducing government intervention." See http://www.who.int/trade/glossary/story084/en/.

[9]WIEGO: Women in Informal Employment: Globalizing and Organizing, "Garment Workers," http://wiego.org.

[10]Feminist Majority Foundation, "Feminists Against Sweatshops," http://www.feminist.org.

[11]WIEGO, "Garment Workers."

[12]United Students against Sweatshops, "Campaign to Affiliate with the Worker Rights Consortium (WRC)," http://usas.org.

[13]Living wage refers to "a theoretical wage level that allows the earner to afford adequate shelter, food and the other necessities of life . . . The goal of the living wage is to allow employees to earn enough income for a satisfactory standard of living"; http://www.investopedia.com/terms/l/living_wage.asp. In most poor nations, there is a significant gap between the minimum monthly wage garment workers earn and that nation's definition of a living wage that covers minimum levels of a worker's or family's food, shelter, clothing, and other necessities.

[14]For details of the USAS campaign on behalf of the workers in Choloma, Honduras, see United Students against Sweatshops, "Details of the Historic Victory by Honduran Factory Workers," http://usas.org.

[15]Bangladesh Accord Foundation, "Accord on Fire and Building Safety in Bangladesh," http://bangladeshaccord.org.

[16]Alliance for Bangladesh Worker Safety, http://www.bangladeshworkersafety.org.

[17]For an overview of the collapse of the Rana Plaza building and subsequent international response, see "2013 Savar Building Collapse," http://en.wikipedia.org/wiki/2013_Savar_building_collapse.

[18]Witness for Peace, "Charter Cities: The New Neoliberal Experiment in Latin America," http://witness4peace.blogspot.com; see also Central-American Business Council, "Unpredictable Minimum Wage Kills Jobs," http://www.centralamericadata.com.

[19]The eight Millennium Goals are (1) eradicate extreme poverty and hunger; (2) achieve

universal primary education; (3) promote gender equality and empower women; (4) reduce child mortality; (5) improve maternal health; (6) combat HIV/AIDS, malaria, and other diseases; (7) ensure environmental sustainability; and (8) global partnership for development; http://www.un.org/millenniumgoals.

[20] *The UN Millennium Development Goals Report 2014* (New York: United Nations, 2014), 4–5, http://www.un.org/millenniumgoals.

[21] Jeffrey Sachs, *The End of Poverty: Economic Possibilities for Our Time* (New York: Penguin, 2005), 11.

[22] "The ecological footprint is a measure of human demand on Earth's ecosystems. It is a standardized measure of demand for natural capital that may be contrasted with the planet's ecological capacity to regenerate." "Ecological footprint," http://en.wikipedia.org. See also Global Footprint Network, http://www.footprintnetwork.org.

[23] By 2014 emissions from the global shipping industry totaled one billion tons a year, accounting for 3 percent of the world's total GHG emissions. Unless addressed, shipping emissions are expected to triple by 2050. See Transport and Environment, "Shipping and Climate Change," http://www.transportenvironment.org. Aviation emissions for both cargo and passenger travel amount to about 1.5 percent of global GHG emissions and are expected to quadruple by 2050. See Center for Climate and Energy Solutions, "Aviation," http://www.c2es.org.

[24] Witness for Peace, "Fact Sheet: The Winners and Losers of DR-CAFTA in Nicaragua's Free Trade Zones," http://www.witnessforpeace.org.

[25] *The Global Social Crisis: Report on the World Social Situation 2011* (New York: United Nations, 2011), 28, http://www.un.org.

[26] For a good overview of the history and tactics of nonviolent conflict and civil disobedience, see Nonviolent Conflict, http://www.nonviolent-conflict.org.

Resources for Teaching

This appendix contains various teaching resources for courses in Earth ethics. These resources include the description of an ecological autobiography assignment as well as several spectrum exercises that help students locate themselves in key debates about social and environmental ethics. In addition, the appendix contains instructions for examining power dynamics in cases as well as guidelines for how students can write brief papers or make group presentations about the cases in this volume. These resources are addressed to students and their teachers; thus the style and tone are informal.

Reflection Paper: Ecological Autobiography

Personal experiences shape the way ethical issues are perceived, analyzed, and assessed. The purpose of this exercise is to reflect on the following question: "How has my relationship to nature influenced the way that I approach environmental issues?" In a brief paper, structure your reflection around the following questions:

Individual Factors

- What have been your most direct experiences of nature and how have they influenced you? Have your primary experiences been through work (farming, trail management, etc.), recreation (hiking, fishing, hunting, etc.), and/or through participation in various organizations (like 4H, Boy/Girl Scouts, church camps, etc.)?
- How has growing up in a rural, urban, or suburban context influenced your environmental values for good or ill?

Family/Historical Factors

- How has your relationship to nature been influenced by the experience of your parents, grandparents, and ancestors? How did they use the land and relate to nature? Have these familial experiences shaped the way you experience and value nature?

287

- What have been some of the important historical, social, cultural, and economic factors that have shaped your *family's* relationship with nature (western settlement, encounters with indigenous persons, slavery, economic depression, wars, 1960s social movements, etc.)?
- How have important historical, social, cultural, and economic factors during *your* life shaped or influenced your experiences of and attitudes toward nature?

Personal Insights

- Are your ethical views about nature grounded in a particular religious faith or philosophical tradition? If so, how?
- How has nature impacted your life? Conversely, to what extent has your life impacted nature?

Spectrum Exercises: Key Debates in Environmental Ethics

The following set of spectrum exercises enables students to locate themselves physically in five key debates in environmental ethics. The first spectrum exercise involves a dialogue between an anthropocentrist and a biocentrist over the value of other forms of life and the rights of nature. The second exercise focuses on the value of individual forms of life versus protecting the welfare of ecosystems as a whole. The third exercise involves a debate between a proponent of critical ecology and an advocate for environmental reform and free market approaches to protecting the environment. The fourth exercise examines early debates between the conservation perspective advocated by Gifford Pinchot and the preservationist viewpoint John Muir argued—a debate that still reverberates today. The final exercise presents the four main perspectives on the global economy discussed in Chapter 2 and summarizes the main points of each perspective. (For this spectrum exercise readers should stand in the four corners of the room with students beginning in the center.)

Students begin these exercises by standing in the middle of the room, equidistant from two readers who stand at opposite corners. As the dialogue unfolds between the readers, students are invited to locate themselves physically in the debate after each numbered paragraph is read. That is, they are encouraged to draw themselves closer to the perspective with which they most agree or to distance themselves from arguments with which they disagree. Often, students find themselves drawn back and forth as they recognize the strengths and weaknesses of either position. When the dialogue ends, students are asked to explain why they are standing where they are in relation to the arguments that were presented. After this experiential introduction, students find it much easier to understand and critique key figures or positions in the field of environmental ethics as they are presented in lectures and readings.

Dialogue 1: Biocentrism vs. Anthropocentrism

BIOCENTRISM	ANTHROPOCENTRISM
1. When I look at the environmental mess we have gotten ourselves into, I think a big part of the problem is our attitudes toward other forms of life. We don't really appreciate or value the diversity of life forms. I've come to believe that *all* forms of life have *equal* value. All forms of life have an equal right to live and flourish, not just humans. Until society believes that, we aren't going to be able to resolve the environmental crisis.	2. I agree with your concern for the environment, but I disagree with your views of other forms of life. There's a basic difference between human life and all other forms of life. It is obvious to me that a human life is *more valuable* than the life of a mosquito or some plant.
3. I knew you would say that! In your view, everything has to be subordinated to humanity. But I believe that *all* forms of life have intrinsic value, not just instrumental value. *All* forms of life have *value for their own sake*, not just for how important they might be to us humans. Mosquitoes may seem obnoxious to us, but they have a place in the scheme of things. And we should care about the plants in the rain forest, not merely because they might some day be useful to us but because they're living organisms and therefore are valuable.	4. Okay. I can agree that all forms of life have *some* value (even mosquitoes), but that doesn't mean that everything has *equal* value. Different forms of life have different levels of value, and it's clear that human beings have the *highest* value. We need to keep the environment healthy so our children and future generations can thrive—but we also need to use different parts of the environment to meet human needs. Are you telling me that if your child had cancer and that plant in the rainforest held the cure, that you wouldn't want someone to harvest it? In a world of many human needs, we have a right, even a duty, to use other parts of nature to make life better for humanity. And when there is a conflict between humans and other forms of life, we should side with humans.
5. That's the attitude that's at the root of our problems: Thinking that nature exists for our sake. Like all other organisms, humans should only use other parts of nature to satisfy our basic human *needs*—and we need to rethink what those really are. We have no right to destroy other forms of life just to satisfy our supposed needs that are often just forms of greed. The human species is one species among all the others and part of an interdependent whole, and we are *all* of equal value.	6. We're back to where we started, and I still don't believe that all creatures and species are equal. Our rational and moral powers set us apart from all other species. We are the only creatures that can transcend instinct in order to choose whether to do good or evil to another creature. For this reason there is a qualitative difference between the value of human life and all other forms of life.
7. I agree with you that human beings have some outstanding abilities that are superior to those of other animals. But other animals also have abilities far superior to ours, such as flying, or the hearing abilities of whales. Isn't it convenient and a bit self-serving that we choose the qualities we do best and construct a hierarchy of values that places us at the top? It's just this tendency toward up-down thinking that gets us into problems in the first place!	8. I agree that hierarchical thinking has led to serious problems in Western civilization, but we can't throw the baby out with the bath water. We need to avoid rigid either-or thinking, but we also need to make key distinctions where there are valid differences. Not all forms of life are of equal value; some are more important than others. It is our responsibility to discern and act on these differences in order to be good stewards of Earth.

Dialogue 2: Ecological Holism vs. Concern for Individual Life Forms

ECOLOGICAL HOLISM	INDIVIDUAL CONCERN
1. Do you remember the expensive efforts that were made a few years ago to save two whales that were trapped under the ice in Canada? I think that was a waste of money. We should be more concerned about maintaining the health of the ocean ecosystems that whales depend on instead of becoming fixated on the plight of two individual whales.	2. You're right that we should be concerned about the health of entire ecosystems that support all forms of life. But I disagree with you that protecting those ecosystems is more important than the individual lives of those creatures that live within them. The thought that we should not have tried to save those whales is morally repugnant. Each individual animal is a living being with rights that should be respected.
3. I appreciate your moral sensitivity, but I think that it is a little misguided. We have limited resources available, and we need to focus them on keeping whole ecosystems and habitats healthy, rather than on the particular animals within them. I think that whenever creatures or species act in ways that undermine the health and integrity of an ecosystem, they can and should be limited—and in some cases eliminated—for the greater ecological good. We see this with invasive species that threaten the ability of ecosystems to function. Invasive plants and animals should be eliminated from the ecosystems they threaten. And concern for healthy ecosystems must include human beings. Whether it's overpopulation of deer or people, it has become clear that there are far too many of us, and our numbers are destroying the planet.	4. There's a term for your position and it's called *environmental fascism*. We must never try to protect the common good by abandoning individual rights. I think the best way to protect ecosystems is by protecting the rights of all creatures in the environment. Sacrificing the lives and rights of individual creatures for the sake of the whole is never morally acceptable—whether those creatures are human or other animals. Ecosystems are dynamic and all plants and animals were once *invasive*—including humans. I've read about conservationists poisoning entire lakes and streams to rid them of tens of thousands of nonnative fish for the sake of the ecosystem. That is morally wrong. Those fish were introduced by humans and did nothing wrong. Ecosystems can and do adapt to new species—including to us.
5. I'm sorry, but I disagree. The survival of the planet's ecosystems is more important than what happens to individual creatures that live within them. The overall well-being of nature and its ecosystems as a whole is more important than the individual rights of creatures, and we must act accordingly. Responsible management of ecosystems requires that we protect their health and integrity, whether that is limiting humans and other species, or eliminating some entirely.	6. Your position is exceedingly dangerous. In effect you have declared yourself God—deciding who lives and who dies. If we don't keep a clear focus on the moral value of *each* individual creature, we become morally desensitized to all life and start down a slippery slope of trying to calculate who is worthy to survive and who is not. We have no business doing that!
7. I admit that my position may sound strange at first. But when you think about it, it's humans who have set ourselves up as God with respect to the ecosystem. Always putting emphasis on the individual rights of creatures, regardless of their effects on ecosystems, is just a way to maintain domination over the ecosystem rather than finding our appropriate place in it.	8. It is outrageous to suggest that a legitimate emphasis on rights can result in the domination of others. The whole concept of rights evolved precisely to protect those who were threatened with domination by others. What we need to do is figure out what to do when rights conflict. This is a task that involves responsibility, not domination.

Dialogue 3: Critical Ecology vs. Environmental Reform

CRITICAL ECOLOGY	ENVIRONMENTAL REFORM
1. Let's face it, the world is a mess! It seems the more we try to solve things, the more we mess things up. What we need is a completely different understanding of our relationship to, and our place in the natural world. We will not be able to transform our ecological problems until we transform ourselves and our societies. We need to understand that humans are fully part of the ecosystems where we live and adapt our societies to the needs of these ecosystems.	2. Yes, we do need to be more careful and intelligent about our relationship to nature, but we don't need some profound change in our worldview or philosophy to see what is wrong and take action. Our democratic, free market societies have provided us with many benefits, including the resources needed to protect the environment. We can correct our environmentally harmful behaviors by using better technologies, by updating our economic theories, and by passing laws with incentives to reduce environmental degradation.
3. Don't get me wrong. I'm not saying that we shouldn't take action where we can, but even those actions will inevitably be flawed until we change some of our basic assumptions about our relationship to the world. For example, we need to get rid of our false ways of thinking that see our minds as separate from our bodies and see humans as separate from the rest of nature. We need to get rid of our false sense of thinking that we are independent from the laws of nature and ecology, and accept our true *inter*dependence with other forms of life.	4. It is true that our narrow human-centered ways of thinking have caused enormous harm. We are deeply indebted to people like you who stress the interdependence of all forms of life. I think we are beginning to understand how we as human beings are dependent on other forms of life and how we need to take care of them in order for all of us to live. It's clear that we need to reform our ways of living to be better stewards of Earth than we have been.
5. Excuse me, but your stewardship model assumes precisely the paternalistic attitude that I'm talking about! It flows out of an up-down, dualistic mind-set that always has someone or something on top of somebody or something else—*managing* and controlling things for the good of those *underneath.* Historically, that has meant men in charge of women, one race in charge of another, owners in charge of workers. The only difference here is it's humans on top of the rest of nature! I think that this attitude is the underlying root of not only the ecocrisis, but also of racism, sexism, and class exploitation. Until we demolish this way of thinking and acting, all our efforts will only exacerbate the ecocrisis.	6. Whoa! That was a fast jump from steward-ship to patriarchy! The point is that we have to be realistic about what we can change. We don't have a lot of time for philosophical introspection and creating the new culture you desire. Unless we act quickly and wisely in the next ten to twenty years, the ecological systems that support life on Earth may collapse. We don't have the luxury to spend much time reflecting on *why* we are in this mess; we need to direct our energies toward *how* we can get out of it. We can't simply go back to some earlier, simpler time—the world is too complex for that. For better or worse, given the enormity of the problems that face us, this means working *within* the system we already have in place, and using the technology and political power already available to us.
7. Everyone agrees that we have to act now, immediately, but working within the system is no long-term answer—the system itself *is* the problem! It's what has caused our current problems. We might be able to limit some of the damage in the short term by working within the system, but the only effective long-term solution will require a total transformation of both the system and the culture that supports it.	8. I think you are too pessimistic about our abilities to change our behaviors and our culture. Utopian thinking will get us nowhere. Reform of the system is possible. Just look at the significant accomplishments of environmental legislation in the United States over the last thirty years such as the Clean Water Act and the Endangered Species Act. Reforming human behaviors and our social systems is possible, but it takes place one step at a time.

Dialogue 4: Conservation (Pinchot) vs. Preservation (Muir)

CONSERVATION	PRESERVATION
1. I've been reading about Teddy Roosevelt and the early conservation movement. It makes a lot of sense to me. His first director of the Forest Service, Gifford Pinchot, said "conservation is the application of common sense to the common problems for the common good." We can use our forest resources, but we must use them wisely and efficiently. *Sustainability* is the main value in conservation.	2. I think conservation is important, but I don't think it gets to the bottom of the issue. It's still too anthropocentric and utilitarian, valuing nature for what it can provide us. I'm reminded of what John Muir once said: "Mountain parks and reservations are useful not only as fountains of timber and irrigating rivers, but as fountains of life." He understood that wilderness, like all of nature, exists for its own sake, and we have a responsibility to preserve it.
3. But in terms of public policy, one of the strengths of conservation is that it's based on democratic principles. The resources of the public domain are used for the benefit of all people, not just the powerful. Government agencies accountable to elected officials administer sustainable-use policies on behalf of us all, so that resources are not exhausted and are used sustainably. It's a true *wise-use* policy.	4. That democratic basis is a strength, and to the extent that conservation preserves natural areas for future generations, I agree with you. But I think we need to ask, sustainable in what sense, and for whom? When you build dams to use water sustainably or log forests at a so-called sustainable rate, something precious is lost in the process: the integrity of natural places themselves. Some places are too precious to be used as resources. They should be preserved in all their natural integrity instead.
5. I don't agree that we should lock up the resources of nature by locking humans out—especially since we can use nature sustainably over time. Forestry now teaches scientific management techniques to maintain forest health. Some of the unhealthiest forests we now have are those that have been preserved from human use—as catastrophic fires keep reminding us. We need to be actively involved in managing forests to better protect them and conserve the resources in them for sustainable use.	6. I disagree. Muir understood the basic insights of ecology—that everything is hitched to everything else in the universe. Ecosystems are too complex to be managed successfully—we simply can't understand all the consequences of our actions. Preserving the integrity of natural places is the most effective way to conserve nature—*not* seeing nature as yet another thing to be managed for *our* benefit.
7. Preservation of some places and resources is important to protect the health of the environment, but it's not the main answer. The Clinton administration's attempt to keep millions of acres in a roadless category was a mistake—locking up all the resources those lands can offer. The environmental movement should focus primarily on *conservation*—drawing on science to use resources sustainably while protecting the environment. Conservation is a middle ground between the excesses of either exploitation or elitist preservation. It's a place where we can build consensus on environmental issues.	8. I have to disagree. The environmental movement should continue to focus primarily on *preservation*. We need to emulate John Muir in his passion for wilderness and recognize that too much already has been lost. I agree with Muir when he echoes Thoreau in arguing, "wildness is a necessity; the mountain parks and reservations are useful not only as fountains of timber and irrigating rivers, but as fountains of life." We need to preserve as many wild places as we can. The Clinton administration's Roadless Rule was a necessary step in that direction. It's too bad that later administrations have tried to overturn it.

Dialogue 5: Four Responses to Globalization, Poverty, and the Environment

Round 1:

A	B	C	D
I've been reading a lot about economic globalization and free trade lately. It seems to offer a promising way for poor nations to help their people get out of poverty by creating jobs through stimulating the free market in each country. By allowing international businesses to invest freely in poor nations without a lot of government controls, their economies can grow rapidly. Poor people then have a chance to earn more than they can now through their more traditional subsistence lifestyles, and lift themselves out of poverty. In addition, economic growth provides needed resources to protect the environment.	I agree with you that economic globalization offers a lot of promise for poor nations, but there is still an important role for governments to play to make sure that economic growth is accompanied by equity and a *fair* distribution of wealth. History has shown that unfettered laissez-faire capitalism can lead to great accumulation of wealth for the few, while the majority in society fail to benefit. It also can devastate the environment without government checks on it. Development agencies, such as the United Nations and the World Bank, are a necessary part of the equation to make sure economic growth is socially just and environmentally sustainable.	I disagree strongly with both of you! Neoliberal economic globalization is simply the latest way for the rich to exploit the poor and nature. It's *neocolonialism*—just the latest form for wealthy nations to take advantage of the lack of political power in poor nations. Corporations outsource jobs from First World nations like the United States to exploit poor workers in places like Honduras or China, and the majority of people and the environment in *both* places end up worse off. This in turn fuels the immigration crisis as millions of poor, displaced farmers and workers try to get into the United States to support their families. Only the rich are winners in this global game.	I agree that the current model of economic globalization is problematic but mostly because it is *environmentally disastrous*. Global trade is premised on unlimited access to cheap oil and further fuels global warming by all the greenhouse gases it produces. It's crazy that apples grown in New Zealand and shipped across the Pacific Ocean should be cheaper than apples grown here in the United States, but that's what's happening! And continuous economic growth only degrades nature. It's an environmentally unsustainable economic movement. We need to be *localizing* our economies, and making them more environmentally sustainable, *not* making them more globally dependent.

Round 2:

A	B	C	D
I admire your moral sentiments, but I think all of you fail to understand the basics of Economics 101: when different individuals or nations are allowed to make what they produce best and then trade them on the free market, *everyone* benefits. Protectionist measures that try to protect inefficient local producers, and costly environmental and labor rules make the economy inefficient and everyone loses. They are especially hard on the poor, by costing them jobs and leaving them in poverty. Too often government regulations and interference—while well intentioned—cause more problems than they resolve. We need to help poor nations restructure their economies to allow the free market to operate so their economies can grow and provide jobs for everyone. After all, *a rising tide lifts all ships!*	I agree with you that a growing market economy is key to lifting poor nations out of poverty, but free markets by themselves often only exacerbate long-standing problems of poverty, inequality, and environmental degradation. For example, markets provide no safety net to buffer some of the effects of unemployment, inflation, and dislocation of people and communities that economic globalization inevitably brings. Government actions are needed to correct market deficiencies. The *best* solution involves strengthening local and national democratic governance, and using globalization as a means to achieve social transformation. Good government *plus* free markets is the best combination to reduce poverty, protect the environment, and bring about much-needed social transformation in poor nations.	You both seem to assume that the so-called free market is both *free* and *fair* when it is anything but! It is stacked against poor nations and poor people, leading to even greater forms of dependency and exploitation. It's fundamentally undemocratic: unelected international organizations, such as the World Trade Organization and the International Monetary Fund, are controlled by wealthy nations— they force poor nations to restructure their economies and governments against the will and interests of their own people. So-called free trade leads to continued exploitation of poor nations: of both their natural resources *and* their cheap labor. What we need instead is global solidarity between workers everywhere and a new global economy that benefits the least well off, not just the rich.	You've described some of the problems with economic globalization but have missed the *central* problem: its thorough-going anthropocentrism that sees everything in the world as simply a resource for human consumption. It ignores basic ecological principles and the notion that there are planetary limits to human activity. And it ignores the value of anything other than human well-being—or, actually, the well-being of the rich. We need to start by recognizing the interdependence of *all* life and develop a truly ecological economics—locating the human economy *within* nature's economy. That means smaller economies of scale and returning our economies to a more local scale, like we see in the sustainable agriculture movement. *Some* trade is of course good and necessary, but it should be truly *fair* trade that allows everyone involved to make a decent living.

Power Dynamics Exercise

Ethical reflection presumes that those engaged in moral deliberation have the power they need to put their values into action. This exercise helps individuals and groups identify and understand the role that power dynamics play in ethical situations.[1]

For individuals engaged in moral deliberation, it is helpful to identify the main characters or forces of power in a case and then develop a diagram or picture that sketches the power dynamics between them. Poster boards, crayons, and other drawing materials can be used in creative ways to complete this exercise.

Groups engaged in moral reflection about a case may want to use various props and draw upon fellow classmates to create a human sculpture that probes the distribution of power in the case. In classroom settings, these sculptures tap into the creativity of students and allow them to step into a case physically in order to identify with certain characters or institutions in the case.

When shared with others, these diagrams and sculptures help identify forces that empower or disempower key players or stakeholders. They can also expose whose voices are heard or not heard within the case. Sometimes they help identify key stakeholders or forces that are invisible in the case as it is presented.

When creating a diagram or sculpture, consider that power can be manifested in many ways. For example, individuals and institutions can wield power politically, economically, socially, or religiously. The following questions may help expose some of the power dynamics in a case:

- How is economic power distributed among characters in the case?
- To what extent do class, race, or gender play a role in the power dynamics?
- Who has the power to make decisions? Why?
- Do laws protect or adversely affect certain people or institutions?
- Are religious or cultural values powerful or disempowered?

Finally, in a book focused on Earth ethics, it is also important to recall the power of nature and the consequences of violating ecological limits.

Guidelines for Case Briefs

Chapter 3 in this volume offers a three-stage method to address the moral problems posed by the cases in this volume. The following guidelines can be used to structure moral deliberation about these cases in written assignments. These guidelines should be revised or supplemented to accommodate diverse learning situations.

The case study method is a participatory method of learning. It involves the study and discussion of a life situation for the purpose of discovering general insights. There is no *one* right answer, and both the students and the instructor bear responsibility for sharing their insights and points of view in class. Careful preparation is in order not just to ensure a good grade, but more importantly to learn and help others to learn. The following notes are some basic suggestions on how to study cases and write case briefs. You will soon develop your own style of working through these cases.

A. *Preparation*: Immerse yourself in the case and get to know the details.
- Read the case at least twice;
- Write out the cast of characters;
- Develop a chronology of events;
- Identify the primary ethical problem(s) and possible solutions;
- Consult the case commentary, lectures, readings, and friends for relevant norms;
- Think critically about the various alternatives offered by the case and the positions of key characters in the case;
- Remember: there is no *one* right answer, but you do need to give reasons for your decision in the end.

B. *Writing the Case Brief*
1. The length of the brief is to be five to six typed, double-spaced pages.
2. Several skills are crucial in writing a case brief:
- Ability to be concise and to summarize well;
- Capacity to identify the ethical problems, the decisions to be made in the case, and the ethical resources relevant to the problems;
- Openness to innovation. You can use a variety of formats beyond the standard paper. For example, some students have written briefs in the form of journal entries, letters to friends, hypothetical dialogues, etc. Don't be afraid to be creative.
3. Consider one of the following approaches:
- Exploratory: Carefully explore conflicting or contrasting positions on the issue. Put an emphasis on being *objective*. Think with an open mind, then decide.
- Persuasive: After you have carefully thought through the alternatives, pick one position and develop it in depth. Do not dismiss other perspectives, but concentrate on making your position as persuasive as possible. An alternative to a longer paper is a five-hundred-word persuasive essay in the form of an OpEd that succinctly supports one position while acknowledging the strengths of opposing perspectives.
4. Utilize the following questions to structure your ethical reflection about the case:

Stage 1: Analysis.
   Personal Factors
   - How does your personal experience shape the way you view this case? Do you have something at stake?

   Power Dynamics
   - Who are the key players or stakeholders?
   - How is power distributed between them?
   - What forces disable or empower them?
   - Whose voices are heard or not heard?
   - Is the question of motive and self-interest relevant here for key players or stakeholders? Why or why not? If so, how does it affect your reflection about the case?

   Factual Information
   - Are there historical roots to the problem?
   - What are the key facts?
   - Are these facts in dispute?
   - Are stakeholders using different theories to interpret key facts?

   Complicating Factors
   - Are there things that make it hard to grasp the context of the case? Is important information unavailable or very complex?

   Relationships
   - Are there relational or character issues that complicate the choices facing key players or stakeholders?

   Ethical Issue(s)
   - What do you perceive to be the primary moral problem or ethical issue?
   - Are there secondary or additional moral problems that need to be resolved?

   Alternatives and Consequences
   - What realistic alternatives exist to address the primary ethical issue?
   - What are the likely consequences of each alternative? What are both good and bad, and short-term and long-term consequences of each?
   - Who will reap the benefits and bear the costs of each alternative?

Stage 2: Assessment.
   Ethical Vision and Moral Imagination
   - Ideally, how would you like to see the ethical problem(s) resolved?
   - What philosophical or religious theories or ideas shape your moral vision and imagination about this case?

   Moral Norms
   - How is your moral vision expressed in specific norms?

- How are the *ecojustice* norms relevant? (Sustainability, Sufficiency, Participation, Solidarity)
- Are these moral norms in conflict with each other or other moral, legal, economic, or religious norms?

Moral Theory
- What are the contributions or important questions from different moral theories for clarifying the moral dimensions of this case?
  - *Duty*—to other persons, future generations, nature.
  - *Character*—relevant virtues and ecological virtues and values.
  - *Relationships*—what is the extent of our moral community?
  - *Rights*—social and environmental conditions necessary for human dignity.
- What role does moral theory (deontology, teleology, virtue ethics) play in shaping your assessment of this case?

Ethical Assessment
- What conclusions do you reach as you assess the various alternatives and consequences in relation to the moral norms you have identified and the moral theory you feel is most relevant or appropriate?

Stage 3: Action.
Justification
- Which alternative is morally preferable, and how will you justify it in relation to the moral norms, principles, and values you identified and the alternatives you rejected?

Viability
- Do the key players or stakeholders have the power they need to put the decision into action?

Strategy
- What strategies will be necessary to implement the alternative you have selected?

Reflection
- How do you feel now that you have reached a decision about how this case should be resolved ethically? What insights have you gained from working through these three stages of ethical analysis?

Guidelines for Group Case Presentations

The following guidelines can be used by groups to structure moral deliberation about cases in this volume. These guidelines should be revised or supplemented to accommodate diverse learning situations.

Students are assigned to a group and a case, either randomly or by expressing which case most interests them. Each group will facilitate analysis about and ethical assessment of the assigned case. (See *Guidelines for Case Briefs* above.) These presentations should last no more than two-thirds of the class period, leaving one-third of the time for discussion and questions by the rest of the class. To the degree that it is possible, the goal is for the group to reach consensus about the appropriate course of moral action. If consensus is not possible, a brief minority report is permitted.

All members of the group are expected to participate fully in the various aspects of this project (meetings, research, presentations). While responsibilities will be divided among the members, care should be taken to ensure that the information presented is coherent and reflects the consensus of the group.

Groups are welcome to be creative. You may wish to use skits, talk-show formats, role-plays, audio-visual resources, etc., in your presentations. A word of caution, however. Creative formats often work well for analyzing a case but not for assessing it ethically. The goal is to do ethics as a group; it is not to entertain each other—though there's nothing wrong with having some fun!

The following are possible guidelines for the in-class presentation.

1. Pick a format that is engaging and interactive (such as role-playing in a public hearing, talk show, etc.).
2. Make sure relevant background information is included (but assume class members have read the case and commentary).
3. Make sure all relevant stakeholders are represented.
4. Make sure the primary ethical issues and ethical dilemma(s) are identified and explored.
5. Draw on the relevant moral theories that help to assess the issues.
6. Involve the class in deciding the case.
7. Make sure you offer a specific resolution to the case and explain how you arrived at your decision.

Group projects can be evaluated in several ways. Group members may be asked to write brief papers in which they reflect on what it was like to do moral deliberation as a group. The professor may also choose to meet with the whole group to evaluate the presentation. Alternatively, the group could write an outline of their ethical analysis following the three-stage analysis described above and use this as the basis of an oral examination with the professor. Students may also be asked to complete peer evaluation sheets assessing the contributions of each group member to the group project and presentation.

Note

[1]This exercise is adapted from "The Three-Storey Building: An Exercise in Social Analysis," in Center for Global Education, *Crossing Borders, Challenging Boundaries: A Guide to the Pedagogy & Philosophy of the Center for Global Education* (Minneapolis, MN: Center for Global Education, Augsburg College, 1988), 11:9–10.

Index

Numbers in *italics* indicate images.